D1571881

Music Theory
FOR
The Music Professional

Music Theory

FOR

The Music Professional

A Comparison of Common-Practice and Popular Genres

---◆---

Richard Sorce

NEW YORK UNIVERSITY

ARDSLEY HOUSE PUBLISHERS, INC., ◆ NEW YORK

Address orders and editorial
correspondence to:
Ardsley House, Publishers, Inc.
320 Central Park West
New York, NY 10025 4967040

ISBN: 1-880157-20-9

Printed in the United States of America

10 9 8 7 6 5 4 3 2

To

Barbara

*an
incessant
and endearing
talent*

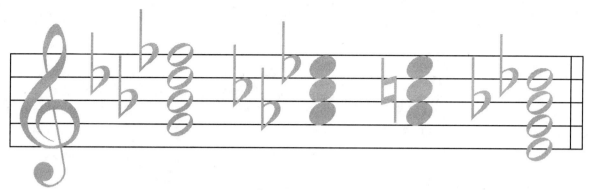

Contents

Preface ◆ *xxi*

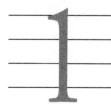

CHAPTER

A Review of Fundamentals ◆ *1*

Pitch Representation ◆ *1*

Pitches ◆ *1*   *Staves* ◆ *1*   *Accidentals and Enharmonic Spellings* ◆ *3*

Time and Meter ◆ *4*

Note and Rest Values ◆ *4*   *Beats* ◆ *5*

Chapter Review ◆ *6*   *Anthology References* ◆ *6*   *Self-Test* ◆ *7*
Exercises ◆ *7*

CHAPTER

RHYTHM ◆ 9

The Temporal Factor ◆ 9

Meter ◆ 10

Time Signatures ◆ 10   Beaming ◆ 10   Dots and Ties ◆ 11   Simple,
Compound, and Asymmetrical Meter ◆ 12   Historical Perspective ◆ 13
Compound Meter Expanded ◆ 13

Other Divisions and Interpretations of the Beat ◆ 14

Triplets ◆ 14   Duplets ◆ 16

Complex Groupings ◆ 16

Constant Values over One Beat ◆ 16   Variable Values over One or
More Beats ◆ 18   Rhythmic Notation ◆ 18

Counting and Rendering of Rhythmic Figures ◆ 19

The Half-Beat Concept ◆ 19   Intrinsically Normal Accents ◆ 20
Anacrusis ◆ 21   Syncopation ◆ 21   Counting Beat Divisions of
Less Than Half ◆ 23

Articulation and Interpretation ◆ 24

CHAPTER REVIEW ◆ 25   ANTHOLOGY REFERENCES ◆ 26   SELF-TEST ◆ 26
EXERCISES ◆ 27

CHAPTER

SCALES, KEYS, AND MODES ◆ 32

Scales ◆ 32

Major-Scale Construction ◆ 33

Minor-Scale Construction ◆ 35

Relative Minor Scales ◆ 35   The Natural or Pure Minor Scale ◆ 36   The
Harmonic Minor Scale ◆ 36   The Melodic Minor Scale ◆ 37   Technical
Names of Scale Degrees ◆ 38

Keys and Key Signature ◆ 38

Parallel Scale and Key Relationships ◆ 40   Several Other Commonly Used
Scale Types ◆ 41   The Circle of Fifths ◆ 41   Tetrachords ◆ 42

Modes ◆ 44

Mode Transposition ◆ 45

*CHAPTER REVIEW ◆ 49   ANTHOLOGY REFERENCES ◆ 50   SELF-TEST ◆ 51
EXERCISES ◆ 52*

CHAPTER

INTERVALS ◆ 56

Basic Notions ◆ 56

Interval Distance ◆ 57

Using Key and Scale ◆ 57   Using the Major Key of the Lower Note ◆ 57

Interval Quality ◆ 59

*Major Intervals ◆ 59   Perfect Intervals ◆ 60   Minor Intervals ◆ 61
Augmented Intervals ◆ 62   Doubly Augmented Intervals ◆ 62
Diminished Intervals ◆ 62   Doubly Diminished Intervals ◆ 63
Simple and Compound Intervals ◆ 63   Inversion of Intervals ◆ 63*

Interval Characteristics ◆ 64

*Consonance and Dissonance ◆ 64   Subjective Aural Evaluation ◆ 64
Consonant Intervals ◆ 65   Dissonant Intervals ◆ 65   Pitch Tendency ◆ 66
Interval-Resolution Tendency ◆ 66*

*CHAPTER REVIEW ◆ 68   ANTHOLOGY REFERENCES ◆ 69   SELF-TEST ◆ 70
EXERCISES ◆ 70*

CHAPTER

TRIADS ◆ 77

Triad Qualities ◆ 78

*Major Triads ◆ 78   Minor Triads ◆ 78   Diminished Triads ◆ 78
Augmented Triads ◆ 78*

Triad Construction ◆ 79

Numerical Designation and Identification of Triads ◆ 80

Triads in Scales and Modes ◆ 81

Triads Derived from Major and Minor Scales ◆ 81   Triads in Modes ◆ 83

Inversions of Triads ◆ *84*

Note-Spacing in Triads ◆ *85*

The Figured-Bass System ◆ *85*

Identifying Root Position and Inversions of Triads ◆ 88

Identifying Spread-Position Triads ◆ *89*

Popular-Music Formats ◆ *91*

*CHAPTER REVIEW ◆ 93   ANTHOLOGY REFERENCES ◆ 94   SELF-TEST ◆ 95
EXERCISES ◆ 96*

CHAPTER

SEVENTH CHORDS ◆ *104*

Seventh-Chord Qualities ◆ *105*

*Diatonic Sevenths in Major Scales ◆ 105   Diatonic Sevenths in
Minor Scales ◆ 106*

Inversions of Seventh Chords in Traditional Practice ◆ *106*

Root Position ◆ 108   Inversions ◆ 108

Numerical Labeling ◆ *110*

*Precise Labeling of Seventh Chords ◆ 110   Seventh Chords in
Popular Music ◆ 112*

Diatonic Sevenths and Hybrid Types ◆ *112*

Inversions of Seventh Chords in Popular Music ◆ *115*

Intervallic Configuration of Seventh Chords ◆ *115*

More on Hybrid Types ◆ *118*

Dominant and Nondominant Seventh Chords ◆ *118*

Extension of Tertian Construction ◆ *122*

*CHAPTER REVIEW ◆ 122   ANTHOLOGY REFERENCES ◆ 123   SELF-TEST ◆ 124
EXERCISES ◆ 125*

CHAPTER

VOICE LEADING AND FOUR-PART WRITING ◆ *132*

Pitch Tendency within the Major Scale ◆ *133*

The Tonic ◆ 133   The Supertonic ◆ 133   The Mediant ◆ 134   The Subdominant ◆ 134   The Dominant ◆ 135   The Overtone Series ◆ 135 The Submediant ◆ 136   The Leading Tone ◆ 137

Chorale Style and Four-Part Writing ◆ *137*

Chorale Style ◆ 137   Why Four-Part Writing? ◆ 138   Overview of Chorale Style ◆ 138   General Procedures for Four-Part Writing ◆ 141

Voice Leading of Triads and Dominant Seventh Chords ◆ *146*

Triads ◆ 146   Six-Four Inversions ◆ 148   Dominant Seventh Chords ◆ 150

Voice Leading of Diminished and Augmented Chords ◆ *153*

Resolution of Seventh Chords ◆ 154   The III+7 Chord ◆ 156   The viiº7 and viiø7 Chords ◆ 157   Deceptive Resolution of the viiº, viiº7, and viiø7 ◆ 159

CHAPTER REVIEW ◆ 161   ANTHOLOGY REFERENCES ◆ 162   SELF-TEST ◆ 163 EXERCISES ◆ 164

CHAPTER

HARMONIC PROGRESSION ◆ *176*

Chordal Tendencies and Musical Style ◆ *176*

Similarities among Triads and Sevenths ◆ 177   Common-Practice and Popular Genres ◆ 178

Chord Movement ◆ *179*

The Circle Progression ◆ 179   Progressive and Retrogressive Movements ◆ 179

Substitution, Factors, and Chord Choice ◆ *182*

Substitution by Extension of a Lower Third ◆ 185   Substitution by Extension of a Higher Third ◆ 186

More on Choosing Chords in a Progression ◆ *186*

The Control of Tension ◆ 187   Structural and Embellishing Chords ◆ 187

Harmonizing a Melody ◆ *188*

The Structural Component • 189   Determining the Key • 189
Rhythmic Stress • 189   Chord Selection in SATB Format • 190
The Harmonic Accompaniment to a Melody • 192

CHAPTER REVIEW • 193 ANTHOLOGY REFERENCES • 194 SELF-TEST • 194
EXERCISES • 195

CHAPTER

NONHARMONIC TONES ◆ *199*

Types of Nonharmonic Tones • *201*

The Passing Tone • 201   The Neighboring Tone • 201
The Appoggiatura • 202   The Escape Tone • 203   The Suspension • 204
The Retardation • 206   The Anticipation • 207   The Free Tone • 207
The Pedal Tone • 209   The Organ Point • 209   The Cambiata • 209
Changing Tones • 210

Embellished Nonharmonic Tones • *210*

Nonharmonic Tones in Four-Part Writing • *210*

Nonharmonic Tones as a Function of Melody • *213*

CHAPTER REVIEW • 215   ANTHOLOGY REFERENCES • 216   SELF-TEST • 217
EXERCISES • 218

CHAPTER

MELODY ◆ *224*

Melody Perception • *224*

Components of Melody • *226*

The Cell • 226   The Motive • 226   The Phrase • 227

Types of Melodies • *230*

Melodic Development • 238

Composing Melodies • *240*

Popular-Song Writing and Traditional Composition • 240

CHAPTER REVIEW • 240   ANTHOLOGY REFERENCES • 241   SELF-TEST • 243
EXERCISES • 243

CHAPTER

MUSICAL STRUCTURE ◆ *248*

The Elements of Structure ◆ *248*

The Single Note ◆ *248   Structure and Relationship* ◆ *248   Structural Elements at the Macro Level* ◆ *249*

Cadences ◆ *250*

The Perfect Authentic Cadence ◆ *250   The Imperfect Authentic Cadence* ◆ *251   The Semicadence* ◆ *251   The Plagal Cadence* ◆ *251 The Deceptive Cadence* ◆ *253   The Phrygian and Landini Cadences and the Picardy Third* ◆ *253   Cadential Modifications* ◆ *254*

Cadences in Popular Music ◆ *255*

The Tritone Substitution ◆ *256*

The Phrase ◆ *256*

Phrase Analysis of Two Works ◆ *258   Period and Phrase Types* ◆ *262*

Binary and Ternary Structure ◆ *262*

Binary Structure ◆ *262   Ternary Structure* ◆ *266*

Popular-Song Structure ◆ *267*

The SDR Principle ◆ *268*

Structure and Improvisation ◆ *270*

An Introduction to Modulation ◆ *270*

Recognizing a Modulation ◆ *271   Types of Modulation* ◆ *273*

CHAPTER REVIEW ◆ *275   ANTHOLOGY REFERENCES* ◆ *276   SELF-TEST* ◆ *277 EXERCISES* ◆ *278*

CHAPTER

SECONDARY DOMINANTS AND DOMINANT SEVENTHS ◆ *284*

Chromaticism and Diatonicism ◆ *284*

Secondary-Dominant Chords ◆ *286*

Origin and Derivation ◆ *286   Inversions* ◆ *287   Assessment* ◆ *287*

Secondary-Dominant Seventh Chords ◆ *288*

Inversions and Introductory Remarks on Resolution ◆ *288*

Resolutions of Secondary-Dominant Chords ◆ *289*

Deceptive Resolutions ◆ *289*   *V/V and V7/V to the Tonic Six-Four* ◆ *292*
Circle Progressions ◆ *292*   *The V7/IV* ◆ *292*   *Unusual Resolutions* ◆ *294*

CHAPTER REVIEW ◆ *298*   *ANTHOLOGY REFERENCES* ◆ *299*   *SELF-TEST* ◆ *299*
EXERCISES ◆ *300*

CHAPTER

FUNCTIONS OF DIMINISHED CHORDS ◆ *307*

Description and Location of Diatonic Diminished Chords ◆ *307*

Embellishing Function of Diminished Chords ◆ *308*

Origin of Diminished Chords ◆ *308*   *The vii° and V7* ◆ *308*
The viiø7, vii°7, and V7 ◆ *308*

Applications ◆ *309*

The Secondary vii° ◆ *309*   *Secondary Fully and Half-Diminished
Sevenths* ◆ *310*   *Deceptive Resolution of Diminished Chords* ◆ *310*
Inversions of Diminished Chords ◆ *312*   *vii°6, the Predominant
Inversion* ◆ *313*   *Preparation and Resolution of the Tritone and Seventh* ◆ *313*

Additional Characteristics of Diminished Chords ◆ *314*

Pitch Spellings of Fully Diminished Sevenths ◆ *314*   *Alteration of Fully
Diminished and Half-Diminished Seventh Chords* ◆ *316*   *The ø7 and
m7♭5* ◆ *319*

CHAPTER REVIEW ◆ *322*   *ANTHOLOGY REFERENCES* ◆ *323*   *SELF-TEST* ◆ *323*
EXERCISES ◆ *324*

CHAPTER

**BORROWED FUNCTIONS:
MOVEMENTS AND REGIONS** ◆ *330*

Chromaticism ◆ *330*

Borrowed Chords ◆ *331*

Function ◆ *331*   *Borrowed Chords and Secondary Chords* ◆ *332*
Qualities ◆ *332*   *Part Writing* ◆ *333*

Change-of-Quality Chords ◆ *333*

Characteristics ◆ *335*

Related and Remote Movement ◆ *336*

Key Regionalizing ◆ *337*

CHAPTER REVIEW ◆ *339*   *ANTHOLOGY REFERENCES* ◆ *340*   *SELF-TEST* ◆ *341*
EXERCISES ◆ *341*

CHAPTER

THE NEAPOLITAN CHORD ◆ *346*

Spelling of the N6 ◆ *346*

Characteristics of the Neapolitan ◆ *347*

Part Writing of the N6 ◆ *352*

The Neapolitan as a Tritone Substitution ◆ *355*

CHAPTER REVIEW ◆ *356*   *ANTHOLOGY REFERENCES* ◆ *357*   *SELF-TEST* ◆ *357*
EXERCISES ◆ *358*

CHAPTER

**GERMAN, FRENCH,
AND ITALIAN AUGMENTED SIXTH CHORDS** ◆ *363*

Augmented Sixths ◆ *363*

Root Origin ◆ *363*   *Implications of Intrinsic Augmented Sixths* ◆ *364*
Passing-Tone Motion and Approach ◆ *364*

Structure and Function of German Sixths ◆ *365*

Intervallic Structure ◆ *365*   *Resolution* ◆ *365*

Structure and Function of French Sixths ◆ *368*

Intervallic Structure ◆ *368*   *Resolution* ◆ *368*   *French Sixths and
Supertonics* ◆ *369*   *Seventh Flat-Five Chords and French Sixths* ◆ *370*

Structure and Function of Italian Sixths ◆ *371*

Intervallic Structure ◆ *371*   *Resolution* ◆ *371*

More on Augmented Sixths ◆ *371*

Popular Genres ◆ *372*   *Alternative Origin: the ♯4* ◆ *374*

CHAPTER REVIEW ◆ 374   ANTHOLOGY REFERENCES ◆ 375   SELF-TEST ◆ 375
EXERCISES ◆ 376

CHAPTER

UPPER-PARTIAL CHORDS:
NINTHS, ELEVENTHS, AND THIRTEENTHS ◆ 382

Characteristics of Upper-Partial Chords ◆ 382

Ninth Chords ◆ 383

*Diatonic Ninths ◆ 383   Ninth Factors ◆ 385   Major Ninths and
Dominant Ninths ◆ 385   Hybrid Structures ◆ 386   Add 9 Chords ◆ 386*

Eleventh Chords ◆ 387

*Dominant Elevenths and 4–3 Suspensions ◆ 387   The "Sus 4" Symbol in
Popular Music ◆ 388   Augmented Eleventh Chords ◆ 389   Minor Eleventh
Chords ◆ 389   9,11 Chords ◆ 390   Elevenths on Other Scale Degrees ◆ 390*

Thirteenth Chords ◆ 390

Add 9, Sus 4, and Add 6 Chords ◆ 391

General Remarks on Upper-Partial Chords ◆ 392

Other Scale Degrees ◆ 392   Symbols in Popular Music ◆ 392

Embedded Harmonic Structures ◆ 393

Triads ◆ 393   Sevenths ◆ 394   Implications ◆ 395

Inversions of Ninths, Elevenths, and Thirteenths ◆ 396

Rerooting and Root Ambiguity ◆ 397

Voice Leading of Upper-Partial Chords ◆ 398

Necessary Chord Factors ◆ 398

Pitch Tendency ◆ 400

*Ninths ◆ 400   Elevenths ◆ 400   Thirteenths ◆ 401   Adapting the
Rules ◆ 401*

Authentic and Appoggiatura Upper-Partial Chords ◆ 402

Chapter Review ◆ *408*   *Anthology References* ◆ *409*   *Self-Test* ◆ *410*
Exercises ◆ *410*

CHAPTER

STEPWISE, MEDIANT,
AND TRITONE RELATIONSHIPS ◆ *417*

Cyclic Movement ◆ *417*

Noncyclic Movement ◆ *417*

Stepwise Movement ◆ *420*
Planing and Parallelism ◆ *423*

Mediant Movement ◆ *423*

Tritone Relationship and Movement ◆ *424*

Tritones and Augmented Sixths ◆ *426*
German Sixths ◆ *426*   *French Sixths* ◆ *427*   *Implied Roots* ◆ *429*

Applications ◆ *431*
Chord Identification in Unconventional Root Movements ◆ *431*

Chapter Review ◆ *433*   *Anthology References* ◆ *433*   *Self-Test* ◆ *434*
Exercises ◆ *434*

CHAPTER

MODULATION ◆ *440*

Establishing a New Key Center ◆ *440*

Why Modulate? ◆ *442*

Common-Chord Modulation ◆ *443*

Pivot-Chord Modulation ◆ *445*

Chromatic Modulation ◆ *449*
Neapolitan Chords ◆ *450*   *Borrowed Pivots in Target Keys* ◆ *452*

Enharmonic Modulation ◆ 453

Augmented Sixths as Pivots ◆ 454   Major-Minor Sevenths ◆ 454
Fully Diminished Sevenths ◆ 456   Augmented Triads as Pivots ◆ 457

Implied Modulation ◆ 459

Static Modulation ◆ 461

Common-Tone Modulation ◆ 461

Further Remarks on Modulation ◆ 462

Extensive Chromaticism ◆ 462   Embedded Structures ◆ 463   Harmonic
Structures Generated from Melodies ◆ 464   Unimplied Roots ◆ 465

Chapter Review ◆ 466   Anthology References ◆ 467   Self-Test ◆ 467
Exercises ◆ 468

CHAPTER

Secundal, Quartal, and Quintal Harmony ◆ 477

The Secundal System ◆ 478

Chords in Seconds ◆ 478   Inversions ◆ 478   Voicings ◆ 479   Multinote
Secundal Chords ◆ 479   Clusters ◆ 480

The Quartal System ◆ 481

Chords in Fourths ◆ 481   Perfect-Perfect Fourths ◆ 481
Perfect-Augmented Fourths ◆ 481   Augmented-Perfect Fourths ◆ 483
Nonfunctional Augmented-Augmented Quartal Chords ◆ 483
Voicings ◆ 484   Consonance and Dissonance ◆ 484   Compound Quartal
Chords ◆ 486   Inversions ◆ 486   Implied Roots ◆ 487   Identification of
Inversions ◆ 488   Analysis of Fourth Chords ◆ 488

The Quintal System ◆ 490

Chords in Fifths ◆ 490   Perfect Fifth Dyads ◆ 491   Superimposed
Fifths ◆ 492   Consonant and Dissonant Perfect Fifths ◆ 493
Perfect Fifths and Perfect Fifth Anchors ◆ 493

Chapter Review ◆ 495   Anthology References ◆ 496   Self-Test ◆ 497
Exercises ◆ 498

APPENDICES

A *Several Scale Constructions from C* ✦ *503*

B *More on Chord Construction and Function* ✦ *506*
Harmonic Construction and Progression Revisited ✦ *507*

C *Instruments and Voices* ✦ *511*
Transposing Instruments ✦ *511*   Instrument and Voice Ranges ✦ *513*

D *The Major Scales and the Three Forms of the Minor Scales* ✦ *516*

E *Historical Perspective* ✦ *523*

F *Common Structures in Common-Practice and Popular Music* ✦ *527*

Glossary ✦ *531*

Index ✦ *543*

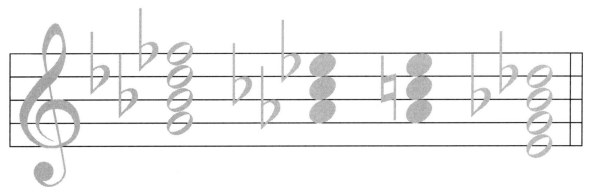

Preface

It is assumed that the reader of this text has already had at least a minimum of musical training and that he or she possesses a rudimentary knowledge of the principles of music theory. Nevertheless, Chapter 1 presents a brief review of music fundamentals; this review is primarily geared to students returning to theoretical studies after a long absence. Others can refer back to it, as needed. The concepts discussed and illustrated in this chapter are perhaps the most important in the understanding of music theory. As they relate to theoretical practice, these materials are analogous to mastering an alphabet as a prerequisite to learning a foreign language, such as Russian.

The reader will notice that most music-literature examples are in piano or lead-sheet format and draw from many styles of music. The purpose in presenting these various styles is to familiarize the reader/student with many styles as soon as possible.

Most chapters address the application of theoretical concepts as they occur in both traditional and popular styles of music. If one principal theme is observed in this book, it is the idea that Western music has changed minimally throughout the past several hundred years. While progressing through the chapters, the reader should come to realize that classical music is not as mysteriously complex as some think, and that popular-music practice is not significantly different from traditional practice.

A complete general knowledge of the many facets of musical materials will be gained through diligently reading the text, observing the examples, and completing the exercises. The reader should always remember that the component parts and principles of music, as we know it, have been in use for many centuries; over time, the elements and syntax of music have remained essentially the same.

The majority of this book investigates the available tools employed in music composition and the methods by which these tools are applied. Theory examines musical practice; musical practice dictates theory. Theoretical principles and concepts were not written as a guide for composers and songwriters. The "rules" of music theory were deduced after thousands of pages of music had been analyzed. These rules, then, are nothing more than the practices employed in the majority of cases in the creation of music.

To the Aspiring Musician

This book is meant to prepare the professional musician for any opportunity that may present itself in which a knowledge of the mechanics of music is a prerequisite. Since one can never predict where he or she will ultimately arrive in the music profession, there is no choice but to possess as complete an understanding of music as possible. One must know the constitution of a musical piece, regardless of the style in which it is written and/or performed. Diligent study of this book will result in the following benefits:

1. It should improve the music professional's performance and creative endeavors through the understanding of theoretical practice and application.

2. It will offer the reader those fundamental principles necessary to understand all of the musical styles, and ideally, it will foster a desire for further information concerning the creation, performance, and presentation of Western music.

3. The reader will examine many of the concepts of music theory as they relate to the styles of music from the Baroque period to current practice while expanding and diversifying one's creative understanding — thereby increasing the scope of opportunity.

Observing the principles of theory as they relate to all the styles of Western practice enables the reader to understand the development of music more easily. A person engaged in the creation, performance, and promotion of music in any style should be knowledgeable about its syntax. In this profession the opportunities are many, and one never knows where one will find oneself. A musician may be asked to do something outside of his or her specialty when it is least expected; in such a fiercely competitive profession, it is definitely beneficial for the aspiring musician to accept this challenge.

As recently as the early '70s, the multitude of opportunities now available in the music profession did not exist. A formal music education consisted of a traditional course of study that was exclusively based on classical practice. If one chose to pursue an alternative other than performance, composition, or education, one did so by applying that which was learned in a traditional course of study.

This book, however, bridges what may be termed a "theory gap." Its content will demonstrate to the reader and music student that, indeed, there is no vast difference between the syntaxes of traditional practice and popular music. Undeniably, most discussions are about and most examples are drawn from what is referred to as *common practice*. Common practice includes those works written between approximately 1650 and 1875 that provided the principles and practices that have influenced the present course of music and will undoubtedly continue to influence music in the future. Whether a performer, writer, arranger, recording engineer, or publishing agent, the professional musician must know the components of music if he or she expects to sustain a successful career.

There is no quick method of becoming a competent composer, songwriter, arranger, orchestrator, harmonist, improvisor, or theorist. For example, developing a proficiency at harmonizing takes years of practice, experimentation, and study of the great works, not to mention the mastering of the multitude of rules of composition that have been the practice of every composer. The rules employed in composition and harmony have become rules because they were, and still are, the practice of all successful composers.

"Breaking the rules" is a widely used phrase — one which is often uttered by novice musicians with hardly enough experience and training to speak with any authority. Too many "artists" are ready to break the rules without first learning the principles of their art as best they can. In this high-tech society, many have come to expect results with minimal effort. This is witnessed in theory, composition, and other types of music courses; students want to score, arrange, and compose "great" music before they learn how to connect two chords properly! This enthusiasm is indeed beneficial, but one must crawl before one can walk. Perhaps with the aid of sophisticated synthesizers and computers one is able to impress others with one's creations; but it is highly doubtful that one could conceive, develop, and present a worthy piece of art without mastering the basic techniques of composition.

Years of formal study will not guarantee the success of any creative work if the artist does not possess the necessary creative spirit. However, formal education in music does guarantee exposure to the multitude of styles, practices, and procedures that have developed throughout the history of composition, and thus will prepare the student musician to function competently in several facets of the music profession.

Curiously, a significant proportion of musicians do not listen attentively; indeed, some musicians possess a "hearing" ear while others possess a "listening" ear. For the truly serious musician enough musical "information" is available daily to whet the appetite of the "listening" ear. Simply hearing music is not enough for the music professional; the professional must *listen,* listen carefully, listen theoretically, and listen critically.

Why listen critically at all? What will listening to Baroque or Classical music do for a pop musician? What will listening to jazz or contemporary classical music do for a musicologist specializing in Renaissance music? Remember that the syntax — the tools of musical creation — have remained virtually unchanged for the last three hundred years. There are no new pitches, chords, rhythms, or dynamics. Every element of syntax that was available in 1700 is still used today. What has changed is the *style* in which these syntactical elements are employed.

Consider, for example, Johann Sebastian Bach, the quintessential Baroque composer (1685–1750), who has often been credited as a great jazz musician. Why would anyone make this statement? Although stylistically Bach's music sounds nothing like modern jazz, syntactically Bach employed rhythms, harmonies, and developmental techniques witnessed in modern jazz compositions and improvisations.

All professional musicians, regardless of the genre in which they choose to work, need the ability to compare styles and techniques as inspiration for their own works. This is because musicians are often called upon to recognize similarities between styles, and to either emulate or draw from a particular style or practice, or even to blend various styles and practices. True musicianship thus requires a command of the variety of musical material that has survived the ages, and that therefore demands intelligent, thoughtful, and concentrated listening.

Will the concern for the "theoretical" eliminate or hinder the appreciation of music for music's sake? After all, music is made to be enjoyed, however one chooses to listen to it. Theorists and musicologists are often accused of being too preoccupied with syntax to appreciate the emotional effects of music. An analogous situation occurs in the appreciation of a visual art work — a painting, for instance. Does the observer concentrate on the essential features of the painting — the faces, the objects, the background scene, — or on the elements contained in the painting — the texture of the canvas, each individual color, the layering of the paint, the underpainting, the size of the painting, the frame? The trained observer can do both — in music or in painting, or in any other art form. It is often the initial impact of the art work that attracts the attention of the observer; it is the study of the elements — the syntax — that eventually either holds one in awe of the work or renders the work less than expert. With music, a knowledge of theoretical concepts augments one's appreciation of the work beyond the impact of a first hearing. Effecting a separation from the initial hearing and an attentiveness to the elemental components does require practice and concentration, but it is nothing that the listening ear cannot do.

In the study of music theory it is not sufficient to function with the techniques and practices presented in a book such as this. There are several other facets of music education necessary for becoming literate, competent, and comfortable with the workings of music; these include the diligent and continuous study and review of theoretical principles, listening with an astute and attentive ear to all genres of music — not only those which are currently popular — listening while following the score of a work, and analyzing music for the purpose of understanding the mechanics of the syntax. Whether or not one chooses to study music composition, following these procedures will surely lead to a thorough comprehension of the art. It is an assiduous process requiring perseverance and dedication.

Acknowledgements

I would like to thank the following people for their thoughtful reviews of my manuscript: Richard Agee of The Colorado College, Allen Brown of the University of the Pacific, Andrew Fox of the University of Mississippi, Donald Hopkins of The Pennsylvania State University, and Toba Kramer of the Wisconsin Conservatory of Music. A special thanks is due to David Loberg Code of Western Michigan University, who did a detailed line-by-line review of the entire manuscript. Each of these reviewers made numerous helpful comments and criticisms which allowed me to clarify the focus and direction of the book. Finally, I would like to thank Linda Jarkesy of Ardsley House for her careful editing of the manuscript.

A REVIEW OF FUNDAMENTALS

Pitch Representation

◆ *Pitches*

In Western practice the term **pitch** is used to define the highness or lowness of a sound, and is based upon the number of vibrations per second of a sounding body, such as a string, air column, or membrane. Pitches are represented by the first seven letters of the alphabet:

A–B–C–D–E–F–G

◆ *Staves*

Pitches, represented by *note* symbols, can be displayed on a **staff** (pl. *staves*) consisting of five lines and four spaces, as in *Example 1–1*.

Example 1–1. Note symbols, representing pitches, displayed on a staff.

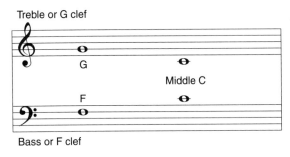

Example 1–2. *The grand staff.*

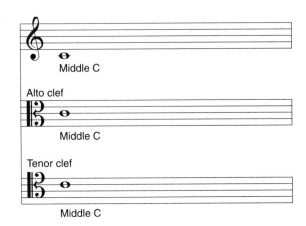

Example 1–3. *The movable C clef.* The locations of middle C in the treble, alto, and tenor clefs are compared.

Any staff used to identify variable pitches must contain a symbol, known as a **clef**, at the beginning, which determines the pitch names of the notes placed on the various lines and spaces of the staff. The two most commonly employed clefs are the *treble* and *bass* clefs. The **treble** or **G clef** locates the note G on the second line of the staff. The two dots immediately following the curve of the **bass** or **F clef** locate the pitch F on the fourth line of the staff. A combination of the two staves, used for notation for certain instruments, such as harps and keyboards, produces the **grand staff**. See *Example 1–2*.

In addition to the treble and bass clefs, the **movable C clef** is also utilized for certain instruments. This clef locates middle C on any line where the two curves intersect. In current practice only the **alto** and **tenor clefs** are employed. See *Example 1–3*.

Since the pitches of many notes exceed the available lines and spaces of the staff, it is often necessary to extend the staff in either direction by the use of **ledger lines**, as illustrated in *Example 1–4*.

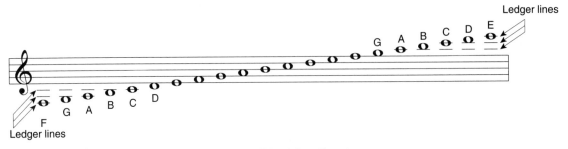

Example 1–4. *Ledger lines, extending the staff in either direction.*

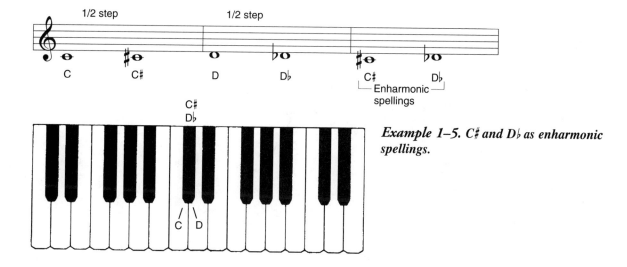

Example 1–5. C♯ and D♭ as enharmonic spellings.

◆ Accidentals and Enharmonic Spellings

A **half step** is the distance on a keyboard from one key to the next adjacent key, black or white. A **whole step** consists of two half steps. Black keys, called **sharps** or **flats**, serve to raise or lower pitches one half step. The black key between C and D *(Example 1–5)* raises C one half step and is known as C-*sharp* (C♯); it also lowers D one half step, in which case it is called D-*flat* (D♭). These alternate spellings for the same pitch, such as C♯ and D♭, are known as **enharmonic spellings** (or **enharmonic equivalents**). See *Example 1–5.*

In the case of adjacent white keys, enharmonic spellings are also used. Thus, B♯ is an alternate spelling of C, as is C♭ of B. The same applies to alternate spellings of E and F. See *Example 1–6.*

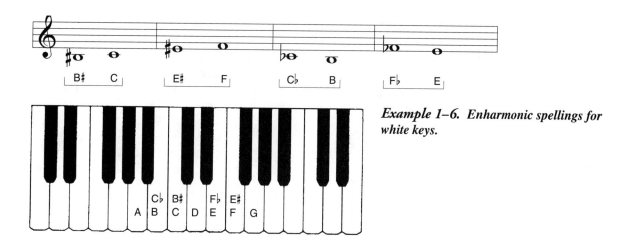

Example 1–6. Enharmonic spellings for white keys.

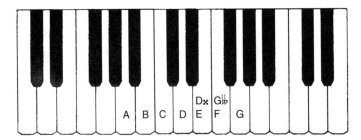

Example 1–7. The use of double sharps and double flats.

For various theoretical reasons, to be discussed, it is sometimes necessary to raise or lower a pitch two keys to the right or left without resorting to the next alphabetical letter name. For this procedure a **double sharp (x)** or **double flat (♭♭)** is employed. See *Example 1–7*.

To restore a pitch after it has been altered by a sharp, double sharp, flat, or double flat, a **natural sign (♮)** is applied. When restoring a double sharp (x), simply to a single sharp, the symbol ♮♯ is used; when restoring a double flat (♭♭) to a single flat, the symbol ♮♭ is used. Collectively, sharps, flats, double sharps, double flats, and natural signs are known as **accidentals**. See *Example 1–8*.

Time and Meter

◆ Note and Rest Values

A **note** symbol not only represents a pitch but also indicates the **duration** or length of time the sound is produced. To indicate the duration of a pitch, a **stem**, a vertical line, can be attached to the **note head**, or circular part of the note symbol. Also, a **flag**, which is shaped like a banner, can be attached to the right of the stem to shorten time durations, as illustrated in *Figure 1–9*.

Example 1–8. The use of accidentals.

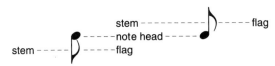

Example 1–9. Note heads, stems, and flags.

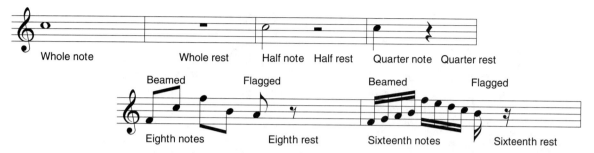

Example 1–10. *Note and rest values.* In single-line music (for one voice or instrument), any stemmed note head placed below the third staff line has its stem attached to the right side and pointing upward. Generally, a stemmed note above the third line has its stem attached to the left and pointing downward. If the note head appears on the third line, either method can be used. However, in certain groupings stems are left in one direction to facilitate reading. Eighth notes, sixteenth notes, and notes of lesser duration can be either beamed or flagged, depending on the context.

Just as a note symbol represents the sounding length of a pitch, a **rest** symbol indicates the length of time of silence. *Example 1–10* illustrates several types of note and rest values.

Beams are thick horizontal lines that join stems in note-value groupings. In *Example 1–10,* notice that eighth notes and sixteenth notes can be written using either beams or flags. These, and notes of lesser value, are written either one way or the other to facilitate reading or to correspond to particular methods of grouping. The discussion of rhythm in Chapter 2 explores beaming in more detail.

◆ *Beats*

A **beat** is a unit of time. If a whole note (or whole rest) receives four beats, for example, a half note (or half rest) will receive two beats (one-half of four); a quarter note (or quarter rest) will receive one beat (one-quarter of four); an eighth note (or eighth rest) will receive one-half beat (one-eighth of four), etc. This is illustrated in *Example 1–11.*

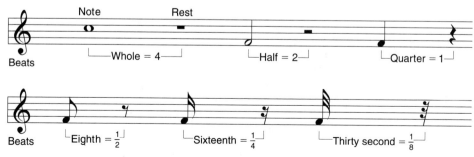

Example 1–11. *Beats.*

Chapter Review

The musical alphabet in Western practice consists of the letters A–B–C–D–E–F–G. Each letter represents a particular sound, referred to as a pitch. *Pitch* is the highness or lowness of a sound, based on the number of vibrations per second.

Pitches, which are represented by *note* symbols, are placed on, above, or below a *staff,* which consists of five lines and four spaces. Lines used to extend a staff are known as *ledger lines.* A staff must contain a *clef sign,* which determines the location of a particular pitch. The four clefs in current use are: the *treble* or *G clef,* which locates G on the second line of the staff, counting from the bottom line; the *bass* or *F clef,* which locates F on the fourth line; the *alto* or *C clef,* which locates middle C on the third line; and the *tenor* or *C clef,* which locates middle C on the fourth line. The C clef is known as a *movable clef.* The *grand staff* is a combination of two staves, usually containing two different *clefs,* the *treble* and *bass.*

In visualizing notes on a keyboard, notes can be raised one *half step* (one adjacent key) to the right by the addition of a *sharp* sign (♯), or lowered one half step to the left by the addition of a *flat* sign (♭). A note can be raised two half steps *(one whole step)* by the addition of a *double sharp* (𝄪), or lowered two half steps by the addition of a *double flat* (♭♭). A raised or lowered note can be restored to the original by the addition of a *natural* (♮). The term *enharmonic* refers to a note with an alternative spelling, for example, C♯–D♭, E♯–F, B♭♭–A, etc.

In addition to the pitch of a note, the length of sound must be represented. The longest single note symbol in modern use is the whole note (𝅝). If the whole note receives four beats, all other note values receive a proportional number of beats. *Rest values,* which correspond in length to the various note values, determine the length of silence between notes. Note values can be extended by the use of *dots* and *ties.* Rest values can be extended by the use of dots.

Anthology References

For additional usage and analysis, see the following examples in Distefano, Joseph P. and James A. Searle, *Music and Materials for Analysis: An Anthology.* New York, Ardsley House, Publishers, Inc., 1995.

beaming
> *Example 63.*   *Concerto for Nine Instruments,* Op. 25, First Movement, Anton Webern, pp. 373–82.

double sharps
> *Example 36.*   *Impromptu,* Op. 5, No. 5, Robert Schumann, pp. 201–6.

clefs, time signatures
> *Example 43.*   *Pictures at an Exhibition,* "Promenade," Modest Mussorgsky, pp. 247–52.

Self-Test

1. *Pitch* is defined as _____ .
2. *Notes* represent _____ .
3. *Rests* represent _____ .
4. Describe the four *clefs* in current use.
5. Describe the *grand staff*.
6. Explain the function of *ledger lines*.
7. Describe how *sharps, double sharps, flats, double flats,* and *naturals* affect notes.
8. Describe *half steps* and *whole steps*.
9. Define the term *enharmonic*.
10. Provide one enharmonic spelling for each given pitch: (a) E♭ (b) F♯ (c) A (d) B♭ (e) C (f) C♯ (g) D𝄪 (h) E♭♭ (i) E♯.

Exercises

1. Name the notes.

2. Locate on the piano.

3. Write a correct enharmonic, as in the first measure of the treble clef.

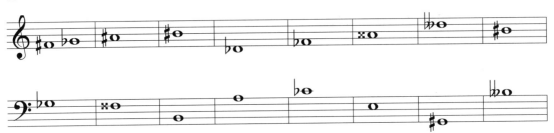

4. Indicate whether the distance between the two notes is a whole step (1) or half step (1/2), as in the first measure of the treble clef.

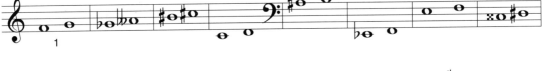

RHYTHM

The Temporal Factor

Rhythm, derived from the Greek, "rhythmos," meaning flow or continuity of motion, is the broad term used to describe and encompass all the elements of duration in music. This temporal factor is probably the most basic and important element in the structure of music since music is conceived in time, perceived in time, and experienced in *micro* (small) as well as *meso* (middle) and *macro* (large) time segments. This chapter examines the *micro* portion of rhythm.

To grasp the effects of rhythm fully, one must be able to sense rhythmic divisions. A listener who truly experiences rhythm is able to track rhythmic movement in *pulsations* and can easily continue along with the music at the designated rate of speed (**tempo**). The **pulse** of a musical work is its regular recurring beat. A listener who really "feels" the pulse will not be affected by any extrinsic factors. A totally developed rhythmic sensitivity can transcend the most complex audible disturbances.

Dancers spend much of their time moving with the pulse or beat. After a particular dance routine is learned, the dancer is no longer consciously aware of the pulsations; he or she simply *feels* the rhythm. Whether or not you are a dancer, you must, as a musician or music professional, be fully cognizant of rhythm.

Meter

◆ *Time Signatures*

Meter is a repetitive pattern, combining accented and unaccented beats. Most music written within the last several hundred years divides groups of beats into specific units. These units, referred to as **measures**,[1] are separated by **bar lines**; the proportional time contained within each measure is determined by a *time or meter signature*. A **time signature** consists of an upper and lower number and is placed at the beginning of a musical work or at any place where the meter changes. In its literal interpretation, the upper number of the time signature represents the number of beats in a measure, and the lower number determines the note type that will receive one beat. For example, in $\frac{3}{4}$ time, each measure contains three beats and the quarter note (♩) receives one beat. In $\frac{6}{8}$ time, each measure contains six beats and the eighth note (♪) receives one beat. In $\frac{3}{2}$ time, each measure contains three beats and the half note (♩) receives one beat. See *Example 2–1*.

◆ *Beaming*

In certain situations, flagged notes can be replaced by notes that are joined by one or more beams. A single eighth note, for example, is represented as ♪; it con-

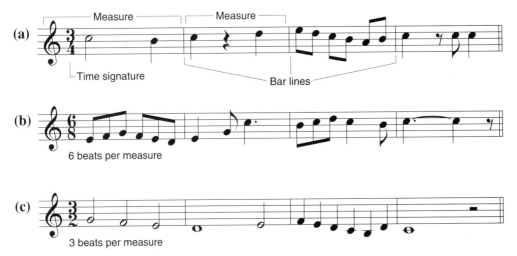

Example 2–1. Three commonly used time signatures. In Part (a), the combined beat value of notes and rests in each measure equals 3. The $\frac{6}{8}$ time signature in Part (b) is considered "compound" and is often interpreted in an alternate manner. Compound meter is discussed later in this chapter.

---

1. m. = measure; mm. = measures

tains a single flag. A sixteenth note is represented as ♪ and contains two flags. When joined to another note, the flag of an eighth note can be replaced by a beam; for example, ♪♪ yields ♫. Two sixteenths joined will appear as ♬. Two sixteenths joined to an eighth produce ♬. Beams can appear above or below the note heads as ♫ or ♫, for example.

Beaming is a method for facilitating reading and for conforming to particular practices for notating rhythm in various time signatures. The rhythmic figure ♪ ♪♪♪♪♪♪ ♪ ♪♪ ♪ is much easier to read as ♫♬♬ ♪ ♫

◆ *Dots and Ties*

A **dot** after a note or rest increases the value of the note or rest by *one-half* its original value. Also, multiple dots or rests increase the value by one-half of the increase of the preceding dot. Thus, if a whole note receives four beats, then a dotted whole note receives six (4 + 2) beats and a double-dotted whole note receives seven (4 + 2 + 1) beats. See *Example 2–2*. Rarely are more than two dots ever used to increase note or rest values.

A **tie** is a curved line connecting two notes of the same pitch, thereby creating a durational value equal to the sum of the values of the two notes. This is necessary when a note is to be sustained over a bar line, and under certain conditions, within the same measure. See *Example 2–3* on page 12.

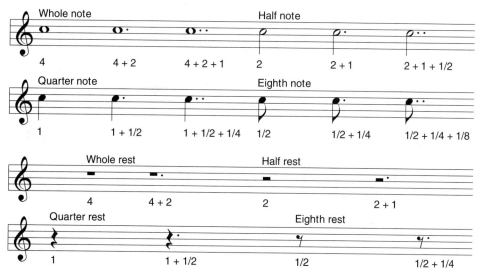

Example 2–2. The use of dots.

Example 2–3. The use of ties.

◆ Simple, Compound, and Asymmetrical Meter

A discussion of rhythm is intrinsically concerned with *meter*. Essentially, there are two types of meter — *simple* and *compound*. A **simple meter** is one that contains an equal *two-part* division of the beat, whereas a **compound meter** contains an equal *three-part* division.

In simple meter, for the time signatures $\frac{2}{2}$, $\frac{3}{2}$, and $\frac{4}{2}$, the beat is the half note (♩) and the two-part division is into two quarter notes (♩♩). For $\frac{2}{4}$, $\frac{3}{4}$, and $\frac{4}{4}$ meters, the beat is the quarter note (♩) and the division is into two eighth notes (♫).

Compound meters can be considered as meters that operate on two levels. In the literal interpretation of $\frac{6}{8}$, for example, six beats occur in each measure and the eighth note receives one beat. However, at fast tempi it is common to group sets of three beats into *beat units*. In $\frac{6}{8}$, then, beats 1, 2, and 3 are combined to form the first beat unit, and beats 4, 5, and 6 form the second beat unit. Thus, $\frac{6}{8}$ is interpreted in "two" (**compound duple meter**). *Table 2–4* illustrates these meters.

Compound meter signifies that each beat is divided into equal groups of three parts with each pulse incorporating a dotted note. Recall that a dot increases the value of a note by one-half its original value; thus, a dotted half note receives the same number of beats as a half note plus a quarter note, or as three quarter notes ($\frac{1}{2} + \frac{1}{4} = \frac{3}{4}$). For $\frac{6}{4}$, $\frac{9}{4}$, and $\frac{12}{4}$ meters, the beat is the dotted half note (♩.) and the division is into three quarter notes (♩♩♩). For $\frac{6}{8}$, $\frac{9}{8}$, and $\frac{12}{8}$ meters, the beat is the dotted quarter note (♩.) and the division is into three eighth notes (♫♫). An eighth note (♪) receives one-third of a beat; a quarter note (♩) receives two-thirds of a beat. For $\frac{6}{16}$, $\frac{9}{16}$, and $\frac{12}{16}$ meters, the beat is the dotted eighth note (♪.) and the division is into three sixteenth notes (♬). *See Table 2–4.*

An **asymmetrical meter** is one in which the measure cannot be divided into *equal* groups; there may be *unequal* groups of two, three, or four parts. Examples of asymmetrical meter are $\frac{5}{4}$, $\frac{7}{4}$, $\frac{5}{8}$, and $\frac{7}{8}$. *Example 2–5* illustrates simple, compound, and asymmetrical meters.

SIMPLE METERS			COMPOUND METERS		
DUPLE	TRIPLE	QUADRUPLE	DUPLE	TRIPLE	QUADRUPLE
$\frac{2}{2}$	$\frac{3}{2}$	$\frac{4}{2}$	$\frac{6}{4}$	$\frac{9}{4}$	$\frac{12}{4}$
$\frac{2}{4}$	$\frac{3}{4}$	$\frac{4}{4}$	$\frac{6}{8}$	$\frac{9}{8}$	$\frac{12}{8}$
$\frac{2}{8}$	$\frac{3}{8}$	$\frac{4}{8}$	$\frac{6}{16}$	$\frac{9}{16}$	$\frac{12}{16}$
$\frac{2}{16}$	$\frac{3}{16}$	$\frac{4}{16}$			

Table 2–4. Simple and compound meters. In simple meters, the upper number for duple is 2, for triple, 3, and for quadruple, 4. In compound meters, because of the groups of three beats, the upper number for duple is 6, for triple, 9, and for quadruple, 12.

◆ *Historical Perspective*

In the sixteenth century, triple meter was believed to be the only natural meter since it was representative of the Trinity. A meter in "three" was referred to as "tempus perfectum," and the meter was represented by the symbol "O." Music that was not in triple meter was indicated by a broken circle or "C," and later became known as **common time**. Common time was referred to as "tempus imperfectum." The ℂ for common time in modern usage represents $\frac{4}{4}$; it is employed extensively in popular music as well as in **common-practice** works (c. 1650–1875). The symbol ¢ represents $\frac{2}{2}$ meter, which is called **cut time** or **alla breve**.

◆ *Compound Meter Expanded*

As previously discussed, compound meter signifies that the beat unit can be divided into groups of *three parts*. Thus, in $\frac{6}{8}$ time, each measure contains two groups

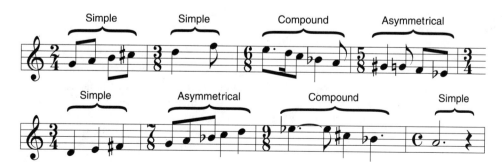

Example 2–5. Simple, compound, and asymmetrical meters.

Values in "12"

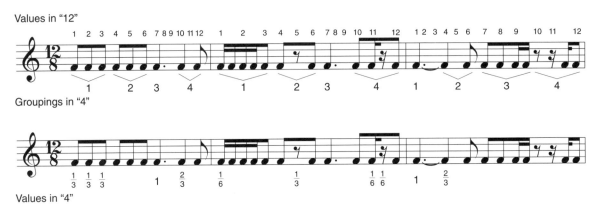

Groupings in "4"

Values in "4"

Example 2–6. Interpreting a ¹²⁄₈ time signature. On the first staff, the literal beats are placed above the corresponding notes and rests. The numbers below represent the actual beat units as they are realized in compound meter. The second staff analyzes the values of the notes as they are realized in compound meter.

consisting of any note or rest values equal to (♩♫♫) or (♩. ♩.). A rapidly moving musical work in ⁶⁄₈ can be interpreted in "two" and is thus referred to as *compound duple meter.* Similarly, a time signature of ⁹⁄₈ can be interpreted in "three" and is referred to as *compound triple meter;* and ¹²⁄₈ interpreted in "four" would be referred to as *compound quadruple meter.* Before attempting to group various combinations of note and rest values into compound meter, it is advisable to analyze the actual beat content of a measure. *Example 2–6* demonstrates the process of interpreting a ¹²⁄₈ time signature.

Other Divisions and Interpretations of the Beat

◆ Triplets

It has been demonstrated how beats may change when certain meters are interpreted as compound meters; so too, beats may be divisible into fractional parts. A common grouping in which a simple beat is divided into thirds is referred to as a *triplet*. A **triplet** is a group of three notes and/or rests equal in duration to the normal time value of two of these notes (rests). Three eighth notes in ⁴⁄₄ time are equal to one and one-half beats; but if they are grouped as a triplet (♫♪) they are equal in time value to two eighth notes, or one beat. Likewise, if three quarter notes in a "four" time signature are grouped into a

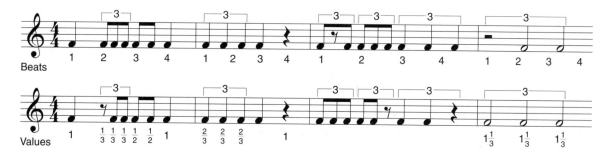

Example 2–7. Eighth-, quarter-, and half-note/rest triplets in 4/4.

triplet configuration ($\overline{}$), the entire triplet is equal to the value of two of the quarter notes, or two beats. Similarly, three half notes in a "four" time signature ($\overline{}$) are equal in time value to two half notes, or four beats. To calculate the durational value of each note in the triplet figure, it is necessary to divide the total number of beats of the entire triplet by the number of notes (3 in each case). Hence, in the eighth-note triplet, 1 would be divided by 3 and each eighth note would receive one-third of a beat; in the quarter-note triplet, 2 would be divided by 3 and the result would be two-thirds of a beat for each note; in the half-note triplet, 4 would be divided by 3 and the result would be one and one-third beats for each note. See *Example 2–7*.

It is clear that a triplet figure can become a complex rhythmic idea. To add further to the intricacies inherent in the triplet, the individual notes can also be divided. In *Example 2–8*, various note values of the triplet have been subdivided and their resultant values are indicated. In this example, note that in measure 1, the triplet encompasses one beat; in measure 2, the triplet encompasses two beats; in measure 3, the third triplet encompasses two beats; in measure 4, the triplet encompasses four beats.

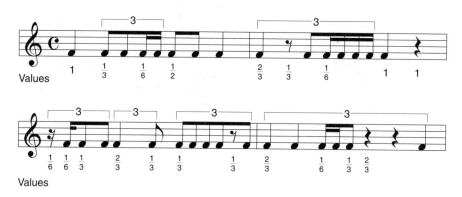

Example 2–8. A subdivision of various note values of the triplet.

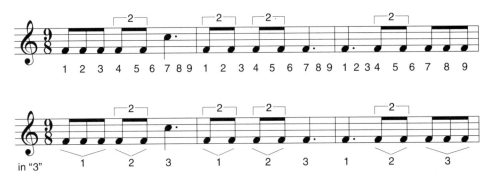

Example 2–9. The use of duplets in dividing beats.

◆ *Duplets*

Duplets, most often written as ♪♪ but also appearing as ♩ ♩ and as ♩. ♩. , provide another method for dividing beats. A **duplet** usually occurs in a meter containing an eight as the lower numeral; it is defined as an even grouping of two notes played over a group of three beats. *Example 2–9* illustrates the use of duplets.

Complex Groupings

◆ *Constant Values over One Beat*

Various groupings of notes and/or rests to be executed over one or more beats are also common in various styles. There are many possibilities for dividing beats. A single beat in ⁴⁄₄ time, for example, may consist of one quarter note (♩); two eighth notes (♪♪); an eighth-note triplet (♪♪♪); four sixteenth notes (♬♬); five sixteenth notes to one beat, or a **quintuplet** (♬♬♬); six sixteenth notes to one beat, or a **sextuplet** (♬♬♬); or seven sixteenth notes to one beat, or a **septuplet** (♬♬♬♬). *Example 2–10* illustrates a group of 29 thirty-second notes spread over two and one-half beats.

When a grouping of eight notes to a beat is written, the note values are changed to thirty-second notes (♫). This is because the thirty-second note is the next naturally occurring value in the normal subdivision of beats, that is, whole note (o), half note (♩), quarter note (♩), eighth note (♪), sixteenth note (♬), thirty-

Polonaise, Op. 9, No. 6

I. J. Paderewski

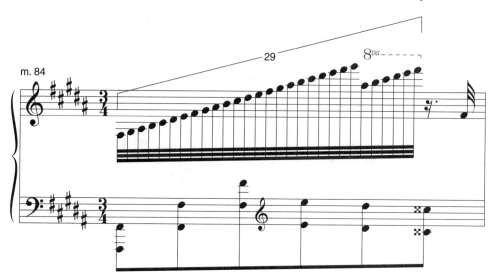

Example 2–10. A group of 29 thirty-seconds over two and one-half beats.

second note (♪), sixty-fourth note (♬), one hundred twenty-eighth note (♬), etc.
Similarly, the thirty-second note can also be categorized from a group of eight to a group of fifteen notes to one beat. A group of sixteen notes to one beat is notated as sixty-fourth notes. See *Example 2–11.*

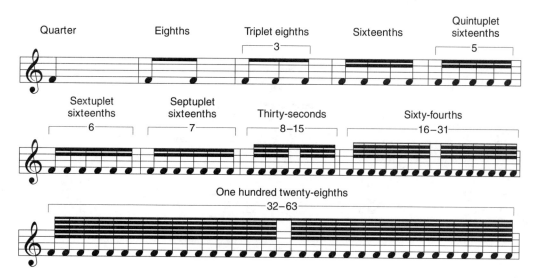

Example 2–11. Decreasing values of notes over one beat.

◆ *Variable Values over One or More Beats*

It is also possible to have a grouping in which the values of the notes are not consistent throughout. This adds to the complexity of calculating the values of each note and approaches an interpretive approximation of time-value distribution in performance. Notice the groupings in the Liszt piece (*Example 2–12*). The interpretation is strictly improvisational. Not only are there "too many beats" in measure 81, but the notes of the quintuplet are not all equal.

◆ *Rhythmic Notation*

The method of rhythmic notation is far from accurate from an interpretive perspective. In the early stages of musical development, bar lines were not employed; but as music became more intricate, it became necessary to indicate metric division in order to facilitate the comprehension and execution of rhythm. A certain rigidity evolved during the Classical period, which resulted in the containment of music within certain boundaries — that is, time signatures remained virtually constant throughout a work. This yielded to more liberal notation beginning in the Romantic period. (See Appendix E.) Composers of this later period would alter the time signature when necessary to accommodate variables in rhythmic patterning. As cultures become more complex and intricate, so do art forms, and artists become more sensitive to the need to portray these intricacies.

The rhythmic notation of melody in popular songwriting is not as accurate as in classical notation. In a significant number of song sheets for popular hits, it is apparent that the rhythmic notation is not quite that of the recorded version. Much of this has to do with the vocalist's interpretation of the melody, and, additionally, with the sheet-music publisher's objective of producing an easily readable and uncomplicated score.

Les Cloches de Genève

F. Liszt

Example 2–12. Too many beats. The total value of the notes in the second measure (m. 81) is three. Also, notice the uneven quintuplet figure.

Counting and Rendering of Rhythmic Figures

Although the following is not an exhaustive study of interpretations of or counting procedures for rhythmic figures, it will facilitate the reader's ability to decipher rhythms. This discussion will examine a method of determining the correct division of beats in "common time," or $\frac{4}{4}$, but can also be applied to any simple meter as well as to any literally interpreted meter.

◆ *The Half-Beat Concept*

Tobias Matthay's statement, "Without rhythm there is nothing" is true not only in music but in the natural universe as well. We live in a rhythmic universe. We expect certain events to occur at specific times. There is rhythm in the passage of day and night and in the seasonal changes. There is rhythm in walking, in sleeping and waking, and in working and relaxing. And there is a beginning and an end to virtually everything.

Many phenomena occur in what can be termed *binary events*. Examples of this are day and night, positive and negative, up and down, left and right, in and out, good and evil, departure and arrival. This binary concept can be applied to the comprehension of the single beat in a musical context. The process of counting a note or rest value is rather simple if the component parts of a single beat are considered. Beating time can be done in several ways — verbally, by tapping one's foot, by the use of a **metronome** (a mechanical device expressly for this purpose), or with the aid of a conductor. For any of these methods a beat consists of only two parts — the "down" part of the beat and the "up" part; thus, a beat is a binary event. Moreover, if the beating process is regular, that is, without variation, a complete beat consists of two *equal* (or *even*) halves.

Consideration of the half-beat values of notes and rests contributes to a far more accurate method of determining the correct placement of the "down" and "up" beats. Since one beat consists of two half beats, each half beat must be either a "down" or an "up" beat. A quarter note in a $\frac{4}{4}$ time signature, for example, receives one full beat or two half beats, and a half note receives two full beats or four half beats. To facilitate the counting process, we can represent the "down" beat by the number "1" and the "up" beat by "and." The quarter note will then be counted as "1 and," or as "1 +." If four quarter notes appear in a measure, the counting procedure will be:

♩ ♩ ♩ ♩

1 + 2 + 3 + 4 +

If two quarter notes followed by a half note appear in a measure, the procedure will be:

♩ ♩ ♩

1 + 2 + 3 + 4 +

Each quarter note receives two half beats and the half note receives four half beats. *Example 2–13* illustrates several rhythmic figures in various "four" meters with correct "down" and "up" beat distribution.

◆ *Intrinsically Normal Accents*

The interpretation of rhythmic figures is greatly facilitated by considering note or rest values in half beats, especially when the rhythm is *syncopated*. **Syncopation** refers to a shifting of the normal accents inherent in a particular time signature, which is usually accomplished by redistributing time values so that normally weaker beats are durationally increased and normally stronger beats are durationally decreased. Intrinsically normal accents for several time signatures are as follows:

$\frac{2}{4}$ — first beat;

$\frac{3}{4}$ — first beat;

$\frac{4}{4}$ — first and third beats, although the third beat is weaker;

$\frac{5}{4}$ — varies, but usually beats one and three, or beats one and four;

$\frac{6}{4}$ — first and fourth beats, although the fourth beat is weaker;

$\frac{7}{4}$ — varies, but usually beats one, three, and five, or beats one, four, and six;

$\frac{8}{4}$ — an atypical time signature, with the strongest accent on the first beat and next strongest on the fifth beat;

$\frac{9}{4}$ — (which usually appears as $\frac{9}{8}$) accents on the first, fourth, and seventh beats;

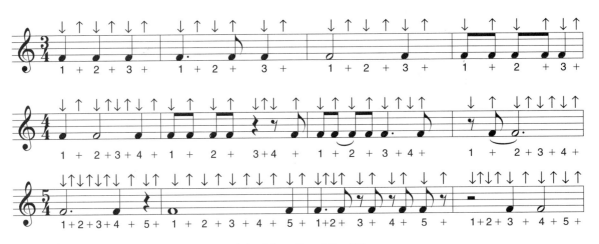

Example 2–13. The correct placement of the "down" and "up" beats.

$\frac{10}{4}$ — an atypical time signature with varying accents;

$\frac{11}{4}$ — also an atypical time signature with varying accents;

$\frac{12}{4}$ — (which usually appears as $\frac{12}{8}$) accents on the first, fourth, seventh, and ninth beats.

These intrinsically normal accents occur in any time signatures with the *same* upper numbers. Thus, for $\frac{2}{8}$ or $\frac{2}{4}$, the accent is on the first beat; for $\frac{4}{8}$ or $\frac{4}{4}$, it is on the first and third beats. See *Example 2–14*.

◆ *Anacrusis*

In a musical work, each complete measure begins with a "down" beat. Often, however, a piece will begin with an incomplete measure; that is, the first measure will not contain the full number of beats prescribed by the time signature. In a short or a moderate-length piece, the combination of the first and last measures will contain the total number of beats required by the time signature. Actually, the incomplete first measure contains the remainder of the beats of the last measure. Those beats in the initial incomplete measure are referred to as an **anacrusis**, an **arsis**, or as "**pick-up**" **beats**. To determine the correct beat with which to begin the count in the incomplete measure, calculate the number of "missing" beats in the incomplete measure and subtract it from the upper number of the time signature. This is illustrated in *Example 2–15* on page 22.

◆ *Syncopation*

Syncopation, though prevalent in all styles of music, is often bewildering to both the neophyte and the experienced musician. However, the concept of applying the half-beat rhythmic method to counting note and rest values may quickly alleviate

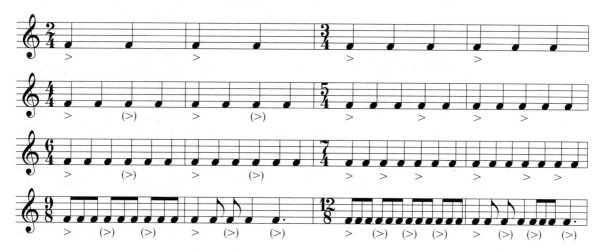

Example 2–14. Normally occurring accents. (>): *weak.*

Example 2–15. Anacrusis. The incomplete measure at the beginning, the anacrusis, is actually the remainder of the final measure. Alternatively, there are 2 beats in the incomplete first measure and the lower number of the time signature is 4; because 4 − 2 = 2, begin on beat 3.

the mystery that many musicians associate with syncopation. Syncopation is simply the displacement of one or more normally accented beats by means of time-value redistribution. While there is more than one method of achieving syncopation, durational-value alteration will be the focus of this discussion.

In *Example 2–16*, syncopation begins with the third beat. Beats one and two are complete because each quarter note receives two half beats, "1 + 2 +" or "1 and 2 and." The eighth note that begins the third beat receives one half beat. Since the second beat of the measure (the second quarter note) is complete and ends with an "and," the beginning of the third beat (the eighth note) must begin with a numeral, in this case the numeral 3. The eighth note can only receive the numeral 3 since an eighth note is equal to one half beat and a numeral or an "and" represents a half beat. The quarter note that follows the eighth note must receive one full beat; but since the eighth note receives only the 3 of the third beat, this quarter note must begin with the "and" of 3 and continue through the first half of the fourth beat — or only the 4. Therefore, the quarter note receives the count "and 4." The last eighth note, which, of course, is equal to a half beat, receives the final "and" of the measure. The resultant beat designation is shown in *Example 2–16*.

In *Example 2–17*, the rhythm is further complicated by the use of ties over the bar line. This, however, should present no problems if the half-beat method is applied. Once again, the meter is $\frac{4}{4}$. Immediately, it can be seen that a syncopation begins the measure. The half-beat value of the first note in measure one causes a weakening of this normally strong beat and an anticipation of the second beat, thus resulting in a syncopation. Since the first note is an eighth note, it can only receive a half beat; moreover, it must begin on the count of 1 since measure one is complete. The second note is a quarter note and must receive two half beats; these are counted "and 2." The ensuing eighth note receives only the "and" of the second beat. Beat three is a quarter note; since

Example 2–16. Syncopation, beginning with the third beat.

Example 2–17. Syncopation incorporating the tie.

the preceding beat was completed with an "and," this quarter note will receive the counts "3 and." Beat four consists of two eighth notes; each, of course, receives a half beat. The count designation is therefore "4 and." The tie that connects the last eighth note of the first measure to the first eighth note of the second measure has absolutely no effect on the counting procedure. The tie means that the first note of the second measure is not to be articulated as a separate note; it is simply held over from the preceding measure for exactly a half beat because it is an eighth note. Therefore, the first eighth note of measure two is held only for the count of 1; the "and" following 1 must be applied to the second eighth note. The third and fourth eighth notes receive "2 and." The fourth eighth note is tied to a quarter note; this quarter note receives the counts "3 and." The eighth rest that follows must be treated exactly as an eighth note. Here, there is one half beat of silence, which is designated by the count of 4. The last eighth note of the measure receives the "and" of the fourth beat.

No durational syncopation occurs in measure three. Although the first beat is weakened by the tie, the measure is quite simple in its rhythmic construction. The first quarter note receives "1 and"; the second quarter note receives "2 and"; the half note receives "3 and 4 and." The resultant count designation is shown in *Example 2–17.*

◆ Counting Beat Divisions of Less Than Half

Obviously, the half-beat concept works well with note and rest values that are no less than a half beat in duration. How, then, are note values with beats less than a half beat counted? In the case of sixteenth notes (♪), two sixteenth notes are placed on each half beat since each sixteenth note in a "four" meter receives one quarter of a beat. With thirty-second notes, four thirty-seconds are placed on each half beat since a thirty-second note (♪) receives one-eighth of a beat.

Although the preceding discussion attempts to give the reader some insight into the process of counting rhythmic figures, it is not, by any means, entirely thorough instruction in rhythmic interpretation. Rhythmic skill can only be achieved through diligent study of and familiarity with the extant musical literature. The primary purpose in presenting this material has been to orient the reader and even the experienced music practitioner to several concepts concerning the interpretation of conventional rhythmic figures employed in a significant portion of common-practice and popular music. One must always keep in mind the infinite variety possible in the creation of music. This applies to elements such as harmony, melody, rhythm, and structure.

Articulation and Interpretation

In music performance, **articulation** means the execution of the written notation as it represents the notes, rests, rhythms, and any other required written directives. **Interpretation** involves the idiosyncratic requirements of specific genres of music as well as the individual ideas that performers and conductors glean from a musical work. Anyone who has heard a musical work performed by various artists knows that from one performance to another a work may sound radically different, although the musical syntax remains fixed. One reason for this can be attributed to **editing**, a procedure common in traditional works, whereby one attempts to clarify, elucidate, correct, and in many instances change particular elements. However, this process does not affect the delivery of a work nearly to the extent that individual interpretation does.

The topic of articulation has been placed in this chapter because the execution and resultant sound of notes is often affected by subtleties that are attributed to rhythmic variation, both slight and drastic. Numerous directives occur in printed music; these include tempo indications, meter signatures, approach and attitude, **attack** (the force applied in the initial production of a sound) and **decay** (the rate at which a sound is permitted to cease), **intensity** (energy), **volume** (loudness), and **timbre** (color). Add to this the individual interpretive aspect and the idiosyncratic requirements of certain styles and it becomes obvious why printed music is only a guide to performance.

Music of the common-practice genre may be considered more rigid than, say, jazz. However, conductors and performers of common-practice works are quite able to convey their personal ideas while leaving the syntax on the printed page intact.

Interpretation of the beat is often a characteristic difference among various styles. Does one play "on the beat," "behind the beat," or "ahead of the beat"? How are certain rhythmic figures interpreted in a particular style? Quite often, the rhythmic figure ♩♩ in a jazz composition is performed as ♩ ♪ . Dots placed above or below note heads (♩ ♩ ♩ ♪) indicate that a note is to be played **staccato** (short or detached). But how short is "short"? This depends upon many factors, such as tempo, approach, and style; these factors also apply to other symbols used to convey various articulations. When a quarter note (♩) is played short, this implies that a certain amount of silence must follow the sound. Does

$$♩ \quad \text{then equal} \quad ♪ ~ \text{ or } ~ ♪ ~ \cdot ~ \text{ or } ~ ♪ ~ ~ \cdot$$

or something else?

When a musical passage is marked "*mf*" (*mezzo forte,* meaning medium loud), how loud is "loud"? In what sense is it "medium"? Terms of this nature are dependent on other terms as a means of comparison. They are not measured in decibels; they are approximated and are contingent upon style, performer, and approach. It must be remembered that musical directives are not one hundred percent accurate and that their interpretation is affected by many factors. It is strongly recommended that the reader become acquainted with the multitude of symbols and directives intrinsic to all genres of music. (See the Glossary.) In the pursuit of understanding musical symbols and their interpretations, there is no substitute for following the score while listening to different performances of a musical work.

Chapter Review

Music as an art form that exists in time is controlled by *rhythm*. Rhythm functions on the micro, meso, and macro levels. The temporal dimension of music is dependent not only on *tempo, pulse, time value,* and *meter,* but also on conceptual and perceptual factors.

A feel for rhythm is a necessary attribute for the music professional; for without it, one's ability to assess, and hence to make valid and authoritative comments regarding musical syntax and performance, is limited.

A time signature consists of an upper number, which, in its literal interpretation, represents the number of beats (units of time) in a measure (a grouping of beats), and a lower number, which indicates the note type that receives one beat.

Several of the elements of rhythm presented and discussed in this chapter were: *common time, alla breve, simple* and *compound meters* — including *compound duple, triple,* and *quadruple meter, asymmetrical meter, note values* and their interpretation in the various meters, the effects of *dots* on notes and rests, and other divisions and interpretations of the beat. Note values are frequently joined by *ties;* notes can also be *beamed* to facilitate reading.

Divisions of the beat include *duplets* (an even grouping of two notes and/or rests played over a division of three), and *triplets* (three evenly distributed notes and/or rests played in the normal time value of two of these). Groupings of notes and rests include the *quintuplet* ($\tilde{}$), *sextuplet* ($\tilde{}$), and *septuplet* ($\tilde{}$). As illustrated, many other groupings are possible.

The counting and interpretation of rhythmic figures based on the concept of the *half-beat* method was demonstrated and applied to simple counting and beat distribution as well as to *syncopation*.

Anacrusis was defined as an *incomplete measure* at the beginning of a work; the counting process here is calculated by subtracting the number of "missing" beats in this incomplete measure from the top number of the time signature.

The section pertaining to *articulation* and *interpretation* was presented to show the element of ambiguity inherent in music notation — often affected by rhythmic variation — and the process and result of music performed in various genres and by individual performers.

Anthology References

For additional usage and analysis, see the following examples in Distefano, Joseph P. and James A. Searle, *Music and Materials for Analysis: An Anthology.* New York, Ardsley House, Publishers, Inc., 1995.

simultaneous simple and compound meters resulting in polymeter
Example 36.   *Impromptu,* Op. 5, No. 5, Robert Schumann, pp. 201–6.
simple and asymmetrical meters
Example 64.   *Structures Ia,* Book I, Pierre Boulez, pp. 383–90.
no initial meter, simple meters, compound meters
Example 56.   *Sonata for Violin,* No. 2, Third Movement, "The Revival," Charles Ives, pp. 325–34.
triplets, complex triplets, sextuplets
Example 44.   *Poème,* Op. 69, No. 1, Alexander Scriabin, pp. 253–58.
quintuplets and complex quintuplets; double whole note; syncopation
Example 54.   *Prelude and Fugue on a Theme of Vittoria,* Benjamin Britten, pp. 305–16.

Self-Test

1. Define *rhythm.*
2. Define the terms *tempo, meter,* and *pulse.*
3. Define the terms *micro, meso,* and *macro.*
4. Define the term *beat.*
5. Explain the meaning and effect of the *time signature.*
6. Describe *simple meter.*
7. Describe *compound meter.*
8. Describe *asymmetrical meter.*
9. Describe *common time* (c).
10. Describe *alla breve* (¢).
11. Popular music uses a time signature of _____ extensively.
12. Explain how (a) a dot and (b) a double dot affect a note or rest.
13. Calculate the time value of (a) a dotted eighth note, (b) a double-dotted half note, and (c) a dotted sixteenth note in common time.
14. Calculate the value of (a) a thirty-second note, (b) a dotted eighth note, and (c) a double-dotted eighth note in $\frac{6}{8}$ meter.
15. Calculate the value of (a) a dotted quarter note and (b) a double-dotted half note in $\frac{3}{2}$ meter.
16. Calculate the time value of a quarter note in $\frac{9}{8}$ meter when the meter is interpreted in "three."
17. Calculate the value of each half note in a half-note triplet in $\frac{6}{4}$ meter interpreted in "two."
18. Calculate the value of a sixteenth note in an eighth-note triplet in $\frac{2}{4}$ meter.
19. What is the value of a sixty-fourth note in $\frac{12}{16}$ meter interpreted in "4"?

20. Define *syncopation*.   **21.** Define *anacrusis*.

22. Define *articulation*.

23. A group of seven notes and/or rests spread evenly over a beat is known as a _____ .

24. Several factors affecting interpretation include _____ , _____ , and _____ .

Exercises

1. Insert bar lines as determined by the time signature.

(a)

(b)

(c)

(d)

2. The first measure of Part (a) indicates notes and rests that satisfy $\frac{4}{4}$ time. Fill in various notes and rests in the other measures to satisfy the time signatures indicated in Parts (a), (b), and (c).

(a)

(b)

3. Write equivalent values using dots and ties.

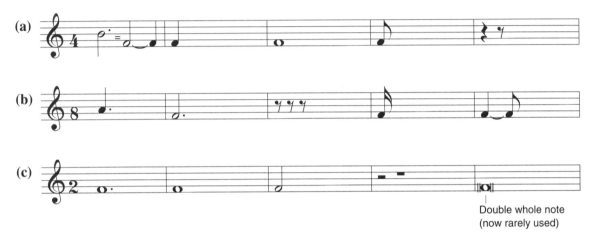

Double whole note
(now rarely used)

4. Add notes and rests to satisfy the time signatures. Use dots, double dots, and ties.

5. Add bar lines to create measures according to the time signature.

6. Bracket the beat units in these compound meters. See Part (a).

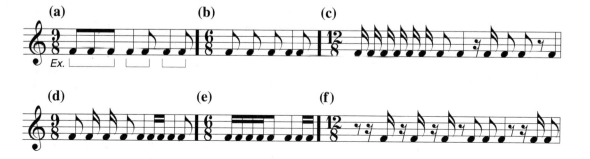

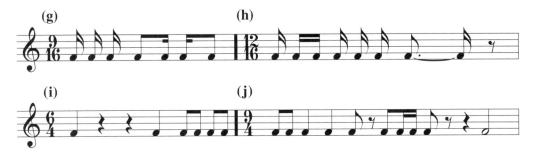

7. Indicate the time values for each of the notes, tied notes, rests, and groupings. Rewrite particular values and groupings correctly to correspond to the time signature.

8. Determine the note and rest values for the following interpretations.

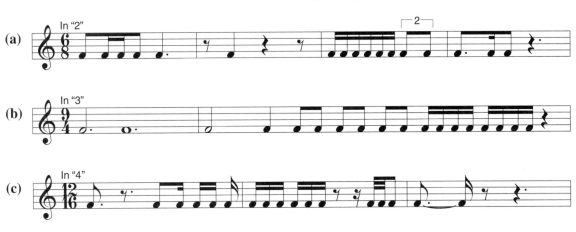

9. Apply the Arabic numeral in counting the following:

(a)

(b)

(c)

(d)

10. Indicate the down beats by numerals and the up beats by the use of +.

(a)

(b)

(c)

(d)

3

SCALES, KEYS, AND MODES

Scales

A **scale** is a series of pitches produced in an ascending and/or descending direction with each succeeding pitch *usually* within an *alphabetical distance* of three letters. Among the most widely used scale structures beginning on C are:

C–D–E–F–G–A–B–C

C–D–E♭–F–G–A♭–B–C

C–D–E–G–A–C

C–D–E–F♯–G♯–A♯–C

Notice that in the first and second scales, each succeeding pitch letter is one alphabetical letter away from the preceding one (with A immediately following G). In the third scale, a distance of an **alphabetical third** (3rd) is present between the E and G (because the series E–F–G contains three notes) and between the A and C. In the fourth scale, an alphabetical 3rd is present between the A♯ and C. Note that sharps and flats do not affect *alphabetical distances* (as opposed to *interval distances,* which will be discussed in Chapter 4).

For the past three hundred years, Western composers and songwriters have relied primarily on two types of scales, the *major* scale and the *minor* scale, from which to fashion their compositions. The major and minor scales are comprised of combinations of whole and half steps; each consists of a series of seven different pitches, usually beginning and ending on the note of the same pitch an **octave** (eight alphabetical scale pitches, inclusive of the initial pitch) removed. These beginning (and ending) pitches identify the letter name of the scale; thus, C major (CM) begins on C. See *Figure 3–6* on page 36.

Major-Scale Construction

The **whole-step (1)/half-step (½) pattern** for a **major scale** consists of:

$$1 - 1 - \tfrac{1}{2} - 1 - 1 - 1 - \tfrac{1}{2}$$

Following this whole-step/half-step pattern and beginning on any pitch, a major scale can be constructed, as shown in *Example 3–1*.

The C major scale is the simplest in that no sharps or flats are necessary:

$$C - D - E - F - G - A - B - C$$
$$\text{1} \quad \text{1} \quad \tfrac{1}{2} \quad \text{1} \quad \text{1} \quad \text{1} \quad \tfrac{1}{2}$$

In all major scales except C major, it is necessary to alter at least one pitch in order to maintain the correct step configuration. For example, the series

$$E - F - G - A - B - C - D - E$$
$$\tfrac{1}{2} \quad \text{1} \quad \text{1} \quad \text{1} \quad \tfrac{1}{2} \quad \text{1} \quad \text{1}$$

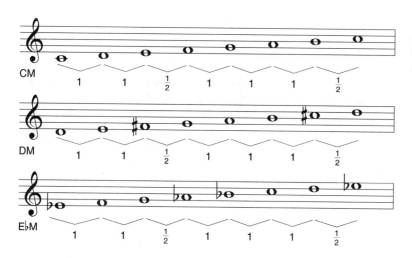

Example 3–1. Construction of major scales using whole steps and half steps.

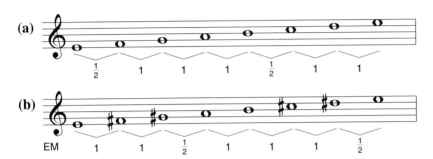

(a)

$\frac{1}{2}$ 1 1 1 $\frac{1}{2}$ 1 1

(b)

EM 1 1 $\frac{1}{2}$ 1 1 1 $\frac{1}{2}$

Example 3–2. Alteration of pitches to maintain the whole-step/half-step pattern. The first staff in Part (a) is a series from E to E. This same series with the correct application of sharps results in the E major scale in Part (b).

does not produce a major scale. Therefore, the **distances** between pitches (as measured in whole and half steps) must be adjusted to conform to the whole-step/half-step pattern so as to form a major scale. Here, it is necessary to *raise* certain pitches to produce the required whole steps as follows:

$$E - F\sharp - G\sharp - A - B - C\sharp - D\sharp - E$$
$$\lor \quad \lor \quad \lor \quad \lor \quad \lor \quad \lor \quad \lor$$
$$1 \quad 1 \quad \tfrac{1}{2} \quad 1 \quad 1 \quad 1 \quad \tfrac{1}{2}$$

See *Example 3–2.*

In many scales, it is necessary to *decrease* the distances between the notes in order to satisfy the required pattern; this is illustrated in *Example 3–3.*

Although *conventional* practice limits the practical application of the preceding major-scale pattern to beginning on specific pitches, namely:

C♭, C, C♯, D♭, D, E♭, E, F, F♯, G♭, G, A♭, A, B♭, and B

it is possible to construct major scales beginning with any pitch. Adhering to the whole-step/half-step pattern *(Example 3–4)* demonstrates several major scales commencing on pitches other than those mentioned.

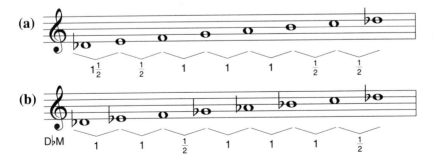

(a)

$1\frac{1}{2}$ $\frac{1}{2}$ 1 1 1 $\frac{1}{2}$ $\frac{1}{2}$

(b)

D♭M 1 1 $\frac{1}{2}$ 1 1 1 $\frac{1}{2}$

Example 3–3. Decreasing the distance between pitches to maintain the whole-step/ half-step pattern. A series from D♭ to D♭ is shown in Part (a). The distance between D♭ and E is one and one-half (1¹/₂) steps. It is necessary to decrease this distance as well as others in this series to obtain the D♭ major scale in Part (b).

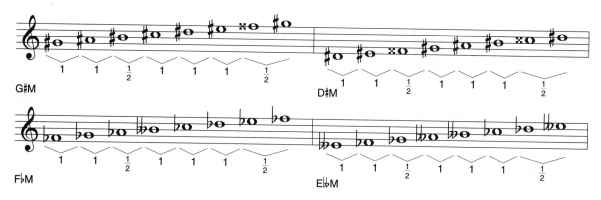

Example 3–4. Major scales commencing on unusual pitches.

Minor-Scale Construction

Although there is only one pattern of the major scale, the **minor scale** can be constructed to produce three different types, namely the *natural* or *pure* minor, the *harmonic* minor, and the *melodic* minor (see *Example 3–5*). The **whole-step/half-step ascending patterns** for each are as follows:

Natural (pure) minor:	$1 - \frac{1}{2} - 1 - 1 - \frac{1}{2} - 1 - 1$
Harmonic minor:	$1 - \frac{1}{2} - 1 - 1 - \frac{1}{2} - 1\frac{1}{2} - \frac{1}{2}$
Melodic minor:	$1 - \frac{1}{2} - 1 - 1 - 1 - 1 - \frac{1}{2}$

◆ *Relative Minor Scales*

Every major scale has what is referred to as a *relative minor* scale, and conversely, every minor scale has a *relative major* scale. A **relative minor scale**

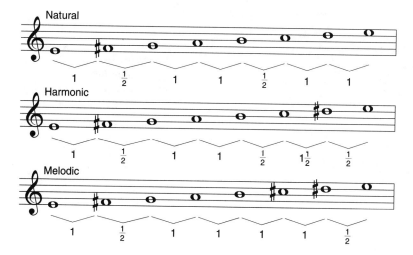

Example 3–5. The natural minor, the harmonic minor, and the melodic minor, beginning on E.

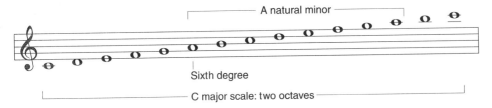

Example 3–6. The relative minor scale of C major. This scale, A minor, begins on the sixth degree of C major.

employs as its initial pitch the *sixth* **degree** (scale step) of its major scale. Thus, as shown in *Example 3–6,* in the C major scale, C–D–E–F–G–A–B–C, the sixth degree is the pitch A. To construct the A minor (Am) scale, begin with A and proceed *alphabetically* until the series is completed; hence

$$A - B - C - D - E - F - G - A$$
$$1 \quad \tfrac{1}{2} \quad 1 \quad 1 \quad \tfrac{1}{2} \quad 1 \quad 1$$

◆ The Natural or Pure Minor Scale

The relative minor scale shown in Example 3–6 is referred to as the **natural** or **pure** form of the **minor scale.** There is absolutely no adjustment of the pitches in the natural minor scale; it is simply derived from the relative major scale as it appears, beginning on the sixth degree. Two other natural minor scales are shown in *Example 3–7.*

◆ The Harmonic Minor Scale

The **harmonic minor scale** differs from the natural minor scale in the distance between the sixth and seventh degrees. In the natural minor scale, the distance

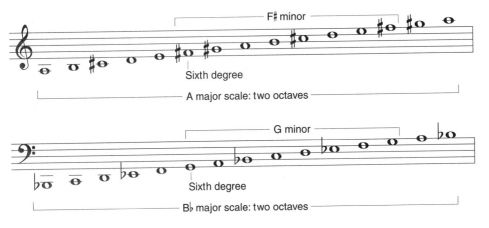

Example 3–7. The natural (pure) form of the minor scale.

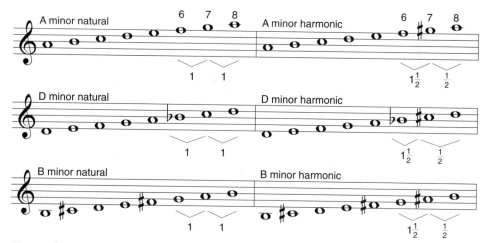

***Example 3–8.** The distance between the sixth and seventh degrees in the natural minor and harmonic minor scales.*

between the sixth and seventh degrees constitutes a whole step; in the harmonic minor scale this distance is *increased* to a whole step *plus* a half step by raising the seventh degree, as illustrated in *Example 3–8*.

◆ *The Melodic Minor Scale*

The **melodic** form of the **minor scale** contains an alteration of the sixth and seventh degrees. Both sixth and seventh degrees are each raised in pitch by a half step. It should be noted that when constructing the melodic minor scale in an autonomous exercise of scale writing, the sixth and seventh degrees are *raised in ascending order* and *restored in descending order* so as to form the natural minor. (See *Example 3–9*.) However, in actual music composition this practice varies, depending on the context.

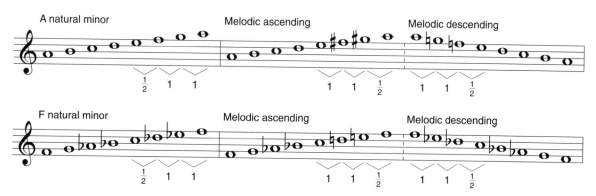

***Example 3–9.** Melodic minor scales in which the sixth and seventh degrees are raised in ascending order and restored in descending order.* The descending order produces the natural minor.

◆ *Technical Names of Scale Degrees*

For reference purposes, it is useful to refer to scale degrees by the following traditional names:

1st Degree:	**Tonic**
2nd Degree:	**Supertonic**
3rd Degree:	**Mediant**
4th Degree:	**Subdominant**
5th Degree:	**Dominant**
6th Degree:	**Submediant**
7th Degree:	**Leading Tone**

The seventh degree in the natural minor scale and in the descending form of the melodic minor scale is referred to as **subtonic**.

Keys and Key Signature

To say that a composition is in a certain **key** means that it derives its pitch content from a particular scale. If the composition in question is *exclusively* in a key (for example, in D major), that is, without *any* pitch alterations, then the only pitches present are those found in that scale (D major), and the composition is said to be **diatonic**. Compositions containing notes foreign to the prevailing scale or key are said to be **chromatic**.

In notating a musical work the clef is followed by a **key signature**, which alerts the performer as to the initial scale in which the piece is constructed. For example, if the E major scale *(Example 3–2(b)* on page 34) is used, the key

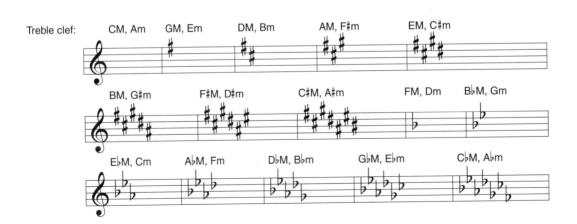

signature would contain the four sharps that appeared as a result of the correct whole-step/half-step pattern. The four sharps must be placed on the correct lines and spaces of the staff to indicate their use in the music.

In the case of the C major scale, which contains no sharps or flats, none will appear in the key signature. *Example 3–10* on pages 38–39 illustrates all the major and relative minor key signatures in treble, bass, alto, and tenor clefs.

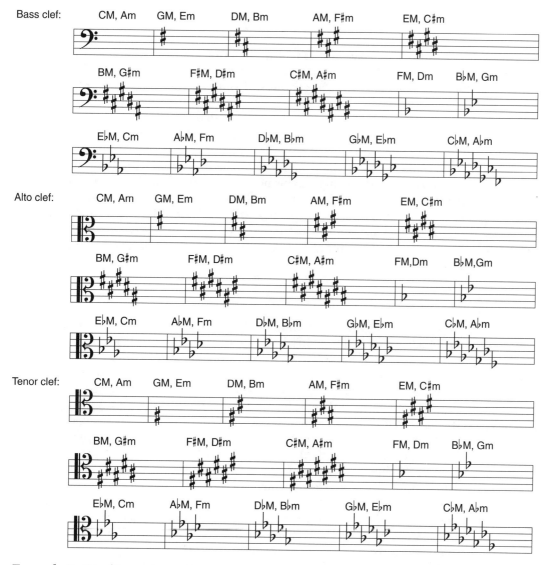

Example 3–10. The major and relative minor key signatures. Note that for the first eight key signatures, each successive one contains one additional sharp; the same is true of the number of flats in the remaining key signatures.

Example 3–11. Notes that are foreign to the major key. Although the key signature is C major, the appearance of G♯ suggests A minor. The last two pitches, F♯–G♯, suggest the use of the melodic minor (♮6, ♯7).

Since every key has a relative major or minor key, how is it possible to know if a musical composition is in a major or minor key by simply observing the key signature? In fact, one must look further into the actual music. If the notes at the beginning are only from the major scale, then it is highly likely that the work is in the major key. However, if notes appear that are *foreign* to the major key, then the relative minor key should be considered.

In the construction of the harmonic minor scale, for example, recall that the seventh degree of the scale is raised one half step. Therefore, if the key signature is C major, which contains no sharps or flats, and if it is determined that the key may be the relative minor, the harmonic form of the A minor scale would contain a raised seventh degree (G♯). With a key signature having no sharps or flats and with the appearance of a G♯ in the pitch content at or near the beginning of the piece, the key center of A minor is virtually assured. See *Example 3–11.*

◆ *Parallel Scale and Key Relationships*

Although not useful for determining the major or minor key of a musical composition, a relationship referred to as *parallel* exists among scales and keys. A parallel key, unlike a relative key, does not contain the same key signature. **Parallel** in this context means the relationship of a major and minor key by **tonic** (pitch) letter name only. Thus, C major and C minor are said to be parallel keys only because they begin with the same pitch. Their key signatures are quite different; C major contains no sharps or flats, whereas C minor contains three flats. Likewise, E major contains four sharps, whereas E minor, the parallel key, contains one sharp.

Determining the key signature for a parallel key is a more complex process than that for a relative key. One may arrive at the parallel minor key signature of a major scale by counting the distance of three half steps up to the *alphabetical* 3rd from the tonic of the major scale. For example, to determine the parallel key signature for G major, the following process produces the correct key signature: begin with G and move up three half steps, that is:

$$G - G\sharp - A - B\flat$$
$$\vee \quad \vee \quad \vee$$
$$\text{½} \quad \text{½} \quad \text{½}$$

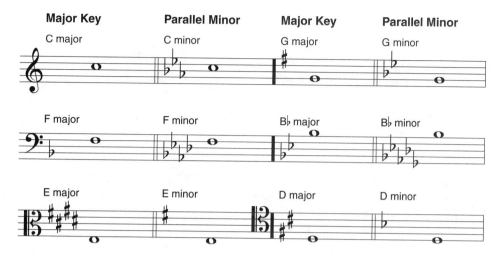

Example 3–12. *A comparison of major and parallel key signatures.*

Note that B♭ must be spelled as such in order to satisfy the *alphabetical* 3rd distance from G to B (G–A–B). If A♯ (enharmonic of B♭) were used, the *alphabetical* distance from G would appear as a 2nd, G–A. The key signature for G minor, then, is the same as the key signature for B♭ major — two flats. *Example 3–12* compares major with parallel key signatures.

◆ Several Other Commonly Used Scale Types

The majority of Western music composition derives its components from the major and minor scales, and as a result, this discussion has been limited to an investigation of the major scale and three forms of the minor scales. However, even though key signatures denote either major- or minor-scale content, many other types of scales are incorporated into the major/minor system. Several of these are listed in *Table 3–13*, on page 42 and their derivations are often extracted from major or minor scales.

◆ The Circle of Fifths

Example 3–14 on page 43 illustrates all the major and relative minor keys and the principle of the **circle** or **cycle of fifths**. These fifths are actually *perfect fifths*. A **perfect fifth** (5th) is the distance between two pitch names an *alphabetical* 5th apart, for example, C to G, containing seven half steps. Beginning with C major, the circle proceeds in an *ascending* direction of 5ths. From C to G is a 5th; thus, G major is the next key in the circle, and it contains one sharp, F♯. To determine the next key in the circle, use the present scale and its correct sharps or flats to locate the next 5th. Thus, in the G major scale, the next 5th is D, whose major key contains two sharps. In the D major scale, the next 5th is

CHROMATIC SCALE

Beginning on any pitch and proceeding in half steps:

Ascending: C, C♯, D, D♯, E, F, F♯, G G♯, A, A♯, B

Descending: C, B, B♭, A, A♭, G, G♭, F, E, E♭, D, D♭

(Various pitches are enharmonically spelled under certain conditions.)

WHOLE-TONE SCALE

Beginning on any pitch and proceeding in whole steps:

Ascending: C, D, E, F♯, G♯, A♯

Descending: C, B♭, A♭, G♭, E, D

PENTATONIC SCALE

A five-note scale often thought of as the first, second, third, fifth, and sixth degrees of a major scale. The black keys of a piano keyboard beginning with the group of three black keys imitates the distances of this pattern.

BLUES SCALE

This may be considered as a major scale with lowered third and seventh degrees. It often contains an additional raised fourth (flatted fifth), as well.

DIMINISHED SCALE

This consists of alternating whole and half steps:

C, D♭, E♭, E, F♯, G, A, B♭ or

C, D, E♭, F, G♭, A♭, A, B

Table 3–13. Scale construction for several commonly used scales other than major or minor.

A; A major yields E as the next 5th; E major yields B as the next 5th; B major yields F♯ as the next 5th since F is sharp in the B scale. Each time a succeeding 5th is located, one additional sharp is added, which is also a 5th from the preceding sharp. For keys containing flats, observe the pattern in *Example 3–14*. Under certain conditions, spellings of key signatures are enharmonic; for example, when a key center exceeds seven sharps or flats, its spelling most often becomes enharmonic in order to avoid double sharps or double flats in the key signature.

◆ *Tetrachords*

Of extreme importance in the relationship between keys and key signatures is the concept of the *tetrachord*. A **tetrachord** consists of the first four-note group and the last four-note group of a scale. (Tetrachord relationships normally apply to major scales.) The second tetrachord of a major scale, for example, is the first tetrachord of the major scale whose tonic lies a perfect 5th above. Hence, in the C major scale,

C – D – E – F – G – A – B – C

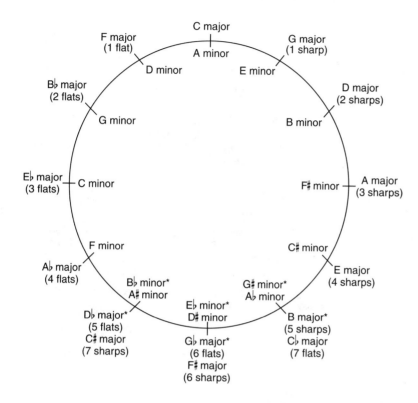

*indicates enharmonic equivalents.

Example 3–14. The circle of fifths.

the first tetrachord is

$$C - D - E - F$$

the second tetrachord is

$$G - A - B - C$$

which is the first tetrachord of the G major scale,

$$G - A - B - C - D - E - F\sharp - G$$

a perfect 5th above C major. Similarly, the second tetrachord of the G major scale,

$$D - E - F\sharp - G$$

is the first tetrachord of the D major scale,

$$D - E - F\sharp - G - A - B - C\sharp - D$$

a perfect 5th above the G major scale (see *Example 3–15* on page 44). A tetrachord relationship also exists between the second tetrachord of an ascending melodic minor scale and the first tetrachord of the major scale a perfect 5th higher. For example, the second tetrachord of Am melodic,

$$E - F\sharp - G\sharp - A$$

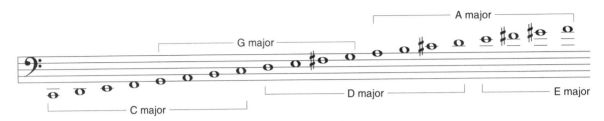

Example 3–15. Tetrachord relationships. The last tetrachord of C major (G–A–B–C) is the first tetrachord of G major. Each subsequent scale is a 5th higher than the preceding one.

is the same as the first tetrachord of EM. The tetrachord relationship is crucial for understanding the relationship between keys and the circle of 5ths.

It will be seen that the theory of music consists of a multitude of patterns, relationships, and logical developments. An understanding of these relationships among keys is one of the first steps in conceptualizing music.

Modes

Although the majority of music composed within the last several hundred years has primarily utilized the major and minor scale systems, much music, even within these systems, has incorporated *modes*. The original modes date from antiquity. The modern system of mode construction formed the basis for Western music composition from approximately 800 to 1500, and was used primarily in church music. Modal usage is still existent in contemporary styles, but its use has been extensively varied and adapted.

Essentially, a **mode** can best be envisioned as beginning on any white key on a piano keyboard. From C to the next C will produce one mode; from D to the next D will produce another, etc. Each series beginning on any white key of the piano will produce a different mode, since each series contains differing whole and half steps. *Example 3–16* lists the various modes and displays them on a staff, as they relate to the key of C major.

Each mode can best be remembered by its position relative to a major scale. An **Ionian** mode always begins on the first degree of a major scale and consequently, the major scale is essentially an Ionian mode. The **Dorian** mode begins on the second degree of a major scale; the **Phrygian**, on the third degree; the **Lydian**, on the fourth degree; the **Mixolydian**, on the fifth degree; the **Aeolian** (natural minor scale), on the sixth degree; and the **Locrian**, on the seventh degree.

Ionian mode (major scale)	C, D, E, F, G, A, B, C
Dorian mode	D, E, F, G, A, B, C, D
Phrygian mode	E, F, G, A, B, C, D, E
Lydian mode	F, G, A, B, C, D, E, F
Mixolydian mode	G, A, B, C, D, E, F, G
Aeolian mode (natural minor scale)	A, B, C, D, E, F, G, A
Locrian mode	B, C, D, E, F, G, A, B

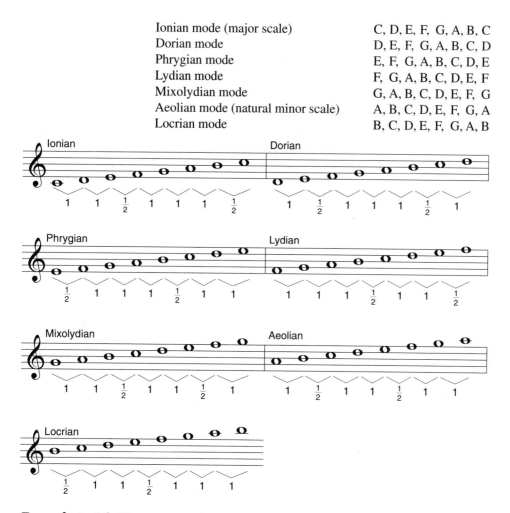

Example 3–16. The seven modes, as they relate to the scale of C major. Note the whole-step/half-step pattern for each mode.

◆ *Mode Transposition*

Modes, like major and minor scales, can be constructed beginning on any pitch. In music, to **transpose** means to recreate a pattern beginning with a different pitch. Just as major or minor scales can be constructed to begin on any pitch by following the whole-step/half-step pattern, so too, any mode can be transposed by simply following its whole-step/half-step pattern. *Example 3–17* on page 46 illustrates the whole- and half-step configurations for the Dorian and Mixolydian modes, two commonly used modes, together with several transpositions.

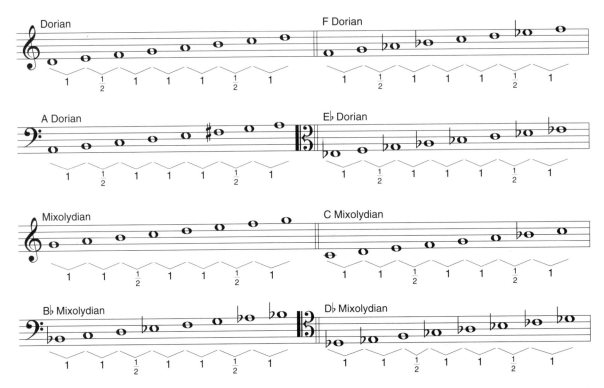

Example 3–17. *The whole-step/half-step pattern for the Dorian and Mixolydian modes with several transpositions.*

A more direct method for transposing modes involves consideration of the relationship of the mode to the tonic of the major scale. Consider, for example, transposing the Dorian mode so that it begins on the pitch F. Recall that the Dorian mode is constructed beginning on the second degree of a major scale. If the pitch F is considered the second degree of a major scale, then the tonic of that scale, which must lie a whole step below F and must be spelled alphabetically as E♭, determines the major scale from which the Dorian mode beginning on F is constructed. Since the E♭ major scale contains the pitches

E♭, F, G, A♭, B♭, C, D, E♭

a Dorian mode on F will contain the same pitches but will begin and end on F:

F, G, A♭, B♭, C, D, E♭, F

As another example of mode transposition, to construct a Lydian mode beginning on the pitch A, consider A as the fourth degree (Lydian) of the E major scale. The A Lydian mode will contain the pitches

A, B, C♯, D♯, E, F♯, G♯, A

Beginning with the pitch A, each ensuing note will be derived from the E major scale. See *Example 3–18.*

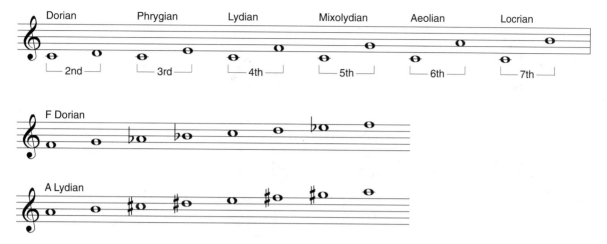

Example 3–18. Modes in relation to C. On the first staff, each mode is illustrated in its relationship to C. To apply this method of transposition, consider a mode as that particular degree of a major scale. On line 2, F Dorian begins a whole step above E♭ and contains the pitches of the E♭ major scale. On line 3, A Lydian begins on the fourth degree of the E major scale.

Although strict or conventional modal usage is not presently in vogue, *Example 3–19* on pages 47–49 illustrates modes in various styles, both past and present.

(a)   **"Scarborough Fair"**

(b)   *Austiefer Not Schrei' Ich Zu Dir*

(c)   **"Bessey Bell and Mary Gray"**

(d)   **"Eleanor Rigby"**

Words and Music by John Lennon and Paul McCartney

El - ea - nor Rig - by,   picks up   the   rice ___ in   the church ___
Fa - ther - Mc Ken - zie,   writ - ing   the words ___ of   a   ser -
El - ea - nor Rig - by,   died   in   the church ___ and was bur -

where a wed - ding has been, _____
mon that no _____ one will hear, _____
ied a - long _____ with her name, _____

lives in a dream. _____
no one comes near. _____
no - bod - y came. _____

Waits at the win - dow,
Look at him work - ing,
Fa - ther - Mc Ken - zie,

wear - ing the face _____ that she keeps _____ in a jar _____ by the door, ___
darn - ing his socks _____ in the night _____ when there's no - bod - y there, ___
wip - ing the dirt _____ from his hands _____ as he walks _____ from the grave, ___

_____
_____
_____

who is it for? _____
what does he care? _____
no one was saved. _____

Example 3–19. Modes in various styles. (a) Although the key signature of one flat (indicating F major or D minor) is used, the melody stresses D as a tonic. The use of B♮ and C♮ (the sixth and seventh of the D scale) does not fit the possible minor scales. The D up to D with no degree alterations yields D Dorian. (b) With D as a tonic and a key signature in a relationship a 3rd below, the Phrygian mode is established: D–E♭–F–G–A–B♭–C–D. (c) With the addition of A♭ throughout this melody, a Mixolydian mode is established. The scale of B♭ major with A♭ yields B♭–C–D–E♭–G–A♭–B♭. (d) E Dorian: E–F♯–G–A–B–C♯–D–E. Note that the encircled C♯s define the mode of the piece.

Chapter Review

The two predominant scale types currently in use are the *major* and *minor*. A multitude of other scales are also used, but not as widely.

With the minor scale, three forms are possible; these are the *natural minor*, the *harmonic minor*, and the *melodic minor*. Each particular type or form of scale consists of a unique *whole-step/half-step pattern*. For the major scale this pattern is:

$$1 - 1 - \tfrac{1}{2} - 1 - 1 - 1 - \tfrac{1}{2}$$

The pattern for the natural minor is:

$$1 - \tfrac{1}{2} - 1 - 1 - \tfrac{1}{2} - 1 - 1$$

for the harmonic minor:

$$1 - \tfrac{1}{2} - 1 - 1 - \tfrac{1}{2} - 1\tfrac{1}{2} - \tfrac{1}{2}$$

for the melodic minor in the ascending form:

$$1 - \tfrac{1}{2} - 1 - 1 - 1 - 1 - \tfrac{1}{2}$$

The term *key* denotes scale use for a particular piece or part of a musical work. The key refers to the scale from which all or the vast majority of the pitches are derived. Musical works or portions of works that use pitches exclusively from one key are said to be *diatonic*. If pitches foreign to the prevailing key are introduced, the piece is said to be *chromatic*. A *key signature* accounts for any pitches that are either sharp or flat within the scale of the employed key.

A major key has a *relative* minor key; similarly, a minor key has a relative major key. There is also a *parallel* relationship between keys. Relative keys share the same key signature; parallel keys share only the tonic letter-name of the key or scale.

Keys and/or scales can be viewed as proceeding in a particular order concerning their numbers of sharps or flats. This order is known as the *circle* or *cycle of fifths*. For example, as each additional sharp is added to a key signature, the scale whose initial note (tonic) lies a perfect 5th above the prevailing key is next in the circle of fifths.

Other scales in current use include, but are not limited to, the *chromatic, whole tone, pentatonic, blues,* and *diminished*.

Modes are types of scales that formed the basis for Western music composition from about 800 to 1500. Essentially seven modes exist, namely: *Ionian, Dorian, Phrygian, Lydian, Mixolydian, Aeolian,* and *Locrian*. The Ionian mode and the major scale are one and the same in their whole-step/half-step pattern; the Aeolian mode and the natural minor scale are also the same in this respect. As with the major and minor scales, modes can be *transposed* to begin on any pitch. Currently, the two most commonly employed modes other than the Ionian and Aeolian are the Dorian and Mixolydian.

Anthology References

For additional usage and analysis, see the following examples in Distefano, Joseph P. and James A. Searle, *Music and Materials for Analysis: An Anthology*. New York, Ardsley House, Publishers, Inc., 1995.

modes

Examples 1–3.   Gregorian Chant, Kyrie, Agnus Dei, Communion. pp. 1–10.
Examples 4–5.   *Le Jeu de Robin,* Adam de la Halle.
                   C'est la Fine, Guillaume d'Amiens. pp. 11–16.

harmonic and melodic minor scales
>   *Example 22.*   *Invention No. 4,* Johann Sebastian Bach, pp. 81–88.

chromaticism
>   *Example 33.*   *Waltz,* Franz Schubert, pp. 179–84.

parallel-key relationship
>   *Example 34.*   *Die Winterreise,* Op. 89, "Muth," Franz Schubert, pp. 185–92.

chromatic scale; circle of fifths
>   *Example 32.*   *Sonata,* K. 333, Wolfgang Amadeus Mozart, pp. 149–78.

whole-tone and pentatonic scales
>   *Example 45.*   *Preludes,* Book I, No. 2, "Voiles" ("Sails"), Claude Achille Debussy, pp. 259–66.

Self-Test

1. The two predominant types of scales in current use are the _____ and _____ .
2. The whole-step/half-step pattern of the major scale is given by _____ .
3. The whole-step/half-step pattern of the natural minor scale is given by _____ .
4. The whole-step/half-step pattern of the harmonic minor scale is given by _____ .
5. The whole-step/half-step pattern of the melodic minor scale is given by _____ .
6. The relative minor is derived from the _____ degree of the major scale.
7. Define the term *key.*
8. The term *diatonic* means_____ .
9. The term *chromatic* means _____ .
10. A *key signature* represents _____ .
11. Describe the *circle of fifths.* What does it represent and in what manner is it ordered?
12. Describe a *parallel* key relationship.
13. Describe the concept of the *tetrachord* relationship.
14. The seven modal types are _____ , _____ , _____ ,
    _____ , _____ , _____ , and _____ .
15. Two commonly utilized modes other than the Ionian and Aeolian are the _____
    and _____ .
16. Write the whole-step/half-step patterns for each of the modes.
17. Describe two methods for transposing modes.

Exercises

1. Construct a major scale beginning on each note. Label all whole and half steps.

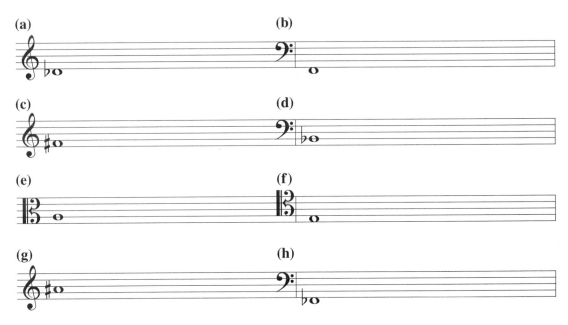

(a)

(b)

(c)

(d)

(e)

(f)

(g)

(h)

2. Construct the required minor scales. Label all steps.

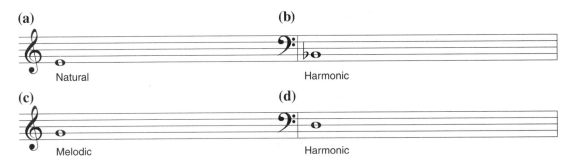

(a)

Natural

(b)

Harmonic

(c)

Melodic

(d)

Harmonic

3. Determine the relative minor for each of the major tonics (several are hypothetical).

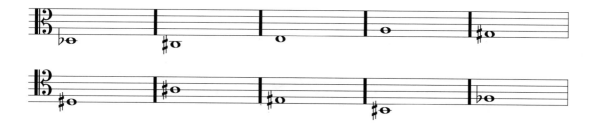

4. Construct the major scale and its parallel minor in each of the indicated forms. Use key signa-tures. (See *Example 3–10.*)

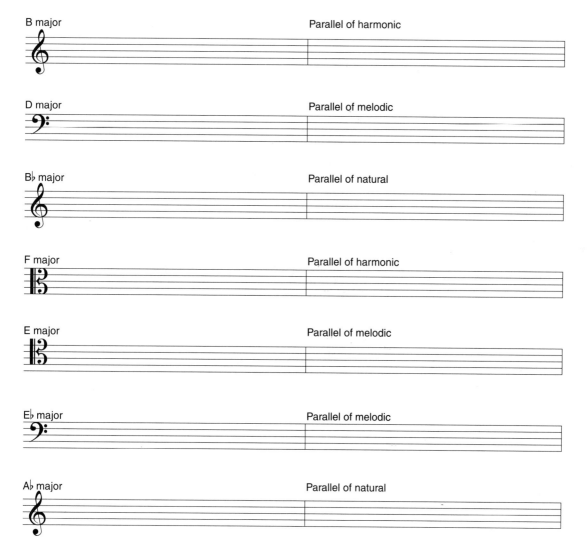

5. Construct the indicated modes.

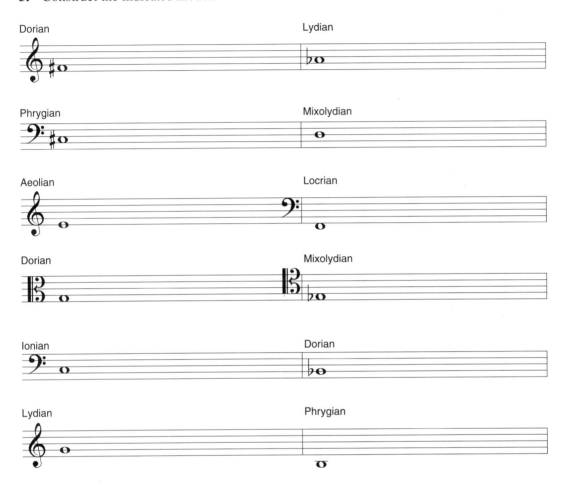

6. Determine which sequences are major scales, which are minor scales, and which are modes. Identify each type of minor scale.

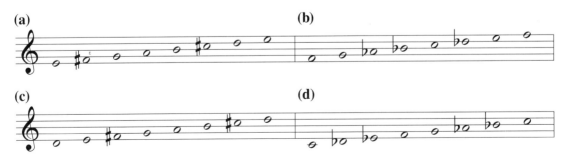

4

INTERVALS

Basic Notions

An **interval** is the numerical and qualitative distance between two notes. Intervals appear either **melodically** (in horizontal or linear form) or **harmonically** (in vertical or simultaneous form). A harmonic interval is also referred to as a **dyad**.

Intervals are described in terms of the distance between their lower and upper notes, as illustrated in *Example 4–1*. In writing and identifying intervals, only the *letter names* are considered in the numerical determination. Thus, both the intervals from D to F and from D to F♯ are 3rds. Moreover, even though the interval from F♭ to A♯ sounds the same as the more common E to B♭, the former is a 3rd, and the latter is a 5th.

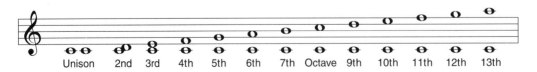

Example 4–1. Intervals. Unison, second (2nd), third (3rd), fourth (4th), fifth (5th), sixth (6th), seventh (7th), octave, ninth (9th), tenth (10th), eleventh (11th), twelfth (12th), thirteenth (13th).

Interval Distance

◆ Using Key and Scale

The ability to identify the distance between two arbitrary notes in any **scale formation** (scales, modes, etc.) is a necessity for the practicing musician. For example, when required to identify the distance between the notes D and E, you must know that this is a whole step. You must be completely familiar with the key signatures of all the major and minor scales so that if the interval from F to G appears in the key of G major, you will know that the F is sharp in this key and produces a half-step distance (F♯–G). If the F–G interval appears in the key of C major, which lacks sharps or flats, the distance is a whole step; if the F–G interval appears in the key of A major, the distance is a whole step because the key of A major contains three sharps, two of which are F and G. Also, if the F–G interval appears in the mode of E Dorian, the distance is a half step. *Example 4–2* illustrates these intervals. Whole- and half-step relationships must be completely understood before the study of intervals can be fully comprehended. (The major scales and three forms of the minor scales and their enharmonic equivalents are listed in Appendix D for reference purposes.)

◆ Using the Major Key of the Lower Note

When determining an interval, it is helpful to calculate the distance between the notes by considering the *major key* of the lower note. Thinking in the major key

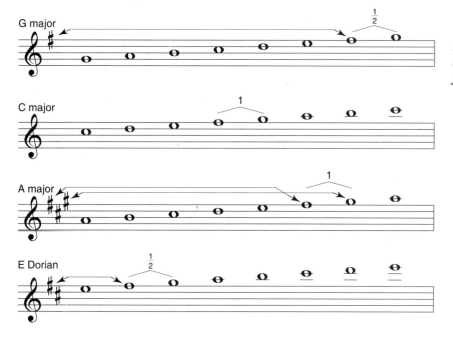

Example 4–2. The F-G interval in various scale formations.

will facilitate the calculation of interval qualities, which will be discussed in the following section. For example, when determining the intervals D–E, D–F♯, D–G, or any interval in which D is the lower note, the process is facilitated by thinking in the key of D major and counting up the scale. Remember to include *both* the lower and the upper notes when counting the distance between them. The interval of D up to F♯ is a 3rd because D–e–F♯ contains three notes in alphabetical order. (Here, for emphasis, only the first and last notes are written in upper case.) When naming the interval E♭ up to C, think in E♭ major. The distance will be a 6th —

$$E♭–f–g–a♭–b♭–C$$

See *Example 4–3(a)*.

Often, it is necessary to identify an interval from a lower note that is not the tonic of any major key — for example, the interval from D♯ up to C𝄪. The key signature of D♯ major (though it is hypothetical) would include nine sharps. The process for determining this interval involves dropping the sharp from D♯ and one sharp from C𝄪 and thinking in D major. See *Example 4–3(b)*. What happens, essentially, is that the interval is transposed down a half step and is placed in a practical key. A similar process can be applied in situations in which the lower note is in a hypothetical flat key. The object in both situations is to retain the *letter names* of the interval and perform a *transposition* to a normal key.

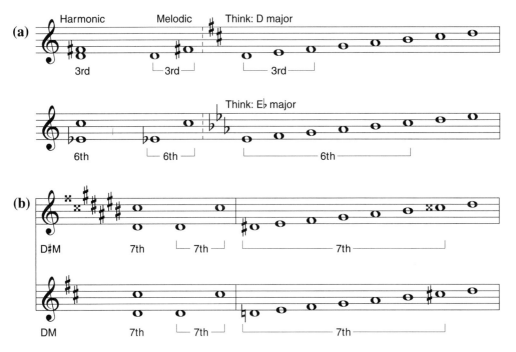

***Example 4–3.** **Intervals determined by key signature.** **(a)** The intervals of a 3rd and a 6th are affected by the key signature. **(b)** Transposition facilitates the determination of interval quality, as will be immediately seen.*

Later, interval determination will become a facile process in which no transposition is necessary.

Interval Quality

Interval quality refers to the classification of intervals as they appear diatonically and as they may be affected by chromatic alteration.

◆ *Major Intervals*

An interval, whether harmonic or melodic, is **major** when the upper note appears in the major scale of the lower note, but the lower note does *not* appear in the major scale of the upper note. Seconds, for example, are major because the upper note is in the major scale of the lower note, but *not* vice versa. Unisons, 4ths, 5ths, and octaves are not major; in each case, *both* upper and lower note appear in the major scale of the other. See *Example 4–4*. Major intervals are denoted by M; in particular, M2 denotes a major 2nd, etc.

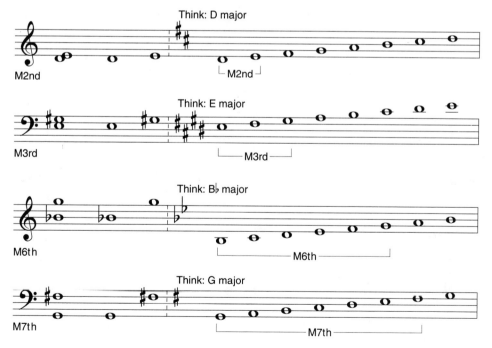

Example 4–4. Major intervals. In a major scale, 2nds, 3rds, 6ths, and 7ths are major intervals.

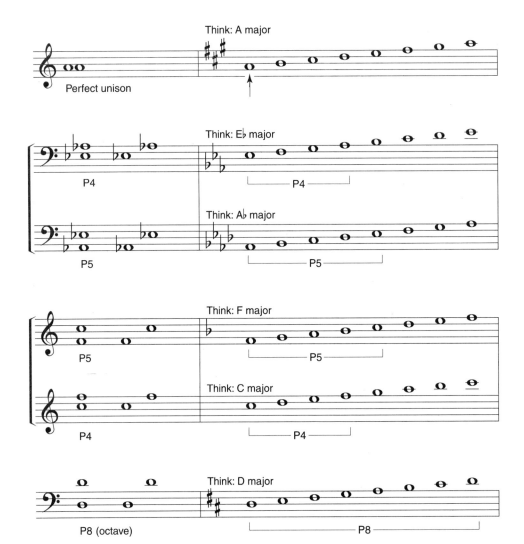

Example 4–5. Perfect intervals.

◆ *Perfect Intervals*

An interval is considered **perfect** when both the lower and the upper notes appear in the major scale of the other. See *Example 4–5*. Perfect intervals are denoted by P; thus, P5 indicates a perfect 5th.

    The interval from C to G is considered perfect since G appears in the scale of C major and C appears in the scale of G major. The interval from A to D is perfect since D appears in the scale of A major and A appears in the scale of D major. The interval from C to E is not perfect: although E appears in the scale of C major, C does not appear in the scale of E major; in E major it is, instead, C♯. See *Example 4–6*.

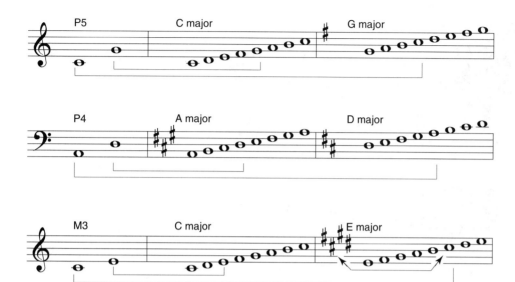

Example 4–6. *Perfect intervals compared with a major interval.*

◆ *Minor Intervals*

A minor interval is obtained by reducing a major interval by one half step provided that the spelling of the pitch names remains the same. For example, C up to E is a major 3rd, and C up to E♭ is a minor 3rd. Here, the pitch spellings remain the same while the distance is decreased by one half step by the alteration of the E to an E♭. Any major interval can be made minor by either lowering the upper note by one half step or by raising the lower note by one half step. In the latter case, the major key signature of the lower note is altered. See *Example 4–7*. Minor intervals are denoted by m; thus, m7 indicates a minor 7th.

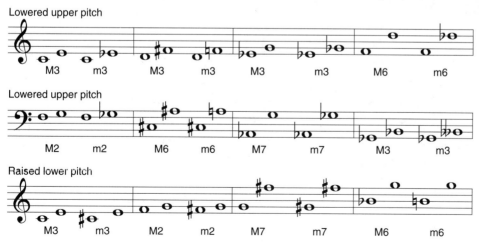

Example 4–7. *Minor intervals.*

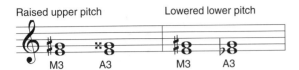

Example 4–9. Doubly augmented intervals.

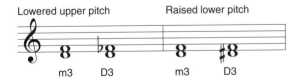

Example 4–8. Augmented intervals.

◆ Augmented Intervals

Any major or perfect interval can be **augmented** by raising the upper pitch one half step or by lowering the lower pitch one half step. See *Example 4–8*. Augmented intervals are denoted by A, so that A6 indicates an augmented 6th.

◆ Doubly Augmented Intervals

Augmented intervals can be further augmented by one half step to produce **doubly augmented** intervals, as illustrated in *Example 4–9*. Doubly augmented intervals are denoted by DA, so that DA6 indicates a doubly augmented 6th.

◆ Diminished Intervals

When minor or perfect intervals are made smaller by one half step, they become **diminished**. Minor and perfect intervals can also be made smaller by raising the lower note one half step. Thus, a major interval becomes diminished by reducing it by a whole step. See *Example 4–10*. Diminished intervals are denoted by D, so that D4 indicates a diminished 4th.

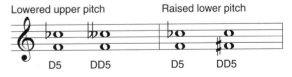

Example 4–11. Doubly diminished intervals.

Example 4–10. Diminished intervals.

	INCREASE		DECREASE	
INTERVAL	**BY ½ STEP BECOMES**	**BY 1 STEP BECOMES**	**BY ½ STEP BECOMES**	**BY 1 STEP BECOMES**
Prime	Augmented	Doubly augmented	Diminished	Doubly diminished
M2	Augmented	Doubly augmented	Minor	Diminished
M3	Augmented	Doubly augmented	Minor	Diminished
P4	Augmented	Doubly augmented	Diminished	Doubly diminished
P5	Augmented	Doubly augmented	Diminished	Doubly diminished
M6	Augmented	Doubly augmented	Minor	Diminished
M7	Augmented	Doubly augmented	Minor	Diminished
PO	Augmented	Doubly augmented	Diminished	Doubly diminished

Table 4–12. Interval alterations.

♦ *Doubly Diminished Intervals*

Diminished intervals can be further reduced by one half step to produce **doubly diminished** intervals. This is achieved by lowering the upper note of a diminished interval one half step or by raising the lower note one half step, as shown in *Example 4–11*. Doubly diminished intervals are denoted by DD, so that DD5 indicates a doubly diminished 5th.

Table 4–12 summarizes the preceding discussion concerning intervals and their alterations.

♦ *Simple and Compound Intervals*

Simple intervals are those that are contained within an octave. **Compound intervals** are those in which the distance between the lower and upper notes exceeds an *alphabetical* spelling of an octave. Thus, D up to the next octave D♯ is an augmented octave and is therefore classified as simple. However, D up to the next E♭, while sounding the same as D–D♯, is actually an *alphabetical* 9th above the initial D. This interval (D up to E♭) is referred to as a compound minor 2nd. In general, intervals exceeding an alphabetical octave are either referred to as compound — for example, compound major 3rd (CM3), compound perfect 5th (CP5), etc. — or by their actual numerical distance — for example, major 9th, perfect 11th, etc. The more common terminology, however, is compound. See *Example 4–13* on page 64.

♦ *Inversion of Intervals*

Simple intervals can also be *inverted*. A simple interval is **inverted** by either raising the lower note by an octave or lowering the upper note by an octave; in either case, the other note remains the same. The "numerical sum" of a simple interval and its inversion is always 9. Thus, 4ths and 5ths are inversions (4 + 5 = 9), as are unisons and octaves (1 + 8 = 9). Interval pairs are illustrated in *Example 4–14* on page 65.

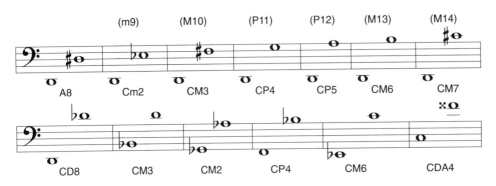

Example 4–13. Compound intervals, beginning in the second measure. Several of these intervals contain two methods of identification.

The process of inversion is used to determine the lower pitch when one is required to construct an interval given the upper pitch. For example, what is the correct lower pitch necessary to construct a perfect 5th *down* from B♭? Knowing that perfect 5ths and perfect 4ths are inversions of one another facilitates this process. Hence, B♭ up to E♭, a perfect 4th that is easily determined in the major scale of B♭ major, will produce a perfect 5th when the E♭ is placed below the B♭.

Interval Characteristics

◆ *Consonance and Dissonance*

Consonance means a sounding together in agreement, free of elements causing discord or harshness. **Dissonance**, conversely, means a lack of agreement in the acoustical sense of sound.[1] It is the author's opinion that qualitative judgment concerning consonance and dissonance is culturally determined. We are taught to accept consonance as pleasing to the ear and we manipulate dissonance so as to cause its resolution to a state of consonance. Eastern and Western listeners often disagree as to what is pleasing. A single vibrating medium cannot be judged as either consonant or dissonant. The concern, then, is the consonance or dissonance caused by the simultaneous sound of two or more vibrating media, as they affect musical pitches. In the study of intervals, the assessment of consonance or dissonance is limited to the simultaneous sounding of two pitches.

◆ *Subjective Aural Evaluation*

Perhaps the best method for evaluating the tendency of an interval is to *test it by ear.* Play several intervals and listen carefully to determine whether they possess

---

1. See *The New Grove Dictionary of Music and Musicianship*, (London: Macmillan Pub. Ltd., 1980), vol. 4, p. 668 and vol. 5, p. 496.

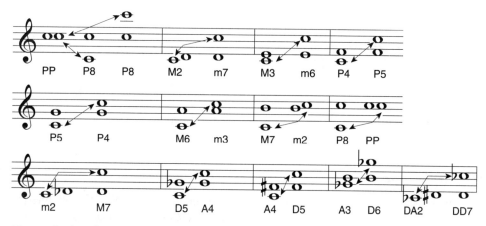

Example 4–14. Inversion of intervals. Note: PP = perfect prime (unison).

an *active* or *static* tendency. Your decision, of course, will be subjective. The theory upon which the practice of music is based is presented throughout this book, but for now, a bit of experimentation is in order. A thorough familiarity with intervals is an absolute necessity for the understanding of harmony, transposition, and melodic structure and development, as well as for virtually every aspect of music. Intervals are the building blocks for all musical construction.

◆ Consonant Intervals

Because of the acoustical and musical reasoning upon which Western musical practice and current theoretical principles depend, the following serves as a basic foundation for the understanding of consonant and dissonant intervals and their individual characteristics.

Perfect unisons, major and minor 3rds, perfect 5ths, major and minor 6ths, and perfect octaves are considered consonant and do not require resolution, provided that their spellings are in agreement with their numerical designations. For example, the minor 3rd from C to E♭ is considered consonant; but if the interval were spelled C–D♯ (same sound, different spelling), its tendency, due to its notation, may be to resolve to some other note or interval. This principle of implied tendency of resolution will be explored in the discussion of upper-partial chords in Chapter 17.

◆ Dissonant Intervals

Major and minor 2nds, perfect 4ths, diminished 5ths, and major and minor 7ths are considered dissonant intervals; by traditional musical practice, they require resolution to a consonance.

The *perfect 4th* is a questionable interval; it is classified as being either consonant or dissonant depending on its use and function. The reader should keep in mind that resolution does not always imply resolution to a consonance.

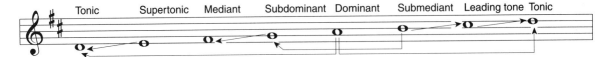

Example 4–15. Pitch tendency.

Musical composition in any style requires the constant increase and decrease of tension, and this can be achieved in many ways.

◆ Pitch Tendency

The tension within an interval is the result of the individual pitches contained in the interval. Intervals possess resolution tendencies dependent on their inherent tension. To begin a discussion regarding interval-resolution tendency, it is first necessary to be familiar with pitch tendency in scalar configurations.

In any major or minor scale, the *tonic* evokes the most complete rest; it requires no resolution and is considered stable. The *supertonic* requires resolution and will most likely gravitate toward the tonic or mediant. The *mediant* is quite stable, yet not as stable as the tonic. The *subdominant* requires resolution and most often tends to gravitate toward the mediant. Although the *dominant* is reasonably stable in a scale configuration, it nevertheless has a strong tendency to move toward the tonic. The *submediant* is also a rather stable degree in the scale, but usually gravitates toward the subdominant or leading tone. Finally, the *leading tone* in most situations possesses a restiveness that compels resolution to the tonic. See *Example 4–15*. The preceding presents *pitch tendency within a scalar configuration;* however, it must be understood that any pitch can move to any other pitch at virtually any time. A familiarity with these movements will prove beneficial to the understanding of interval-resolution tendency.

◆ Interval-Resolution Tendency

Example 4–16 on pages 66–67 indicates where various consonant and dissonant intervals appear in a major scale and where they tend to *resolve.*

(a)

INTERVALS	APPEAR BETWEEN	INTERVALS	APPEAR BETWEEN
Minor 2nds	3–4, 7–8	Minor 6ths	3–8
Major 2nds	1–2, 2–3, 4–5, 5–6, 6–7	Major 6ths	1–6, 2–7
Minor 3rds	2–4, 3–5, 6–8	Minor 7ths	2–8
Major 3rds	1–3, 4–6, 5–7	Major 7ths	1–7
Perfect 4ths	1–4, 2–5, 3–6, 5–8	Perfect octaves	1–8
Perfect 5ths	1–5, 2–6, 3–7, 4–8		

Example 4–16. Appearance and resolution tendencies of intervals in a major scale. **(a)** Unisons appear as the result of a duplicated pitch, for example, 1–1, 2–2, 3–3, etc. Here, the numerals refer to scale degrees. **(b)** Intervals as they appear in F major are shown together with their resolution tendencies, indicated by arrows.

(b)

INTERVAL	CHARACTER OF SOUND	VISUAL SUGGESTION	RESOLUTION
Unison	Consonant	Consonance	No
AU	Dissonant	Dissonance	Yes
m2	Dissonant	Dissonance	Yes
M2	Dissonant	Dissonance	Yes
A2	Consonant	Dissonance	Yes
m3	Consonant	Consonance	No
M3	Consonant	Consonance	No
A3	Dissonant	Consonance	Yes
D4	Consonant	Dissonance/Consonance	Yes
P4	Dissonant/Consonant	Dissonance/Consonance	Depends on context
A4	Dissonant	Dissonance	Yes
D5	Dissonant inversion of A4	Consonance	Yes
P5	Consonant	Consonance	No
A5	Consonant	Consonance	Yes
m6	Consonant	Consonance	No
M6	Consonant	Consonance	No
A6	Dissonant	Consonance	Yes
D7	Consonant	Dissonance	Yes
m7	Dissonant	Dissonance	Yes
M7	Dissonant	Dissonance	Yes
P8	Consonant	Consonance	No

Table 4–17. Consonance and dissonance in intervals. Note: AU = augmented unison.

A thorough assessment of the traits of intervals should alleviate much of the confusion that is likely to occur in their treatment. *Table 4–17* lists various types of intervals, together with their character of sound, visual suggestion of quality, and resolution tendency.

Chapter Review

An *interval*, the measured distance between two pitches, occurs either *melodically* (in horizontal linear form) or *harmonically* (in vertical simultaneous form); harmonic intervals are also referred to as *dyads*. In the calculation of numerical distance both the lower and the upper pitches are always counted. *Interval quality* — for example, *major, minor, augmented, diminished* — is best determined by considering the major key of the lower note. This alerts the observer to those pitches that are "in the key," and to an assessment of whether the diatonic intervals are major or perfect. Within a major scale the major intervals are the 2nds, 3rds, 6ths, and 7ths; the perfect intervals are the unisons, 4ths, 5ths, and octaves. Major intervals become minor when reduced by one half step and diminished when reduced by one whole step; they become augmented when increased by one half step and doubly augmented when increased by one whole step.

Perfect intervals become augmented when increased by one half step and doubly augmented when increased by one whole step; they become diminished when decreased by one half step and doubly diminished when decreased by one whole step.

Simple intervals are those within an octave; *compound intervals* exceed an octave. Simple intervals can be inverted. *Inversion* occurs when either the lower note is placed an octave above the upper note or the upper note is placed an octave below the lower note; in either case, the other note remains the same and the "numerical sum" of the simple interval and its inversion is 9.

Intervals are also classified as *consonant* (free of discord) or *dissonant* (harsh). Unisons, major and minor 3rds, perfect 5ths, major and minor 6ths, and perfect octaves are considered consonant. Major and minor 2nds, augmented 4ths, diminished 5ths, and major and minor 7ths are considered dissonant. The perfect 4th is ambiguous and may be considered as either consonant or dissonant, depending on usage.

Intervals also possess certain resolution tendencies, depending on the amount of tension contained therein. Tension is the result of acoustical characteristics (vibrations of the individual pitches contained in the interval).

Anthology References

For additional usage and analysis, see the following examples in Distefano, Joseph P. and James A. Searle, *Music and Materials for Analysis: An Anthology.* New York, Ardsley House, Publishers, Inc., 1995.

augmented fourths, diminished fifths, augmented sixths; compound intervals
    Example 30.   *Rondo,* Wolfgang Amadeus Mozart, pp. 135–40.
compound augmented seconds, diminished sevenths
    Example 31.   *Sonata,* Hob. XVI, No. 27, First Movement, Franz Joseph Haydn, pp. 141–48.
augmented fifths, compound augmented thirds, major sevenths
    Example 32.   *Sonata,* K. 333, Wolfgang Amadeus Mozart, pp. 149–78.
diminished fourths
    Example 36.   *Impromptu,* Op. 5, No. 5, Robert Schumann, pp. 201–6.
diminished sixths, diminished thirds
    Example 37.   *Du Bist Wie Eine Blume,* Op. 25, No. 24, Robert Schumann, pp. 207–12.
augmented and diminished octaves
    Example 47.   *Mikrokosmos,* No. 59, Béla Bartók, pp. 267–72, 274.
augmented sevenths, diminished thirds, diminished fourths
    Example 45.   *Preludes,* Book I, No. 2, "Voiles" ("Sails"), Claude Achille Debussy, pp. 259–66.

Self-Test

1. An interval is the distance between _____ .
2. When an interval appears in linear (horizontal) format, it is known as _____ .
3. When an interval appears in harmonic (vertical) format, it is known as _____ .
4. When calculating *interval distance* and quality, it is best to consider _____ .
5. When determining the numerical distance between two notes, it is necessary to include _____ _____ .
6. What does *interval inversion* mean?
7. When major intervals are increased by one half step, they become _____ .
8. When major intervals are increased by one whole step, they become _____ .
9. When major intervals are decreased by one half step, they become _____ .
10. When major intervals are decreased by one whole step, they become _____ .
11. When perfect intervals are decreased by one half step, they become _____ .
12. When perfect intervals are decreased by one whole step, they become _____ .
13. The definition of a *compound interval* is one that exceeds an _____ .
14. When the lower note of an interval is not a degree of a commonly used major scale, the process for measurement is accomplished by _____ .
15. Which intervals within a major scale are classified as major?
16. Which intervals within a major scale are classified as perfect?
17. What does *consonant* mean?
18. What does *dissonant* mean?
19. Which intervals are consonant?
20. Which intervals are dissonant?
21. Which interval is consonant or dissonant, depending on its function?
22. What determines the degree of tension within an interval?

Exercises

1. Identify as either a whole step or half step.

(a)

(b)

(c)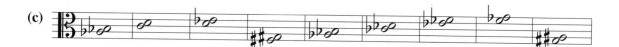

(d)

2. Write the indicated numerical interval within the major key of the lower pitch. See the first measure of Part (a).

(a)

3 5 4 7 2 8 4 6 5 4

(b)

5 3 7 7 3 2 3 5 3 7

(c)

2 7 6 6 7 4 7 4 7 6

(d)

5 6 2 7 3 4 6 6 5 2

3. Write the numerical distance of each interval. See the first measure of Part (a).

(a)

6

(b)

(c)

4. Spell the upper note enharmonically and label the numerical result. See the first measure of Part (a).

5. Identify numerically the distance between consecutive notes, as shown in the first measure of Part (a).

6. Write the upper note necessary to form the indicated interval.

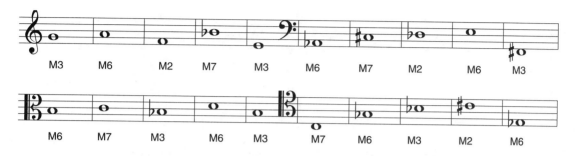

M3   M6   M2   M7   M3   M6   M7   M2   M6   M3

M6   M7   M3   M6   M3   M7   M6   M3   M2   M6

7. Locate and identify the perfect intervals by number and quality.

(a)

(b)

(c)

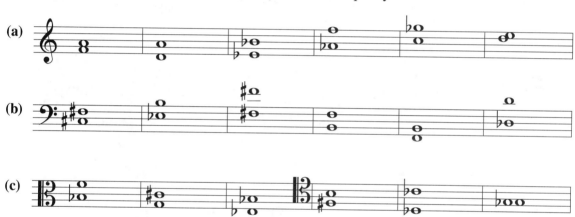

8. Identify the major and minor intervals by number and quality.

(a)

(b)

(c)

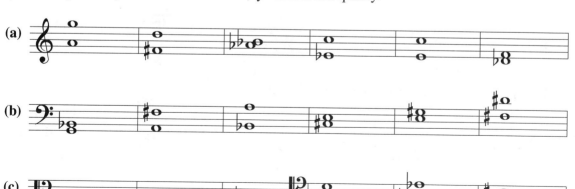

9. Determine which intervals are perfect and which are diminished.

(a)

(b)

10. Determine which intervals are major, which are perfect, and which are augmented.

(a)

(b)

11. Determine which intervals are minor and which are diminished.

(a)

(b)

12. Determine which intervals are doubly augmented.

(a)

(b)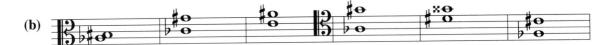

13. Determine which intervals are diminished and which are doubly diminished.

(a)

(b)

14. Invert each interval and identify both the given interval and its inversion, as in the first measure of Part (a).

(a)

(b)

15. Create compound intervals by raising the upper note one octave. Identify both the given interval and its inversion, as in the first measure of Part (a).

(a)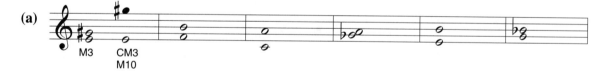

(b)

16. Mark with a "C" those intervals that are consonant and with a "D" those that are dissonant.

(a)

(b)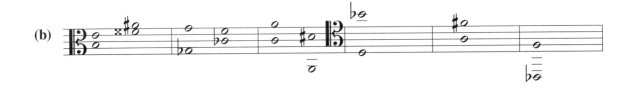

TRIADS

Letter class refers to all notes that have the same letter name; thus, all Cs are in the same letter class, as are all Ds.

The literal meaning of the term **triad** is a harmonic structure consisting of three pitches each belonging to a different letter class. Most often these three pitches are derived from a *superimposition* (or *stacking*) of two intervallic thirds, as when the thirds 𝄞𝄰 and 𝄰 are superimposed to form the triad 𝄰

Triads can appear vertically (in **harmonic** form) or horizontally (in **melodic** form). Notice the method of constructing triads on each scale degree in *Example 5–1*. The lowest note is the *root,* the second note is the *third,* and the highest note is the *fifth;* these three notes are called the **factors** of the triad.

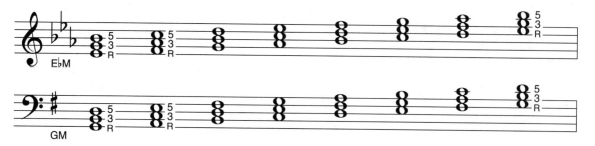

Example 5–1. Triads on each degree of the E♭ major and G major scales with their roots (R), 3rds, and 5ths.

Triad Qualities

There are four types of *triad qualities: major, minor, diminished,* and *augmented.* The **quality** of a triad is determined by the size or quality of each 3rd contained between the factors.

◆ *Major Triads*

A **major triad** consists of a **root** (the initial note and the letter name of the triad); a second note, the **third** (3rd), which is a major 3rd above the root; and a third note, the **fifth** (5th), which is a minor 3rd above the second note and therefore a perfect 5th above the root. See *Example 5–2.*

◆ *Minor Triads*

A minor triad consists of a *root*; a second note, the *third*, which is a minor 3rd above the root; and a third note, the *fifth*, which is a major 3rd above the second note and therefore a perfect 5th above the root. See *Example 5–3.*

◆ *Diminished Triads*

A diminished triad consists of a *root*; a second note, the *third*, which is a minor 3rd above the root; and a third note, the *fifth*, which is a minor 3rd above the second note and therefore a diminished 5th above the root. See *Example 5–4.*

◆ *Augmented Triads*

Lastly, an augmented triad consists of a *root*; a second note, the *third*, which is a major 3rd above the root; and a third note, the *fifth*, which is a major 3rd above

Example 5–2. Major triads.

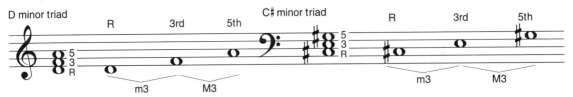

Example 5–3. Minor triads.

Example 5–4. Diminished triads.

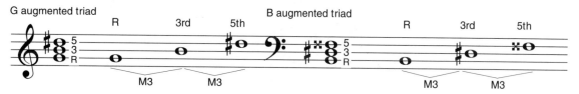

Example 5–5. Augmented triads.

the second note and therefore an augmented 5th above the root. See *Example 5–5*.

To remember these triads, it is helpful to consider the actual meaning of the identifying labels of each triad quality. A major triad is the most commonly heard and utilized triad in Western practice. It therefore can serve as the basis for measuring the qualities of the other triads. If the first 3rd (which is a major 3rd) of a major triad is decreased by a half step, thus resulting in a minor 3rd, the triad becomes minor; "minor" can now be considered as smaller than major. If the second 3rd is also decreased, thereby creating another minor 3rd, the triad is smaller still, hence resulting in a diminished triad — "diminished" inferring less than minor. Reverting back to the major triad, if the second 3rd is increased by a half step, thereby creating two major 3rds, the resultant triad is larger in intervallic distance than the major triad and hence is augmented. *Example 5–6* on page 80 illustrates the four triad qualities and their intervallic configurations.

Triad Construction

A triad of any quality (major, minor, diminished, or augmented) can be constructed on any note provided that certain conditions are met, namely:

1. the initial note is considered as the root,

2. the second note is either a major or minor 3rd above the root, and

3. the third note is either a major or minor third above the second note.

It is essential that each 3rd be spelled so as to be alphabetically correct.

Example 5–6. **The four triad qualities and their intervallic configurations shown on single staves and on a grand staff.**

Numerical Designation and Identification of Triads

The term **chord** applies to the simultaneous sounding of three or more pitches.[1] In the discussion of triads and later in more complex structures, the term *chord*

---

1. Occasionally, a dyad, or two-note harmonic interval, is also referred to as a chord.

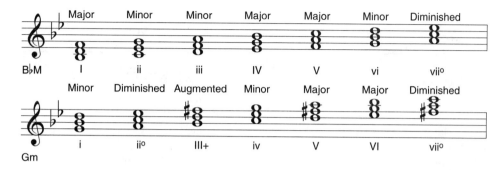

Example 5–7. **Triad qualities in major and harmonic minor.**

can be considered synonymous with the structure under discussion. Chords constructed of stacked 3rds are referred to as **tertian harmony**.

In the analysis of classical music, chord content is most often illustrated by the use of Roman numerals. These numerals refer to chord structures constructed on the various scale degrees. For example, in a major key any triad constructed on the first degree is referred to as a I chord; a triad on the fourth degree is a IV chord. Triad qualities determine the use of upper- or lower-case Roman numerals. Triads of major quality are specified by upper-case Roman numerals; triads of minor quality employ lower-case Roman numerals, for example, ii, iii; triads of diminished quality use lower-case Roman numerals usually followed by a degree sign, for example, ii°, vii°. Augmented triads are indicated by upper-case Roman numerals followed by a plus sign, for example, III+.[2] See *Example 5–7.*

Triads in Scales and Modes

◆ *Triads Derived from Major and Minor Scales*

The I, IV, and V triads in a major scale are often referred to as the **primary triads,** whereas the ii, iii, vi, and vii° triads are called the **secondary triads**. These labels should not be taken literally in all situations. A close examination of the corresponding triad qualities in the various minor scales and modes reveals many dissimilarities on respective scale degrees. The terms *primary* and *secondary* can be employed, but only as general locations of triad appearances.

Example 5–8 on page 82 illustrates the qualities of each triad in the four types of scales discussed in Chapter 3 — namely, major, harmonic minor, melodic minor, and natural minor.

---

2. Some authors use upper-case numerals for all qualities.

MAJOR

SCALE DEGREE	NAME	QUALITY	ROMAN NUMERAL
1st	Tonic	Major	I
2nd	Supertonic	Minor	ii
3rd	Mediant	Minor	iii
4th	Subdominant	Major	IV
5th	Dominant	Major	V
6th	Submediant	Minor	vi
7th	Leading tone	Diminished	vii°

HARMONIC MINOR

SCALE DEGREE	NAME	QUALITY	ROMAN NUMERAL
1st	Tonic	Minor	I
2nd	Supertonic	Diminished	ii°
3rd	Mediant	Augmented	III+
4th	Subdominant	Minor	iv
5th	Dominant	Major	V
6th	Submediant	Major	VI
7th	Leading tone	Diminished	vii°

MELODIC MINOR

SCALE DEGREE	NAME	QUALITY	ROMAN NUMERAL
1st	Tonic	Minor	i
2nd	Supertonic	Minor	ii
3rd	Mediant	Augmented	III+
4th	Subdominant	Major	IV
5th	Dominant	Major	V
6th	Submediant	Diminished	vi°
7th	Leading tone	Diminished	vii°

NATURAL MINOR

SCALE DEGREE	NAME	QUALITY	ROMAN NUMERAL
1st	Tonic	Minor	i
2nd	Supertonic	Diminished	ii°
3rd	Mediant	Major	III
4th	Subdominant	Minor	iv
5th	Dominant	Minor	v
6th	Submediant	Major	VI
7th	Subtonic	Major	VII

Example 5–8. Triad characteristics in the four types of scales.

TRIAD NOTES	QUALITY	ROMAN NUMERAL
E–G–B (in thirds)	Minor	i
F♯–A–C♯	Minor	ii
G–B–D	Major	III
A–C♯–E	Major	IV
B–D–F♯	Minor	v
C♯–E–G	Diminished	vi°
D–F♯–A	Major	VII

E Dorian

i   ii   III   IV   v   vi°   VII

Example 5–9. *Triad characteristics in the Dorian mode.*

◆ *Triads in Modes*

Triad qualities are also affected by modal use. If the mode of E Dorian were used and the triad qualities were to be determined, the results would be as shown in *Table 5–9.*

For each mode — Ionian (major scale), Dorian, Phrygian, Lydian, Mixolydian, Aeolian (natural minor scale), and Locrian — the triad qualities vary according to the configuration of the major and minor 3rds that occur. Several triads are compared in *Example 5–10.* For practice, determine all the triad qualities in every mode.

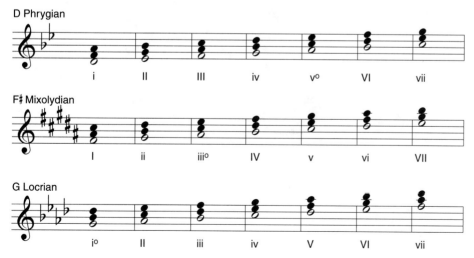

D Phrygian

i   II   III   iv   v°   VI   vii

F♯ Mixolydian

I   ii   iii°   IV   v   vi   VII

G Locrian

i°   II   iii   iv   V   VI   vii

Example 5–10. *Triad qualities in the Phrygian, Mixolydian, and Locrian modes.*

Thus, triads can be constructed by stacking 3rds or they can be derived directly from a particular scale or mode. It is absolutely necessary that both methods be fully understood.

Inversions of Triads

In the triads thus far considered, all three notes appear in 3rds; such triads are said to be in **closely spaced root position**. A rearrangement of the notes of a triad in which a note other than the root appears in the lowest part (the bass) is called an **inversion** of the triad. Triads that appear with the 3rd as the lowest note are said to be in **first inversion**. Triads with the 5th appearing as the lowest note are in **second inversion**. See *Example 5–11*.

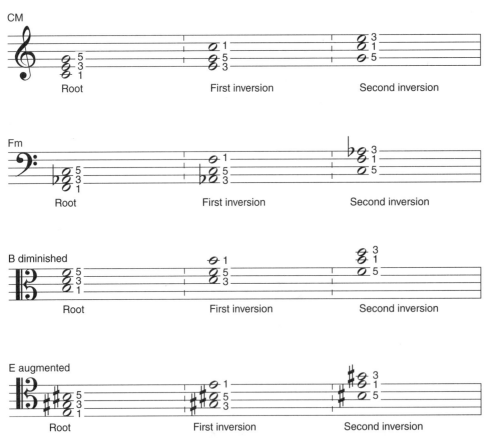

Example 5–11. Root positions and inversions of the four triad qualities.

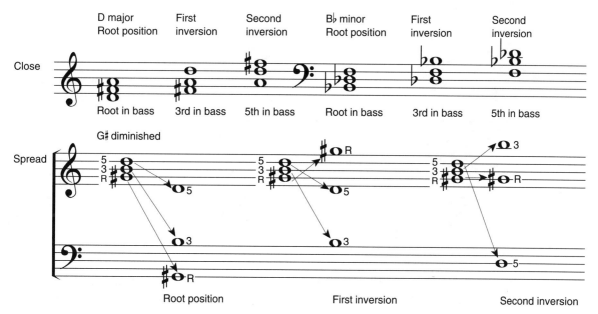

Example 5–12. Note spacing in triads.

Note-Spacing in Triads

Triads in root position and inverted triads can be either **closely spaced**, meaning that their intrinsic notes are as compactly arranged as possible, or **spread**, meaning that any note of a particular letter can be placed in any octave above the bass. The spacing of the notes has absolutely no effect in determining the inversion of the triad. Regardless of the spacing, the only factor considered in the determination of root position or inversions is the bass note:

if the root is in the bass, then root position
if the 3rd is the bass, then first inversion
if the 5th is the bass, then second inversion

See *Example 5–12.*

The Figured-Bass System

In music analysis as well as in certain styles of performance it is necessary to identify the Roman numeral of a triad as well as the correct inversion. The *figured-bass*

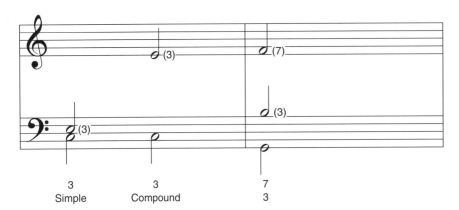

Example 5–13. An Arabic numeral below a bass note, indicating inclusion of the interval in the harmonic content.

3
Simple

3
Compound

7
3

system of chord identification originated in the **Baroque** period (c.1600–1750). Below a given bass line, numbers and symbols are written that represent various intervals above the bass note; these numbers and symbols provide a guide to help the performer realize the harmonic content of the work without every pitch being notated. **Figured bass**, then, is a short-hand method for indicating harmonic content. Figured-bass directives illustrate interval content and occasionally complete chord structures.

1. Any (Arabic) numeral appearing below a bass note indicates that the interval (simple or compound) is to be included in the harmonic content. One or more numerals may be present. See *Example 5–13.*

2. A slashed numeral or a numeral followed by a plus sign, +, indicates that the interval above the bass is to be raised one half step. See *Example 5–14.*

3. A numeral preceded or followed by an accidental indicates the corresponding modification of that numerical interval. See *Example 5–15.*

4. A free-standing accidental affects the 3rd above the bass. See *Example 5–16.*

5. Any numeral or pitch-altering symbol in parentheses indicates that the interval is already represented and notated in the music. See *Example 5–17.*

6. Any numeral or pitch-altering symbol followed by a horizontal line indicates that that particular interval is sustained through the length of the line. See *Example 5–18.*

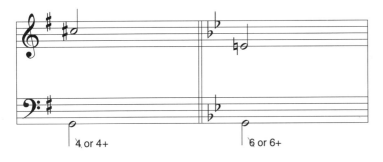

4 or 4+

6 or 6+

Example 5–14. A slashed numeral or a numeral followed by a plus sign, indicating that the interval above the bass has been raised by one half step.

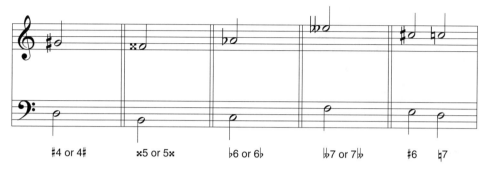

Example 5–15. *A numeral preceded or followed by an accidental, indicating a modification of the corresponding numerical interval.*

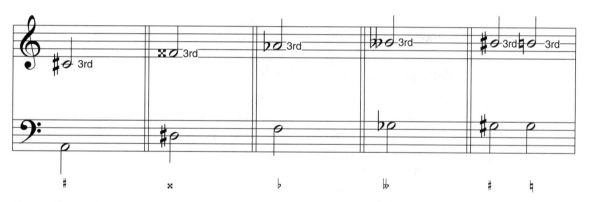

Example 5–16. *A free-standing accidental, affecting the third above the bass.*

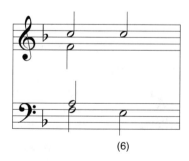

Example 5–17. *A numeral or pitch-altering symbol in parentheses, indicating that the interval is already represented and notated in the music.*

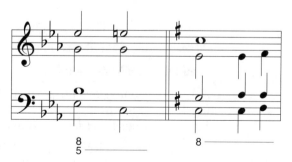

Example 5–18. *A numeral or pitch-altering symbol followed by a horizontal line, indicating that that particular interval is sustained through the length of the line.*

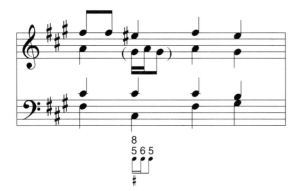

Example 5–19. Rhythmic figures below figured bass, indicating the exact time-value designations for each interval.

7. Rhythmic figures, occasionally placed below the figured bass, advise as to the exact time-value designations for each interval. See *Example 5–19.*

◆ *Identifying Root Position and Inversions of Triads*

A triad in root position can be represented solely by its Roman numeral in the key. A triad in first inversion can be indicated by its Roman numeral followed by 6 — for example, I6, ii6, iii6, etc. A triad in second inversion can be indicated by its Roman numeral followed by $\substack{6\\4}$, for example, ii$\substack{6\\4}$, iii$\substack{6\\4}$, etc. The Arabic numeral(s) following the Roman numeral represent(s) the (simple or compound) intervals appearing above the bass note in each particular inversion. These Arabic numerals do not indicate the quality of each interval; rather, they represent the numerical distance above the bass and within the prevailing key.

With the use of figured bass, each interval contained within a chord structure can be indicated. For example, a triad in root position contains a root, a 3rd, which is an intervallic 3rd above the root, and a 5th, which is an intervallic 5th above the root. Therefore, a figured-bass notation for a I-chord in root position might read "I$\substack{5\\3}$," a figured-bass notation for a I-chord in first inversion might read "I$\substack{6\\3}$," and a figured-bass notation for a I-chord in second inversion might read "I$\substack{6\\4}$." It has become standard practice, however, to employ only those Arabic numerals necessary to determine the actual inversion; thus, a Roman numeral designates root-position triads, a Roman numeral followed by 6 represents first-inversion triads, and a Roman numeral followed by $\substack{6\\4}$ stands for second-inversion triads. Although the Arabic numerals pertain to triads or chords as they appear in closely spaced position, these numbers do not change when the triad or chord appears in spread position. The only important determining factor in correctly identifying an inversion is the note present in the bass of the triad or chord, that is, the root, 3rd, or 5th. See *Example 5–20.*

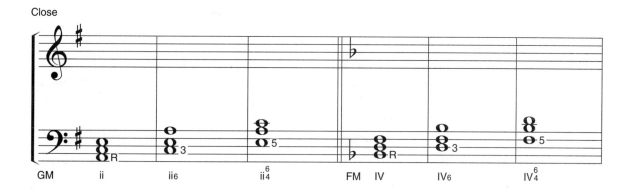

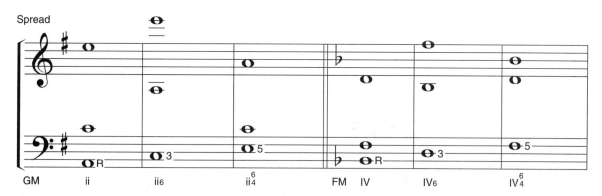

Example 5–20. Close and spread positions of several triads.

Identifying Spread-Position Triads

Determining the triad root, inversion, and quality in spread position is a fairly simple process. The span of the triad has no effect on this identification — nor does **note duplication** (multiple factors of the same letter class).

The process for determining a spread triad with or without note duplication is as follows:

1. Extract only one note belonging to each particular letter class. Thus, if a chord contains five Ds, three Fs, and two A's, extract only one of each to arrive at the three principal notes.

2. Arrange these extracted notes in alphabetical 3rds either by visualizing the arrangement or by placing each note on the staff on three adjacent lines or three adjacent spaces. The lowest note will yield the root.

3. Examine the intervallic distance between each 3rd. In the case of the example in item 1, D–F yields a minor 3rd and F–A yields a major 3rd. Therefore, the quality of the triad is minor.

4. Observe the lowest note in spread position. If it is the D, then the triad is in root position and it need only be identified by its Roman numeral within the prevailing key. If F is the lowest note, the triad is in first inversion and is identified by the correct Roman numeral followed by 6. If A is the lowest note, the triad is in second inversion and the Roman numeral is followed by $^6_4$.

If in item 2, the arrangement were "A up to D up to F" and if the key were B♭ major, the correct label would be iii$^6_4$, a D minor triad in second inversion. See *Example 5–21.*

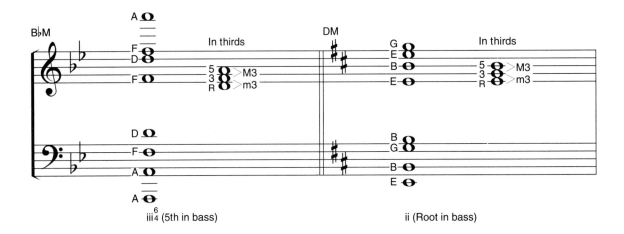

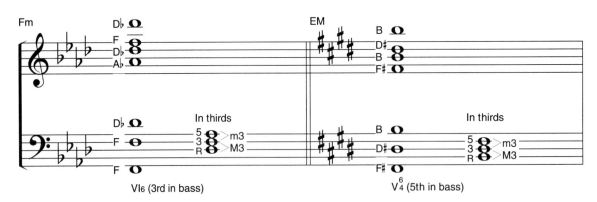

Example 5–21. Reduction of multiple-note duplication to determine the triad.

Popular-Music Formats

In popular music, especially in sheet-music form, one often sees chord symbols indicated above the written notes of the treble clef. This practice of indicating the harmonic content of a musical work is relatively new in the overall history of Western notation. Common-practice notation does not incorporate chord symbols for the identification of harmonic content; however, occasionally, publishers edit these symbols into their publications.

In popular-music formats, such as lead sheets, in which only the melody and chord symbols are present, and even in fully notated piano scores, chord content is indicated by letter name, quality, and in the case of inversion, by a fractional notation, such as $\frac{D}{F\sharp}$ or $\frac{D}{F\sharp}$. Either notation for inversion indicates a D major triad over an F♯ bass note. An upper-case letter standing alone or followed by an (upper-case) M represents a major triad; an upper-case letter followed by a (lower-case) m indicates a minor triad; an upper-case letter followed by either dim or º indicates a diminished triad, and an upper-case letter followed by aug or + indicates an augmented triad. Some confusion can occur in popular-music notation since these symbols have not become totally standardized. In applying these symbols to the performance of a musical work instrumentalists must use their discretion in the arrangement and duplication of chord factors. The process described is referred to as **voicing** and will be considered in greater detail in forthcoming chapters. *Example 5–22* on pages 91–93 illustrates chord and triad identification in popular music.

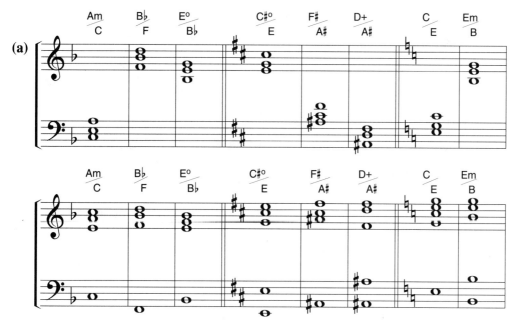

(b)

"Ego"

Elton John, Bernie Taupin

(c) MAJOR	MINOR	DIMINISHED	AUGMENTED
C	Cm	Cdim.	Caug
Cmaj	Cmin	C°	C+
CM	C−		C+5
CΔ			
C5 (no third, perfect			
5th dyad)			

Example 5–22. Triad and chord identification in popular music.
(a) A typical method of indicating chord quality and inversion in popular music. **(b)** Compare the chord symbols, indicated by asterisks, with the written notes. Notice the discrepancies. This disparity is a frequent occurrence in song sheets and is the result of facilitating the reading, thus producing a visually smoother melodic line, a part-writing alternative, or an error. (See Chapter 7.) **(c)** Several methods of triad identification from a C root.

Chapter Review

A *triad* is a harmonic structure consisting of three different notes each belonging to a particular *letter class*. Every triad consists of a *root*, a *third*, and a *fifth*, each separated by a major or minor 3rd when the triad appears in *closely spaced root position*. There are four types of *triad qualities: major, minor, diminished*, and *augmented*.

The *primary triads* are those constructed on the first (tonic), fourth (subdominant), and fifth (dominant) degrees of the scale. Those triads that are constructed on the second degree (supertonic), third degree (mediant), sixth degree (submediant), and seventh degree (leading tone

or subtonic) are considered *secondary triads*. Triad qualities are affected by the prevailing type of scale. These include but are not limited to scales of major, natural minor, harmonic minor, and melodic minor, and in certain styles, modes.

Triads can appear in *closely spaced* or *spread root position, first inversion*, and *second inversion*. The duplication of chord factors does not affect the quality of a triad nor does the spacing between chord notes. In the descriptive analysis of triads found in common-practice works, identification is made by use of Roman and Arabic numerals. The *Roman numeral* identifies the location of the triad within the scale — for example, I, ii, iii, etc.; the *Arabic numeral* identifies the inversion — 6 for first inversion, $\overset{6}{4}$ for second inversion. No Arabic numeral is required for root position. The identification of triads (and other chords) contained in popular works is achieved by indicating the letter name, quality, and inversion in a more direct fashion. For example, $\frac{Dm}{F}$ translates to a D minor triad with F in the bass; $\frac{E+}{G\sharp}$ translates to an E augmented triad with G♯ in the bass.

In the Baroque period, keyboardists were guided in their accompaniments by the inclusion of *figured bass*. This technique of harmonic notation consists of a written bass line with Arabic numerals and other pitch-altering symbols below. The numerals indicate the required intervals (simple or compound) above the bass that are necessary for the performer to include in order to "realize" the harmonic content. In popular nomenclature this is achieved by the use of chord symbols, for example, $\frac{C}{G}, \frac{F\sharp o}{A}$, etc.

Voicing, which refers to the relative placement of chord notes, is not affected by figured bass or chord symbols; it is the performer's responsibility, based on the style, mood, and the rhythmic content of the piece, to arrange the order of the chord notes correctly.

Anthology References

For additional usage and analysis, see the following examples in Distefano, Joseph P. and James A. Searle, *Music and Materials for Analysis: An Anthology.* New York, Ardsley House, Publishers, Inc., 1995.

inversions and spacing of triads

Examples 15–21. Lord Jesus Christ, the Prince of Peace, Johann Sebastian Bach
O Darkest Woe! Ye Tears that Flow, Johann Sebastian Bach
If God Withdraweth, All the Cost, Johann Sebastian Bach
O Lord! How Many Miseries, Johann Sebastian Bach
My Cause Is God's, and I Am Still, Johann Sebastian Bach
O Thou, of God the Father, Johann Sebastian Bach
Blessed Jesu, at Thy Word. Johann Sebastian Bach, pp. 69–80.

figured bass

Example 14. *Trio Sonata,* Op. 4, No. 7, Corrente, Arcangelo Corelli, pp. 63–68.

chord symbols in popular music

Example 58. *Tar River Blues,* Joseph P. Distefano, pp. 341–48.
Example 59. *A Little Duet (for Zoot and Chet),* Jack Montrose, pp. 349–54.

Self-Test

1. Define a *triad.*
2. The four types of triad qualities are _____ , _____ , _____ , and _____ .
3. Triads in root position are constructed by the intervals of _____ .
4. Every triad consists of three factors. They are _____ , _____ , and _____ .
5. Identification of triads in common-practice works is achieved through the use of _____ .
6. Triad content in popular music is achieved through the use of _____ .
7. The triad qualities on each degree of a major scale are _____ , _____ , _____ , _____ , _____ , _____ , and _____ .
8. The triad qualities on each degree of a natural minor scale are _____ , _____ , _____ , _____ , _____ , _____ , and _____ .
9. The triad qualities on each degree of a harmonic minor scale are _____ , _____ , _____ , _____ , _____ , and _____ .
10. The triad qualities on each degree of a melodic minor scale are _____ , _____ , _____ , _____ , _____ , and _____ .
11. Name the primary triads.   12. Name the secondary triads.
13. What does *interval stacking* refer to?
14. Identify the qualities of all the triads in each mode.
15. What does *close position* mean?   16. What does *spread position* mean?
17. What does *voicing* mean?   18. What does a Roman numeral indicate?
19. What does an Arabic numeral indicate?
20. A major triad consists of the stacking of two 3rds from the bass upward. They are _____ and _____ .
21. A minor triad consists of the stacking of two 3rds from the bass upward. They are _____ and _____ .
22. A diminished triad consists of the stacking of two 3rds from the bass upward. They are _____ and _____ .
23. An augmented triad consists of the stacking of two 3rds from the bass upward. They are _____ and _____ .
24. In figured bass, a free-standing accidental affects the _____ above the bass.
25. In figured bass, what does a slash through a numeral indicate?
26. What does a figured-bass symbol appearing within parentheses indicate?
27. How do popular-chord symbols compare with figured bass?

Exercises

1. By measuring the 3rds, determine whether each triad is major, minor, diminished, or augmented.

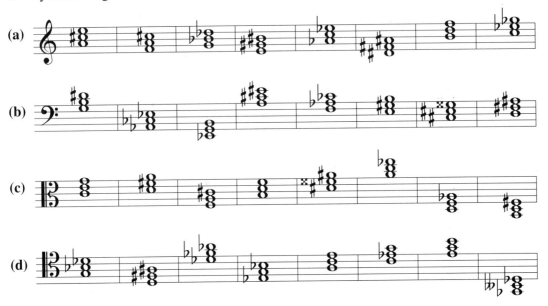

2. Construct the indicated quality for each triad.

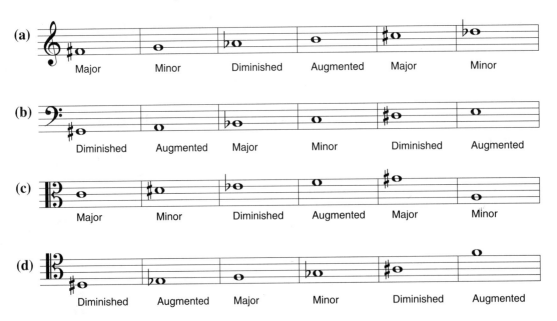

3. Apply the Roman numeral indicating triad identification within each key.

4. Spell each triad as it appears in the indicated scale, as in the first measure of Part (a).

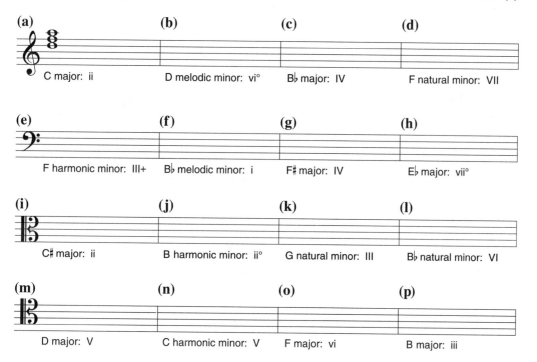

(a) C major: ii

(b) D melodic minor: vi°

(c) B♭ major: IV

(d) F natural minor: VII

(e) F harmonic minor: III+

(f) B♭ melodic minor: i

(g) F♯ major: IV

(h) E♭ major: vii°

(i) C♯ major: ii

(j) B harmonic minor: ii°

(k) G natural minor: III

(l) B♭ natural minor: VI

(m) D major: V

(n) C harmonic minor: V

(o) F major: vi

(p) B major: iii

5. Spell each triad according to the type of mode indicated, as in the first measure of Part (a). (Roman numerals signify position only, not quality.)

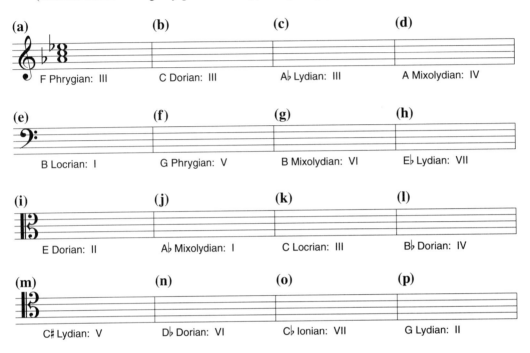

(a) F Phrygian: III **(b)** C Dorian: III **(c)** A♭ Lydian: III **(d)** A Mixolydian: IV

(e) B Locrian: I **(f)** G Phrygian: V **(g)** B Mixolydian: VI **(h)** E♭ Lydian: VII

(i) E Dorian: II **(j)** A♭ Mixolydian: I **(k)** C Locrian: III **(l)** B♭ Dorian: IV

(m) C♯ Lydian: V **(n)** D♭ Dorian: VI **(o)** C♭ Ionian: VII **(p)** G Lydian: II

6. Arrange in 3rds and determine quality, as in the first measure of Part (a).

7. Indicate whether each triad is in root position, 1st inversion, or 2nd inversion, as in the first measure of Part (a). Identify each triad by letter name and quality.

8. Identify by Roman numeral and popular nomenclature, as shown in the example.

9. Write each triad in spread position. See the example.

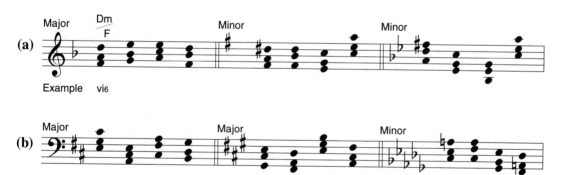

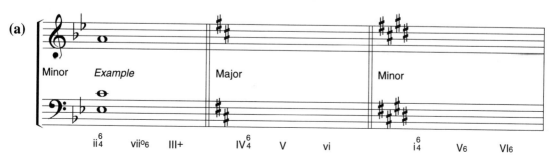

(b)

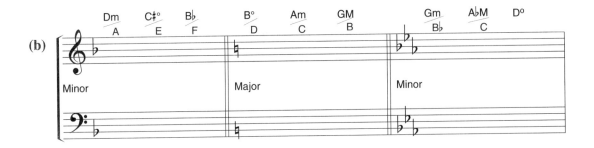

(c)

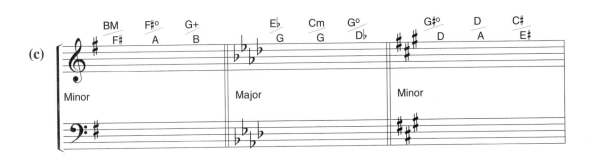

10. Complete the required triads. Use spread position.

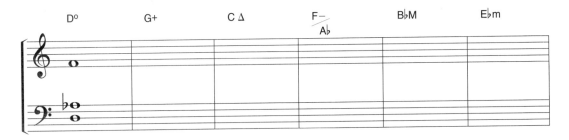

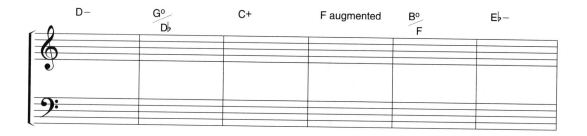

D−   G°/D♭   C+   F augmented   B°/F   E♭−

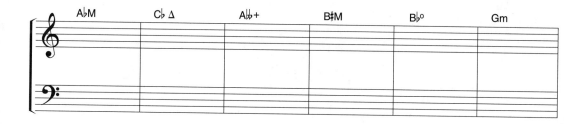

A♭M   C♭ Δ   A♭♭+   B♯M   B♭°   Gm

11. Add the correct intervals.

(a)   (b)   (c)   (d)

(e)   (f)   (g)   (h)

12. Identify by Roman numeral and inversion, as in the first measure of Part (a).

13. Label, using popular nomenclature, as in the first measure of Part (a).

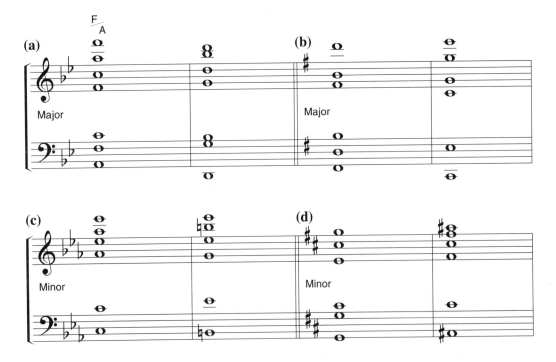

14. Write figured bass. Account for every note. See the example. (Several resultant chord structures have not been discussed; the object is to access intervallic content.)

Example: 8
        5
        3

SEVENTH CHORDS

A **seventh** (7th) **chord** in root position consists of a triad together with a note that is an interval of a 7th above the root.[1] In keeping with *tertian* construction, a 7th chord is a triad together with a fourth note an intervallic 3rd above the 5th of the triad. See *Example 6–1.*

C major

E minor (harmonic)

Example 6–1. Seventh chords in the C major and E minor scales.

---

1. Originally, the pitch producing the 7th above the root was a result of melodic motion whereby the dissonant 7th was a descending melodic tone between the dominant (5) and mediant (3) of the scale. Since the supporting harmony of the dominant and passing subdominant scale degrees was typically a dominant triad, the practice of increased stress as a result of duration and rhythmic configuration eventually rendered the dissonant 7th a chord tone.

Seventh-Chord Qualities

Sevenths add an additional dimension of color to a triad. All 7th chords contain a *dissonant-appearing seventh* interval in their tertian stacking, and depending on the arrangement of the chord factors, the pitch producing the 7th above the root can appear anywhere in the chord.

Essentially, three qualities of 7th intervals above a given root are possible: a *major seventh* interval, as found on a I7 and IV7 in a major key; a *minor seventh* interval, as found on a ii7, iii7, and vi7 in a major key; and a *diminished seventh* interval, as found on a vii°7, which occurs in minor keys that utilize the harmonic minor scale. Enharmonically, the diminished 7th sounds like a major 6th, which is a consonant interval. The diminished 7th is, however, dissonant in its appearance due to its context, and is treated as such.

The interval of the major 7th produces the greatest degree of dissonance because in inversion (to a minor 2nd) it can appear in closest proximity to the root. The minor 7th interval is less strident since in inversion it is a major 2nd from the root. Lastly, the diminished 7th interval is the least dissonant of the three, and in inversion yields an augmented 2nd. If spelled enharmonically, the diminished 7th interval yields a major 6th. When incorporated as the 7th of a chord, it is a highly unstable interval. These matters are illustrated in *Example 6–2*.

◆ *Diatonic Sevenths in Major Scales*

The diatonic triads and 7ths available on the seven degrees of the major scale are indicated in *Table 6–3* on page 106. In the third column, under the heading of "Precise Description," the triad quality and intervallic 7th quality of each are given. A chord description of a major-major 7th, for example, indicates a major triad with a major 7th interval above the root. This assures accurate assessment of the entire chord structure. In popular-music formats, chord qualities are regularly abbreviated; these abbreviations are listed in the fourth column.

With regard to the bottom row of *Table 6–3*, the half-diminished 7th chord appearing on the seventh degree of a major scale and ordinarily on the second degree of a minor scale (harmonic and natural) is often written as minor 7th, flat 5 (Am7♭5, A–7♭5) in popular formats. This is done in order to eliminate any

Example 6–2. Seventh chords illustrating the dissonant seventh or second interval. The last measure illustrates the enharmonic spelling of the diminished seventh interval.

TRADITIONAL ROMAN NUMERAL	PITCHES	PRECISE DESCRIPTION	POPULAR SYMBOL
I	B♭–D–F	Major	B♭M
I7	B♭–D–F–A	Major-major 7th	B♭M7
ii	C–E♭–G	Minor	Cm
ii7	C–E♭–G–B♭	Minor-minor 7th	Cm7
iii	D–F–A	Minor	Dm
iii7	D–F–A–C	Minor-minor 7th	Dm7
IV	E♭–G–B♭	Major	E♭M
IV7	E♭–G–B♭–D	Major-major 7th	E♭M7
V	F–A–C	Major	FM
V7	F–A–C–E♭	Major-minor 7th	F7
vi	G–B♭–D	Minor	Gm
vi7	G–B♭–D–F	Minor-minor 7th	Gm7
vii°	A–C–E♭	Diminished	A dim or A°
vii∅7	A–C–E♭–G	Diminished-minor 7th	A∅7

Table 6–3. Characteristics of triads and seventh chords in the major scale of B♭.

confusion in the construction of the chord since this structure is not nearly as common as 7ths constructed on major and minor triads. In actuality, this structure is an A dim m7th.

In both *Tables 6–3 and 6–4*, it should be noted that some of the chords are almost never used; nevertheless, they do exist.

◆ *Diatonic Sevenths in Minor Scales*

Since three forms of the minor scale exist, the results of the triads and 7th structures also vary, as illustrated in *Table 6–4*. In the fourth and fifth rows, the i7 extracted from the harmonic and melodic minors is often labeled iM7 or i+7, indicating that the 7th is a major 7th interval above the root; this is preferable when employing the interval of a major 7th above the root with minor triads.

Inversions of Seventh Chords in Traditional Practice

As discussed in Chapter 5, inversions of 7th chords can also be indicated by figured bass. Whereas a triad consists of three factors, and hence, three positions — namely, root position, first inversion, and second inversion — a 7th chord consists of four factors, and consequently can appear in *root position, first inversion, second inversion,* and *third inversion*. As with triads, note duplication and spacing has no effect on 7th-chord quality and inversion.

Table 6–4. Characteristics of triads and seventh chords from D minor, indicating actual content and popular symbols.

TRADITIONAL ROMAN NUMERAL	SCALE	NOTES	PRECISE DESCRIPTION	POPULAR SYMBOL
i	Harmonic minor	D–F–A	Minor	Dm
i	Melodic minor	D–F–A	Minor	Dm
i	Natural minor	D–F–A	Minor	Dm
i7*	Harmonic minor	D–F–A–C♯	Minor-major 7th	Dm+7
i7*	Melodic minor	D–F–A–C♯	Minor-major 7th	Dm+7
i7	Natural minor	D–F–A–C	Minor-minor 7th	Dm7
ii°	Harmonic minor	E–G–B♭	Diminished	E°
ii	Melodic minor	E–G–B	Minor	Em
ii°	Natural minor	E–G–B♭	Diminished	E°
iiø7	Harmonic minor	E–G–B♭–D	Diminished minor 7th	Eø7
ii7	Melodic minor	E–G–B–D	Minor-minor 7th	Em7
iiø7	Natural minor	E–G–B♭–D	Diminished minor 7th	Eø7
III+	Harmonic minor	F–A–C♯	Augmented	F+
III+	Melodic minor	F–A–C♯	Augmented	F+
III	Natural minor	F–A–C	Major	FM
III+7	Harmonic minor	F–A–C♯–E	Augmented major 7th	FM7+5
III+7	Melodic minor	F–A–C♯–E	Augmented major 7th	FM7+5
III7	Natural minor	F–A–C–E	Major-major 7th	FM7
iv	Harmonic minor	G–B♭–D	Minor	Gm
IV	Melodic minor	G–B–D	Major	GM
iv	Natural minor	G–B♭–D	Minor	Gm
iv7	Harmonic minor	G–B♭–D–F	Minor-minor 7th	Gm7
IV7	Melodic minor	G–B–D–F	Major-minor 7th	G7
iv7	Natural minor	G–B♭–D–F	Minor-minor 7th	Gm7
V	Harmonic minor	A–C♯–E	Major	AM
V	Melodic minor	A–C♯–E	Major	AM
v	Natural minor	A–C–E	Minor	Am
V7	Harmonic minor	A–C♯–E–G	Major-minor 7th	A7
V7	Melodic minor	A–C♯–E–G	Major-minor 7th	A7
v7	Natural minor	A–C–E–G	Minor-minor 7th	Am7
VI	Harmonic minor	B♭–D–F	Major	B♭M
vi	Melodic minor	B–D–F	Diminished	B°
VI	Natural minor	B♭–D–F	Major	B♭M
VI7	Harmonic minor	B♭–D–F–A	Major-major 7th	B♭M7
viø7	Melodic minor	B–D–F–A	Diminished minor 7th	Bø7
VI7	Natural minor	B♭–D–F–A	Major-major 7th	B♭M7
vii°	Harmonic minor	C♯–E–G	Diminished	C♯°
vii°	Melodic minor	C♯–E–G	Diminished	C♯°
VII	Natural minor	C–E–G	Major	CM
vii°7	Harmonic minor	C♯–E–G–B♭	Diminished-diminished 7th	C♯°7
viiø7	Melodic minor	C♯–E–G–B	Diminished minor 7th	C♯ø7
VII7	Natural minor	C–E–G–B♭	Major-minor 7th	C7

*Can also be written as i M7 or i+7 (a minor triad with a major seventh interval above the root).

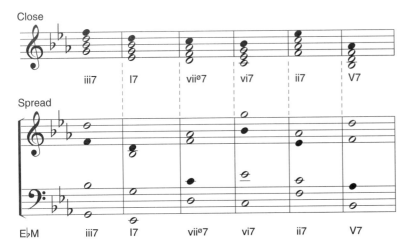

Example 6–5. Seventh chords in root position.

◆ Root Position

Seventh chords that appear in **root position**, that is, with the letter name of the chord in the lowest part (bass), are indicated by the proper Roman numeral followed by 7, as shown in *Example 6–5*.

◆ Inversions

First Inversion: Seventh chords that contain the 3rd in the bass are identified by a Roman numeral followed by $\frac{6}{5}$, as shown in *Example 6–6*.

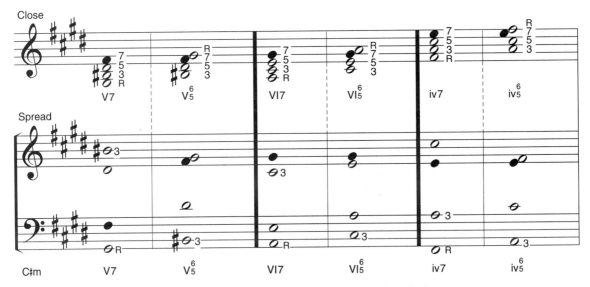

Example 6–6. First inversion: seventh chords that contain the third in the bass.

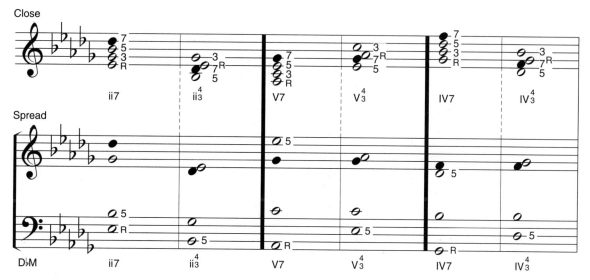

Example 6–7. Second inversion: seventh chords that contain the fifth in the bass.

Second Inversion: Seventh chords that contain the 5th in the bass are identified by a Roman numeral followed by $^4_3$, as shown in *Example 6–7*.

Third Inversion: Seventh chords that contain the 7th in the bass are identified by a Roman numeral followed by $^4_2$, or sometimes by just 2. See *Example 6–8*.

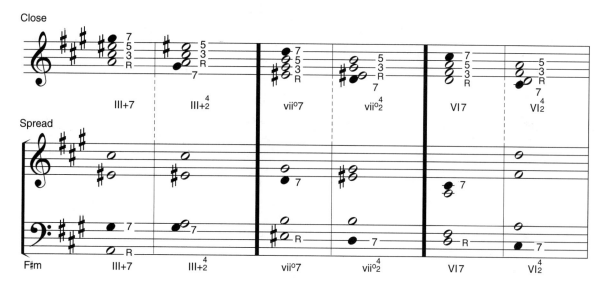

Example 6–8. Third inversion: seventh chords that contain the seventh in the bass.

Numerical Labeling

◆ *Precise Labeling of Seventh Chords*

The Arabic numerals used to identify each position of the 7th chord are traditional, but they do not account for every interval present. This was also the case in the labeling process of triads. Recall that a triad in root position requires only a Roman numeral to indicate its position, rather than a measurement of each interval present in close position. A first-inversion triad requires a Roman numeral followed by an Arabic 6, and a second-inversion triad requires a Roman numeral followed by 6/4.

A closer look at the structure of 7th chords is presented in *Example 6–9*. The encircled Arabic numerals indicate those intervals used to identify the

Example 6–9. The intervallic structure of seventh chords.

inversion of the chord. Technically, all the intervals could be identified — for example, we could write

$$I\overset{7}{\underset{3}{5}}, \; I\overset{6}{\underset{3}{5}}, \; I\overset{6}{\underset{3}{4}}, \; I\overset{6}{\underset{2}{4}}$$

but, as was the case with triads, this is unnecessary.

Several examples of 7th chords taken from the extant common-practice literature are given in *Example 6–10* on pages 111–12.

(a)   *Soldier's March*

F. Schubert

GM

I   V7

(b)   *Little Dance in F*

F. J. Haydn

FM $V\overset{4}{3}$ $V\overset{6}{5}$

(c)   *Hunter's Song*

L. v. Beethoven

CM   I7 $V\overset{4}{3}$

(d)   *Study #46 for Piano,* **Op. 45**

S. Heller

CM   ii$\begin{smallmatrix}4\\2\end{smallmatrix}$ V$\begin{smallmatrix}6\\5\end{smallmatrix}$

Example 6–10. Common-practice examples of seventh chords. **(a)** A root-position dominant 7th. **(b)** A second-inversion dominant 7th in measure 3 and a first-inversion dominant 7th in measure 4. **(c)** A tonic 7th in measure 2 and a second-inversion dominant 7th in measure 3. **(d)** A third-inversion supertonic 7th in measure 2 and a first-inversion dominant 7th in measure 3.

◆ Seventh Chords in Popular Music

Seventh chords in popular music are virtually the same in structure as those used in common practice. One important difference, however, is the manner in which chords are notated in popular music. Although chord symbols are not incorporated in classical music scores, these symbols play an important role in popular forms. Most sheet-music scores, lead sheets, and fake books contain a melody with chord symbols written above it.[2] The performers — usually keyboardists, guitarists, and/or bassists — are required to improvise an accompaniment based on the chord structures indicated by these symbols, as did the keyboardist in past centuries with figured bass. Several types of symbols are illustrated in *Table 6–11*.

Diatonic Sevenths and Hybrid Types

Which of the chords listed in *Table 6–11* can be located as diatonic sevenths? The chord C7 (C–E–G–B♭) can be found in the key of F major as the V7 and also in the key of F minor (harmonic and melodic scales). Cm7 (C–E♭–G–B♭) can be located in C minor (natural scale) as a i7, in B♭ major as a ii7, in A♭ major as a iii7, in E♭ major as a vi7, and in G minor as a iv7. C dim7 (C–E♭–G♭–B♭♭)

2. A **fake book** is a volume of lead sheets.

SYMBOL	MEANING	CHORD NOTES
CM7, CMaj7, CΔ7	Major triad with major 7th interval above the root: major-major 7th	C–E–G–B
C7	Major triad with minor 7th interval above the root: major-minor 7th	C–E–G–B♭
Cm7, Cmin7, C–7	Minor triad with minor 7th interval above the root: minor-minor 7th	C–E♭–G–B♭
Cdim7, C°7	Diminished triad with diminished 7th interval above the root: diminished-diminished 7th	C–E♭–G♭–B♭♭
Cø7, Cm7♭5	Diminished triad with minor 7th interval above the root: diminished minor 7th	C–E♭–G♭–B♭
Cm+7, Cmin+7	Minor triad with major 7th interval above the root: minor-major 7th	C–E♭–G–B
Caug7, C+7, C7+5, C7♯5	Augmented triad with minor 7th interval above the root: augmented minor 7th	C–E–G♯–B♭
C+M7	Augmented triad with major 7th interval above the root: augmented major 7th	C–E–G♯–B
C7♭5	Major triad with the 5th lowered and a minor 7th above the root	C–E–G♭–B♭

Table 6–11. Seventh-chord symbols from a C root and their interpretations in popular music.

can be located in the hypothetical key of D♭ minor as a vii°7 (relative to F♭ major with *eight flats*). Cø7 (C–E♭–G♭–B♭) can be located in D♭ major as a viiø7 and in B♭ minor as a iiø7. Cm+7 (C–E♭–G–B) can be found in C minor (harmonic and melodic scales). Caug7 (C–E–G♯–B♭) cannot be found in any diatonic major or minor scale; it is considered a hybrid. C+M7 (C–E–G♯–B) can be located as a III+7 in A minor (harmonic and melodic scales). C7♭5 (C–E–G♭–B♭) cannot be found in any diatonic major or minor scale and is also considered a hybrid.

Any of the chords discussed can be identified with Roman and figured-bass numerals; but in popular-music formats this would become unwieldy and impractical.

"Cry Me a River"

Words and Music by Arthur Hamilton

Example 6–12. An example (above) with analysis (right) of several types of seventh chords used in popular nomenclature.

Examining the various qualities of diatonic 7th chords as they appear in modes is a good mental exercise. Means of identification remain the same as for seventh chords from major and minor scales.

Inversion of Seventh Chords in Popular Music

As discussed in Chapter 5, a triad in inversion is indicated by a fractional notation. Seventh chords are denoted in precisely the same fashion; thus, $\frac{E7}{G\sharp}$ $\left(\text{or } \frac{E7}{G\sharp}\right)$ indicates an E7 chord (E–G♯–B–D) over a G♯ bass note. Since G♯ is the 3rd of the E7 chord, the chord is in first inversion. Also, $\frac{Cm7}{B\flat}$ $\left(\text{or } \frac{Cm7}{B\flat}\right)$ indicates a Cm7 chord (C–E♭–G–B♭) over a B♭ bass. Since B♭ is the 7th of the Cm7 chord, the chord is in third inversion. The execution, spacing, and doubling of chord factors is at the discretion of the performer. See *Example 6–12.*

Intervallic Configuration of Seventh Chords

A knowledge of the various types of 7th chords, their harmonic structures, scale derivatives, and inversions is essential to any musician's ability to function as a

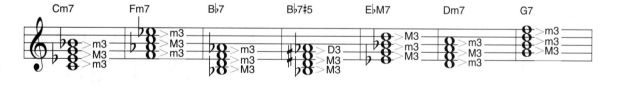

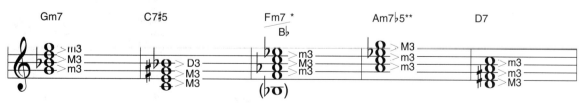

*Notice that the bass note is not a factor in the Fm7 chord. This chord structure is discussed in Chapter 17.

**The m7♭5 is a half-diminished seventh chord which can also be identified by °7.

TRIAD	SUPERIMPOSITION
Major triad	Major 3rd superimposed with a minor 3rd
Minor triad	Minor 3rd superimposed with a major 3rd
Diminished triad	Minor 3rd superimposed with a minor 3rd
Augmented triad	Major 3rd superimposed with a major 3rd

Table 6–13. Qualities of intervallic thirds for each triad type.

performer or writer. A further requirement for the knowledge of harmonic structure is the intervallic configuration of any chord.

A review of the intervallic configurations of triads in *Table 6–13* will provide a smooth transition to the intervallic configurations of 7th chords in *Example 6–14*.

INTERVALLIC CONFIGURATIONS OF SEVERAL SEVENTH CHORDS

	SUPERIMPOSED 3RDS	FROM ROOT
Major-major 7th (Major 7th)	M3, m3, M3	M3, P5, M7
Major-minor 7th (Dominant 7th)	M3, m3, m3	M3, P5, m7
Minor-minor 7th (Minor 7th)	m3, M3, m3	m3, P5, m7
Diminished minor 7th (Half-diminished 7th)	m3, m3, M3	m3, D5, m7
Diminished-diminished 7th (Fully diminished 7th)	m3, m3, m3	m3, D5, D7
Minor-major 7th	m3, M3, M3	m3, P5, M7
Augmented minor 7th (Dominant 7th ♯5)	M3, M3, D3	M3, A5, m7
Augmented major 7th (Major 7th ♯5)	M3, M3, m3	M3, A5, M7
Dominant 7th ♭5	M3, D3, M3	M3, D5, m7

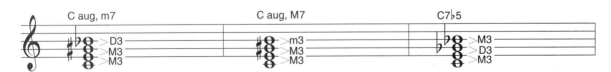

Example 6–14. Intervallic configurations and qualities of intervallic thirds in several seventh-chord types. Notice how the triad C–E–G♭ in the last measure cannot be qualified as either major or minor. It is the only triad presented thus far that contains a diminished 3rd interval.

A knowledge of the pattern of 3rd intervals will enable one to construct any 7th chord from an arbitrarily given pitch, regardless of key, scale degree, or unusual spelling due to enharmonic alteration. *Example 6–15* illustrates several 7th chords originating from various roots with precise identification and popular nomenclature.

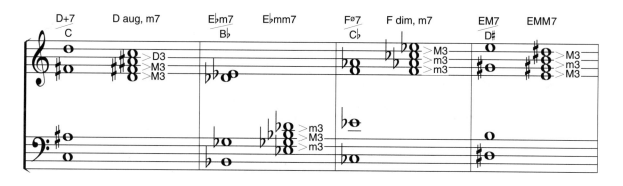

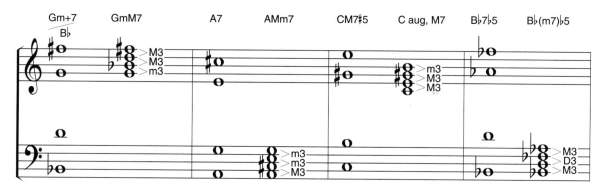

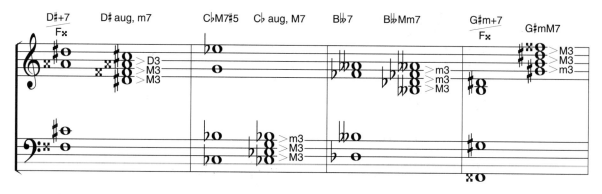

Example 6–15. Spread voicings identified by typical popular symbols. Close voicings are identified by symbols accounting for every superimposed 3rd. These latter symbols are far more accurate, but are not used in popular formats.

More on Hybrid Types

Triads and 7th chords provide the basis of all Western harmonic practice. It is from these harmonic structures that each variant is derived. Triads and 7th chords provide a foundation for the structure of more complex and colorful harmonies.

Although it has been shown that a great proportion of 7th chords emanate from the diatonic pitches of major and minor scales, certain 7th-chord structures are not diatonically available in any major or minor scale. Many of these altered forms are located in uncommon scale types. The chord of C7♭5, for example, is not available in any of the familiar scale types; it does appear in the Oriental scale (C–D♭–E–F–G♭–A–B♭–C), although this is not its Western derivation.[3] Notice scale degrees 1–3–5–7. When certain chord structures are employed in the major/minor key system but do not emanate from the scales of this system, they are referred to as **hybrid** types. Hybrids become more prevalent when chord structures are extended beyond the 7th.

Dominant and Nondominant Seventh Chords

The most prevalent of the 7th chords is the **dominant seventh**. This 7th structure on the dominant degree (V) of a major scale, as well as in the harmonic and melodic minor, is the only one containing a major triad and a tritone interval.

The term *dominant* needs clarification. Literally, *dominant* implies the fifth scale degree; but it may also represent a character exemplified by an affinity of the chord to resolve, and hence, to satisfy its intrinsic tension by movement toward the tonic. The dominant 7th contains a tritone interval inclusive of the leading-tone and subdominant scale degrees. This tritone interval has a tendency toward the tonic and mediant scale degrees. Other 7th chords containing this same tritone are constructed on the leading tone (vii°, vii⌀7, vii°7). Consequently, the leading-tone chord, whether a triad or 7th, is also considered a *dominant function*. See *Example 6–16*.

The **nondominant seventh chords** are those 7th chords of a *nondominant function;* that is, these chords do not include a tritone interval originating from the leading tone.

Although nondominant 7th chords except for the ii7 and ii⌀7 were not as common in practice prior to the **Classical** period (c. 1770–1830), their use

---

3. Many scale types other than major and minor exist. Several of these are illustrated in Appendix A.

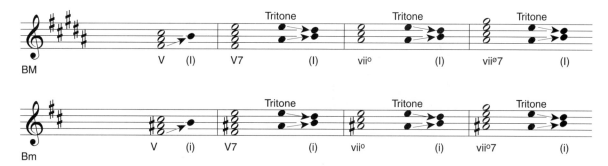

Example 6–16. Tritone intervals in dominant and diminished chords.

steadily increased as music became more harmonically complex. Nondominant 7ths can be found throughout the Classical, **Romantic** (c. 1790–1910), **post-Romantic** (c. 1875–1920), and **contemporary** periods (1920–present), the last including jazz and pop.

Several types of 7th chords in various styles are illustrated in *Example 6–17* on pages 119–21.

(a)   *Gymnopédie No. 1*

E. Satie

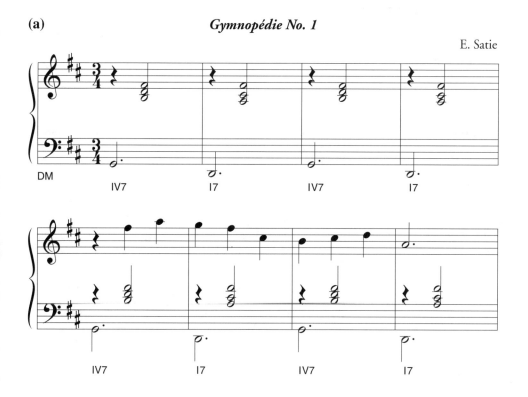

(b)

***Sonata*, K. 332**

W. A. Mozart

(c)

"I've Grown Accustomed to Her Face"

Words by Alan Jay Lerner, Music by Frederick Loewe

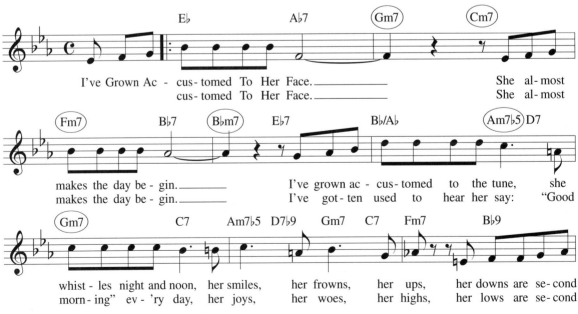

(d)

"They're Playing My Song"

Words by Carole Bayer Sager, Music by Marvin Hamlisch

Example 6–17. Seventh chords in various styles. **(a)** The use of the I7 and IV7. **(b)** The use of the m7, M7, ⁰7 and dominant 7th. **(c)** The use of minor seventh chords in a popular work. Note that Am7♭5 is actually ii⌀7 in the key area of Gm. **(d)** The use of nondominant 7th chords in a popular work. Here, D7 is considered as a dominant 7th in this brief key region of G.

Extension of Tertian Construction

An understanding of the tertian system of chordal construction clearly reveals the fact that chords can be structured to include factors that exceed the interval of a 7th. Although these chords will not be presented in detail at this time, a cursory investigation is in order.

A 7th chord is the last available tertian structure within an octave. Triads in close root position consist of the 1st, 3rd, and 5th factors contained within the octave; the 7th chords in close root position include the 1st, 3rd, 5th, and 7th factors within the octave. It is reasonable, then, that if a scale were extended to two octaves, other pitches would be available for the inclusion of additional 3rds, which could be superimposed over the now-familiar 7th chords. The C major scale extended over two octaves, with corresponding numerical designations, is illustrated in *Example 6–18*.

It is apparent from the preceding that in the tertian system, 3rds can be extended to produce chords of the 9th, 11th, and 13th. When the 15th is reached, the root is duplicated; but is that the end of the tertian order? Just as 7th chords were shown to include many possibilities, so also are chords of the 9th, 11th, and 13th. These will be discussed at length in Chapter 17, on upper-partial chords.

Chapter Review

A *seventh chord* in root position and close voicing consists of a triad — major, minor, diminished, or augmented — (except in the structure of the 7♭5) together with a 7th of some quality (M7, m7, °7) above the root.

Seventh-chord qualities vary according to the scale type from which they are extracted. These include primarily the major, natural minor, harmonic minor, and melodic minor. Seventh chords as well as other chords can be constructed from the superimposition of various qualities of intervallic 3rds.

In the process of 7th-chord identification utilizing Roman and Arabic numerals, root position, first, second, and third inversions — regardless of spacing and pitch duplication — proceed as follows:

Root position: I7, ii7, iii7, etc. — only the 7 is necessary

First inversion: I$\overset{6}{5}$, ii$\overset{6}{5}$, iii$\overset{6}{5}$, etc.

Second inversion: I$\overset{4}{3}$, ii$\overset{4}{3}$, iii$\overset{4}{3}$, etc.

Third inversion: I$\overset{4}{2}$, ii$\overset{4}{2}$, iii$\overset{4}{2}$, etc.

The identification process for 7th-chord inversions in popular works containing chord symbols consists of the 7th quality over a particular bass note. For example, $\frac{B♭7}{A♭}$ $\left(\text{or } \frac{B♭7}{A♭} \right)$ indicates a B♭ major triad with an added minor-7th interval above the bass, thus forming a B♭Mm7th chord over an A♭ bass note. Since the 7th is in the bass, the chord is in third inversion.

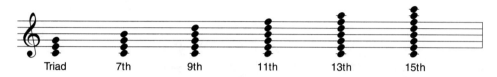

Example 6–18. The C major scale extended over two octaves, with corresponding numerical designations and intervallic third superimposition through the second octave.

Any arrangement of the notes is permissible provided that

1. the resultant arrangement complements the melody,

2. the performance execution is stylistically correct,

3. the bass note is fixed as A♭, and

4. duplication of notes is based on overall musical texture.

Chord structures used within a major/minor key framework that are not derived from a particular major or minor scale are said to be *hybrid forms*. These occur with much greater frequency as the tertian hierarchy is extended.

The primary difference between *dominant sevenths* and *nondominant sevenths* is that dominant 7ths and dominant-function chords contain the active leading-tone tritone interval; nondominant 7ths do not contain the leading-tone tritone interval.

Anthology References

For additional usage and analysis, see the following examples in Distefano, Joseph P. and James A. Searle, *Music and Materials for Analysis: An Anthology.* New York, Ardsley House, Publishers, Inc., 1995.

seventh chords in inversions

Example 31. *Sonata,* Hob. XVI, No. 27, First Movement, Franz Joseph Haydn, pp. 141–48.
Example 36. *Impromptu,* Op. 5, No. 5, Robert Schumann, pp. 201–6.

Self-Test

1. Define a *seventh chord.*

2. What is meant by the "precise description of qualities" of the 7th chords on each of the seven degrees of the major scale?

3. Give the "common" terminology for the 7th chords on each degree of the major scale.

4. Describe the qualities of each of the 7th chords on each of the seven degrees of the natural, harmonic, and melodic scales.

5. The Arabic numeral designation indicating a 7th chord in root position is _____ .

6. The Arabic numeral designation indicating a 7th chord in first inversion is _____ .

7. The Arabic numeral designation indicating a 7th chord in second inversion is _____ .

8. The Arabic numeral designation indicating a 7th chord in third inversion is _____ .

9. In the major keys of B, A, G, F, E♭, and A♭, spell the following upward from the bass in close root position: (a) $I\frac{6}{5}$ (b) $ii\frac{4}{3}$ (c) $iii\frac{4}{2}$ (d) IV7 (e) $V\frac{6}{5}$ (f) $vi\frac{4}{3}$ (g) $vii^{o}\frac{4}{2}$

10. In the minor keys of G♯, F♯, E, D, C, and B♭, spell the following upward from the bass in close root position. Use the harmonic minor. (a) $i\frac{6}{5}$ (b) $ii^{o}\frac{4}{3}$ (c) $III+\frac{4}{2}$ (d) iv7 (e) $V\frac{6}{5}$ (f) $VI\frac{4}{3}$ (g) $vii^{o}\frac{4}{2}$

11. Spell the following chords upward from the bass in close root position: (a) $\frac{FM7}{A}$ (b) D7 (c) $\frac{F\sharp m7}{A}$ (d) A°7 (e) $\frac{E\flat m7\flat5}{G\flat}$ (f) Em+7 (g) G7♯5 (h) B♭+M7 (i) $\frac{D\flat7\flat5}{C\flat}$

12. Determine the quality of the 3rds for each of the following 7ths: (a) MM7 (b) Mm7 (c) mm7 (d) dimm7 (e) mM7 (f) augm7 (g) augM7 (h) dom7♭5

13. List the 7th chords that can be categorized as dominant functions.

14. List the types of 7th chords that can be categorized as nondominant 7ths.

15. The interval that creates the dominant character is the _____ .

16. Explain the processes for identification of 7th chords in common-practice and in popular styles.

17. Provide the alternate popular symbol for the identification of the half-diminished 7th.

18. List all the 7th qualities in the major scale and the three forms of the minor scales.

19. Explain why the diminished-7th interval in the fully diminished 7th chord sounds consonant but appears dissonant.

20. Choose several root-position 7th chords in the major scale and the three forms of the minor scales; for each choice, identify the resultant triad appearing as the 3rd, 5th, and 7th factors of the 7th chord.

21. Choose several root-position triads in the major scale. For each such triad, add a minor 3rd below the root and identify the resultant 7th chord. Do the same for each of the three forms of the minor scale.

22. Choose several root-position triads in the major scale. For each such triad, add a major 3rd below the root and identify the resultant 7th chord. Do the same for each of the three forms of the minor scale.

Exercises

1. In each measure add any seventh quality and indicate the quality of the 3rds. See the first measure of Part (a).

(a)

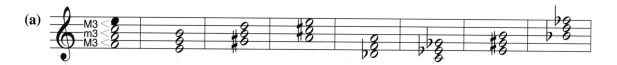

(b)

2. Identify by Roman numeral and indicate the 7th quality, as in the first measure of Part (a).

(a)

(b)

3. Supply both a Roman numeral and a "precise description," as in the first chord of Part (a).

(a)

(b)

4. Write the 7th chord and provide a "precise description," as in the example.

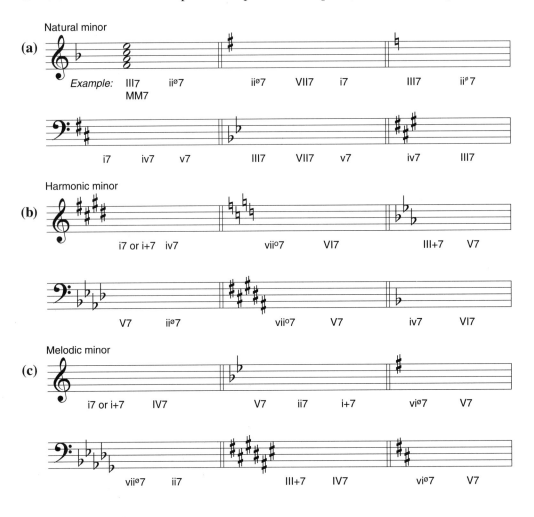

5. Arrange in thirds. Supply both numerals and letter names, as in the first measure of Part (a).

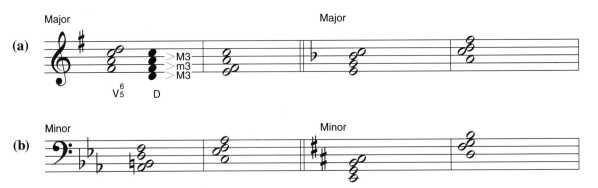

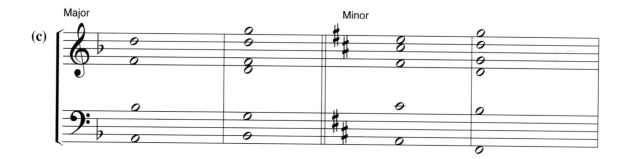

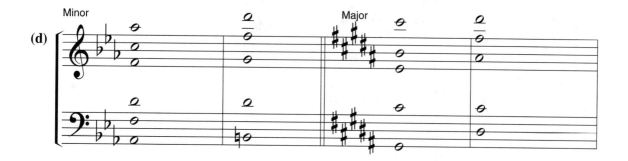

6. Write in spread position. See the example in the first measure of Part (a).

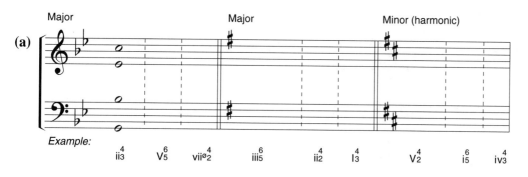

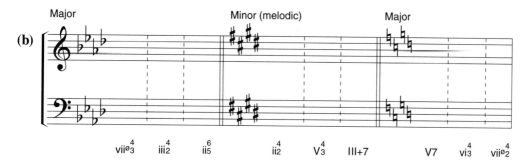

7. Identify the following using popular nomenclature, as in the first measure of Part (a).

(a)

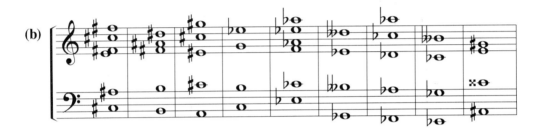

(b)

8. Construct in spread position, as in the first measure of Part (a).

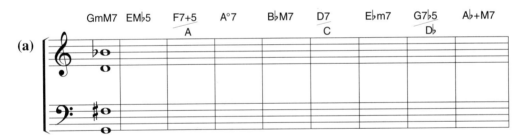

GmM7	EMb5	F7+5	A°7	BbM7	D7	Ebm7	G7b5	Ab+M7
		A			C		Db	

(a)

C aug 7	Db−7	FbM7	Gbø7	Cb7b5	E#+7	C#m+7	D#M7	G#+M7
	Ab			Eb			Cx	

(b)

9. Determine two or three keys in which the 7th chords can be located. To determine the root, arrange in tertian order, as in the first measure of Part (a).

(a)

Fm: i$^6_5$

Cm: iv$^6_5$

E♭M: ii$^6_5$

(b)

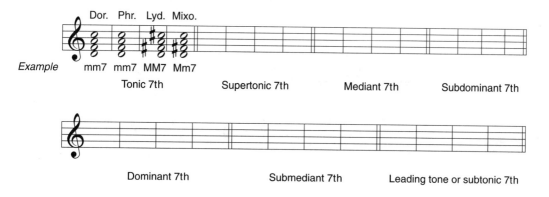

10. Construct in the modes of D Dorian, Phrygian, Lydian, and Mixolydian. Also, label the 7th types. See the example.

Example

Dor. Phr. Lyd. Mixo.

mm7 mm7 MM7 Mm7

Tonic 7th   Supertonic 7th   Mediant 7th   Subdominant 7th

Dominant 7th   Submediant 7th   Leading tone or subtonic 7th

11. Determine a scale in which each tritone exists, as in the first measure.

CM

12. Determine the root of the dominant 7th containing the tritone, as in the first measure.

F dom7

13. Determine the root of a ø7 containing the perfect 5th, as in the first measure.

Bø7

14. Add a diminished 5th to complete a °7, as in the first measure.

B°7

15. Identify with Roman numerals and inversion, as well as with symbols. See the example.

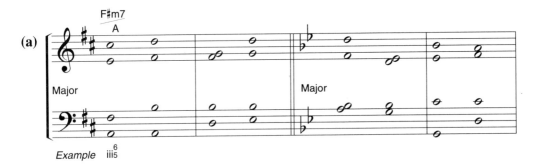

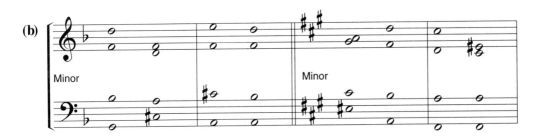

16. Provide a popular chord symbol for each vertical structure.

(a)

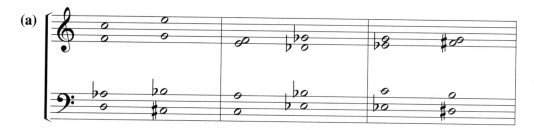

(b)

17. Provide one or more chords containing the notes of each interval, as in the first measure of Part (a).

(a)

Dm B♭M B° G7

(b)

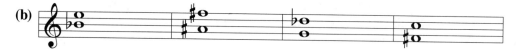

(c)

7

VOICE LEADING
AND
FOUR-PART WRITING

The material in this chapter examines triads and 7th chords. As will be seen in later chapters, the principles of *voice leading* and *four-part writing* can be extended to more complex chord structures; although these structures are not part of the vocabulary of traditional four-part writing practice, their successful usage is contingent upon a knowledge of traditional practice.

Within a tonal format, pitches possess a particular *tendency* concerning their progression toward other pitches. This tendency is further enhanced when pitches are contained within a vertical structure such as an interval or chord. **Voice leading** is the practice of the linear (horizontal) aspect of music, with particular attention given to the vertical context (interval or chord) within which each particular pitch or voice is placed. In the study of voice leading, the term **voice** refers to a note of the chord. See *Example 7–1*.

A **chorale** is a hymn or religious melody, usually set in **SATB** (soprano, alto, tenor, bass) context. Most voice-leading study is normally presented in chorale style; however, knowledge of voice leading is necessary even when the context is nonchordal. Chorale writing dates back to the fifteenth century and was brought to its most-developed stage in the chorale harmonizations of Johann Sebastian Bach (1685–1750). These harmonizations of Protestant hymn tunes exhibit the materials of voice-leading practice upon which most music is dependent, to this day.

The goal of correct voice-leading practice and procedure is not only to treat notes within a chord but also to affect the correct construction of melodic lines and bass lines and to affect any other note movement within a composition.

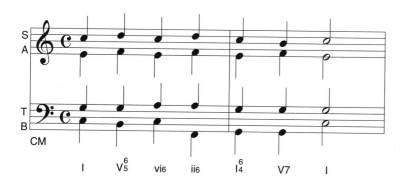

Example 7–1. Voices from the top down: soprano, alto, tenor, bass (SATB). In general, the stems for soprano and tenor face upward, and those for alto and bass face downward.

Specific musical styles or periods are not of concern here. Any style or type of composition demands that the work be "musical"; a knowledge of voice leading contributes in a most significant fashion to the attainment of this requirement.

Pitch Tendency within the Major Scale

◆ *The Tonic*

Perhaps the best approach to the understanding of what is referred to as *pitch tendency* or *progressive tendency* is to begin by reexamining the notes contained in a scale. For the purpose of this discussion, a major scale will be observed. Upon hearing a major scale played from tonic (first degree) to tonic (eighth degree), the first and last note, and especially the last, reinforce the gravitational pull and the final repose of the other notes; the tonic provides the resolution of the entire scalar sequence. To comprehend the various degrees of gravitational tendencies of the other notes in the major scale fully, it is necessary to perform a scale and to listen attentively to the character of each pitch and its *relative stability* or *instability*. Upon playing the tonic, do you hear a tendency toward movement? If so, is the tendency upward or downward? A single pitch out of context has virtually no melodic tendency — it is at rest.

◆ *The Supertonic*

Playing the tonic followed by the second scale degree, the supertonic, in a relatively equal rhythmic distribution immediately causes an attentive ear to surmise two conflicting possibilities, as illustrated in *Example 7–2.*

1. The motion may continue its tendency to ascend.

2. There may be a return to the more familiar tonic, which will therefore be less foreign in its final repose.

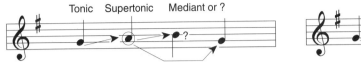

Example 7–2. *Motion of the supertonic.*

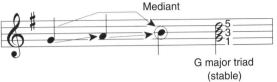

Example 7–3. *Motion of the mediant.*

Since the movement has begun in ascending fashion, the ear may anticipate motion in the same direction. However, if the sequence does continue in
ascending motion, it will move scalewise to an unfamiliar pitch, one that until
now has not been sonically presented. If the supertonic returns to the tonic and
thus descends, it will arrive at a familiar pitch, which has already been heard.

◆ The Mediant

Now examine the mediant; play 1–2–3 of the major scale. What is your opinion concerning this third scale degree? Has the supertonic attained its resolution? Is there a strong, weak, or incalculable progressive tendency of the third
scale degree? You may think that the mediant exhibits a relatively stable degree
of resolution — not as stable as the tonic, but certainly more stable than the
supertonic. Why? This is most likely due to *conditioning*, as are many events
of musical content. The mediant in the context of the major scale is the third
degree of the tonic triad. Essentially, the effect is one of reinforcement of the
tonic by the creation of a major-3rd interval, the initial interval in the close
root-position major I chord. Therefore, although the third degree is not as stable as the tonic, it nevertheless contributes in a melodic interval to create the
required major-3rd interval of the stable tonic triad. See *Example 7–3*.

◆ The Subdominant

This fourth scale degree must be carefully considered. Again, the approach is
by ascending movement, and the normal reaction of the ear is to anticipate continued upward motion. Listen carefully to the fourth degree as it is preceded by
1–2–3. Is the fourth degree active or passive? Is 1–2–3–4 the first tetrachord
of the initial tonic or the second tetrachord of what would prepare the fourth
degree as a tonic? Is the tendency of this pitch upward to a pitch that has yet to
be presented or is the tendency to resolve downward to the third degree, a pitch
already established in the ear? This scale degree, as will be discussed later,
requires careful treatment in vertical harmonic context since its function in
many situations may be ambiguous. See *Example 7–4*.

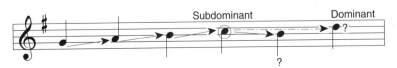

Example 7–4. *Motion of the
subdominant.*

◆ *The Dominant*

The fifth scale degree, the dominant, is the second most important one in the consideration of pitch tendency. Whereas the tonic firmly establishes the final point of motion in a scalar design, it is the dominant scale degree that relentlessly suggests resolution to the tonic. What is the reason for this phenomenon? Examine several musical works from the classical and popular repertories. It may be difficult to find pieces that do not contain V–I or V–i progressions. In fact, numerous works have been written that utilize only the I and V chords.

Why is this tendency for the dominant to resolve to the tonic so apparent? Much of what we are accustomed to anticipate in music is obviously derived from conditioning; but the practice of resolution of notes began at some point, and for good reason. The dominant note of the scale combines with the tonic and third degree to form the tonic triad. However, even when the dominant is sounded in a nonchordal context, its tendency is to resolve to the tonic. Play 1–2–3–4–5 and pause on 5. Does 5 sound as if the sequence is complete? Play 1–2–3–4–5 and resolve 5 to any pitch other than the tonic. Does the sequence sound complete or must 5 continue to a point of resolution? Play 1–2–3–4–5–1. Is this a completed sequence? Play any sequence ending with 5 — for example:

1–2–4–5, 1–6–5, 1–2–6–5, 1–7–6–5, 1–3–4–5

and attempt to bring 5 to a complete resolution on any pitch other than the tonic. The tonic played after the dominant always exudes the most complete degree of rest. This tendency of dominant-to-tonic has been a unifying force in most Western music for the last several hundred years and continues to be so to this day.

◆ *The Overtone Series*

The reason for this compelling gravity of dominant-to-tonic lies in the physical nature of the *overtone series*. When a body is set into vibration, it is not only the **fundamental** (initial pitch) that sounds, but also an infinite number of additional pitches, known as **overtones** or **partials**. See *Example 7–5*. These additional pitches, while considerably less audible than the fundamental pitch, nevertheless add color to the fundamental. When a fundamental is set into

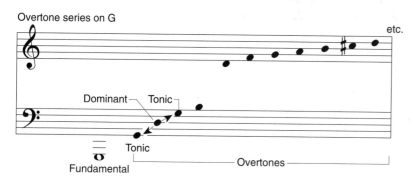

Overtone series on G

etc.

Dominant   Tonic

Tonic

Fundamental   Overtones

Example 7–5. Overtones emanating from a G-fundamental. As the series is extended, pitches become less accurate.

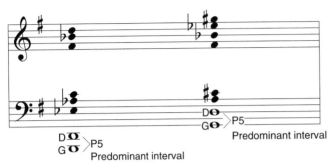

Example 7–6. Relationship between tonic and fifth. The P5 in the bass makes it virtually impossible to destroy the tonic (G)-dominant (D) relationship, no matter how many "unrelated" pitches are stacked above. Both maintain G as a root. (See quintal harmony in Chapter 20.)

motion either by a vibrating string or air column, or by any other device capable of producing sound, the vibrating body divides itself in half and complements the fundamental. The first overtone to be set into motion is the octave; the second is the 5th, or dominant.

This relationship between the tonic and 5th is a natural law in the overtone series, and hence, becomes a unifying factor in the establishment of the tonic-dominant relationship — so unifying, in fact, that it is difficult, if not impossible, to destroy this relationship with any pitches that may be superimposed! See *Example 7–6.*

◆ *The Submediant*

The submediant is located between the dominant and the leading tone, both of which exhibit a significant degree of gravitational tendency toward resolution to the tonic. This sixth degree is perhaps less insistent in its resolution and more neutral than any other scale degree. It is not a note contained in the tonic triad and, unlike the second and fourth degrees, it is adjacent to only one note of the tonic triad, the dominant. Play 1–2–3–4–5–6. Due to the ascending motion of the scalar sequence, the ear anticipates a continual ascent; but if one pauses momentarily on the sixth degree, a careful listening indicates that any direction can be taken with equal results. Furthermore, the major scale and its relative minor share the same key signature; the submediant in the major scale is the tonic of the relative minor, considered a neutral degree — one that does not have a strong tendency in one direction or another. See *Example 7–7.*

Example 7–7. Motion of the submediant.

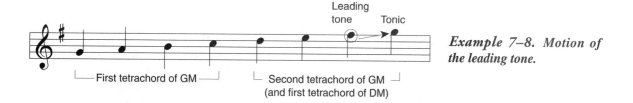

Example 7–8. Motion of the leading tone.

◆ *The Leading Tone*

The seventh scale degree, the leading tone, exhibits the most compelling motion toward the tonic. In the scale pattern 1–2–3–4–5–6–7, it would be difficult to anticipate any resolution of the leading tone other than toward the tonic. One reason for this is the proximity of the leading tone to the tonic. It is, after all, one half step below the tonic. The only other half step in the major scale lies between the mediant and the subdominant — one of the reasons, incidentally, why the subdominant fourth degree has a tendency to resolve downward to the mediant.

In the present configuration in which the leading tone is contained, 5–6–7–8 of the major scale is also a tetrachord. Combine the tendency of the dominant toward the tonic with the proximity of the leading tone and it becomes quite evident why the leading tone contains such a strong tendency for resolution to the tonic. See *Example 7–8*.

Chorale Style and Four-Part Writing

◆ *Chorale Style*

Although the content of the preceding discussion is not meant to be a set of rules or practices in the treatment of notes contained in a melody, chord, or accompaniment, it should alert the musician to the fact that notes contained in certain contexts possess characteristics pertaining to resolution tendencies, ascending or descending motion, and hierarchical significance. Also, the treatment of voices depends largely on the chord presently being utilized as well as those chords that precede and succeed it. Voice leading and four-part writing address these particular tendencies within a chorale format.

Why chorale style? As mentioned at the beginning of this chapter, our practice of music composition is contingent upon the practices established hundreds of years ago, at the time when vertical harmony was first introduced. The methods and procedures established at that time have been, in no small way, the basis for nearly all Western composition in Baroque, Classical, Romantic, Impressionist, contemporary, popular, jazz, and rock styles.

Upon hearing four-part music containing diatonic and chromatic harmony that employs triads and 7th chords, the listener might feel that this music sounds liturgical. It is true that this music had its origin in the church, the Lutheran Church to be specific; but it is also true that our Western musical heritage originated with church music. The purpose of studying four-part writing is not necessarily to become expert at liturgical composition, but rather, to become competent at the writing and analysis of music and to gain an understanding of the techniques of all of Western musical practice, regardless of the style. Even if one never sets an original tune on paper, the music professional is obliged to recognize that which is competently written or performed, why it is well written, and if it is not well written, what can be done to improve the quality of the musical work.

◆ Why Four-Part Writing?

An understanding of four-part writing enables one to comprehend the content of the many diverse styles of music of the past and consequently, music of the present. Virtually any piece of music written in traditional notation can be reduced to four parts, regardless of the harmonic and melodic content. Whether the harmony contains simple triads or complex chord structures, four-part writing offers a view into the structural content of the entire work. The medium of presentation does not affect the content of the music. A work may be for voice, a solo instrument, an orchestra, a chamber, jazz, or rock group, or for any medium of presentation; the four-part reduction, or in some cases, expansion, of the musical material will at once reveal the *primary structural content* of the music. For the composer, analyst, songwriter, theorist, and any other practitioner of music, a knowledge of four-part writing is necessary for the creation of competently written works, arrangements, and orchestrations.

Example 7–9 illustrates a four-part reduction. It provides a skeletal and structural view of the composition. Virtually any musical work from any genre can be reduced and viewed in this manner.

◆ Overview of Chorale Style

The **parts** or **voice designations** employed to represent **four-part harmony** are the *soprano, alto, tenor,* and *bass,* referred to as *SATB* format. In four-part context the soprano is the highest voice, followed by the alto, tenor, and bass in descending order. The *grand staff* is utilized for the placement of the parts with soprano and alto written in the treble clef, and tenor and bass written in the bass clef. The distance between the soprano and alto should not exceed an octave; this is also the maximum distance between the alto and tenor. *Example 7–10* on page 140 illustrates these restrictions. In strict practice, the distance between the tenor and the bass can be as wide as a 12th (compound perfect 5th) or a 13th (compound major 6th). Chords can be either closely spaced or spread apart. **Close position** occurs when the three upper voices of the chord are as close together as possible; otherwise, the chord is in **open position**.

Piano Concerto in Cm, K. 491

W. A. Mozart

Example 7–9. A four-part reduction. The piano reduction, although not strictly SATB, consists of the essential melody and harmony notes. Notice the doubled melody line in the flute and bassoon parts. In a reduction only those parts necessary to illustrate the primary components are written. Virtually any style can be reduced and observed in this manner.

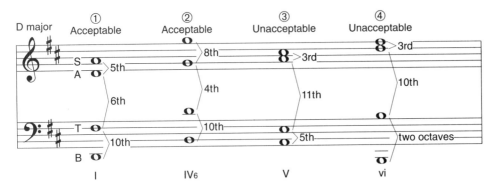

Example 7–10. Restrictions on the distances between parts. In ③, the distance between the tenor and alto exceeds an octave. In ④, the distance between the bass and tenor exceeds a 12th or 13th.

The practice of four-part harmony must not be confused with *chorale style*. Choral music in SATB format utilizes four staves in most cases. The highest staff accommodates the soprano, the staff directly below this is for the alto, the third staff down is for the tenor — the notes of which are written an octave higher than they sound (see Appendix C), and the lowest staff accommodates the

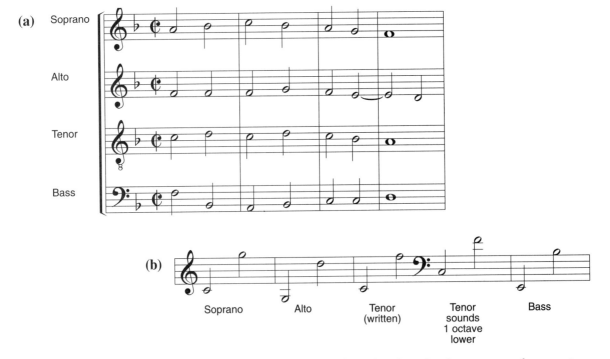

Example 7–11. Chorale style as opposed to piano style. **(a)** In chorale style, the tenor sounds one octave lower than written. **(b)** Approximate ranges are given for soprano, alto, tenor, and bass.

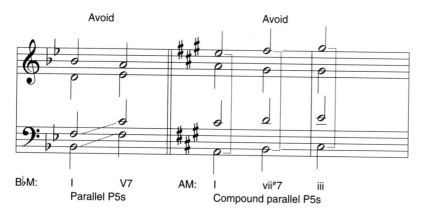

B♭M: I   V7   AM: I   vii°7   iii

Parallel P5s   Compound parallel P5s

Example 7–12. Parallel perfect fifths and compound perfect fifths.
They are to be avoided.

bass voice. See *Example 7–11(a)*. Approximate practical ranges for SATB format are illustrated in *Example 7–11(b)*.

◆ *General Procedures for Four-Part Writing*

Correct four-part writing and voice leading entail numerous procedures. Although the following is by no means a complete list of the "do's and dont's," it will familiarize the reader with various matters that must be considered in correct four-part writing.

1. Avoid parallel perfect fifths or compound perfect 5ths among the same voices. **Parallel movement** occurs when two voices move in the same direction at the same interval. See *Example 7–12*.

2. Avoid parallel perfect octaves and compound octaves for the same pair of voices. See *Example 7–13*.

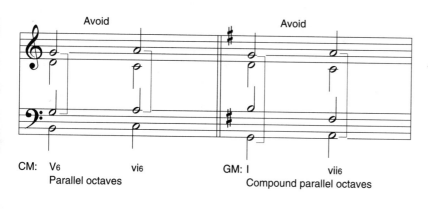

CM: V6   vi6   GM: I   vii6

Parallel octaves   Compound parallel octaves

Example 7–13. Parallel perfect octaves and compound octaves among the same pair of voices. They are to be avoided.

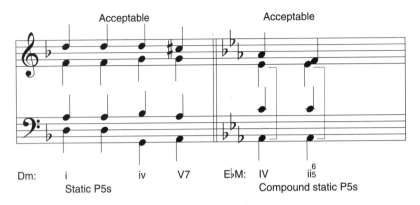

Example 7–14. A static restated perfect fifth. This is acceptable.

3. A static (restated) perfect 5th or perfect octave is not considered parallel and may be used, as shown in *Example 7–14.*

4. The leading tone of the key should not be doubled since its normal resolution in most situations is to the tonic, thus creating parallel octaves. This is illustrated in *Example 7–15.*

5. Avoid melodic leaps of the augmented second interval and of the **tritone** (augmented 4th, diminished 5th) interval in the outer voices. These may be used occasionally in inner voices. See *Example 7–16.*

6. Avoid voice-overlapping whenever possible. Overlapping occurs, for example, when the bass moves to a note higher than the tenor in the preceding chord or when the soprano moves to a note lower than the alto in the preceding chord, as illustrated in *Example 7–17.*

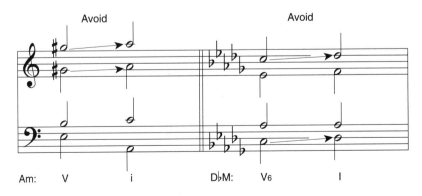

Example 7–15. Doubling of the leading tone of the key. This should be avoided. Note that the doubled leading tone creates parallel octaves.

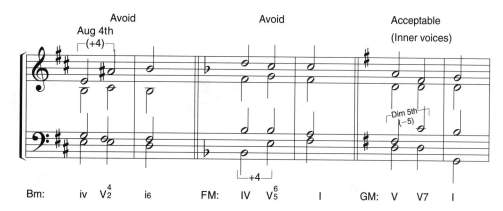

Example 7–16. Melodic leaps of the augmented second interval and the tritone in the outer voices. They should be avoided. The tritone interval in the inner voices is used occasionally.

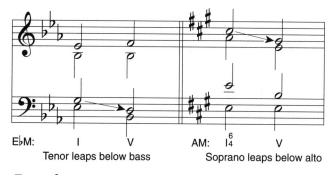

Example 7–17. Voice-overlapping. This should be avoided, whenever possible.

Example 7–18. Voice-crossing. This should be avoided, whenever possible. Notice that here the alto is lower than the tenor on the encircled notes.

7. Avoid voice-crossing whenever possible. Voice-crossing occurs when one voice exchanges its hierarchical position with an adjacent voice, as illustrated in *Example 7–18*.

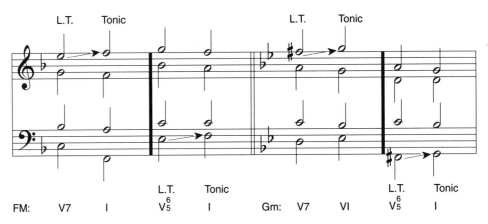

Example 7–19. The correct resolution of the leading tone in an outer voice. (L.T. = leading tone.)

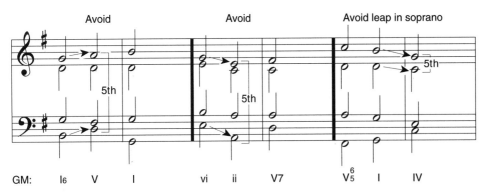

Example 7–20. Hidden fifths. They should be avoided, whenever possible, especially when a leap occurs in the soprano.

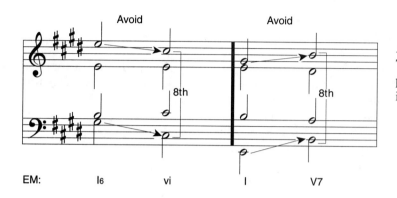

Example 7–21. Hidden octaves. They should be avoided, whenever possible, especially when a leap occurs in the soprano.

8. When the leading tone appears in an outer voice, it should proceed to the tonic. See *Example 7–19*.

9. Whenever possible, avoid *hidden fifths*, especially when a leap occurs in the soprano. A **hidden fifth** occurs when a perfect 5th in the outer voices is approached by **similar motion**; that is, when two voices move in the same direction at different intervals. See *Example 7–20*.

10. Whenever possible, avoid *hidden octaves*, especially when a leap occurs in the soprano. A **hidden octave** occurs when a perfect octave in the outer voices is approached by similar motion. See *Example 7–21*.

11. Keep all voices of the SATB format as close as possible to the designated ranges of the soprano, alto, tenor, and bass. Violations of this "rule" are shown in *Example 7–22*.

12. In general, avoid a reiteration of more than three notes in any one voice. The uniqueness of the line is lost when notes are repeated too often.

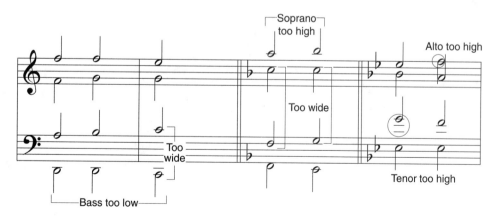

Example 7–22. Voices out of range. All voices of the SATB should be kept as close as possible to their designated ranges.

The preceding list offers general procedures for the attainment of correctly written SATB format. In the ensuing narrative, the study moves to the specific, whereby chords and their intrinsic voices are addressed concerning type, use, stability, resolution tendency, substitute quality, and other factors that contribute to the correct manipulation of the elements contained in SATB format. The procedure for the presentation of this material will be to list the "rule" or practice together with an example. At this time, a review of triad and 7th-chord structures is recommended. See Chapters 5 and 6.

Voice Leading of Triads and Dominant Seventh Chords

◆ Triads

The following describes procedures for the voice leading of triads: much of this will also apply to other chords characterized by particular root movements.

1. **Oblique motion** occurs when one of the voices remains static. In a chord progression involving root-position chords a 4th or a 5th apart, retain the common tones and move the remaining voices stepwise to the nearest chord tones.[1] The use of a common tone creates oblique motion between this note and any other voice that moves either toward it or away from it, as illustrated in *Example 7–23*.

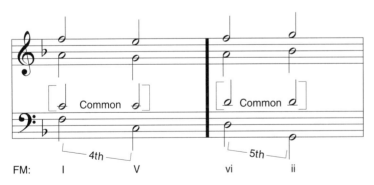

Example 7–23. Oblique motion between the common tone and any other voice in a progression involving root-position chords a fourth or fifth apart.

Example 7–24. Contrary motion. The motion of the upper voices is opposite to that of the bass.

---

1. In this context, *tone* is the same as *note*.

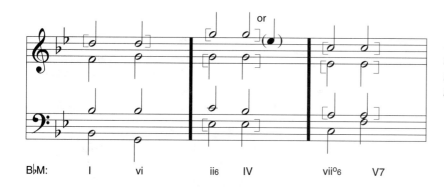

Example 7–25. In root movement by thirds, movement of the other voices to the nearest chord tone.

B♭M: I   vi   ii6   IV   vii°6   V7

2. **Contrary motion** occurs when at least one voice moves in a direction opposite to that of other voices. In a chord progression involving roots that lie a 2nd apart, move the three upper voices to the nearest chord tones in contrary motion to the bass. See *Example 7–24.*

Oblique motion and contrary motion are the most desirable movements between voices.

3. In a chord progression involving roots that lie a 3rd apart, retain the common tones in the same voices and move the remaining voices to the nearest chord tone, as shown in *Example 7–25.*

4. With use of the vii° triad resolving to I or i, double the 3rd, move the diminished 5th interval in similar motion, and move the remaining voices stepwise. (A diminished 5th to a perfect 5th is not a parallel fifth.) However, if possible, avoid the movement of a diminished 5th to a perfect 5th when it occurs in a pair of adjacent voices, for example, soprano-alto or tenor-bass. *Note*: The vii° triad rarely appears in root position. See *Example 7–26.*

5. In first-inversion primary chords, such as I6 or IV6, double the root, 5th, or bass. In the V6, double the root or fifth, but not the bass. See *Example 7–27* on page 148.

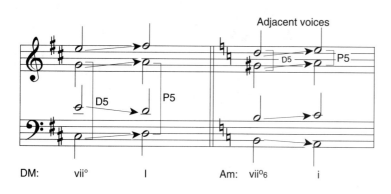

Example 7–26. Diminished fifths approached by similar motion.

DM: vii°   I   Am: vii°6   i

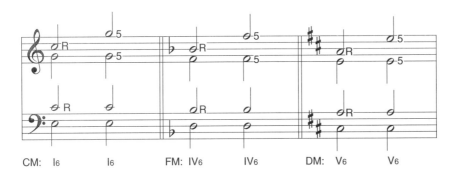

Example 7–27. Doubled roots or fifths in first-inversion primary chords.

6. In first-inversion secondary triads, such as ii6, iii6, or vi6, double the bass note — the 3rd — whenever possible, as is shown in *Example 7–28*.

7. In the first inversion of the vii° triad, that is, vii°6, double the 3rd (bass) or 5th, but never the root — since it is the leading tone. All voices move by step. Be sure to move doublings in contrary motion to avoid parallels. See *Example 7–29*.

◆ Six-Four Inversions

Before a discussion of second-inversion triads and proper voice-leading procedure, it is necessary to examine the character of the six-four triad. This chord contains its 5th factor in the bass and hence, yields a dissonant perfect 4th interval between this 5th and the root of the chord. Perfect 4ths between a bass note and an upper voice are considered dissonant. It is this dissonance that requires careful treatment of six-four inversions. Six-four chords are categorized by type, including the *passing six-four*, the *cadential six-four*, and the *neighbor six-four*.

The dissonance caused by the perfect-4th bass interval renders the six-four an unstable chord; hence, in reality, the bass note of the six-four is considered and treated as the root of the more stable chord that is its V. Six-four chords most often appear on a metrically strong beat. In the progression of

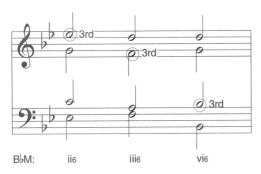

Example 7–28. Doubled bass notes in first-inversion secondary triads.

Example 7–29. Doubled third in the first inversion of the vii° triad.

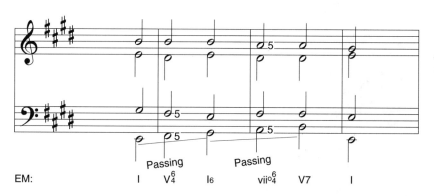

Example 7–30. Doubled fifth in second-inversion chords.

I_4^6 to V in the key of F major, for example, the bass note, C, of the I_4^6 is considered to be the root of the ensuing V; the remaining notes, F and A, are considered neighbors of the E and G of V. Since C is considered to be the actual root of the I_4^6, it is doubled, and the general rules are as follows:

8. In second-inversion chords, such as I_4^6 and ii_4^6, double the 5th (bass). The bass note of a six-four chord within a regular progression is normally approached and left by stepwise motion, and is referred to as a **passing six-four**. See *Example 7–30.*

9. A **cadence** is a point in a musical segment that expresses a particular degree of closure. The **cadential six-four** (a six-four appearing at a cadence) is also normally approached by step or by leap from a chord whose root lies a 4th below. See *Example 7–31.*

Example 7–31. The approach to the cadential $\frac{6}{4}$ chord.

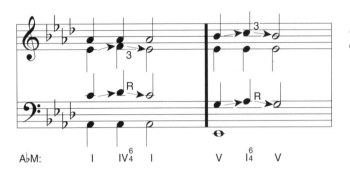

Example 7–32. Neighboring or pedal $^6_4$ chords.

10. A **neighboring tone** is a step-related tone that returns to the initial tone. In the **neighboring** or **pedal six-four**, the root and 3rd are treated as neighboring tones and the bass remains common. See *Example 7–32.*

◆ Dominant Seventh Chords

In examining the voice leading of 7th chords, an intrinsic dissonance must be considered. This dissonance is the interval between the root and 7th of the chord. The 7th is treated in a most careful manner, and its resolution is of utmost significance.

11. The V7 to I or i requires careful treatment. The 7th is best approached by step or common tone. In the resolution of the V7 to I or i, move the 7th downward by step, move the leading tone (3rd) upward by step, move the root of the V7 to the root of the I or i, and, finally, move the 5th of the V7 to the root of the I or i. The 5th of the V7 can be omitted. The complete V7, that is, with all chord factors present, will resolve to an incomplete I

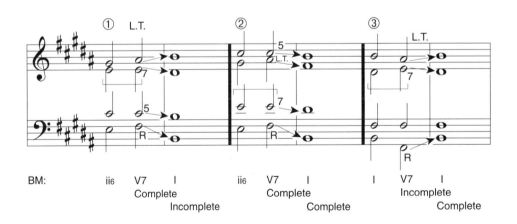

Example 7–33. Downward resolution of a third, as opposed to typical upward resolution of a second. In ②, the inner leading tone may resolve downward a 3rd, thus producing a complete I.

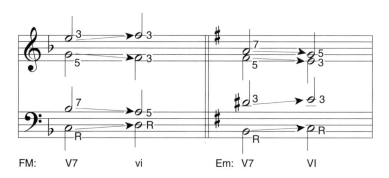

FM:　V7　　　vi　　　　Em: V7　　　VI

Example 7–34. Deceptive resolution of V7 to vi or VI.

or i. However, if the leading tone is in an **inner voice** (alto or tenor), it may resolve downward a 3rd to the 5th of the tonic chord. The incomplete I or i will contain three roots and a 3rd; the 5th is omitted. The incomplete V7 will resolve to a complete tonic triad. See *Example 7–33.*

12. In the V7 to vi or VI (deceptive resolution), move root to root, 3rd upward by step, 5th downward by step — thus, doubling the 3rd of the vi or VI, and the 7th downward by step. See *Example 7–34.*

13. In the V$^6_5$ (first inversion of the V7) to I or i, resolve the bass (3rd) to the tonic, the 5th downward by step, and the 7th downward by step. Retain the root as a common tone. This is shown in *Example 7–35.*

14. In a deceptive resolution of the V$^6_5$, that is, to VI6 or vi6, resolve the bass (3rd) upward by step, the 5th downward by step, the 7th downward by step, and the root upward by step. The case of V$^6_5$ to vi6 is illustrated in *Example 7–36.*

15. In the second inversion of the V7, that is, the V$^4_3$ to I or i, resolve to either the I, I6, i, or i6. Resolve the 7th downward and the 3rd upward by step.

    Note the following: If the bass note of the V$^4_3$ resolves upward to the 3rd of the I or i, thus producing a first inversion, the 7th *may* resolve upward.

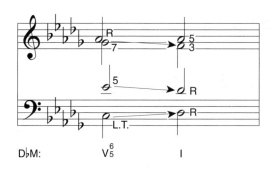

D♭M:　　　　V$^6_5$　　　　I

Example 7–35. V$^6_5$ to I or i.

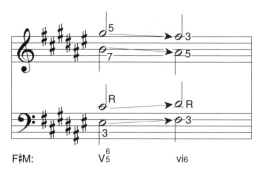

F♯M:　　　　V$^6_5$　　　　vi6

Example 7–36. Deceptive resolution of the V$^6_5$ to vi6.

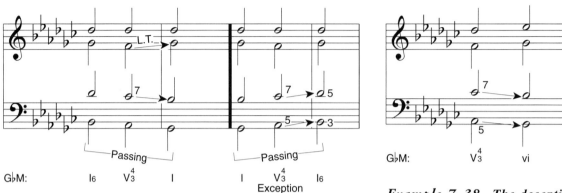

Example 7–37. V $\frac{4}{3}$ to I and I6.

Example 7–38. The deceptive resolution of the V $\frac{4}{3}$.

Approach the V $\overset{4}{3}$ by step in the bass because it behaves like a "passing six-four" (second inversion). See *Example 7–37.*

16. In the deceptive resolution of the V $\overset{4}{3}$, move the bass downward. Follow correct voice-leading practice for the remaining notes. See *Example 7–38.*

17. In the resolution of the V $\overset{4}{2}$ to I6 or i6, resolve the bass (7th) downward and the remaining tones by step, unless they are common. The bass of the V $\overset{4}{2}$ is best prepared by step or common tone since it is the dissonant 7th. Resolution of the V $\overset{4}{2}$ results in a first-inversion triad because the 7th resolves downward by step to the 3rd of the following triad. See *Example 7–39.*

18. In the deceptive resolution of the V $\overset{4}{2}$, that is, to vi or VI, resolve the bass downward by step; follow the correct doubling procedure for the remaining notes. This is shown in *Example 7–40.*

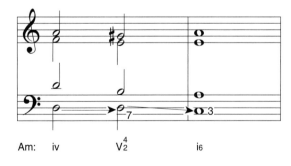

Example 7–39. V $\frac{4}{2}$ to i6.

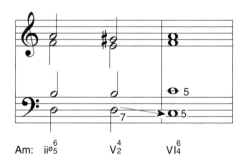

Example 7–40. Deceptive resolution of the V $\frac{4}{2}$ to VI $\frac{6}{4}$.

	MAJOR KEYS		MINOR KEYS (HARMONIC MINOR SCALE)
CHORD	**DOUBLE**	**CHORD**	**DOUBLE**
I	Root	i	Root
ii	Root, 3rd	ii°	3rd, 5th
iii	Root, 3rd	III+	Root, 3rd
IV	Root	iv	Root
V	Root	V	Root
vi	Root, 3rd	VI	Root, 3rd
vii°	3rd, 5th	vii°	3rd, 5th
I6	Root, 5th	i6	Root, 5th
ii6	Soprano, bass	ii°6	Bass
iii6	Soprano, bass	III+6	Root, 3rd
IV6	Root, 5th	iv6	Root, 3rd
V6	Soprano (except if 3rd), root	V6	Soprano (except if 3rd), root
vi6	Soprano, bass	VI6	Root, 3rd
vii°6	Bass	vii°6	Bass, 5th
I^6_4	Bass	i^6_4	Bass
ii^6_4 (rare)	Bass	$\mathrm{ii°}^6_4$ (rare)	3rd
iii^6_4 (rare)	Bass	$\mathrm{III+}^6_4$ (rare)	3rd
IV^6_4	Bass	iv^6_4	Bass
V^6_4	Bass	V^6_4	Bass
vi^6_4 (rare)	Bass	VI^6_4 (rare)	Bass, 3rd
$\mathrm{vii°}^6_4$ (rare)	Bass, 3rd		

Table 7–41. Doubled chord factors in triads and seventh chords.

Table 7–41 will be of assistance in doubling procedures of various triads and 7th chords. Remember that to achieve smooth voice leading, alternate doublings may be considered if they contribute to a more musical line.

Voice Leading of Diminished and Augmented Chords

In the preceding discussion only major, minor, and diminished triads and dominant 7th chords were examined in SATB context. However, the available chord

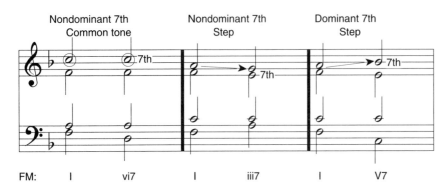

Example 7–42. The dissonant seventh prepared by common tone or by step from either direction.

structures within the octave are far from exhausted. Other diatonic chord structures available within the octave include any chord containing a 7th, such as I7, ii7, iii7, IV7, vi7, and vii7, and their inversions, that is, $\frac{6}{5}$, $\frac{4}{3}$, and $\frac{4}{2}$. Also, remember that when employing the harmonic or ascending melodic forms of the minor scale, an augmented triad is also available on the third degree, III+. Whereas 7ths constructed on the first, third, fourth, and sixth degrees of the scale are not nearly as common as 7ths constructed on the second, fifth, and seventh degrees of the scale in typical SATB format, their proper use must nevertheless be considered and examined; although their "sound" is not typical of traditional common-practice style, these chords are very much in the modern vocabulary, especially in the popular genre.

◆ Resolution of Seventh Chords

The normal resolution of most 7th chords is to the root of a chord that lies up a perfect 4th or down a perfect 5th. The chord of resolution may also contain a 7th. Concerning the correct treatment of 7th chords, the following points will serve as a guide:

1. The dissonant 7th is best prepared as in the V7, by common tone or by step from either direction; this is shown in *Example 7–42*.

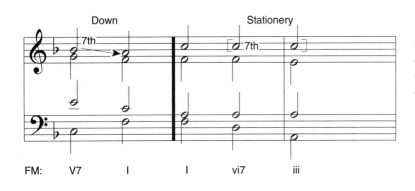

Example 7–43. The seventh resolving downward or else remaining stationary as a chord tone of the succeeding chord.

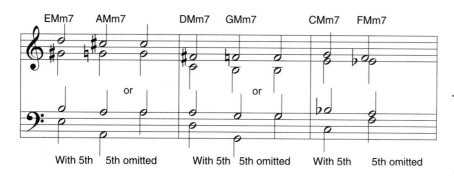

Example 7–44. Omitting fifths in alternate chords to avoid parellel fifths. Notice that the perfect 5ths in the first, third, and fifth chords do not proceed to a perfect 5th in the subsequent chords.

2. The 7th must resolve downward, as in the V7, or else must remain stationary as a chord tone of the subsequent chord. See *Example 7–43.*

3. If parallel fifths occur when progressing from one 7th chord to another, omit 5ths in alternate chords. See *Example 7–44.*

4. In first inversions of all 7th chords, that is, $\overset{6}{5}$, the resolution of the bass note is normally upward by step to the root of the ensuing chord, except for ii$\overset{..6}{5}$ to I$\overset{6}{4}$ or i$\overset{6}{4}$, in which case the bass moves to the 5th of the $\overset{6}{4}$. See *Example 7–45.*

5. In second inversions of 7th chords, that is, $\overset{4}{3}$, resolve upward by step to a first inversion or downward by step to the root in a normal progression. Depending on the voice-leading requirements, the 7th of the $\overset{4}{3}$ may resolve upward, as in the V$\overset{4}{3}$. This is illustrated in *Example 7–46* on page 156.

6. In the third inversion of 7th chords, that is, $\overset{4}{2}$, the bass, a dissonant 7th, is usually prepared by common tone or by step from either direction and resolves to a first-inversion chord, as shown in *Example 7–47* on page 156.

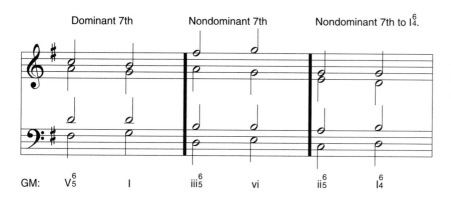

Example 7–45. Resolution of the first inversion of the seventh chord.

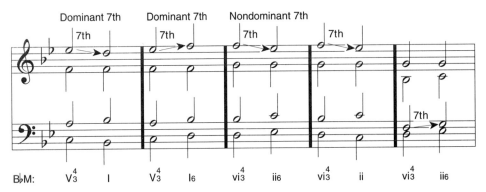

Example 7–46. Resolution of the second inversion of the seventh chord.

◆ *The III+7 Chord*

7. Although the use of the III+7 chord is rare — it is found in the harmonic minor and in the ascending form of the melodic minor — the augmented 5th

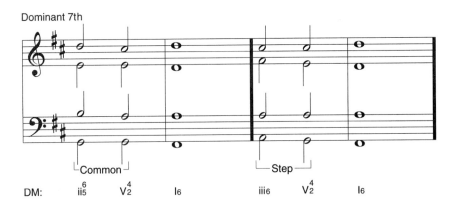

Example 7–47. Preparation and resolution of the seventh in the third inversion of the seventh chord.

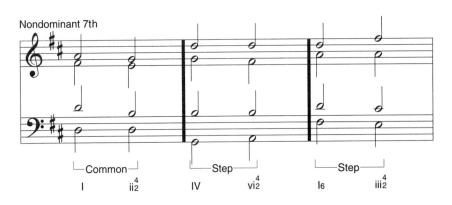

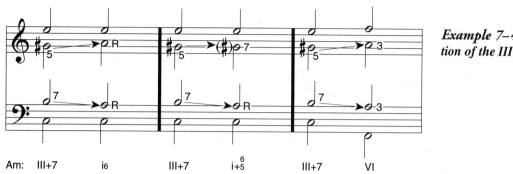

Example 7–48. Resolution of the III+7.

Am: III+7   i6   III+7   i+$^6_5$ III+7   VI

note and the 7th will resolve to the same letter class provided that the resolution is to a triad. If the resolution is to i+$^6_5$, for example, the resolution of
the 5th will be to the 7th of the i7 — a static resolution. A more common resolution of the III+7 is to VI, as in a diatonic circle of fifths. It is worth men-
tioning that composers often use III as a major triad whether or not they use
the harmonic minor. See *Example 7–48*.

◆ *The vii°7 and vii°7 Chords*

In voice leading, the vii°7 and vii°7 chords and their inversions require particular attention. In a major key the vii°7 is identified as a half-diminished 7th. The
intervallic structure of this chord consists of two minor 3rds and a major 3rd, as
discussed in Chapter 6. In a minor key, the vii°7 is constructed on a leading tone;
it is identified as a fully diminished 7th. The intervallic structure consists of
three minor 3rds. For each chord, a diminished triad serves as the primary structure; however, in the half-diminished 7th, the distance from the root to the 7th
is larger by a half step than the distance from the root to the 7th in a fully diminished 7th. The half-diminished 7th chord contains one tritone interval between
the root and the 5th; the fully diminished 7th contains two tritones — one occurring between the root and the 5th, the other, between the 3rd and the 7th. See
Example 7–49.
    The following list indicates voice-leading procedures in resolving the
vii°7 and the vii°7:

Example 7–49. Tritones in the vii°7 and vii°7.

CM: vii°7   Cm: vii°7

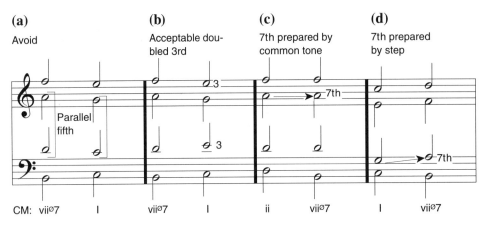

Example 7–50. vii⁰7 to I. In (**b**), the 3rd of the I is doubled. In (**c**), the 7th is prepared by common tone. In (**d**), the 7th is prepared by step.

1. In the resolution of the vii⁰7 to I, the 3rd of the I can be doubled to avoid parallel fifths. The 7th, again, is prepared by common tone or by step. Each note of the vii⁰7 resolves by step. This is illustrated in *Example 7–50.*

2. If the vii⁰7 resolves to I, the root of the I can be doubled provided the 3rd of the vii⁰7 is above the 7th. This is because the perfect 5th interval that is created between the 3rd and the 7th of the vii⁰7 now inverts to a perfect 4th, thereby eliminating a parallel fifth in the resolution of the I. See *Example 7–51.*

3. In the resolution of the vii⁰7 to i, resolve the tritone (the root and 5th forming a diminished 5th) inward by step, and resolve the tritone formed by the 3rd and 7th (diminished 5th) to a perfect 5th. No parallel fifths occur since one 5th is perfect and the other is diminished. See *Example 7–52.*

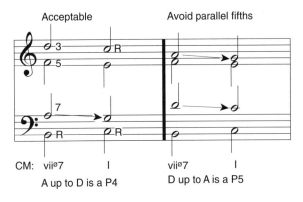

Example 7–51. vii⁰7 to I. Here the root of the I is doubled because the 3rd of the vii⁰7 is above the 7th.

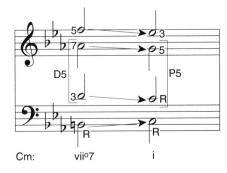

Example 7–52. vii⁰7 to i.

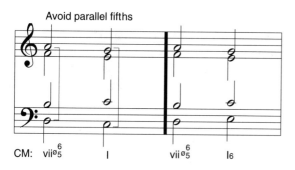
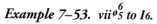

Example 7–53. *vii°⁶₅ to I₆.*

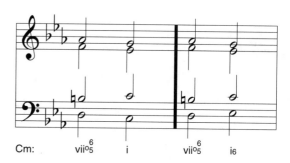

Example 7–54. *vii°⁶₅ to i or i₆.*

4. The vii°⁶₅ (major key) must resolve to I₆ to avoid parallel fifths, as shown in *Example 7–53.*

5. The vii°⁶₅ (minor key) can resolve to i or i₆, as shown in *Example 7–54.*

6. In the vii°⁴₃ (major key) to I₆, double the 3rd of the I₆ to avoid parallel fifths, as illustrated in *Example 7–55.*

7. In the vii°⁴₃ (minor key) to i₆, the 3rd or root of the i₆ can be doubled. See *Example 7–56.*

8. The vii°⁴₂ (major key) and the vii°⁴₂ (minor key), resolve to I⁶₄ or i⁶₄ with doubled 5th. See *Example 7–57* on page 160.

◆ *Deceptive Resolution of the vii°, vii°7, and vii°7*

As in the deceptive (evaded) resolution of V, V7, and their inversions to vi or VI, so too can the vii°, vii°7, and vii°7 chords and their inversions be contained within a deceptive resolution. Remember that a diminished 5th can resolve to

Example 7–55. *vii°⁴₃ to I₆.*

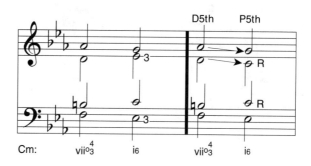

Example 7–56. *vii°⁴₃ to i₆.*

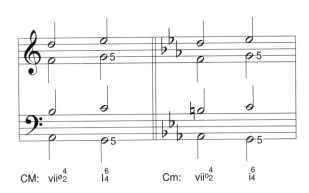

Example 7–57. *vii°$\frac{4}{2}$ to I$\overset{6}{4}$ and vii°$\frac{4}{2}$ to i$\overset{6}{4}$.* Notice that the D5 to P5 in the adjacent alto and tenor voices cannot be avoided. This movement could only be avoided if the 3rd or root of the $\overset{6}{4}$ is doubled.

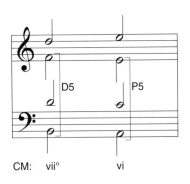

Example 7–58. The vii° triad in a deceptive resolution to a vi.

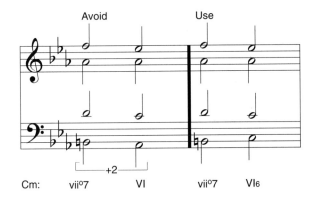

Example 7–59. Use of the first inversion of VI6 to avoid the augmented-second leap in the bass in a deceptive resolution of the vii°7.

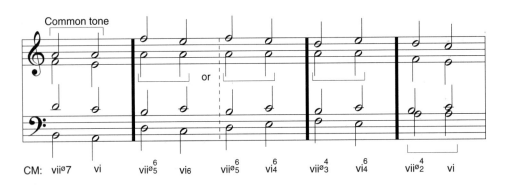

Example 7–60. The deceptive resolution of the vii°7 and the inversions of the vii°7 to vi.

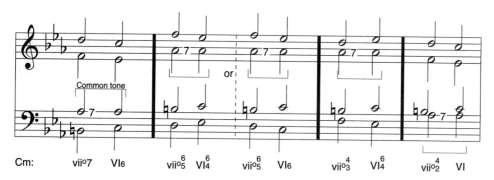

Cm: vii°7   VI6   vii°$^6_5$ VI$^6_4$ vii°$^6_5$ VI6   vii°$^4_3$ VI$^6_4$ vii°$^4_2$ VI

Example 7–61. The deceptive resolution of the vii°7 and its inversions to VI.

a perfect 5th and that an augmented 4th can resolve to a perfect 4th. Thus, the vii° triad in a major key can resolve to a vi in a deceptive resolution, as shown in *Example 7–58*.

In the deceptive resolution of the vii° in a minor key (to VI) does not work as well, however. It is necessary for the leading tone (a raised 7th) to leap downward an augmented 2nd to the root of the VI chord. Recall that leaps of augmented 2nds and augmented 4ths should be avoided in traditional SATB practice, particularly in the outer voices. See *Example 7–59*.

In the deceptive resolution of the vii∅7 (in a major key) to vi, the 7th of the vii∅7 remains as a common tone and becomes the root of the vi chord. Proper voice-leading procedure should be followed for the remaining voices. In the resolution of inversions of the vii∅7, retain the 7th as a common tone and resolve the remaining voices by step. Avoid parallel fifths. See *Example 7–60*.

In the deceptive resolution of the vii°7 (in a minor key) to VI (a major triad in the harmonic form of the minor scale), the 7th of the vii°7 again remains as a common tone — the root of the VI chord — and the remaining voices are resolved by step. In deceptive resolutions of inversions of the vii°7, retain the 7th as a common tone and resolve the remaining voices by step. See *Example 7–61*.

Chapter Review

The study and practice of *voice leading* involves the consideration of pitch tendency within a linear and vertical context. Principles of

voice leading are usually presented in *chorale style (SATB)*, but the practice extends beyond the vertical, leading to harmonic considerations.

Melodic design is affected in no insignificant way by pitch tendency. In this chapter, the seven degrees of the major scale were examined for their potential resolution tendencies; the concepts discussed can also be applied to other scales. The choice of the major scale was a result of its close relationship with the *overtone series* and the fact that a significant proportion of Western music incorporates this scale.

An understanding of voice leading, especially in *four-part style,* is necessary for determining the basic structural, harmonic, and melodic content of virtually any style of Western music. Correct movement, placement, and texture of the inherent notes of a musical score ensure the best possible use and effect of those notes. A few notes used correctly will always be more effective sonically than many notes applied incorrectly, especially in the practice of spacing and duplication.

Several general and specific practices were discussed and illustrated. These practices must become familiar if one expects to gain a thorough knowledge of the mechanics of music theory and composition.

1. When progressing from one chord to another in chorale style, try to have at least one voice moving in contrary motion to the others. Oblique motion, in which one voice remains stationary, is also desirable.

2. Limit leaps in each voice to within a 5th or 6th. Leaps of an augmented 2nd or augmented 4th should be avoided.

3. Avoid voice-crossing and voice-overlapping.

4. Avoid a series of more than three repeated notes in any one voice. The uniqueness of the line is lost when notes are repeated too often.

5. Avoid parallel perfect fifths and octaves as well as compound parallel perfect fifths and octaves. Also, avoid hidden fifths and octaves.

6. Be certain that each voice contains a sense of melodic continuity. This can be achieved by the use of inversions rather than root-position chords. A series of notes that simply fill space, even though correctly placed, is meaningless. The melodic lines of the alto, tenor, and bass, although appearing subordinate to the soprano by virtue of their placement, should nevertheless be of equal melodic interest.

Anthology References

For additional usage and analysis, see the following examples in Distefano, Joseph P. and James A. Searle, *Music and Materials for Analysis: An Anthology.* New York, Ardsley House, Publishers, Inc., 1995.

SATB on four staffs

Example 7.   *Ave Christe* (Part One), Josquin des Prez, pp. 23–32.

voice leading of triads and seventh chords

Examples 15–21. Lord Jesus Christ, the Prince of Peace, Johann Sebastian Bach
O Darkest Woe! Ye Tears that Flow, Johann Sebastian Bach
If God Withdraweth, All the Cost, Johann Sebastian Bach
O Lord! How Many Miseries, Johann Sebastian Bach
My Cause Is God's, and I Am Still, Johann Sebastian Bach
O Thou, of God the Father, Johann Sebastian Bach
Blessed Jesu, at Thy Word, Johann Sebastian Bach, pp. 69–80.

voice leading in piano style

Example 26. *Larghetto,* Wolfgang Amadeus Mozart, pp. 109–14.

Self-Test

1. Describe *pitch tendency.*
2. Describe *voice leading.*
3. Define the term *chorale.*
4. Define *relative stability* as it is applied to scale degrees.
5. What is meant by the term *conditioning?*
6. What are the two most compelling scale degrees with regard to gravitational tendency?
7. Describe the *overtone series.*
8. Define the terms *fundamental* and *overtone.*
9. Describe how *four-part writing* and *voice leading* are applied in the practice of music.
10. What is meant by (a) *parallel motion,* (b) *similar motion,* (c) *contrary motion,* and (d) *oblique motion?*
11. Explain hidden 5ths and octaves.
12. The factor most often doubled in the vii° triad is the _____ .
13. In second-inversion triads the factor most often doubled is the _____ .
14. The 7th of a dominant 7th usually resolves _____ .
15. In the second inversion of a dominant 7th, the 7th may move _____ by step if the bass moves upward by step.
16. Two intervallic leaps in SATB format that should be avoided are _____ and _____ .
17. A term synonymous with *deceptive* is _____ .
18. Describe (a) *the pedal six-four,* (b) the *cadential six-four,* and (c) *the neighboring six-four* chords.

19. Describe *voice-crossing*.

20. Describe *voice-overlapping*.

21. Discuss spacing limitations between adjacent SATB voices.

Exercises

1. Arrange in SATB format. Use correct spacing as well as various inversions. Label all chords and determine at least two keys in which each chord can be located. See the *example*.

Ex: FM as I in F
       and IV in C

2. Arrange in chorale format as in the first measure.

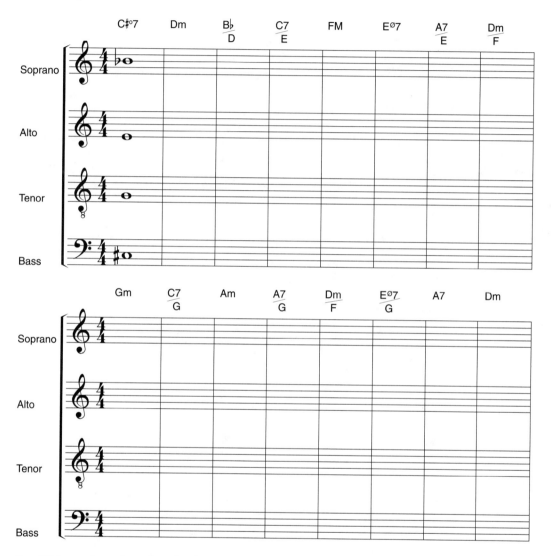

3. Write and resolve. See the first measure of Part (a).

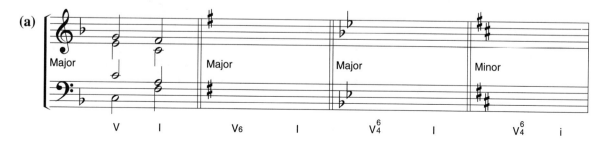

(b)

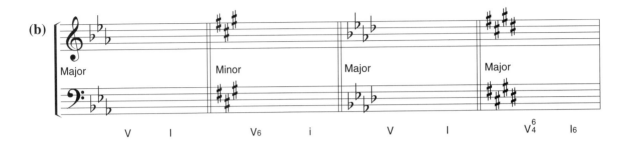

V I   V6 i   V I   V$_4^6$ I6

(c)

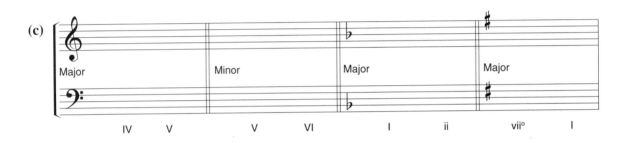

IV V   V VI   I ii   vii° I

(d)

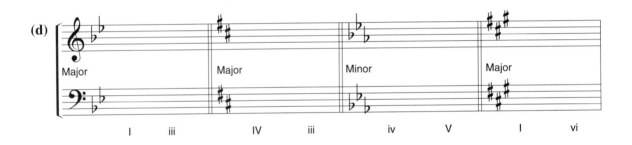

I iii   IV iii   iv V   I vi

4. In each part, list all errors in voice leading, such as spacing, doublings, voice-crossing, parallel fifths and octaves, resolutions, and preparations. Note that Parts (a) and (b) contain only triads; Parts (c) and (d) contains triads and 7ths.

(a)

(b)

(c)

(d)

5. Add soprano, alto, and tenor. Label all chords.

(a)

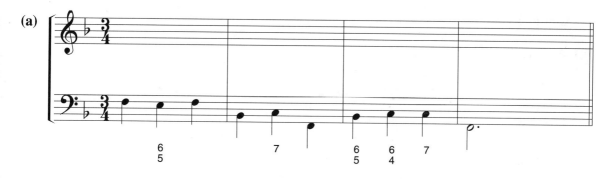

6. Construct passing $^6_4$ chords, cadential $^6_4$ chords, and neighbor $^6_4$ chords.

(a) Passing:

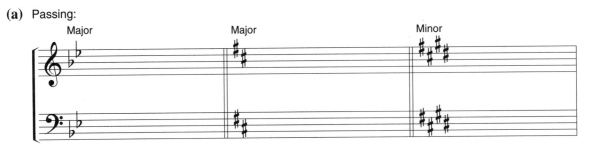

(b) Cadential:

(c) Neighbor:

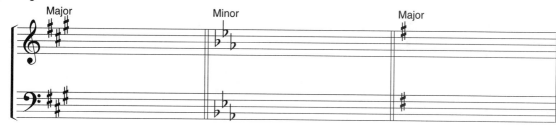

7. Resolve to I or i with the necessary inversions.

(a)

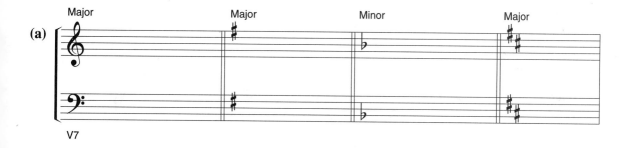

(b)

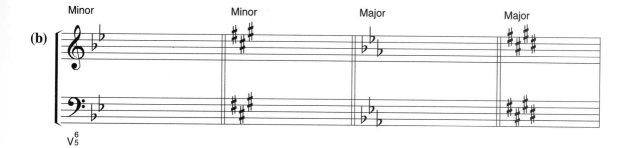

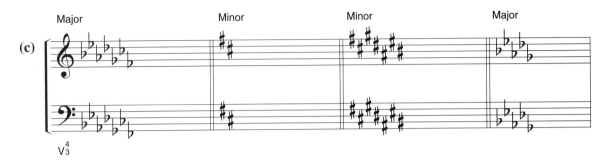

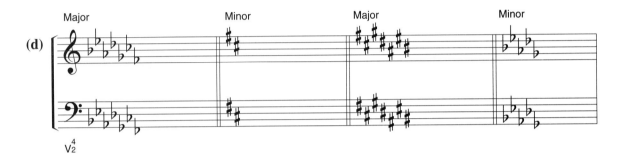

8. Resolve as deceptive resolutions.

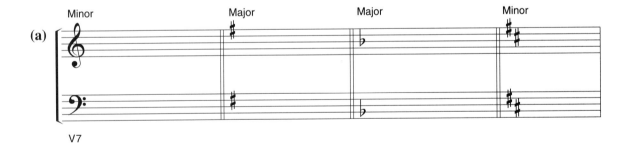

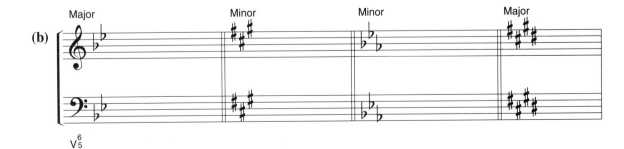

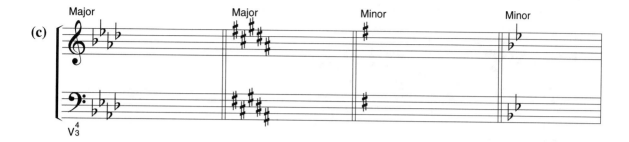

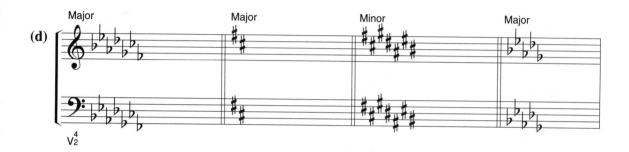

9. Resolve the vii°7 or vii⌀7 and their inversions to I or i and their inversions.

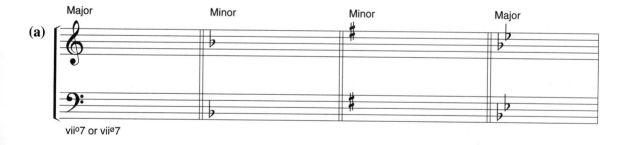

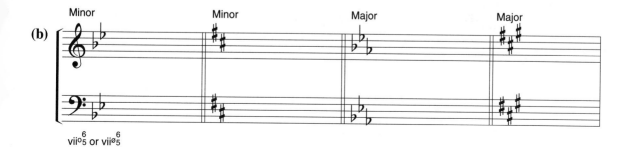

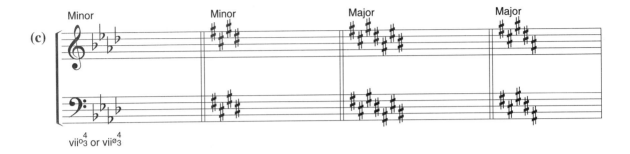

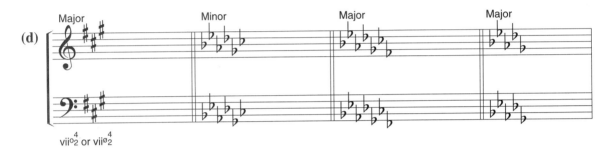

10. Write deceptive resolutions.

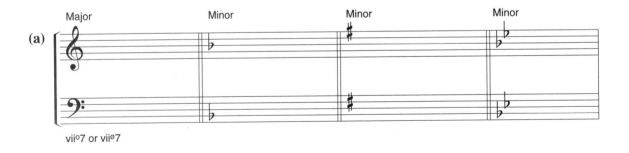

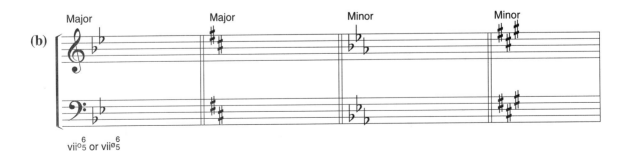

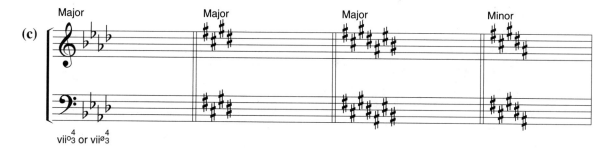

(c)

Major · Major · Major · Minor

vii°$^4_3$ or viiø$^4_3$

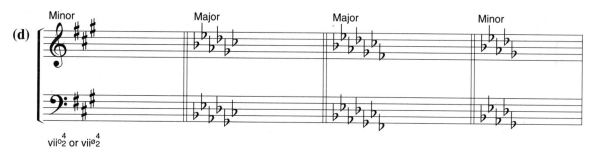

(d)

Minor · Major · Major · Minor

vii°$^4_2$ or viiø$^4_2$

11. Complete the SATB. Label all chords.

(a) Add alto and tenor.

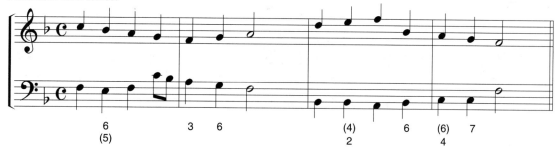

6   3   6   (4)   6   (6)   7
(5)   2   4

(b) Add bass.

(c) Add alto.

(d) Add soprano.

12. Add alto and tenor. Label all chords.

J. S. Bach (adapted)

(a)

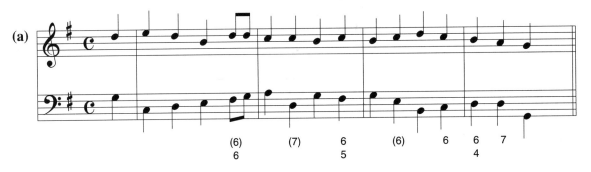

J. S. Bach (adapted)

(b)

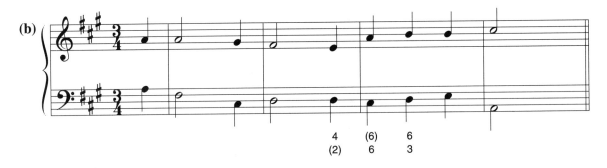

J. S. Bach (adapted)

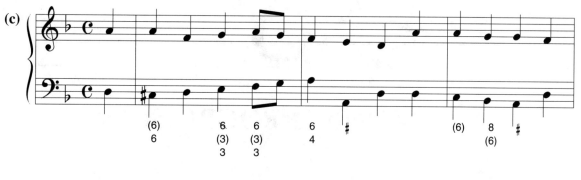

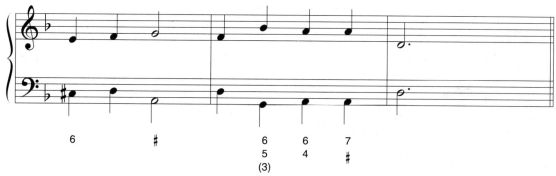

8

HARMONIC PROGRESSION

Perhaps the most compelling forces in sustaining the tension and resolution aspects of a musical work are the manner in which one chord progresses to the next (at the *micro* level), the protracted character of the harmonic movement in phrases (at the *meso* level), and the achievement of the *harmonic goal* of the section, movement, or entire work (at the *macro* level). *Music is essentially a series of tension/resolution events functioning within a temporal framework.* The continuous overlapping of the micro, meso, and macro levels of harmonic content and motion have a major impact on a musical work.

Chordal Tendencies and Musical Style

At the beginning of Chapter 7, the tendency of certain pitches to move toward other pitches within the framework of a major scale was discussed. Chords also move toward other chords; **progression** is a general term used to define chord-to-chord movement. Just as individual notes contained within a melodic con-figuration in a tonal environment, such as a scale, possess characteristics regarding their tonic gravity, so too, chords and intervallic structures possess tendencies toward progression and resolution. Musical works of the common-practice period and many works composed in the contemporary period utilize harmonic relationship as the primary structural element in their development. The movement of one chord to another is always a matter of personal choice. Progression of chords rests solely on the decision of the composer, the song-writer, or in certain styles, the arranger. The degree of tension required at any moment is determined strictly by individual preference. Of course, many other factors contribute to the selection of certain chords; these may include: the character of the melody, the rhythmic content, the instrumentation, and perhaps most importantly, the *style* or *type* of composition. Consequently, there are many correct procedures for harmonizing a melody or selecting chords in a progression. What should initially be considered is the natural tendency of certain chords within the framework of the particular work and the style in which the work is written. Since this book addresses Western music, harmonic tension and resolution will be determined by the tendencies of chords toward one another in the major-minor system.

◆ *Similarities among Triads and Sevenths*

Before commencing the discussion of chord movement, it is necessary to observe similarities among several triads and 7th chords. In *Table 8–1* on page 178, triads and 7th chords in the key of C major are examined.

   A discussion of actual chord progression must be preceded by a comparison of the notes contained in the various chords listed in *Table 8–1*. Beginning with tonic triad I, C–E–G, locate other chords that contain the notes C–E–G, C–E, or E–G. A likely chord to investigate for similarities is the chord of the relative key, A minor. The triad of A minor contains both a C and an E. Upon inspection of the A minor 7th, it is apparent that this chord contains all the notes of the C major triad. Perform the same process with the other primary chords.

   It can immediately be seen that every triad except the vii° has been considered. Although the B diminished triad cannot be tonicized in the major/minor system and thus has no relative-key counterpart, some or all of the notes contained in the B diminished triad do appear in other triads or 7th chords. Compare the B diminished triad with the ii chord, the D minor. Both chords contain the notes D and F. Compare the B diminished with the V7; every note of the B diminished triad is contained in the V7 chord. Can it be assumed, then, that B diminished (vii°), D minor (ii), and G dominant 7th (V7) are intrinsically related to one another? Reverting to the C major triad for a moment, it was seen that C major, A minor, and A minor 7th contained many of the same notes. Inspect the notes of the IV and IV7 chords — F–A–C (in IV) and F–A–C–E (in IV7). Notice that the IV contains two notes of the vi (A–C–E) and that IV7 contains all the notes of the vi. The obvious question at this time concerns the point at which chords cease to be related to one another. Suffice it to say, possible chord relationships, similarities, and substitutions are innumerable, as will be seen in more detail in later chapters.

TRIADS IN C MAJOR

ROMAN NUMERAL	NOTES	CHORD NAME	QUALITY
I	C–E–G	C major	Major
ii	D–F–A	D minor	Minor
iii	E–G–B	E minor	Minor
IV	F–A–C	F major	Major
V	G–B–D	G major	Major
vi	A–C–E	A minor	Minor
vii°	B–D–F	B diminished	Diminished

SEVENTH CHORDS IN C MAJOR

ROMAN NUMERAL	NOTES	CHORD NAME	QUALITY
I7	C–E–G–B	C major 7th	Major-major 7th
ii7	D–F–A–C	D minor 7th	Minor-minor 7th
iii7	E–G–B–D	E minor 7th	Minor-minor 7th
IV7	F–A–C–E	F major 7th	Major-major 7th
V7	G–B–D–F	G dominant 7th	Major-minor 7th
vi7	A–C–E–G	A minor 7th	Minor-minor 7th
viiø7	B–D–F–A	B half-diminished 7th	Diminished minor 7th

Table 8–1. C major triads and seventh chords.

What can be deduced from the preceding, then, is that various chords, when considered in their triad, 7th, and other inherent structures, appear to be closely related. These similarities in note content often determine the progression from one chord to another; ultimately, however, it is the style of the musical work that imposes the most influence on harmonic movement and content

◆ *Common-Practice and Popular Genres*

A contemporary popular composition that relies on the reiteration of one or two chords to establish its harmonic framework certainly will not be convincing as the harmonic framework for a Baroque-style chorale. Stylistically, the two works are quite different; each requires a particular method of unfolding — of progression; each has been stylistically established. Two factors must be considered in determining chord choice and hence, harmonic progression: the natural tendencies of chords within a tonal framework and the style.

Example 8–2 on pages 180–81 contains excerpts of chord progressions from compositions in Baroque and popular styles. Compare the difference in the chord activity in the two styles.

Chord Movement

◆ *The Circle Progression*

In the discussion of scale construction and the order of keys (Chapter 3) it was noted that as each additional sharp is added to the key signature, the center of tonality is shifted by an ascending perfect 5th interval; moreover, as flats are systematically eliminated from the signature, the results are the same.

In the circle of fifths, if we begin with C♯ major, a key signature that contains seven sharps, and proceed to eliminate sharps one by one from the right of the key signature, each resulting key will be a perfect 5th interval lower than the preceding one. Upon reaching C major, the continuation of the series requires the addition of flats until the key of C♭ major, with seven flats, is attained. Thus, the series moves through every possible key.

This movement in 5ths provides perhaps the most compelling gravitational tendency in Western music. Each descending key results in a dominant-to-tonic relationship, thus establishing the circle of fifths. Any chord movement or progression that involves the movement of one chord root to another by a descending 5th or an ascending 4th is known as a **circle progression**. Most often, these 4ths and 5ths are perfect in quality. More than any other type of root movement, the circle progression exudes direction, motion, and tendency toward resolution. See *Example 8–3* on pages 182–83.

◆ *Progressive and Retrogressive Movements*

Progressive (strong) **movement** indicates forward motion, and, conversely, **retrogressive** (weak) **movement** indicates backward motion. A determination of strong or weak movement can be quite a subjective decision; however, in no case should *progressive* signify proper movement and *retrogressive* signify improper movement. The only determining factor in choosing one movement over the other is the musical desirability of each at some moment in a particular harmonization and style. In most cases, progressive or retrogressive movement only approximates a relatively strong or weak harmonic relationship. Through observation and analysis of music of the common-practice period, progressive and retrogressive harmonic movements have been differentiated. In general, *progressive movement* includes those chord roots that move:

1. downward in 5ths or upward in 4ths;

2. upward in 2nds or downward in 7ths, except ii–iii, vi–vii°;

3. downward in 3rds or upward in 6ths, except V–iii, iii–I.

Additionally, movement from the tonic chord to any other chord is considered progressive.

Retrogressive movement includes those chord roots that move:

1. downward in 4ths or upward in 5ths;

2. downward in 2nds or upward in 7ths;

3. upward in 3rds or downward in 6ths.

See *Example 8–4* on page 184.
Inversions do not affect progressive or retrogressive movement.

(a)

Chorale No. 15, *St. John Passion*

J. S. Bach

(b)

"Stranded in a Limousine"

Paul Simon

Example 8–2. Chord progressions in Baroque and popular styles. **(a)** Notice the active chord movement.
(b) Although the chord content is sparse, the melody line is colorful in its use of nonchord tones.

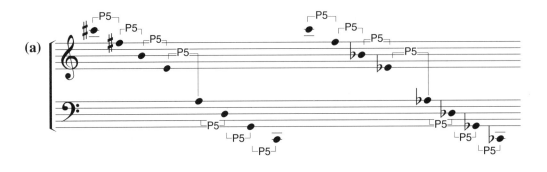

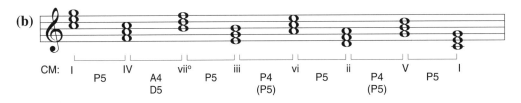

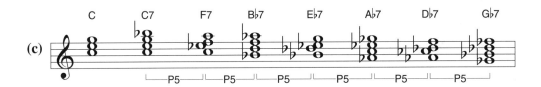

Substitution, Factors, and Chord Choice

In a major key, each primary triad contains two notes that appear in the relative minor chord, which can be considered the relative key. For example, the I chord in the key of C major is closely related to the vi chord of A minor. Both chords contain the notes C and E, and A minor is the relative minor key of C major. The IV chord of F major and the ii chord of D minor also share two common notes, F and A, and F major and D minor are relative keys. Similarly, V and iii share two common notes, G and B, and are relative keys. The vii° triad, B diminished, has no relative key, but is nevertheless closely related to ii and V because two notes of the ii (D and F) and two notes of the V (B and D) are contained in B diminished.

(d) "Ego"

Elton John, Bernie Taupin

I'm on the stage —— to-night and —— if — the price —— is right — I'll ——

I will a-maze —— be-fore — the ———— light, — I — crave — the light, —

—— mmm blind - ing white —— I need the light —— to-night —

Example 8–3. Circle progressions. **(a)** Descending perfect 5ths. **(b)** The circle progression of diatonic triads IV to vii° produces an augmented 4th or diminished 5th, depending on ascending or descending movement. **(c)** Dominant 7ths in root position and inversions in a circle progression. **(d)** Circle progressions between measures 2–5 and measures 7–10.

It is necessary to know pitch similarities when choosing chords in a harmonic progression, especially when considering possible alternatives, known as *chord substitutions*. A **chord substitution** is an alternate choice of one chord for another. Although there are numerous possibilities for chord substitution both within a diatonic and a chromatic framework, the chords that will be considered in this discussion will include only the most obvious ones within a *diatonic* framework.

A progression that continuously utilizes the I, IV, and V chords may provide more interest if certain substitutions are employed. The most readily available substitutions can be found by replacing a primary chord with a relative chord. Instead of the IV, for example, the ii chord can be substituted if the melody and style allow for this, as one learns through experience. Similarly, the vi can be substituted for the I chord. However, if a replacement for the V is desired, will the iii be a good choice? The iii chord is the relative minor of the V, and thus would seem the likely substitution. In many cases it is substituted,

Progressive movement

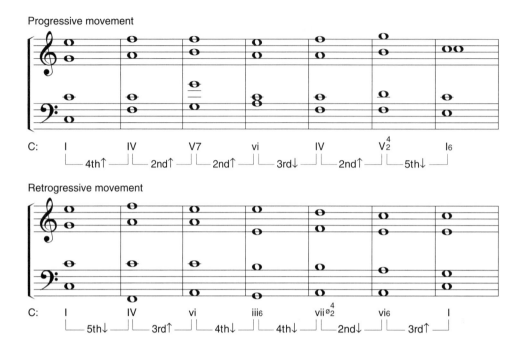

Retrogressive movement

Example 8–4. Progressive and retrogressive movements. Measure 1 of the retrogressive movement is progressive because of the movement of I to another chord.

but it is *not* the best choice. Several problems exist in choosing the iii as an alternate for the V. The V chord provides the most compelling thrust toward the tonic. A comparison of the V chord with the I chord reveals that the only common factor among the two is the root of the V chord, which is the 5th of the I chord. The V chord and the iii chord both contain the leading tone. This is desirable since the leading tone also provides a thrust toward the tonic. The V chord contains the supertonic second degree of the scale as its 5th factor; this is also desirable since the supertonic degree also has a tendency toward the tonic. Although the iii chord contains both the dominant and leading-tone degrees of the scale, it also contains the mediant degree, the note that is the 3rd of the I chord. The presence of the 3rd is what causes the iii triad to be a weak substitution for the V triad. The 3rd factor is a highly stable tone in the I triad; it determines the major or minor quality, and, hence, causes ambiguity when contained in a chordal substitution for V. This does not occur in the V–to–I progression, even though there is a common tone — the root of the V and the 5th of the I — because that common tone is the dominant degree of the scale and, as has been stated, the dominant provides a thrust toward the tonic. See *Example 8–5.*

What, then, is a more appropriate substitute for the V when a strong convincing resolution to the tonic is desired? A chord containing the dominant note would surely be desired; however, no triads other than I, iii, and V contain the dominant note G.

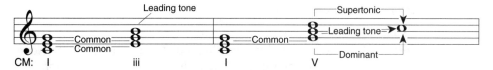

Example 8–5. *All pitches of the V gravitate towards the tonic.*

The next consideration should be those chords that contain a leading tone, since the leading tone provides a high degree of thrust toward the tonic. These chords containing the leading tone are the iii, the V, and the vii°. This last triad contains the leading tone, supertonic, and subdominant notes of the scale. Recall from the discussion concerning note tendency within a scale that the leading tone exudes a strong tendency toward the tonic, the supertonic tends toward the tonic or mediant, and the subdominant tends toward the mediant. The vii° triad also contains the interval of the diminished 5th tritone that is contained between the root, B, and 5th, F. There is much to be said concerning this triad. It is the only triad in the major scale that contains the unstable dissonant tritone interval. The resolution of the tritone — the diminished 5th in the case of a root-position vii° triad — is inward by step. If the two notes included in the tritone contract by step to a major 3rd interval, the resulting notes will be C and E, the root and 3rd of the I chord. If the chord appears in inversion, so that the diminished 5th is inverted to an augmented 4th, the resolution is outward by step to an inversion of the notes C and E. It can be readily seen why the vii° triad is perhaps the best choice as a substitution for the V. See *Example 8–6.*

◆ Substitution by Extension of a Lower Third

If a note that is a major 3rd below the root of the vii° triad is added to the entire structure, the resulting harmony is a V7 chord. The V7 contains all the notes of the vii° triad as its 3rd, 5th, and 7th factors. See *Example 8–7.* This **extension** procedure is applicable to other triads as well.

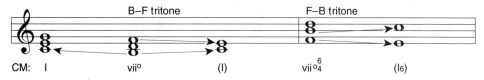

Example 8–6. *Resolution of the tritone in the vii° to I.*

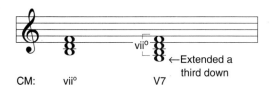

Example 8–7. *Substitution by extension of a lower third.*

◆ *Substitution by Extension of a Higher Third*

To understand substitutions of this type, consider extending the ii triad upward by the addition of the next normally occurring 3rd. The ii triad in C major consists of D–F–A; when extended upward to include the C, the next normally occurring 3rd, the chord becomes a ii7. However, the three upper notes of the ii7 comprise the notes of the IV chord, F–A–C. If the ii chord were extended downward by the addition of the next naturally occurring third, B, the entire structure would read B–D–F–A, the vii⌀7 chord in C major. The B–D–F notes by themselves comprise the vii° triad; with the A added, the chord becomes a vii⌀7 — with the B omitted, it is simply the ii triad. See *Example 8–8*.

The principle of extending triads upward or downward is a significant concept in locating alternate chord choices, tension, and color.

More on Choosing Chords in a Progression

Harmonic progression is not entirely contingent on the degree of tension desired. Chord choice is dependent on several factors, some of which have already been mentioned. Compositional style is important, and this may include the use of certain types of chords. It may be the style of the **harmonic rhythm** (rate of chord changes in a measure) or the use of highly chromatic chords under a rather diatonic melody, or the reverse — diatonic chords under a highly chromatic melody. It may be a piece that contains masses of chordal texture in both melody and accompaniment; it may be harmony achieved through the combination of several independently moving melodic lines.

How, then, should chords and chord progressions be chosen? A songwriter may first improvise a chord progression and then superimpose a suitable melody, or alternatively, may conceive of both melody and chord progression simultaneously. Then again, perhaps a melody might be followed by a suitable chord progression. Composers and songwriters employ the method that best accommodates the particular style in which they are creating; essentially, there is no one correct method of choosing a chord progression.

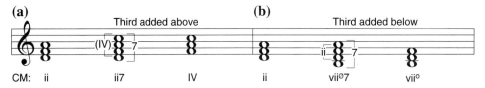

Example 8–8. Extensions of the ii by a third. (a) An extension upward creates a ii7 and produces an embedded IV. (b) An extension downward produces a vii⌀7.

◆ The Control of Tension

If the question, "what is music?" were asked, one answer might be, "the organization of sound and silence within a temporal dimension." The term *organization* applies to several factors involved in the creation of music, one of which is the control of tension. In Western music, control of tension is often affected by the choice of chordal content. Music must have direction; it must breathe. It must strive toward a particular goal, and in the process of reaching that goal, it must behave in a way consistent with a life process. A life process is rarely either completely tranquil or completely stressful. Moments of relaxation, and, of course, tension, are both part of this process. If something remains continually at rest, there is the absence of variation; likewise, if something is continually in a state of flux, turmoil, or stress, that too becomes tedious. Music must also contain variable states of tranquility and tension.

In a work containing rather obvious sections, the conclusive harmony appearing at the end of each section provides a point of relative repose. Tension and resolution must be carefully considered in the harmonic material preceding this conclusive harmony. In any event, the section must exhibit a thrust toward the conclusion; how this thrust is handled and achieved is a matter of personal choice that is always guided by style.

Should the harmonic material begin in a tranquil manner and proceed in graduated degrees of tension to the conclusion? Should the harmony begin with extreme tension and continually evolve to a state of tranquility? Should the harmonic material progress in undulating design? Should the degree of tension or the degree of tranquility remain flat? These questions are continuously considered by the composer during the writing of a musical work.

◆ Structural and Embellishing Chords

Structural harmonies are those that appear at strategic points of the melody and that provide a sense of the tonality of the work. **Embellishing harmonies** are those that are not essential to the tonal establishment of the work and that do not provide the primary structural components of the harmonic content. The entire harmonic content of a work can be reduced to its essential components, thus revealing its basic harmonic makeup. The determination of whether a particular harmony is structural or embellishing is often a subjective decision. However, the following may help clarify the difference.

Investigation of the harmonic content of "Jeanie with the Light Brown Hair," *Example 8–9* on page 188, initially reveals a composition that can be considered chordally and rhythmically active. Accidentals are present in several measures, and these do affect the intrinsic harmony. However, these chromatic chords do not alter the sense of an insistent key of F major. Moreover, they are not structurally necessary in the establishment and reinforcement of F major — and thus are embellishing harmonies. In contrast, in this excerpt there is sufficient use of the tonic and dominant (I and V) to establish the tonal center of F major. Hence, I and V can be considered structural.

"Jeanie with the Light Brown Hair

(Partial)

Stephen Foster

Example 8–9. Arrows indicating strategical strong points (structural harmonies) in the melody. Notice that at each of these points either a I or V7 is present. The vi in measure 3 is a likely substitution for I because vi is the relative minor triad. The chromatic chords do not alter the sense of an F major key center. These chromatic chords are discussed in later chapters.

Harmonizing a Melody

More than any other process, harmonizing an existing melody will improve one's ability to select appropriate harmonic content. A melody without any indication of harmonic content surely tests the inventiveness of the composer, songwriter, or arranger, who must determine the harmonic content and thus the accompaniment based on no factor other than the existing melody. The most crucial aspect in beginning this creative process is the ability to understand the melody. Understanding the melody does not mean merely hearing the pitches; it means hearing melody in its particular style. During which period of music history do you think this melody was written? Should it be performed in a fast or a slow tempo? Do you think it was conceived as a flute melody, a violin melody, a vocal melody, or as a melody for some other instrument? Familiarity with the idiomatic characteristics of particular styles and instruments is achieved only by listening to and examining various styles.

◆ *The Structural Component*

Recognizing the structural component of the melody is of vital importance. How is the motive (the recurring initial idea) treated? How can the harmony be varied upon repetitions of the motive? Will the harmony remain the same each time the melody appears in the work or will it continually evolve? Essentially, the structure of the melody must be assessed before a harmonic background is attempted.

◆ *Determining the Key*

The initial problem is how to begin the piece. What is the key? Is it a major or minor key? If a melody containing two sharps in the key signature is to be harmonized, how do you determine if the melody is in D major or B minor? Do any A♯s occur? If the melody is in B minor, it will most likely utilize the harmonic minor scale and thus contain one or more A♯s. It may be that this particular melody is in B minor, but never incorporates the leading tone of the scale. You must then look further. Do the significant melody notes — those appearing on the stronger beats of the measure or those of longer time duration — suggest they are factors of primary chords appearing in B minor? Does the final melodic content suggest B minor? Are certain groupings of notes factors in chords appearing in B minor or do they suggest D major? If the melody is in B minor and the tonic and dominant chords are implied by the melody, the V chord in B minor will contain the raised leading tone, A♯, since the V chord consists of F♯–A♯–C♯. Even with all this observation it may still be difficult to determine the actual key of the melody. It may remain ambiguous, and it may lend itself to more than one treatment. It is possible and often not unlikely that a particular melody continually shifts between two or more keys.

◆ *Rhythmic Stress*

Assuming that a key center has been determined (see the analysis in *Example 8–10* on page 190), the next process involves the determination of which notes of the melody suggest the most stress, either durationally achieved by accent, by highest or lowest note, or by rhythmic design, ties, and even rests. If, through the determination of stressed melody notes, a key center of D major is revealed, the next process is to determine at which junctures of the melody the I chord might provide a suitable harmony. Following this, possible locations of the V chord should be investigated. A key center is best established by the use of the I (i, if minor) and V chords. Remember that the establishment of the key is the object

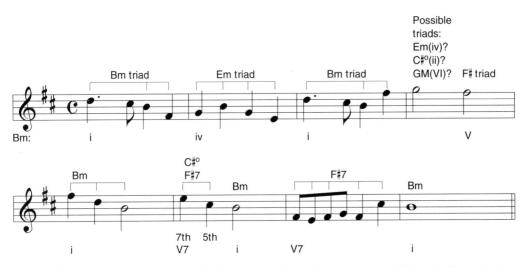

Example 8–10. Determination of a key center. Although the Bm, Em, GM, and C#° triads also appear in the key of D major, it is unlikely that this excerpt is in D major for several reasons:

1. The initial triad implied by the melody is B minor and most likely reinforces a B minor key center.
2. The E minor triad in measure 2 can be considered the iv, a primary chord.
3. The triad in measure 5 is preceded by the dominant degree in measure 4.
4. No support for D major is contained in the final two measures.

Even though no leading tone is present anywhere in this excerpt, the key center is apparently B minor.

in selecting the structural harmonies. It is possible, of course, to place a different chord on every melody note, but that is not the purpose at this time.

◆ *Chord Selection in SATB Format*

As has been noted, the style in which a melody is to be harmonized is a crucial factor in determining which chords will be selected and where they will be placed. Chorale-style harmonization contains an active harmonic rhythm, and there is often a chord assigned to each melody note. Chorale style has provided the most significant insight into the art of harmonization and chord progression.

The following procedures will serve as a guide for harmonizing a melody in SATB format when no indication of the chords is available:

1. Determine the key.

2. Check strategic points to affirm the key selection.

3. Determine where a circle progression can be incorporated. For now, all melody notes should be factors of the chosen chord.

Example 8–11. Harmonizing a melody. The key is F major; D minor (the relative minor) is not supported by the melody. Each melody note is harmonized.

4. Harmonize the notes of the melody with different chords. Each note of the melody can be, but need not necessarily be, harmonized by a different chord. Substitutions can be used when appropriate.

5. Avoid excessive retrogressive movement.

Example 8–11 illustrates these points.

Example 8–12. **A melody harmonized with a piano accompaniment.**

◆ *The Harmonic Accompaniment to a Melody*

Suppose that a rather simple diatonic melody, such as the one in *Example 8–12*, were presented for harmonization in a particular piano-style accompaniment, and the directions called for the melody to be treated as an independent function of the chords; that is, no specific harmonic rhythm, as in SATB format, need be applied. How will suitable chords be determined and where in the rhythmic flow will these chords be placed? Many of the same procedures for SATB format are applied. Note the similarities and differences:

1. Determine the key.

2. Check strategic points to affirm the key selection.

3. Determine where a circle progression can be incorporated.

4. Use substitutions where appropriate.

5. Try to achieve contrary motion between the bass and the soprano whenever possible by use of inversions.

6. Avoid excessive retrogressive movement.

7. For now, do not attempt to provide a chord for every melody note.

8. Apply a suitable accompaniment style.

Chapter Review

Harmonic progression functions at the micro, meso, and macro levels and is essentially the control of tension and resolution. Music is, after all, a series of tension-resolution events occurring within a temporal framework. Chords, like notes, possess particular affinities within certain contexts. This is especially true when observing these chords in a tonal work.

Chord preference, which is a matter of the composer's personal choice, is nevertheless controlled in a significant way by the style of the musical work. A knowledge of chord construction is, of course, a requirement of any musician, but autonomous chords mean little in the control of tension and resolution. It is the similarities among various chords and their gravitational tendencies that are at issue in comprehending harmonic progression.

Progressive and *retrogressive* are two terms used to describe the tension between two chords. *Progressive movement* indicates forward motion and includes the following chords that resolve to other chords: downward in 5ths or upward in 4ths, upward in 2nds or downward in 7ths, downward in 3rds or upward in 6ths. Movement from the tonic to any chord or from a primary chord to its minor or major is also considered progressive. *Retrogressive movement* indicates backward motion and includes the following chords that resolve to other chords: downward in 4ths or upward in 5ths, downward in 2nds or upward in 7ths, upward in 3rds or downward in 6ths. Movement from a secondary chord to its major or minor is considered retrogressive.

Substitution is the process whereby one chord is replaced by another for the purpose of variety or for a higher or lower degree of tension. A substitution may have several notes in common with the original chord or, as will be seen later, no notes in common. Initially, substitutions are derived by extension, that is, by adding one or more notes — a 3rd lower, higher, or both — to the original chord. Notes can also be eliminated from the top as notes are added to the bottom of a chord and vice versa. For example, D–F–A may be extended to D–F–A–C; with the D omitted, the result is F–A–C, a likely substitute.

Structural harmonies are those harmonic structures that appear in strategic points of the melody and provide a sense of the tonality of the work. *Embellishing harmonies* provide substitutions and contribute to the prolongation of the structural harmonic element; they are not essential in providing the primary structural harmonic components.

Ultimately, it is the style of a musical work that determines harmonic motion. It is, however, the composer who injects his or her creativity in manipulating the style to serve the composition.

Anthology References

For additional usage and analysis, see the following examples in Distefano, Joseph P. and James A. Searle, *Music and Materials for Analysis: An Anthology.* New York, Ardsley House, Publishers, Inc., 1995.

accompanied vocal melody

Example 37.   *Du Bist Wie Eine Blume,* Op. 25, No. 24, Robert Schumann, pp. 207–12.

Example 42.   *Morgen,* Richard Strauss, pp. 239–46.

Self-Test

1. Give a brief description of music that incorporates the salient concepts of this chapter.

2. The three levels of musical function are _____ , _____ , and _____ .

3. How does a composer decide on chord selection?

4. The gravitational tendencies of chords is a result of their _____ .

5. Define *chord substitution.*

6. The term *progressive* implies the movement of chords whose roots move by particular intervals. What are some of these intervals?

7. The term *retrogressive* implies the movement of chords whose roots move by particular intervals. What are some of these intervals?

8. Indicate where progressive and retrogressive movement occur in each of the following series:

    (a) I, IV, ii, V, vi, ii, vii°, iii, vi, ii, V, I

    (b) i, V, VI, ii°, vii°, V, iv, i, III+, iv, V, i

9. Discuss similarities and possibilities of substitution for each of the following:

    (a) I and iii   (b) vi and IV   (c) V and vii   (d) ii and vii   (e) I and vi   (f) iii7 and IV
    (g) IV and ii7   (h) vii and iii   (i) ii and iii7

10. Within the key of F major the I chord when extended downward by a 3rd produces _____ ; the ii chord when extended downward by a 3rd produces _____ ; the iii chord when extended downward by a 3rd produces _____ . Continue this for the remaining diatonic chords.

11. Describe *structural harmonies.*

12. Describe *embellishing harmonies.*

13. Discuss the procedure for SATB format in the selection of chords used to harmonize a given melody.

14. Discuss the procedure for the selection of chords used to harmonize any melody.
15. Define the term *circle progression*.

Exercises

1. For each of the given triads, locate and name other chords in and out of the key having two notes in common.

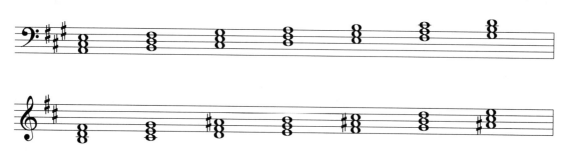

2. Locate and name at least three chords having one note in common.

3. Locate and name at least three chords having two notes in common.

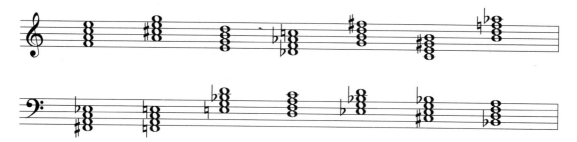

4. Write, then play on the piano, the entire circle of fifths. Use various quality triads and 7th chords.

5. Write a progression of triads and 7th chords incorporating all the root movements in progressive and retrogressive sequence.

6. Write substitutions for each of the following triads. Label all chords. See the first measure of Part (a).

(a)

FM   Dm

(b)

7. Add a major and minor 3rd below each triad. Label the result. See the first measure of Part (a).

GM   Em7   E♭+M7

8. The given chords are structural. Add embellishing chords, as in the first measure of Part (a). Label and describe each type of movement.

B♭   I   vi6   ii²⁴   V6

9. Provide possible chord content in each measure. Circle all nonchord tones. See the example.

NONHARMONIC
TONES

Any note that is not contained in, or is not a factor of, a supporting or implied harmonic structure,[1] such as an interval or chord, is defined as a **nonharmonic tone**.[2] Several qualifications must be considered in the determination of whether a tone is harmonic or nonharmonic, one being the style of the musical work. Certain styles primarily employ triads, whereas others may incorporate triads and 7th chords or more complex chord structures.

Under what conditions does a note cease to be nonharmonic? If a work consists primarily of triads and 7th chords, and if certain melody notes supported by these chords form 9th intervals in relation to the roots of the triads or 7th chords, are these melodic notes nonharmonic or do they actually form 9th chord structures?[3] Again, the work under analysis must be evaluated in its proper context. Jazz-style compositions invariably incorporate 9th, 11th, and

---

1. In certain contexts a chord can be "implied" by, or suggested by, a dyad. For example, the dyad F–A can suggest several chords including, but not limited to: FM, Dm, D♭+, B⌀7, B♭M7.

2. The term *tone* is usually reserved as a description of an aurally perceived pitch. *Tone* in the discussion of nonharmonic tones means literally the same as *note*.

3. In the hierarchical stacking of intervallic 3rds, the next normally occurring chord type after the 7th chord is the 9th. (See Chapter 17 on upper-partial chords.)

FM: V or V7?   GM: I or vi6?   V   Am: i or iv$^6_4$?

Example 9–1. Ambiguous nonharmonic tones.

13th chords and alterations of chord tones.[4] Are notes that form these chords, then, harmonic or nonharmonic?

Another consideration in the harmonic- and nonharmonic-tone designation is their *durational* or *rhythmic* character. If a nonharmonic tone is sustained long enough, does the ear accept it as part of the supporting harmony? Judgments of this nature become psychological, philosophical, or cultural in many cases.

Example 9–1 illustrates several ambiguous nonharmonic tones.

Harmonic and nonharmonic tones are absolutely contingent on the supporting or implied harmony. Without a harmonic frame of reference, an analysis of melodic tones and their harmonic or nonharmonic functions is impossible. In *Example 9–2*, the encircled tones are not related to the designated chord structure as chord tones.

Ecossaise

L. v. Beethoven

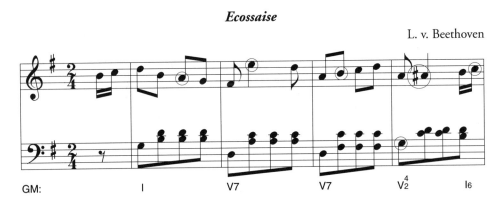

GM: I   V7   V7   V$^4_2$ I6

Example 9–2. Encircled notes not factors in the accompanying chords. This is only one of several possible interpretations of measure 4.

---

4. In the tertian stacking of intervals, for all practical purposes, chords can be extended through the 13th, after which the octave is duplicated. (See also the discussion in Chapter 17.)

Types of Nonharmonic Tones

◆ *The Passing Tone*

The **passing tone** (PT) moves by whole or half step between two chord tones of the same chord or different chords. Passing tones can be diatonic or chromatic. When determining the intervallic distance of whole and half steps, always consider any sharp or flat that is in the key signature. A passing tone can move in ascending fashion (**ascending passing tone** — APT) or in descending fashion (**descending passing tone** — DPT), as illustrated in *Example 9–3(a),* below. Passing tones can be double or, as shown in *Example 9–3(b),* can form decorative chord structures when they exceed a dyad. They can be successive, accented (on the beat), or unaccented (off the beat), as shown in *Example 9–3(c)* on page 202.

◆ *The Neighboring Tone*

The **neighboring tone** (NT) moves by whole or half step and returns to the same note of the chord or to the same note belonging to a different chord. This

Example 9–3. Passing tones. **(a)** Ascending passing tones (APT) and descending passing tones (DPT). **(b)** A decorative passing chord. **(c)** Accented and unaccented passing tones.

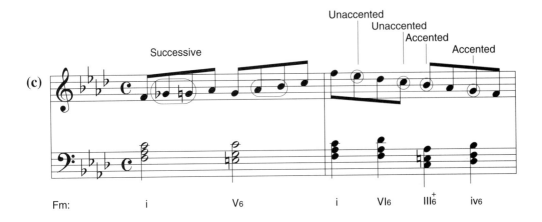

nonharmonic tone can be diatonic or chromatic, and can move upward or downward. It can be accented, unaccented, or a dyad, and it can form a neighboring chord when exceeding a dyad. See *Example 9–4.*

◆ *The Appoggiatura*

The term **appoggiatura** (APP) means "leaning," and this nonharmonic tone is characterized by its tendency to lean toward the note of resolution. The appoggiatura is normally approached by **leap** (a leap constitutes any interval greater than a whole step) and resolves by step. The appoggiatura movement usually consists of a leap upward and a step downward; less commonly, it can leap downward and resolve upward by step, leap upward and resolve upward by step, or leap downward and resolve downward by step. Appoggiaturas can be

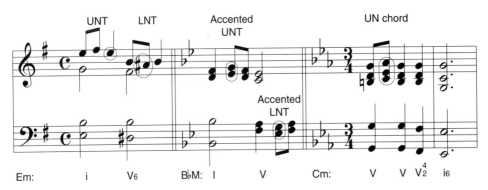

Example 9–4. Upper neighboring tones (UNT) and lower neighboring tones (LNT).

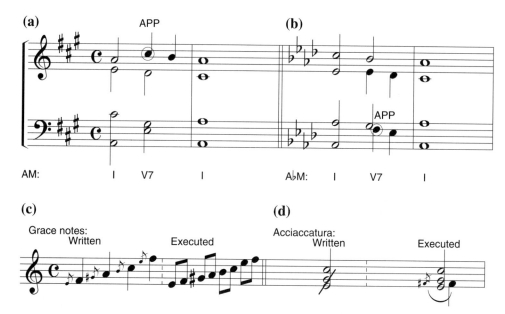

Example 9–5. Various types of appoggiatura. (a) An appoggiatura in the soprano.
(b) An appoggiatura in the bass. **(c)** Grace notes and their execution. **(d)** The acciaccatura
and its execution.

accented or unaccented, but are usually placed in a rhythmically strong position. Accented passing tones are often referred to as appoggiaturas.

Grace notes are also considered a type of appoggiatura. A **grace note**, notated in smaller-than-normal size, frequently with a diagonal line through its stem, is usually accented, and borrows its time value from the note that follows. The interpretation and execution of grace-note appoggiaturas are contingent upon genre, tempo, and other elements of music.

Finally, the **acciaccatura**, probably from *acciaccane* (It.), meaning "to crush," is another type of appoggiatura. This nonharmonic tone is sounded simultaneously with the following note or chord, and is quickly released. The acciaccatura is a common technique in many keyboard jazz melodies and improvisations.

Various types of appoggiatura are illustrated in *Example 9–5*.

◆ The Escape Tone

The **escape tone** (ET) or **échappée** is a nonharmonic tone that steps upward from a chord tone and leaps a 3rd downward to a note of the following chord. An escape tone can also leap upward; larger leaps in either direction are possible, but do not occur frequently. See *Example 9–6* on page 204.

Example 9–6. The escape tone.

CM: I   V   FM: I   V

◆ *The Suspension*

The **suspension** (sus) is a nonharmonic tone that consists of a harmonic tone presented in the initial harmony, sustained or repeated as a dissonance in the succeeding harmony, and resolved as a consonance to a note of the second chord. The term *suspension* is somewhat ambiguous since in common-practice music a suspension normally consists of the following three steps, only one of which is the actual suspension:

1. The *preparation*: the note to be suspended appears as a consonance in the supporting harmonic structure or interval. (With the suspension and the ensuing explanation of a *retardation*, the perfect fourth (P4) interval is considered a dissonance).

2. The *suspension*: the suspended note forms a dissonance on a strong beat with the second harmonic structure or interval.

3. The *resolution*: The suspended note resolves *downward* by step to a consonance within the second harmonic structure or interval.

Suspensions are identified by Arabic numbers. The first number identifies the interval of the suspended note above the bass note. The second number identifies the interval of the resolved note above the bass note. The three most common suspensions occurring in an upper voice are the 4–3, 7–6, and 9–8. One other type of suspension, the 2–3, occurs in the bass. The three-step process is the same, but the preparation, suspension, and resolution occur in the lowest voice. These four types of suspension are shown in *Example 9–7*.

The preceding discussion on suspensions applies primarily to those found in the common-practice genre. Suspensions in popular music may appear in the same manner, but in many instances the preparation step is not present. Two common suspensions employed in popular music are the 4–3 and 2–1, the latter often referred to as the 9–8. In popular style, the sus 4 symbol is used to define a suspension — for example — F sus 4 or A♭ sus 4; for a 9 suspension the symbol is normally "add 9" or "add 2" — for example, F add 9 or A♭ add 2. See *Example 9–8* on pages 205–6.

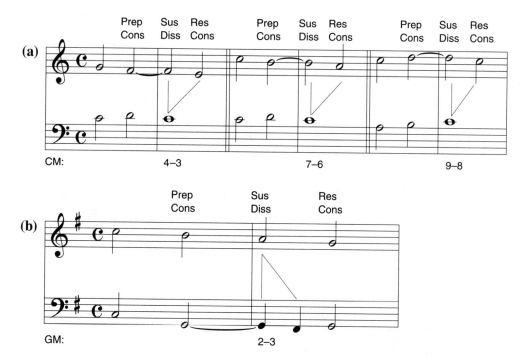

Example 9–7. Suspensions. (a) Suspensions in an upper voice. (b) A suspension in the lower voice. Prep: preparation, Sus: suspension, Res: resolution, Cons: consonance, Diss: dissonance.

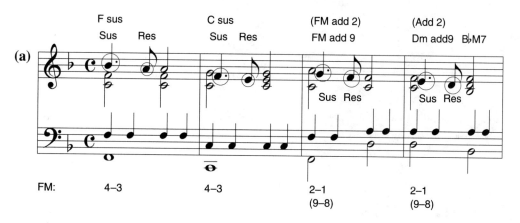

Example 9–8. Suspensions in popular music. (a) The various suspensions used in general. (b) The G sus consists of the pitches G–C–D, where C, the 4th above the G root, replaces B, the 3rd. The same process is applied to the Eb sus.

(b)

"Send in the Clowns"

Stephen Sondheim

◆ *The Retardation*

The **retardation** (RET) is a nonharmonic tone that is essentially the same as the suspension in the preparation and suspension steps, but whose final resolution is upward by step, instead of downward. See *Example 9–9.*

Example 9–9.
The retardation.

Example 9–10.
The anticipation.

Example 9–11.
The free tone.

◆ The Anticipation

The **anticipation** (ANT) literally anticipates a note of the following chord. Its movement is usually by step, but it can also be approached by leap. See *Example 9–10.*

◆ The Free Tone

Though rare both in common practice and in popular music, the **free tone** (FT), illustrated in *Example 9–11,* is a nonharmonic tone that nevertheless requires

Example 9–12. Pedal tones.

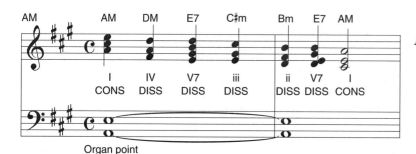

Example 9–13. The organ point.

some attention. It is normally found in "leap-to-leap" situations and is approached by leap and resolved by leap.

◆ *The Pedal Tone*

The **pedal tone** (PED) or **pedal point** is a recurring or sustained note or octave that supports chords which are consonant and/or dissonant to it. Pedal tones are of three types: the **lower pedal tone**, the most common of the three; the **internal pedal tone**, which is contained within an inner voice; and the **inverted pedal tone**, which is contained within the highest part of the harmonic structure. Pedal tones usually consist of the tonic or dominant of the key. In popular music, the lower pedal tone is virtually always employed. See *Example 9–12*.

◆ *The Organ Point*

The **organ point** (ORG PNT) is virtually synonymous with the pedal tone and functions in essentially the same way. However, when the pedal tone actually consists of a dyad that is a perfect 5th, the term "organ point" is employed. Organ points normally appear in the lower part of a harmonic structure and consist of the tonic and dominant of the prevailing key, as is illustrated in *Example 9–13*.

◆ *The Cambiata*

A **cambiata** (CAM) is a group of notes in a melodic configuration in which a descending passing tone is resolved by leaping downward a 3rd and then moving upward a step to a chord tone. See *Example 9–14*.

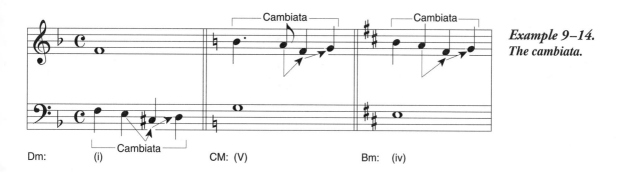

Example 9–14. The cambiata.

◆ *Changing Tones*

These nonharmonic tones are derived from the original cambiata and can be thought of as double neighboring tones. Essentially, **changing tones** (CT) are two nonharmonic tones that surround the ensuing harmonic tone of the second chord by a step from both directions. The first of the two nonharmonic tones is usually approached by step. See *Example 9–15.*

Embellished Nonharmonic Tones

Many of the nonharmonic tones just discussed may not always appear obvious in musical notation. Often, several of these tones appear in **embellished** or **decorated** form. This process occurs primarily in ornamented melodies, which are *virtuosic* or *improvisational* in character. Embellishment also occurs in **melismatic** melodies, in which many notes apply to one syllable of text.[5] The usual procedure for embellishing nonharmonic tones is by the addition of intervening notes, that is, interpolative notes that cause the expected resolution of the nonharmonic figure to be ornamented and/or rhythmically delayed.

In the sonata by Mozart, *Example 9–16,* a decorated appoggiatura appears above the I$_4^6$. The dotted sixteenth, E, and the thirty-second, F♯, are the principal melodic tones; here F♯ is an appoggiatura.

Nonharmonic Tones in Four-Part Writing

In the initial study of voice leading and four-part writing, the texture of the music is **homophonic**, that is, all four voices appear in consistent note values. For example, if the bass voice is a half note, the tenor, alto, and soprano are also half notes. Essentially, there is no rhythmic independence among the inclusive voices.

---

5. Any highly decorated principal melody note can also be referred to as *melismatic style.*

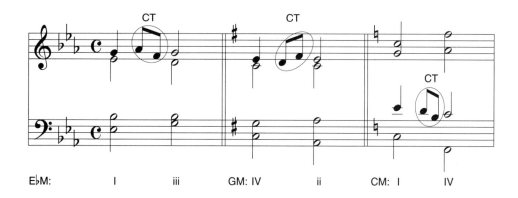

Example 9–15. Changing tones.

Homophonic four-voice texture as well as other textures can be enhanced by the use of nonharmonic tones in one or several voices; this can occur intermittently in any voice or simultaneously in two or more voices. However, it is of paramount importance that all nonharmonic tones be considered in the practice of proper voice leading. For example, although parallel fifths and octaves may not be obvious in a more complex texture that utilizes nonharmonic tones, they nevertheless must be avoided. Doublings and specific resolutions of certain chord factors must be considered as well. Whether the note in question is a chord tone or a nonharmonic tone makes no difference — its proper control must be maintained. In *Example 9–17* on pages 212–13, a homophonic four-voice texture followed by a more complex texture incorporating nonharmonic tones is illustrated. Each nonharmonic tone in the example is assessed as to its relation to the supporting harmony and its resolution to the subsequent harmony.

Sonata XVI

Variation V, m. 8

W. A. Mozart

Example 9–16. The encircled appoggiatura decorated with the preceding four-note figure. This figure is often written as ∞ and is known as a *gruppetto* or *turn*.

Chorale: *Seelen-Bräutigam*

J. S. Bach

Example 9–17. A homophonic four-voice texture followed by a more complex texture with nonharmonic tones. **(a)** A chorale utilizing strictly chord tones. (The nonharmonic tones have been omitted.) **(b)** The same chorale as written by Bach. Notice the usage of various types of nonharmonic tones.

Nonharmonic Tones as a Function of Melody

Diatonic chord progressions may become monotonous upon continued reiteration. Even when the progressions are varied, the diatonic chords, through continued use, lose their aural appeal because of their lack of chromatic content. If a melody is constructed against these chords and if it utilizes only chord tones, the resulting work may not sustain the attention of the listener. This is true in virtually every style of music. Although rhythmic variation, melody, lyric content (in certain styles), production, and dynamic variation are certainly important contributing factors in maintaining the appeal of a work, none of these aspects can replace the tension/resolution element of music that is affected by the continuous interplay of consonance, dissonance, chromaticism, and diatonicism, especially in extended works.

The discussion of chords and harmony to this point has not addressed the virtually limitless possibilities of *chromaticism*, and most explanations have concerned only diatonic harmony; nevertheless, it is still possible to create melodies and melodic figures that sustain interest through the use of diatonic and chromatic nonharmonic tones, both in their simple and their decorated forms. The musician must always consider the genre and, consequently, the harmonic palette of a musical work in the determination of most nonharmonic tones. As harmonic structure becomes more complex, traditional nonharmonic tones become increasingly harmonic, as will be seen later. *Example 9–18* on pages 213–15 illustrates the use of nonharmonic tones in several styles.

(a)

"I've Loved These Days"

Billy Joel

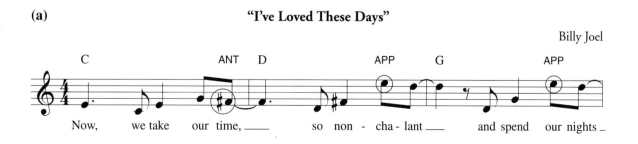

(b)

"Lennie's Pennies"

Lennie Tristano

CLN = Chromatic lower neighbor
CUN = Chromatic upper neighbor
CDPT = Chromatic descending passing tone

(c)

"Fake Your Way to the Top"

Words by Tom Eyen, Music by Henry Krieger

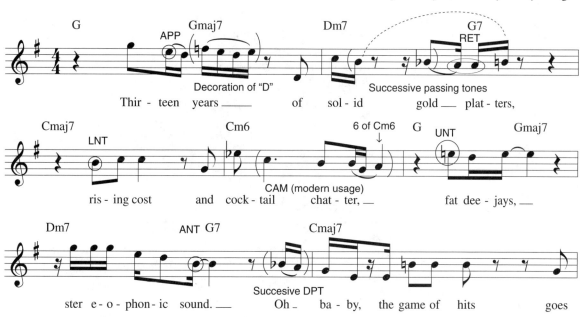

Example 9–18. Nonharmonic tones in various styles. **(a)** Anticipations, appoggiaturas, and lower neighboring tones in a popular style. **(b)** On the fourth line, the C7 chord is actually a C$\flat$11. See Chapter 17. On the last line, the D7 chord is actually D7$\flat$9. **(c)** In the last line, the G is the 4th of D, but does not function as a suspension or as any common nonharmonic tone. Nor does it function as a typical 11th (see Chapter 17). In this context it is a free tone.

Chapter Review

In general, a *nonharmonic tone* can be defined as any tone that is not part of the supporting or implied harmony. A determination of whether a tone is nonharmonic is contingent on the genre of the musical work. What appear to be nonharmonic tones in a simpler style may be chord factors in a more complex harmonic structure. Another important consideration in the determination of what are nonharmonic tones is the rhythmic or durational value of the tones in question. In many cases, the ear must be relied upon in the assessment of certain questionable nonharmonic tones.

The nonharmonic tones presented include *passing tones, neighboring tones, appoggiaturas, grace notes, acciaccaturas, escape tones, suspensions, retardations, anticipations, free tones, pedal tones, organ points, cambiata,* and *changing tones.*

Nonharmonic tones often occur in *decorated* or *embellished* form, which may cause their resolution to be delayed. Rather than moving directly to the note of resolution, other interpolative notes are occasionally added in the melodic design. This does not affect the function of the nonharmonic tone.

Anthology References

For additional usage and analysis, see the following examples in Distefano, Joseph K. and James A. Searle, *Music and Materials for Analysis: An Anthology.* New York, Ardsley House, Publishers, Inc., 1995.

ascending and descending passing tones
  Example 15.   *Lord Jesus Christ, the Prince of Peace,* Johann Sebastian Bach, pp. 69–74.
lower neighboring tones
  Example 17.   *If God Withdraweth, All the Cost,* Johann Sebastian Bach, pp. 69–73, 76.
upper neighboring tones
  Example 33.   *Waltz,* Franz Schubert, pp. 179–84.
appoggiaturas
  Example 32.   *Sonata,* K. 333, Wolfgang Amadeus Mozart, pp. 149–78.
escape tones
  Example 27.   *Allegro,* Wolfgang Amadeus Mozart, pp. 115–20.
suspensions
  Example 21.   *Blessed Jesu, at Thy Word,* Johann Sebastian Bach. pp. 69–73, 80.
retardations
  Example 32.   *Sonata,* K. 333, Wolfgang Amadeus Mozart, pp. 149–78.
anticipations
  Example 19.   *My Cause Is God's, and I Am Still,* Johann Sebastian Bach. pp. 69–73, 78.
free tones
  Example 40.   *Mazurka,* Op. 9, No. 1, Frédéric Chopin, pp. 225–32.
pedal tones
  Example 22.   *Invention No. 4,* Johann Sebastian Bach, pp. 81–88.
  Example 24.   *The Well-Tempered Clavier,* Book I, *Prelude and Fugue No. 16,* Johann Sebastian Bach, pp. 91–100.
  Example 45.   *Preludes,* Book I, No. 2, "Voiles" ("Sails"), Claude Achille Debussy, pp. 201–6.

organ points
Example 40.   *Mazurka,* Op. 7, No. 1, Frédéric Chopin, pp. 225–32.
changing tones, decorated nonharmonic tones
Example 32.   *Sonata,* K. 333, Wolfgang Amadeus Mozart, pp. 149–78.
nonharmonic tones in four-part writing
Examples 15–21. *Lord Jesus Christ, the Prince of Peace,* Johann Sebastian Bach
                    O Darkest Woe! Ye Tears that Flow, Johann Sebastian Bach
                    If God Withdraweth, All the Cost, Johann Sebastian Bach
                    O Lord! How Many Miseries, Johann Sebastian Bach
                    My Cause Is God's, and I Am Still, Johann Sebastian Bach
                    O Thou, of God the Father, Johann Sebastian Bach
                    Blessed Jesu, at Thy Word, Johann Sebastian Bach, pp. 69–80.

Self-Test

1. Describe *nonharmonic tones* in general.
2. Mention several determining factors in the assessment of whether or not a tone is nonharmonic.
3. A note or tone cannot be labeled as harmonic or nonharmonic unless it is supported by or is in a _____ .
4. A tone that steps between F and the adjacent G is _____ .
5. A tone that steps between B and the adjacent A is _____ .
6. A stepwise upper note that exists in a melodic pattern from C and back is _____ .
7. A stepwise lower note that exists in a melodic pattern from G♭ and back is _____ .
8. A nonharmonic tone that is usually approached by upward leap and that resolves downward by step is _____ .
9. A nonharmonic tone that is approached by a step upward and that leaves by the leap of a 3rd downward is _____ .
10. The three steps of the suspension are _____ , _____ , and _____ .
11. The suspended note resolves _____ .
12. Three common suspensions are _____ , _____ , and _____ .
13. In a retardation, the resolution of the suspended tone is _____ .
14. A nonharmonic tone that is approached and that leaves by leap is _____ .
15. The tonic or dominant note of the prevailing key that is sustained, repeated, or reiterated beneath a series of chords which may be consonant and/or dissonant to the note is known as _____ .
16. The tonic or dominant note of the prevailing key that is sustained, repeated, or reiterated above a series of chords which may be consonant and/or dissonant to the note is known as _____ .

17. The tonic or dominant note of the prevailing key that is sustained, repeated, or reiterated within a series of chords that may be consonant and/or dissonant to the note is known as _____ .

18. The sustained, repeated, or reiterated perfect 5th dyad below a series of chords that may be consonant and/or dissonant to it is known as _____ .

19. Added and/or interpolative notes may cause nonharmonic tones to be _____ .

20. Describe the *anticipation.*

21. Describe the *cambiata.*

22. Describe *changing tones.*

Exercises

1. Add various types of passing tones and identify each type. Label all chords.

2. Add passing tones to the melody in measures 1 and 2, and to the bass in measures 3 and 4. Label all chords.

3. Add neighboring tones to the melody. Label all chords.

4. Add neighboring tones to the bass. Label all chords.

5. Add appoggiaturas to the soprano, as shown in the first measure. Label all chords.

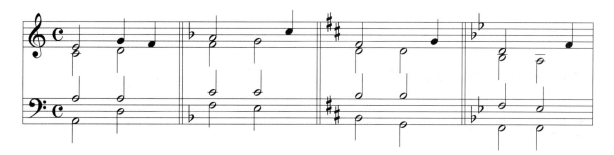

6. Add escape tones to the soprano and complete the harmony, as shown in the first measure. Label all chords.

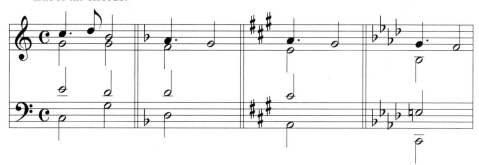

7. Create the suspensions.

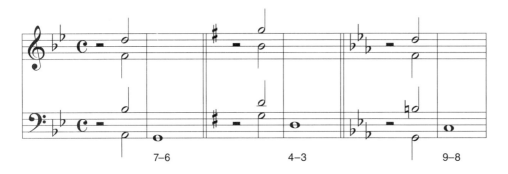

8. Add the notes necessary to form the suspension, as shown in the first measure.

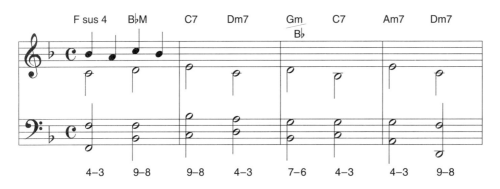

9. Create retardations, as shown in the first measure.

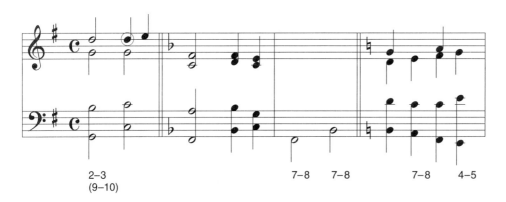

10. Create anticipations. Label all chords.

11. Compose a melodic line containing several free tones. Label all chords.

12. Write a progression above and/or below each pedal tone.

(a) Above.   **(b)** Above.

(c) Above and below.   **(d)** Above and below.

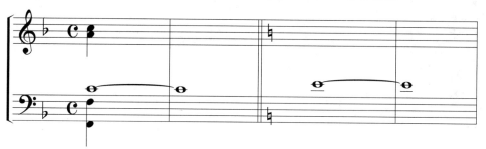

(e) Below. **(f)** Below.

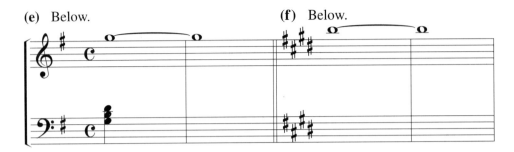

13. Compose cambiata figures.

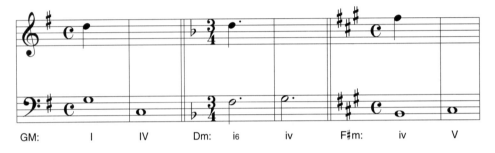

GM: I   IV   Dm: i6   iv   F♯m: iv   V

14. Write changing tones, as shown in the first measure.

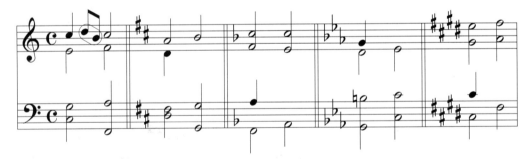

15. Add nonharmonic tones. Label all chords.

(b)
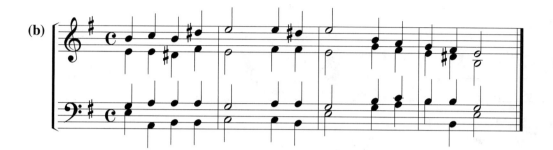

(c)
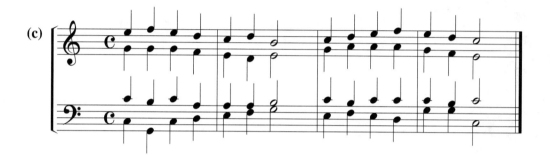

10

MELODY

Melody Perception

The perception of *melody* is subjective. According to Alexander L. Ringer,

> Melody, defined as pitched sounds arranged in musical time in accordance with given cultural conventions and constraints, represents a universal human phenomenon traceable to prehistoric times…wherever music became an intrinsic condition of life, certain common melodic procedures were necessarily adopted, because they satisfied basic physiological and biological requirements, if not the aesthetic imagination, per se…. 'Melodic unity' is configurationally speaking an intrinsic psychoacoustical function of melodic generation in a given historical-cultural context and must in the end be experienced as such.[1]

Essentially, Ringer says that the perception of **melody** is defined by one's cultural influences; what constitutes a melody depends upon how groups of notes are perceived by the listener. Ringer continues:

---

1. *The New Grove Dictionary of Music and Musicians* (London: Macmillan Pub. Ltd., 1980), vol. 12, pp. 118–19.

...Above all, as a social product, melody is part and parcel of the culture or subculture to which it owes its existence...[2]

An objective definition of melody, then, is virtually impossible simply because a melody is not an objectively perceived phenomenon. Its definition, identification, and perception are always contingent upon the observer's *cultural influences*. For this reason, what may be considered melodic and appealing by some may be distasteful to others. Therefore, a qualitative assessment of melody is not the purpose of this discussion. However, the components of melody, for example, *harmonic* and *nonharmonic tones, cells, motives, phrases*, and so on, are the proper subjects of a music theory book. What follows, then, is a presentation of the component factors that contribute to the formation and structure of melodies — a *quantitative* examination of melody — particularly, of those melodies existing in Western music.

A melody consists of a succession of notes — but how many notes? Immediately, one is confronted with a problem that cannot be viewed objectively. Can a melody contain two notes (for example, various lullabies of Greenland and Buddhist chants), three notes (for example, Old Roman chants of the eleventh through thirteenth centuries as well as various Buddhist chants), four notes (for example, the opening melody of Beethoven's Fifth Symphony), or must it contain more than four notes? Or is one note sufficient to construct a melody? If one note is reiterated, and each time it sounds, its character is altered by modifying its duration, intensity, or timbre,[3] does it qualify as a melody (for example, "One Note Samba" by Antonio Carlos Jobim)? These questions cannot be answered objectively because no one person can answer for everyone, everywhere, and in every time. See *Example 10–1.*

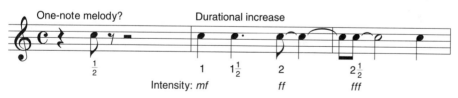

Example 10–1. Melodies as successions of notes.

---

2. Ibid, p. 123.

3. **Timbre** can by defined as sound quality that is a result of the presence or absence of certain overtones. It is this characteristic of sound that enables one to hear the difference between various instruments.

In the light of cultural influence it appears, then, that something audible is a melody because it fulfills certain human needs — biological, emotional, psychological, philosophical, and so on.

Nearly every musician has at one time been confronted with the situation in which he or she has attempted to convey a "wonderful" melody to someone else by means of humming, singing, or whistling; yet the listener has been less than impressed. The reason is that the performer, having either composed the melody or having heard it performed in another context, is unable to convey other supporting elements associated with the melody. A melody can only be sung, hummed, or whistled one note at a time. Hence, the listener can aurally conceive of only the melody notes and has virtually no clue concerning the harmonic and production content. Although it is possible and highly probable that a listener trained in music can deduce certain implied harmonies that are suggested by the melody, the possibilities with which to harmonize a melody are virtually limitless.

Components of Melody

A melody may consist of *cells*, *motives,* and *phrases*. The word "may" is important in that certain melodic elements are not discernable in their autonomous state; that is, their identification is *dependent* upon their ensuing function in the melody or theme.[4]

◆ *The Cell*

A **cell** is defined as the smallest or shortest melodic or rhythmic figure serving as the *germ* from which a melody is developed. Upon initial observation, it is difficult to determine what this smallest figure is; therefore, one must look further into the developmental aspect of the music. *Example 10–2* provides possible cells extracted from a melody. Here, the key word is "possible"; for one cannot be certain that a musical segment is, indeed, a cell until further observation of the music has been made.

◆ *The Motive*

The next component in the hierarchy of melodic construction is the *motive* or *motif.* A **motive** is defined as the shortest *complete* fragment. The motive is a self-contained melodic idea that usually occurs at least twice and that can be modified. How is a complete idea experienced, or for that matter, how is it

---

4. The terms *melody* and *theme* are often used interchangeably.

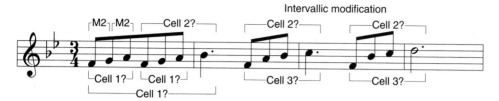

Example 10–2. Cells. In intervallic modification, the general design of a melodic line may remain similar, although the intervals are increased or decreased. Here, in the initial cell, the intervallic distances of the first three notes are M2, M2. In measure 2, the design of the cell is essentially the same, but the intervallic distances of the first three notes are M3, m2. In the last cell, the intervallic distances of the first three notes are P4, M2.

described? Where does it begin and where does it end? Can a motive be identified without tracing its occurrences throughout the music? Can a cell be a motive and vice versa? How long must a group of notes be in order to constitute a motive? Again, these questions usually require the observer to delve deeper into the musical content of the work. See *Examples 10–3 and 10–4,* which follow.

◆ *The Phrase*

Next in the hierarchy of melody construction is the **phrase,** which can be described as a unit of melodic material that is comparable to a clause in a sentence. A phrase can sound complete or incomplete, depending upon what precedes and/or follows it. A phrase can consist of cells, motives, or both, as shown in *Example 10–3.*

(a)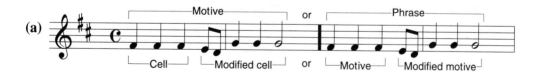

(b)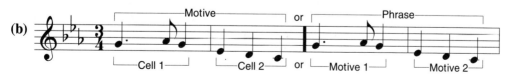

Example 10–3. Motives and phrases. In determining whether a musical segment is a cell, a motive, or a phrase, the ensuing musical material must be considered.

Phrases are usually delineated at their **cadences**, which are points of arrival in the flow of the music, achieved by harmonic, melodic, or rhythmic variation.[5] Less significant cadences or points of delineation, known as **caesuras**, indicated by the sign //, may occur between motives. Often, an **antecedent phrase** precedes a **consequent phrase** that affects completion of the entire melodic and harmonic idea. Whereas most thematic ideas are normally perceived as containing an antecedent and a consequent phrase, numerous themes contain more than one antecedent followed by one or more consequents. See *Example 10–4.*

(a)

Clowns

D. Kabalevsky

Example 10–4. Types of phrases and closure. **(a)** In part (a), play and listen carefully to measures 4 and 8. Notice the high degree of closure in measure 8, due to the root of the I chord in the melody—as opposed to the lack of closure due to the 3rd of the I chord in the melody of measure 4. The tonic in the soprano in measure 8 produces a greater sense of completion than the 3rd or 5th of the I chord. **(b)** Antecedent and consequent phrases.

---

5. Cadences are measured and identified by their degree of "closure" of a melodic or thematic segment. Many types of cadences exist; these are discussed in forthcoming chapters.

(b)

Etude

C. Gurlitt

Types of Melodies

Melodies appear in numerous shapes and lengths; in most instances these physical characteristics are a direct result of the culture and epoch in which the melodies were composed.

Melodies can be derived from conventional *scales, modes,* and *composer-created pitch sequences,* as in *Example 10–5.* Melodies can be *terse, moderate,* or *protracted* in length, as illustrated in *Example 10–6* on pages 231–32. They can have *wide* or *compact* **range** (the distance between the lowest and highest notes) and *wide* or *compact* **tessitura** (the location of the majority of notes). See *Example 10–7* on page 233.

(a)

Prelude in G Major

G. F. Handel

Example 10–5. Melodies from various scales and modes. **(a)** A melody from conventional scales. The encircled notes further suggest scalar content. The parenthesized notes continue the motion in the higher octave. **(b)** An ancient melody written in the Lydian mode. Notice the emphasis on the pitch F and the absence of any B♭s. **(c).** A melody from a composer-created scale.

(b)

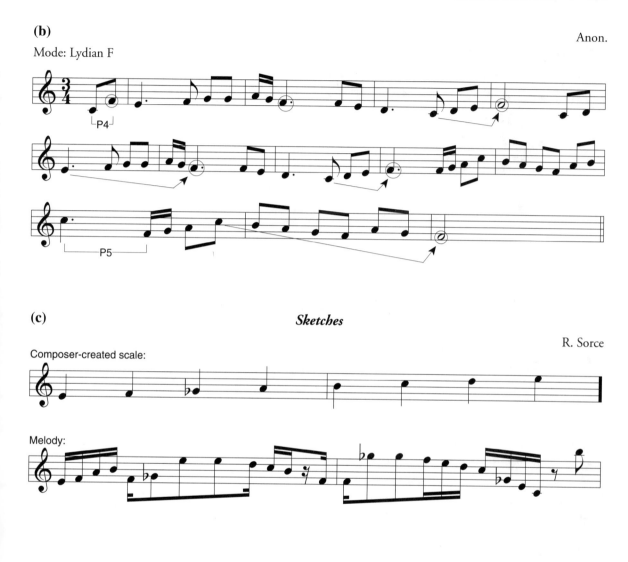

(c) *Sketches*

(a) *La Gracieuse*

Example 10–6. Melodies of varying lengths. **(a)** A terse melody. **(b)** A moderate melody. **(c)** A protracted melody.

(b) **Minuet**

H. Purcell

(c) **Ophelia Theme from *Hamlet and Ophelia***

E. A. MacDowell

Meas. 38

Melodies can involve *primarily stepwise* (scalar) *motion (Example 10–8)*, *skipping motion (Example 10–9)*, or *primarily leaping motion (Example 10–10* on page 234). They can be *diatonic (Example 10–11)* or *chromatic (Example 10–12)*. They can be *primarily ascending (Example 10–13* on page 235), *primarily descending (Example 10–14)*, or *primarily level (Example 10–15)*. They can be **undulating** (wavelike), as in *Example 10–16* on page 236, **sawtooth** in design, as in *Example 10–17*, or **pointillistic** (sparse texture, brief phrases, with angular and widely scattered melodic lines), as in *Example 10–18* on page 237. Melodies can also be *rhythmically active* or *calm*. See *Example 10–19*. Of course, melodies may be combinations of these types.

(a)

Evening Song

A. Khachaturian

(b)

Larghetto

I. Stravinsky

Example 10–7. Melodies with varying ranges. **(a)** A melody with wide range. Here, the range is from middle C to A above the staff. The tessitura is from E to E. **(b)** A melody with compact range, consisting of a perfect 4th.

Toccatina

M. Yordansky

Example 10–8. A melody with primarily stepwise motion.

Humoreske

A. Dvorak

Example 10–9. A melody with skipping motion.

Album Leaf

C. Debussy

Example 10–10. **A melody with primarily leaping motion.**

Minuet in G

J. S. Bach?

Example 10–11. **A diatonic melody.**

Nocturne in E♭ Major

F. Chopin

Example 10–12. **A chromatic melody.**

String Quartet, Op. 64

F. J. Haydn

Example 10–13. *A primarily ascending melody.*

Minuet Scherzando

D. Scarlatti

Example 10–14. *A primarily descending melody.*

Prelude in E minor

F. Chopin

Example 10–15. *A primarily level melody.*

"Memory"

Words by Trevor Nunn, Music by Andrew Lloyd Webber

Mid - night. _____ Not a sound from the pave - ment. _____ Has the moon lost her

mem - 'ry? _____ She is smil - ing a- lone. _____ In the lamp - light the with - ered leaves col -

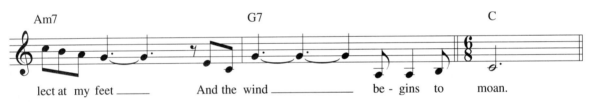

lect at my feet _____ And the wind _____ be - gins to moan.

Example 10–16. A melody with an undulating design. Undulating melodies normally consist of primarily stepwise movement in wave form.

Waltz

J. Brahms

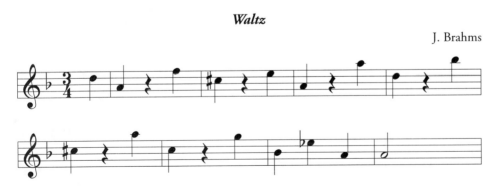

Example 10–17. A melody with a sawtooth design.

Expressions

R. Sorce

Example 10–18. A pointillistic melody.

(a)   *Fantasia, K. 475*

W. A. Mozart

(b)   *Morning Song*

C. Gurlitt

Example 10–19. Melodies that vary rhythmically. **(a)** A rhythmically active melody. **(b)** A rhythmically calm melody.

◆ *Melodic Development*

Melodies are normally derived from an initial idea, which can be a cell, motive, or phrase. In order to extend the melodic line beyond the confines of the initial idea, these contributing elements are often manipulated and developed in various ways. In each of *Examples 10–20 — 10–29*, the original melodic segment is presented and followed by an illustration of the applied technique under discussion. Thus, the idea can be followed:

by **repetition** (one repeat of an idea), as in *Example 10–20*,

by **reiteration** (more than one repeat of an idea), as in *Example 10–21,* or

by **sequence** (a melodic design beginning on another scale degree), as in *Example 10–22*. In general, because of the half and whole steps contained in a scale, the intervals may vary. However, a sequence can also be strict, whereby every interval is exactly the same as the original.

Other extensions of the initial idea include:

inversion, in which the melodic interval movement is reversed, as in *Example 10–23*. With inversion, the direction of each succeeding note is the opposite of the original.

retrograde, a statement of the melodic idea in reverse order *(Example 10–24)*,

retrograde inversion, the reversal of the melody and melodic intervals *(Example 10–25)*,

augmentation, the proportional increase in the durational values of melody notes and rests *(Example 10–26)*,

diminution, the proportional decrease in the durational values of melody notes and rests *(Example 10–27)*,

interpolation, the addition of new melodic material within a previously established motive *(Example 10–28)*, and

rhythmic modification *(Example 10–29)*.

Example 10–20. The initial melodic segment followed by repetition.

Example 10–21. The initial melodic segment followed by reiteration.

Example 10–22. *The initial melodic segment followed by three sequences.*

Example 10–23. *The initial melodic segment followed by inversion.*

Example 10–24. *The initial melodic segment followed by retrograde.*

Example 10–25. *The initial melodic segment followed by retrograde inversion.*

Example 10–26. *The initial melodic segment followed by augmentation.*

Example 10–27. *The initial melodic segment followed by dimunition.*

Example 10–28. *The initial melodic segment followed by interpolation.*

Example 10–29. *The initial melodic segment followed by rhythmic modification.*

Composing Melodies

A knowledge of these extension techniques will not necessarily enable one to compose good melodies. The study of composition requires years of perfecting skills for writing melodies as well as for perfecting other facets, such as harmony, rhythm, structure, and orchestration. In fact, there is no formula for creating good, original, and memorable music. Every creator of music must learn to speak through his or her own voice or personality. Whether or not a composer's work is meritorious essentially depends upon the individual's talent.

♦ *Popular-Song Writing and Traditional Composition*

Composition in the classical sense requires extensive formal training in theory and compositional technique. However, many formally unschooled popular-song writers have achieved success with their songs. The reason for this is quite simple — these writers have assimilated their cultural influences to such a degree that they are able to convey their ideas through appealing songs without an extensive knowledge of music theory. By simply being exposed to their environment and being sensitive to the ideals, practices, and requirements of the styles of popular music, these songwriters are able to accompany their own melodies and set their lyric ideas to music. The popular-song writer need not possess a knowledge of music notation; an instrument, a voice, and a tape recorder are the primary tools. A good "feel" for chords, melodies, and lyrics are the only requirements for successful song writing. Songs composed by "pop" writers are often notated by others after the song has been recorded and has attained some measure of success. Traditional composition, on the other hand, requires a formal knowledge of music notation — a symphonic work simply cannot be sung into a tape recorder.

Chapter Review

Although the perception of melody is depend–ent upon cultural conventions and constraints, we can nevertheless discuss the quantitative aspects of melody in an informative manner.

First and foremost, a melody normally consists of pitched sounds. These are arranged into units, beginning with the tersest group, known as *cells*. Cells are expanded into *motives*, and motives into *phrases*. A determination of what constitutes a cell, motive, or phrase is dependent on the context, total content, and development of the melody.

Phrases, which may be compared to clauses in sentences, are considered the most aurally satisfying segment of a melody or theme. For the most part, they evoke a feeling of a complete, or at least a semicomplete, statement. Again though, phrase interpretation and perception is very often quite subjective. Most phrases appear in pairs, the first being the *antecedent* and the second, the *consequent*. However, other combinations do exist.

Although this chapter is not a guide to composing melodies (just as this book is not a course in music composition), most types and characteristics of melody are outlined and demonstrated here. These include: *melodies derived from conventional scales, modes,* and *composer-created pitch series*; *terse, moderate,* or *protracted* melodies; melodies that incorporate *wide* or *compact range* and/or *tessitura*; melodies whose notes move *stepwise* or by *skipping* or *leaping motion*; melodies that are primarily *diatonic* or *chromatic*; melodies that are primarily *ascending, descending,* or *level* in direction; melodies that are *undulating* (wavelike), *sawtooth* (jagged), or *pointillistic* (disjunct); and melodies that are *active* or *calm*.

In developing melodic components several techniques were presented; these include: *repetition, reiteration, sequence inversion, retrograde, retrograde inversion, augmentation, diminution,* and *interpolation,* as well as *rhythmic modification.*

Anthology References

For additional usage and analysis, see the following examples in Distefano, Joseph P. and James A. Searle, *Music and Materials for Analysis: An Anthology.* New York, Ardsley House, Publishers, Inc., 1995.

wide range
> *Example 35.* *Album Leaves,* Op. 124, Waltz. Robert Schumann, pp. 193–200.

compact range
> *Example 4.* *Le Jeu de Robin,* Adam de la Halle, pp. 11–16.

stepwise motion
> *Example 1.* Gregorian Chant, Kyrie, pp. 1–7.

skipping motion
> *Example 31.* *Sonata,* Hob. XVI, No. 27, First Movement, Franz Joseph Haydn, pp. 141–48.

leaping motion

Example 62.   *Suite for Piano,* Op. 25, Prelude, Arnold Schoenberg, pp. 363–72.

diatonic melody

Example 5.   *C'est la Fine,* Guillaume d'Amiens, pp. 11–14, 16.

chromatic melody

Example 55.   *Twelve Poems of Emily Dickinson,* No. 3, "Why Do They Shut Me Out of Heaven?," Aaron Copland, pp. 317–24.

ascending motion

Example 40.   *Mazurka,* Op. 7, No. 1, Frédéric Chopin, pp. 225–32.

descending motion

Example 35.   *Album Leaves,* Op. 124, Waltz, Robert Schumann, pp. 193–200.

level design

Example 28.   *Sonatina,* First Movement (Allegro), Franz Joseph Haydn, pp. 121–24.

undulating design

Example 26.   *Larghetto,* Wolfgang Amadeus Mozart, pp. 109–14.

sawtooth design

Example 57.   *Divertimento for Band,* Prologue, Vincent Persichetti, pp. 335–40.

pointillistic design

Example 63.   *Concerto for Nine Instruments,* Op. 25, First Movement, Anton Webern, pp. 373–82.

Example 64.   *Structures Ia,* Book I, Pierre Boulez, pp. 383–90.

motives and phrases

Example 22.   *Invention No. 4,* Johann Sebastian Bach, pp. 81–88.

cadences

Example 24.   *The Well-Tempered Clavier,* Book I, *Prelude and Fugue No. 16,* Johann Sebastian Bach, pp. 91–100.

range and tessitura

Examples 60–61. *Six Short Pieces for Piano,* Op. 19, No. 5 and No. 6, Arnold Schoenberg, pp. 335–62.

repetitions

Example 44.   *Poème,* Op. 69, No. 1, Alexander Scriabin, pp. 253–58.

sequences

Example 32.   *Sonata,* K. 333, Wolfgang Amadeus Mozart, pp. 149–78.

Example 39.   *Prelude,* Op. 28, No. 20, Frédéric Chopin, pp. 219–24.

inversions

Example 8.   *Benedictus,* Orlando Lassus, pp. 33–36.

Example 22.   *Invention No. 4,* Johann Sebastian Bach, pp. 81–88.

Example 46.   *Mikrokosmos,* No. 37, Béla Bartók, pp. 267–73.

retrogrades and retrograde inversions

Example 62.   *Suite for Piano,* Op. 25, Prelude, Arnold Schoenberg, pp. 363–72.

tessituras

Example 35.   *Album Leaves,* Op. 124, Waltz, Robert Schumann, pp. 193–200.

Example 37.   *Du Bist Wie Eine Blume,* Op. 25, No. 24, Robert Schumann, pp. 207–12.

augmentations

Example 54.   *Prelude and Fugue on a Theme of Vittoria,* Benjamin Britten, pp. 305–16.

Self-Test

1. Describe *melody*.
2. Define a *cell*.
3. Define a *motive*.
4. Define a *phrase*.
5. Describe the function of a *cadence*.
6. Define a *sequence*.
7. A *theme* can be identified with a _____ .
8. The accurate identification of certain melodic components is dependent on _____ .
9. Two types of phrases are _____ and _____ .
10. The term *caesura* refers to _____ .
11. Explain why a "wonderful" melody may be difficult to convey in an autonomous manner.
12. Explain why an individual may perceive a group of sounds as a melody.
13. List the types and characteristics of melodies.
14. List the techniques employed in melodic development.
15. What is the primary difference between popular-song writing and conventional composition?

Exercises

1. Manipulate according to the indicated techniques.

(a) Reiteration

(b) Sequence

(c) Inversion

(d) Retrograde

(e) Retrograde inversion

(f) Augmentation

(g) Diminution

(h) Interpolation

(i) Rhythmic modification

2. Apply at least three different developmental techniques to each melodic figure. Use additional staff paper where necessary.

(a)

(b)

(c)

(d)

3. Compose simple melodies demonstrating the indicated styles.

(a) Wide range

(b) Skipping

(c) Leaping

(d) Chromatic

(e) Undulating

(f) Rhythmically active

(g) Composer-created pitch series

4. Compose simple melodies based on the chord progressions. Use chord tones and various types of nonharmonic tones.

5. Compose simple melodies to the given chord progressions. Label all chords and nonharmonic tones.

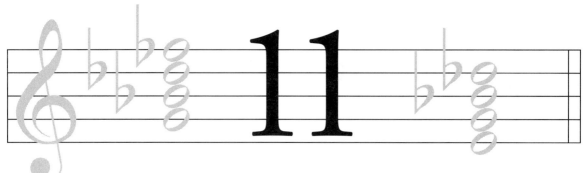

MUSICAL STRUCTURE

The Elements of Structure

◆ *The Single Note*

Structure begins with the most minute detail of a musical work, the single note. This one note possesses many characteristics that can be incorporated into the development of the work. First, the note, when written on a staff, represents a pitch. It also represents a duration when placed in the context of a time signature. It may also represent intensity, provided that some indication of its execution is given. And finally, a single note may represent a particular timbre. How this single note is treated during the evolutionary process of the composition may be quite significant at the structural level. Thus, the single note *is* a structural element.

◆ *Structure and Relationship*

Every element of musical notation relates in some manner to the structural character of a musical work. These elements include, but are not limited to: pitch, time values of notes and rests, chords, rhythm, tempo, texture, dynamics, cells, motives, phrases, periods, and sections. The study of music intrinsically mandates the study of structure.

Theoretical concepts and practices are rooted in the understanding of various structures. Recall, for example, that what was necessary in learning about scales was not the individual notes of each type of scale, but rather, the patterns of the inherent structure. Assuming that the intervallic configurations were learned, one could construct any scale beginning on an arbitrary pitch. Similarly, each of the various types of triads contains certain intervallic distances between the required notes. Once these intervallic distances were learned, it was quite simple to construct any type of triad. Here again, it was not necessary to memorize the notes of every triad, only the intervallic configurations required to structure them.

An understanding of musical structure involves an ability to recognize the relationships among various elements; their similarities or dissimilarities; the repetition or nonrepetition of elements at the micro, meso, and macro levels of the work; the factors contributing to continuity, cohesiveness, and logic. A knowledge of structure is a means to understanding that which is indigenous in any piece of music.

◆ *Structural Elements at the Macro Level*

The elements of the *micro* level include syntactical components, such as notes, rests, time values, intervals, chords, and rhythm, as well as various signs, such as ties, slurs, fermatas, repeat signs, and tempo and intensity directives.

At the *meso* level structural elements include cells, motives, and phrases; these elements were discussed in Chapter 10.

Structural elements at the *macro* level include the following:

1. **period**: A group of at least two adjacent phrases with the following characteristics:

    i.   the first phrase must be weaker than the second in closure;

    ii. a strong sense of closure must be present at the end of the second phrase;

    iii. the phrases must be somehow related, as in a question-answer relationship.

2. **section**: Part material usually consisting of at least two phrases. A section can be a single period, depending on the length and scope of the entire work.

3. **movement**: An autonomous section of a large work, such as a sonata, concerto, suite, or symphony.

Example 11–1 on page 250 illustrates these various elements.

Much of this terminology emanates from the common-practice period; structural components are the same in any style of music, although certain styles exhibit these components more obviously than others. In some compositions in every style certain structural components are missing; nevertheless, the components described here suffice for structural identification in most Western music.

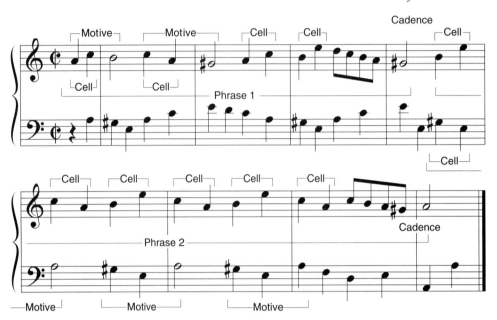

Example 11–1. A section consisting of a period structure. Play this work and listen carefully to where the first significant sense of closure is located. Compare this to the actual ending. Also, observe the cells and motives. Do you think the piece is complete?

Cadences

Cadences are comparable to punctuation marks in sentences. Sentences consist of complete ideas; they may require continuation or a response, and they sometimes seem to end in an unexpected manner. Sentences may evoke an exclamatory character, yet elicit a response in opposition to the presupposed answer. Just as specific punctuation marks characterize types of sentences, the type of cadence used in a musical work is often a determining factor in decisions of structural delineations.

◆ *The Perfect Authentic Cadence*

In the **perfect authentic cadence** (PAC), the most complete sense of closure is achieved. This character of the PAC is contingent upon the progression of

Gypsy Dance

F. J. Haydn

Cm: V7   i

***Example 11–2.** A perfect authentic cadence in the last measure.*

chords and the melodic line. For a cadence to be a PAC, at least two chords are necessary — the V (or V7) and I, or in a minor key, the V (or V7) and i, all in root position. Also, the final melody note must be the *tonic* of the key and must be located in the highest voice. See *Example 11–2.*

◆ The Imperfect Authentic Cadence

The **imperfect authentic cadence** (IAC) is weaker in its effect of closure than the PAC. An IAC is characterized by at least one of the following conditions:

1. the 3rd or 5th of the tonic triad must appear as the highest melody note.

2. An inversion of the V, V7, I, or i must appear in one or both of the chords.

3. A substitution of the vii°, viiø7, or vii°7 for the V or V7 is made.

See *Example 11–3* on page 252.

◆ The Semicadence

A **semicadence** (SC) or **half-cadence** normally requires continuation. This cadence most often rests on the V, but can also rest on the V7, vii°, viiø7, or vii°7. The final chord of the semicadence is usually preceded by the I, i, IV, iv, ii, ii7, ii°, iiø7, or ii°7. See *Example 11–4* on page 252.

◆ The Plagal Cadence

The **plagal cadence** (PC) consists of the progression IV–I, or in the minor key, iv–i. A plagal cadence is **perfect** when the tonic of the key appears as the soprano in both chords of the cadence. A plagal cadence is **imperfect** when the final tonic chord contains the 3rd or 5th in the highest voice and/or the penultimate

(a)

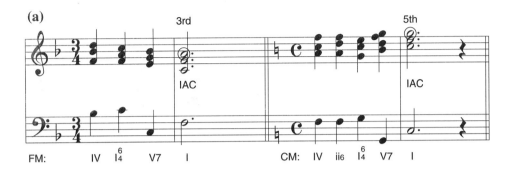

(b)

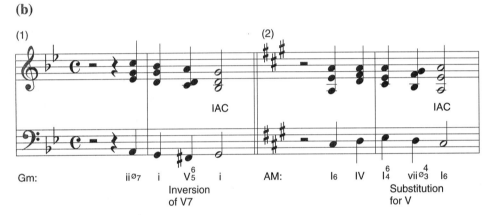

Example 11–3. Imperfect authentic cadences. **(a)** Imperfect authentic cadences with the 3rd and 5th in the soprano. **(b)** (1) An imperfect authentic cadence using an inversion of the V7. (2) An imperfect authentic cadence using a substitution for V.

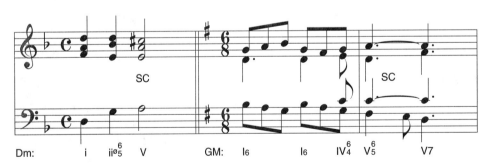

Example 11–4. Semicadences on V and V7.

chord contains its root or 3rd in the highest voice. Another condition that caus-es a plagal cadence to be imperfect is the appearance of either one or both of the cadential chords in inversion. See *Example 11–5.*

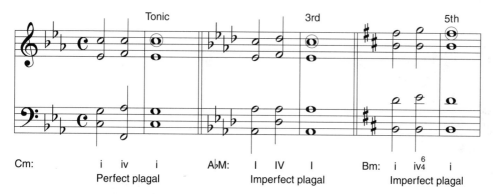

Example 11–5. Plagal cadences.

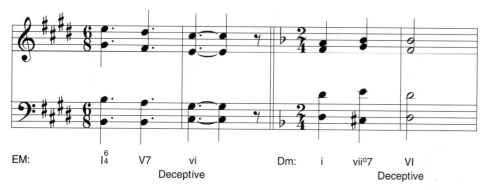

Example 11–6. Deceptive cadences in major and minor keys.

◆ *The Deceptive Cadence*

A **deceptive** or **evaded cadence** (DEC) incorporates the harmonic progression V or any of its substitutes (V7, vii°, viiø7, or vii°7) moving to any chord other than the I or i. The final chord in this progression is normally the vi, if the key is major, or the VI, if the key is minor. (In a major key the vi chord is minor and in a minor key the VI chord is major.) See *Example 11–6.*

◆ *The Phrygian and Landini Cadences and the Picardy Third*

The **Phrygian cadence**, originating from usage in the Phrygian mode, is essentially a semicadence in a minor key in which V is preceded by iv6 — hence, it can be characterized by iv6 to V. This is illustrated in *Example 11–7* on page 254.

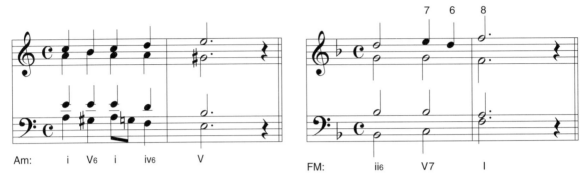

Example 11–7. *A Phrygian cadence.*

Example 11–8. *A Landini cadence.*

The **Landini cadence**, named after Francesco Landini (1325–97), consists of an interpolated sixth-scale degree appearing between the seventh degree and the tonic — hence, it can be referred to as 6 to 8. This type of cadence does not appear regularly in common-practice works; however, it is used quite extensively in popular songs. See *Example 11–8*.

The **Picardy third** or **tierce de Picardie** is a type of authentic cadence in the minor key in which the final i chord is altered to I (a major triad), as shown in *Example 11–9*.

◆ *Cadential Modifications*

Although the perfect authentic cadence consists primarily of two chords — the V and I or the V and i — other chords are often included, interpolated, or substituted in the PAC as well as in other cadences. Preceding the V may be the ii, ii7, or inversions of these, as well as the I^6_4 or the i^6_4.[1] This inversion of the I or

Example 11–9. *A Picardy third.*

---

1. It is suggested that the reader review the discussion of the $^6_4$ in Chapter 6 at this time.

(a) *Allemande*

C. Czerny

CM: ii6   V7   I   PAC

(b) **Chorale:** ***Nun ruhen alle Wälder***

J. S. Bach

AM: ii⁶5   I⁶4   V7   I

Example 11–10. Perfect authentic cadential progressions. **(a)** A perfect authentic cadence with the V7 preceded by ii6. **(b)** A perfect authentic cadence with the V7 preceded by ii$^6_5$ and I$^6_4$.

i functions as a substitute for the V and aids in the prolongation of the cadence, thus reinforcing the idea of an impending resolution. In substitutions for the V chord, the V7 is very often employed. *Example 11–10* provides several perfect authentic cadential progressions incorporating the ii and its variants, the cadential $^6_4$, and variants of the V.

Cadences in Popular Music

Although *extended chords* (upper-partial chords of the 9th, 11th, and 13th, as well as substitute chords) have yet to be discussed, mention of these structures must be made at this time. (Remember that the 9th, 11th, and 13th intervals are compound intervals that are 2nds, 4ths, and 6ths, respectively, in their simple structures.)

Popular music derives the majority, if not all, of its structure from common-practice works. However, a PAC or an IAC may not at first appear to be as obvious in popular music as it is in classical music because the chords are more complex in the popular form. This is usually the result of chord substitution. However, the relationships among the cadential chords are what is of importance.

Cadences in popular music often avoid the "classical sound" of the PAC or IAC through variation or manipulation of the chords contained in the cadential progression. It has been determined that the V-to-I provides the most effective form of closure. In keeping with this progression, final cadences in popular music often embellish the V-to-I progression by adding additional tertian factors to either one or both chords. A 7th, 9th, 11th, or 13th alone or in combination, may be added to the V chord, and it is quite common to see 7ths and 9ths added to I chords. In certain styles, for instance, jazz, it is not unusual to add types of 11ths to I chords.

◆ *The Tritone Substitution*

Several substitutions are available for the V, but perhaps the one that is employed most is that of the chord whose root lies a *tritone* interval apart from the V. In the case of V-to-I in the key of F major, the chord of G♭, a tritone from V, can be substituted. More often than not, the tritone substitution is also embellished by the addition of a 7th, 9th, 11th, or 13th, alone or in combination, as seen in *Example 11–11*. Parallels frequently occur. Correct movement of the 7th (downward, by step) is not always possible. However, smooth voice leading should be maintained. Several alternate PACs and IACs are also demonstrated in *Example 11–11*. The use of the tritone substitution will be further discussed in Chapters 15 and 18.

Other cadential types are also embellished by similar methods. Notes that create various tensions by introducing increased dissonance can be added to any of the other types of cadences discussed. Chords can also be substituted and interpolated. *Example 11–12* on page 258 presents other types of cadences with various substitutions and embellishments.

The Phrase

The human ear naturally assesses the temporal flow of music and attempts to understand and even anticipate what is to follow. The ear strives to form cohesive units; it tries, essentially, to make sense by grouping the sound material that it is assimilating. Music begins to exhibit significant aural delineations with the appearance of the phrase.

Example 11–11. Tritone substitutions and alternate cadence types. (a) The G♭ root is a tritone interval from C, the dominant. (b) Chords of the 9th, 11th, and 13th are fully discussed in Chapter 17.

The phrase is perhaps the initial most cohesive unit of a musical work, as is its counterpart in a sentence; still, its determination is often subjective. However, a characteristic feature of the phrase is that it exhibits a certain degree of completeness and resolution. Nonetheless, it is often difficult to determine exactly where and to what extent completeness and resolution occur.

Example 11–12. Substitutions and embellishments. SUB = substitution, EMB = embellishment.

◆ *Phrase Analysis of Two Works*

To study this problem, two pieces will be analyzed. The melody of "Beautiful Dreamer" *(Example 11–13)* is in D major. In singing or playing this melody most listeners would agree that the first significant point of "relative" completeness is in measure 4. However, this point of completeness is not thorough since the melody does not rest on the tonic, D. Measures 5 through 8 are nearly identical with measures 1 through 4; but in measure 8, the phrase does come to rest on the tonic. It can be said, then, that the first section, which is a period, is actually complete in measure 8. Furthermore, measures 1 through 4 constitute the antecedent phrase and measures 5 through 8 constitute the consequent phrase.

The melodic material in measures 9 through 12 is different than that of measures 1 through 8; this is the beginning of the second section or period. The first phrase of this section consists of measures 9 through 12 and does not evoke a sense of complete closure, as is reinforced by the fact that it ends on the dominant, A. This phrase may be considered an antecedent phrase. Measures 13 through 16 provide a restatement of measures 1 through 4, and measures 17 and 18 provide an extension, thus completing the second section. The section could have closed convincingly in measure 16, had the tied F♯ been a D.

In the excerpt from *Prelude (Example 11–14* on page 260), phrase determination is more difficult because of the changing meters and the more com-

"Beautiful Dreamer"

S. Foster

Example 11–13. Phrase structures and degrees of closure in cadences in a traditional work. The various measures are discussed on page 258.

plex rhythmic scheme. A general observation reveals four contrasting ideas in this excerpt. The first incorporates measures 1 and 2; this is simply an introduction. Measures 3 through 5 establish the second idea, and, as can be seen, the melody is in the graphic shape of an arc, beginning on E, ascending to B, and returning to E. Measures 6 through 9 provide the second melodic idea — an ascending scalar and **arpeggio** (broken chord) design. Measures 10 and 11 and measures 12 and 13 are quite similar to each other and provide the third melodic idea. No melodic idea in the excerpt rests on the tonic, A♭.

Although it is not difficult to determine the origin of melodic ideas, their termination poses specific problems. Does the beginning of a new melodic motive delineate the point at which the previous idea ends? The E♭ in measure 5 is the dominant note of the key and exudes a tendency toward the tonic. Hence, the listener anticipates continuation. Measure 6 provides this continuation, but proceeds by development through measure 9, again resting on the dominant, E♭. Measure 10 begins with yet another E♭, proceeds to a more pronounced arrival of the dominant note by its leading tone, D, in measure 11, is then reinforced by an octave-higher D in measure 12, and finally resolves to C, the 3rd of A♭ major in measure 13. The question then remains: are measures 1 through 13 one phrase or is this a chain of phrases? From a rhythmic-content standpoint, measures 3 through 9 contrast with measures 10 through 13. Measures 6 through 9 serve as a continuation of measures 3 through 5, and measures 10 through 13 provide a significant change from measures 3 through 9. Generally speaking, then, two contrasting melodic phrases exist — measures 3 through 9 and measures 10 through 13.

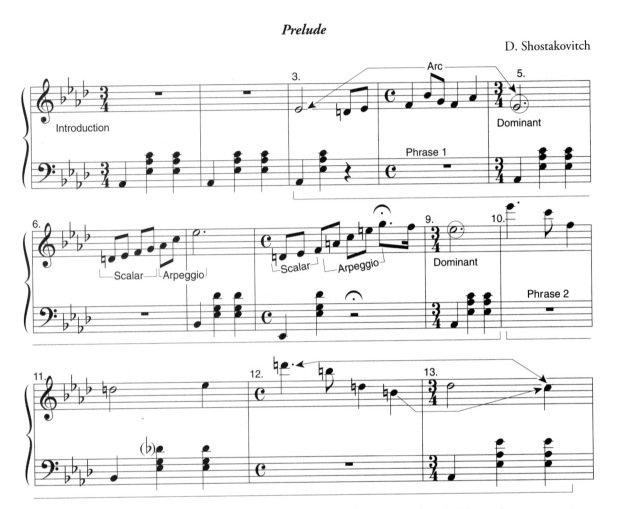

Example 11–14. Phrase structures and degrees of closure in a modern work. The various measures are discussed on page 259.

Although the determination of a phrase can be made strictly from its melodic content, the harmonic content also plays a significant role in locating its resolution. Notice the varying degrees of resolution in the phrases of the Chopin waltz *(Example 11–15)* as a result of the melodic motion, design, and harmonic content.

Example 11–15. Varying degrees of resolution. It would seem as though the i in measure 8 should serve as a relatively strong chord of closure; but since the melody begins on a dominant 7 (measures 1 and 9), measure 8 only serves to bridge measures 7 through 9. Listen to this work and notice the strength of closure exuded by the i in the final measure. There is no doubt that this is the end of this section of music.

Waltz, Op. 64, No. 2

F. Chopin

◆ *Period and Phrase Types*

Phrases are often paired as an *antecedent* and *consequent*. Phrases can be combined to form *periods*, *phrase groups,* and *phrase chains.* At least two phrases are required to form any period, phrase group, or phrase chain.

Various types of period and phrase structures include:

1. **Symmetrical period**: This consists of an antecedent phrase balanced by a consequent phrase of the same or similar length.

2. **Parallel period**: A symmetrical period that consists of antecedent and consequent phrases with quite similar musical elements is referred to as *parallel.*

3. **Double period**: This consists of a double antecedent and a double consequent.

4. **Asymmetrical period**: This consists of an antecedent and a consequent of dissimilar lengths. An asymmetrical period can also consist of at least two antecedents followed by a consequent, or one antecedent followed by at least two consequents.

5. **Contrasting period**: This consists of antecedent and consequent phrases with dissimilar musical elements.

6. **Phrase group**: This consists of at least two, or more often, three or more, phrases. At least two of the phrases must be similar, and no phrase can end with a conclusive cadence, such as a PAC, IAC, or plagal.

7. **Phrase chain**: This consists of three or more dissimilar phrases, none of which ends with a conclusive cadence.

These period and phrase structures are illustrated in *Example 11–16* on pages 263–66. It should be noted that in all period structures, the final cadence of the period supplies the resolution of the harmonic movement presented in the preceding phrases.

Binary and Ternary Structure

◆ *Binary Structure*

Like other facets of music, musical structure is vast and complex; it would require volumes to present, analyze, and formulate conclusions concerning its virtually infinite varieties. For the purpose of this introductory discussion, it is necessary to examine several musical structures that provide the fundamental foundation for many of the larger and more complex ones.

Example 11–16. Types of period and phrase structures. (a) A symmetrical period with an 8-measure antecedent and an 8-measure consequent. It is also a parallel period. (b) A parallel period. Notice that the melody is in the bass. The treble can be considered an inverted pedal tone. (c) A double period. The final cadence supplies the resolution of the entire period. (d) An asymmetrical period with two consequent phrases. (e) A contrasting period. (f) A phrase group. Phrases 3 and 4 are similar. None of the phrases end with a conclusive cadence. (g) A phrase chain. None of the three dissimilar phrases ends with a conclusive cadence.

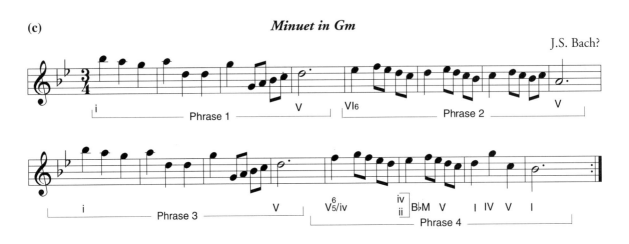

Minuet in Gm

J.S. Bach?

Folk Song

E. Grieg

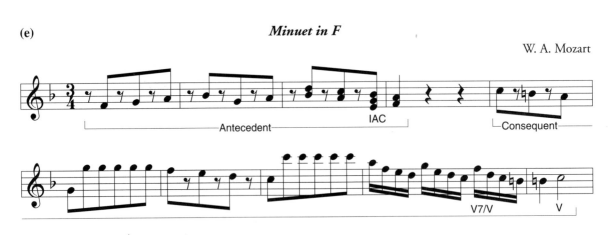

Minuet in F

W. A. Mozart

(f)

Etude in A Minor

S. Heller

(g)

Intermezzo in C Major, Op. 119, No. 3

J. Brahms

(g) continued

A musical work is usually perceived in sections. These sections are delineated by a number of factors, which may include various types of cadences, melodic contours, rhythmic figures, rests, texture, and pauses. Essentially, two quite general types of sections exist; *closed* and *open*. A section is considered **closed** if it cadences on the tonic triad, and **open** if it cadences on any other chord. Open sections frequently cadence on a semicadence, a deceptive cadence, or appear in another key, thus suggesting, if not necessitating, a return to the tonic key.

The **binary** or **two-part structure**, common in many styles of music, consists of *two* principal sections, referred to as A and B. Remember that a section is often only a period construction. Therefore, a binary structure can consist of an A-section, comprising a period, as well as a B-section, comprising another period. The A-section can be open or closed and can be extended to a double-period construction. The B-section can consist of a period or can be extended to a double period; it is usually a closed structure. Typically, the material in the two sections is related. A binary structure can be either simple or compound.

A popular variant of the binary structure is the **rounded binary**, often referred to as an **incipient three-part structure**. See *Example 11–17*. A feature of this structure is the repetition of the A-section in whole or part.

◆ Ternary Structure

Ternary structure consists of *three* principal sections (A–B–A), each of which is a complete statement and can be expanded by repetition through either repeat signs or rewriting. Section B contrasts with section A; the return of A is a restatement of the initial section. A significant difference between binary and ternary designs is the degree of resolution in the cadences. The A-section of the ternary design is normally closed; that is, it ends on the tonic chord. The B-section normally cadences as open, is written in another key, and requires a return of the A-section. As with the binary structure, the ternary structure can be simple or compound. A simple ternary structure can be as terse as three phrases or three periods; yet in an expanded version it can be compound (sections within sections) and incorporate an entire movement. See *Example 11–18* on page 268.

Alla Polacca

C. Reinecka

Example 11–17. A rounded binary structure.

Popular-Song Structure

The structure of popular songs and instrumental works does not depart radically from established structures utilized in common-practice composition. The ternary design offers the most successful method for song construction. ("Song" in this context refers to any popular work, whether it contains lyrics or is solely instrumental.)

Example 11–18. A ternary structure.

◆ The SDR Principle

Perhaps the most persuasive argument for the success of the ternary design lies in the **statement-departure-return principle** (SDR). This sequence is familiar to people because it is common to many everyday routines — a beginning in a familiar place (the statement), a trip to the unknown, fraught with apprehension (the departure), and the anticipated arrival at the place of origin (the return). Thus, ternary structure allows the listener to experience a familiar and psychologically satisfying sequence.

In ternary design, material is presented and often repeated in order to create a sense of familiarity. A departure from familiar musical materials — the A-section — takes the listener on a musical excursion — the B-section. When the A-section finally returns, the listener then arrives in familiar territory and is satisfied with the completed journey.

In the popular format, **expanded ternary structure**, in which each large section (A, B) can contain more than one phrase or period and can be repeated, is usually employed. The A-section is called the **verse** and the B-section, which repeats, is the **chorus**, or **hook**. In popular music, the chorus is often the most musically and/or lyrically appealing, and is crafted to be the most memorable part of the song, thus becoming the part with which the listener most readily identifies. In terms of musical interest, then, B, the chorus, is more significant than A, the verse. (Interestingly, B-sections, or **subordinate themes**, in larger works of the common-practice period were in many instances musically more appealing than A-sections, or **principal themes**. An example of this is the second theme in the first movement of Rachmaninoff's *Piano Concerto No. 2 in C Minor.*)

A typical format for the construction of many popular songs is the *verse-chorus-verse-chorus* structure. However, in practice there is usually more involved. An **introduction**, that utilizes a portion of the material from either verse or chorus, usually precedes the verse; a verse may be repeated before the chorus enters. In many repeated first-verse structures, the repeated second verse usually leads to the chorus via a **verse-bridge**, which often consists of one to several measures of musical material that alerts the listener to the likelihood that something significant is about to occur — namely, the chorus.

Popular songs appear in a variety of structures. Some seem to contain no verse material; they begin immediately with a chorus, progress to a bridge, and continue with the chorus. Others seem to contain only chorus material. When all three of these elements are present, verses can be referred to by A, choruses by B, and bridges by C. A bridge can occur between a verse and a chorus or after a chorus. In any event, bridge material is characterized by its thrust or sense of urgency. In terms of this system of identification, several well-known works and their corresponding structures are listed:

AB: *Greensleeves, America*

B (repeated): *Sunny, Happy Birthday, Try to Remember*

BBCB: *Close to You, Satin Doll*

ACB: *God Bless America*

AABB: *That's What Friends Are for*

BBCBCB: *Yesterday*

ABABCB (repeated): *I Write the Songs*

AABBCBB: *One Moment in Time*

ABABCBBAB: *Saving All My Love for You*

In these structures, the final B (chorus) can be repeated as many times as desired since in many instances the chorus provides the final ending in a **decrescendo** (fade). Any section, A, B, or C, can be immediately repeated, although the bridge, C, usually is not.

It is safe to say that virtually any format is possible in popular-song construction provided that at least a chorus, B, is present somewhere in the material.

Structure and Improvisation

Composition is not limited to written notes, and hence, structural as well as other syntactical considerations must be addressed in *extemporaneous* or *improvisational* composition. Musical improvisation dates back to the beginning of musical performance. Even in the highly structured music of the Classical period, composers permitted and encouraged performers to improvise both within the work proper and in **cadenzas**, elaborate passages that were inserted near the end of certain concerto movements and were either improvised by the performer or written out by the composer.[2] In any event, cadenzas were of an improvisational nature and their success was contingent upon the performer's or composer's ability to assimilate materials presented earlier in the movement into a virtuosic improvisational solo section.

Improvisation, currently referred to as "soloing" in popular formats, must be understood structurally, if it is to be musically successful. Performing as many notes to a beat as possible does not create a successful solo. Solos or improvisations must be carefully rendered in their developmental aspect. This is generally best achieved by careful and thoughtful consideration of the elements of structure, through an ability to develop these elements extemporaneously by compositional technique, and, above all, by being an alert and acute listener. The structural aspect of an improvised solo is perhaps the most important consideration in the development of successful improvisation. Live performances are rife with unsuccessful improvisations and incompetent improvisers. Why? Simply because the improvisor or soloist has not considered or studied the structural-developmental aspect of extemporaneous composition or knows little about composition at all for that matter. Improvisation and composition require the methodical and calculated unfolding of musical events in a temporal dimension. They are never successful when random and thoughtless events are permitted to occur. An understanding of structural development will not necessarily guarantee competency in solo performances, but it will certainly aid in the process of becoming a more musical musician.

An Introduction To Modulation

The ensuing chapters deal extensively with chromaticism, the introduction of pitches foreign to the prevailing key. Chromaticism often suggests **modulation**,

---

2. A **concerto** is a musical composition for orchestra and one or more solo instruments.

which is the process whereby the key of a musical work is changed and the new key is firmly established. A modulation can occur once or several times within a work.

Modulation can range from a simple to a complex process; it is best understood when a comprehensive knowledge of chromatic harmony is attained. Therefore, a detailed investigation of modulation is deferred until Chapter 19, which presents an exhaustive discussion of tertian harmony.

Essentially, three conditions must exist in modulation:

1. The initial key must be established.

2. Movement toward the intended key must be initiated. This can be gradual or abrupt.

3. The new key must be firmly established.

◆ Recognizing a Modulation

A high percentage of modulations occur between closely related keys, those that differ by no more than the addition or deletion of one sharp or flat. If, for example, the initial key is C major, the closely related keys are F major, G major, and the relative minors of C, F, and G. If the initial key is B minor, the closely related keys are E minor, F♯ minor, and their relative majors.

A modulation can be detected by the appearance of a chromatic pitch in the melody or harmony, possibly in both. However, a chromatic pitch may be a nonharmonic tone, and one must assess whether its function is purely that of a nonharmonic tone or whether it is the first indication of an impending modulation. These matters are illustrated in *Example 11–19*.

Example 11–19. Recognizing a modulation by the appearance of a chromatic pitch. The appearance of F♯ in measures 1 and 2 might suggest key movement toward G major. However, close observation reveals that these chromatic pitches are chromatic lower neighbors of G. Similarly, the C♯ in measure 3 might suggest movement toward the closely related key of D minor. Again, this chromatic pitch is also a lower neighbor. Also, neither G major nor D minor is supported by the chord progression in the lower staff.

[I]   [V] in C   [V]   [I]   [V]   [I] [V] [I]
             [I] in G

Example 11–20. Recognizing a modulation from the emphasis of various diatonic pitches. The key of C major is established in measure 1. In measure 2, the V chord, G, is outlined; but the A tends to reinforce G as an impending tonic, and the outlined G triad becomes ambiguous as to its function. The D and A pitches in measure 3 suggest dominant and supertonic scale degrees in support of G as a new tonic. Bracketed chord numerals indicate implied chords.

A modulation can occur when certain diatonic pitches are simply empha-sized. It is quite possible to modulate from C major to G major, for example, and avoid the leading tone, F♯. Thus, G major is established by stressing certain scale degrees that serve to reinforce G as a new key center. These scale degrees are very often repetitions of the dominant degree and factors of the I chord. See *Example 11–20.*

A Regal Dance

Daniel Gottlob Turk

GM

Example 11–21. Recognizing a modulation from multiple occurances of chromatic pitches. It is apparent that the occurrences of the C♯s in measures 5, 6, and 7 and the finali-ty of the phrase in measure 8 reveal a modulation to D major.

Minuet in C

F. J. Haydn

Example 11–22. A modulation from C major to G major. A modulation is suggested by the inclusion of F♯ in measure 4. This F♯ is retained, establishing the key of G major, and the section concludes with a PAC in measure 8.

Multiple occurrences of one or more chromatic pitches can serve as evidence that a modulation is in progress, as is shown in *Example 11–21.*

The most convincing proof that a modulation has occurred can be seen at the cadence in what is assumed to be the new key. The authentic and plagal cadences are typically used to establish a new key, and appear at strategic points in a phrase. Cadences must be more carefully considered after more complex chromaticism has been introduced. A cadence must *not* be interpreted as any progression of V-to-I, for example, that may appear to be in a new key. See *Example 11–22.*

◆ *Types of Modulation*

Three broad types of modulation exist.

Common-chord or **diatonic modulation** occurs when a chord that is diatonic in both the initial key and the ensuing key is used in what is referred to as a *pivot.* The **pivot** serves to provide a common link between the two keys. A

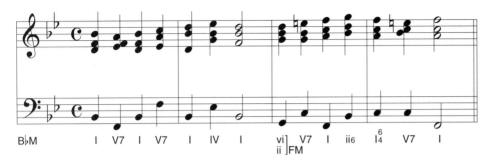

Example 11–23. Common-chord modulation. In measure 3, Gm is common to both the keys of B♭M and FM. Here, Gm serves as a pivot; it is bracketed and identified. The bracket literally means, "this becomes this"; hence, vi in B♭ becomes ii in F. (Sometimes, the bracket is placed to the left; either placement is acceptable.)

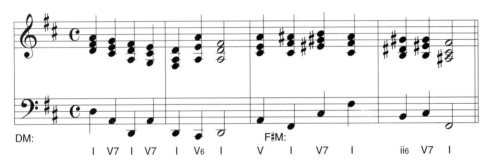

Example 11–24. Chromatic modulation. In measure 3, the chromatic inflection of A♯ creates a chromatic chord, which is subsequently established as a new tonic. Since no common chord exists, no bracket is necessary.

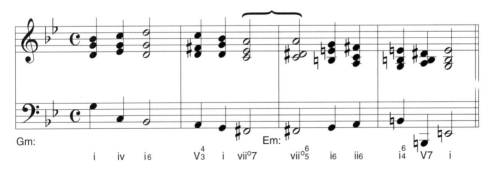

Example 11–25. Enharmonic modulation. This enharmonic modulation is accomplished through a respelling of the vii°7 in Gm. The enharmonic spelling of E♭ in the vii°7 in Gm as a D♯ causes the creation of a vii°7 in Em (D♯–F♯–A–C). An alternative method for indicating this type of modulation is to bracket the chord as follows:

$$\left.\begin{array}{l} \text{vii°7 en} \\ \text{vii°}{}^{6}_{5} \end{array}\right] \text{Em}$$

pivot chord in any type of modulation is indicated with a bracket and the pivot is identified in both keys, as is illustrated in *Example 11–23*.

Chromatic modulation can occur both between closely related keys and between remote keys; it is distinguished by the use of a chromatic chord in one or both keys. Chromatic modulation is shown in *Example 11–24*.

Enharmonic modulation involves the enharmonic spelling of one or more chord tones or melodic tones so as to construct a pivotal chord tone, and hence, a link to the ensuing key. See *Example 11–25*.

Chapter Review

The structural components of a work include those elements belonging to the micro, meso, and macro levels; for example, notes develop into phrases and phrases may develop into complete works. The study of music inherently involves the study of structure — structure as it relates to the construction of scales, intervals, chords, rhythm, and melody, through entire large-scale works and even groups of works. The ability to recognize these relationships is a necessity in understanding musical structure.

Basic terms employed in the analysis and description of structure include *cell, motive, phrase, period, cadence, section,* and *movement.* Some of these components are prevalent in nearly every style of Western music. The human ear and psyche are determining factors in the conceptual, perceptual, and ultimately, the developmental aspects of music. It is the requirement of the ear that finally shapes and organizes musical events both within individual works and within general practices, and mandates a requirement for continuity and coherence.

Two fundamental structures that are prevalent in virtually all styles of Western music were discussed — *binary* and *ternary.* It was shown how the structure of ternary design satisfies a human condition as it pertains to familiarity. This concept was defined as *Statement, Departure, Return* (SDR).

The structure of music in the popular style was presented and discussed and the significant parts were defined as *verse, chorus,* and *bridge.*

Although most music is ultimately preserved in written or recorded form, much is of an improvisational nature. *Improvisation,* or *extemporaneous composition* is successful only when the performer is aware of structural development.

In the process of *modulation* three conditions must occur:

1. the establishment of the initial key,

2. a movement toward the intended key, and

3. the firm establishment of the new key.

In most cases modulation can be detected by the

presence of nondiatonic pitches. However, these nondiatonic pitches may simply be nonharmonic tones, and it is therefore necessary to assess the musical passage carefully in a broader sense by examining cadence points to determine whether a modulation has actually occurred.

The three broad types of modulation discussed were: *common-chord modulation, chromatic modulation,* and *enharmonic modulation.*

Anthology References

For additional usage and analysis, see the following examples in Distefano, Joseph P. and James A. Searle, *Music and Materials for Analysis: An Anthology.* New York, Ardsley House, Publishers, Inc., 1995.

perfect authentic cadences
    Example 15.   *Lord Jesus Christ, the Prince of Peace,* Johann Sebastian Bach, pp. 69–74.
Landini cadences
    Example 6.   *Quam Pulcra Es,* John Dunstable, pp. 17–22.
Phrygian cadences
    Example 7.   *Ave Christe* (Part One), Josquin des Prez, pp. 23–32.
imperfect authentic cadences
    Example 5.   *C'est la Fine,* Guillaume d'Amiens, pp. 11–14, 16.
deceptive cadences
    Example 20.   *O Thou, of God the Father,* Johann Sebastian Bach, pp. 69–73, 79.
semicadences
    Example 21.   *Blessed Jesu, at Thy Word,* Johann Sebastian Bach, pp. 69–73, 80.
Picardy thirds
    Example 24.   *The Well-Tempered Clavier,* Book I, *Prelude and Fugue No. 16,* Johann Sebastian Bach, pp. 91–100.
period types
    Examples 15–21. Lord Jesus Christ, the Prince of Peace, Johann Sebastian Bach
        O Darkest Woe! Ye Tears that Flow, Johann Sebastian Bach
        If God Withdraweth, All the Cost, Johann Sebastian Bach
        O Lord! How Many Miseries, Johann Sebastian Bach
        My Cause Is God's, and I Am Still, Johann Sebastian Bach
        O Thou, of God the Father, Johann Sebastian Bach
        Blessed Jesu, at Thy Word, Johann Sebastian Bach, pp. 69–80.
rounded binary structure
    Example 25.   *Minuet and Trio,* Franz Joseph Haydn, pp. 101–8.

Example 26.   *Larghetto,* Wolfgang Amadeus Mozart, pp. 109–14.
Example 27.   *Allegro,* Wolfgang Amadeus Mozart, pp. 115–20.
Example 29.   *Variations on a Swiss Song,* Ludwig van Beethoven, pp. 125–34.
Example 30.   *Rondo,* Wolfgang Amadeus Mozart, pp. 135–40.
Example 32.   *Sonata,* K. 333, Wolfgang Amadeus Mozart, pp. 149–78.
Example 33.   *Waltz,* Franz Schubert, pp. 179–84.
Example 35.   *Album Leaves,* Op. 124, Waltz, Robert Schumann, pp. 193–200.

ternary structure
Example 30.   *Rondo,* Wolfgang Amadeus Mozart, pp. 135–40.

Self-Test

1. Why does the study of music intrinsically involve the study of structure?

2. List several components contributing to (a) the micro level, (b) the meso level, and (c) the macro level of a musical work.

3. Define each of the following:

   (a) *cell,* (b) *motive,* (c) *phrase,* (d) *period,* (e) *cadence,* (f) *movement.*

4. Describe each of the following cadences and indicate the elements necessary to establish each:

   (a) *perfect authentic cadence,* (b) *imperfect authentic cadence,* (c) *semicadence,* (d) *plagal cadence,* (e) *deceptive cadence.*

5. Describe (a) the *Phrygian cadence,* (b) the *Landini cadence,* and (c) the *Picardy third.*

6. Which cadence provides the highest degree of closure?

7. What is meant by the term *substitution?*

8. What is the function of the ear in the perception of structure?

9. Two types of phrases are _____ and _____ .

10. Define each of the following:

    (a) *symmetrical period,* (b) *double period,* (c) *asymmetrical period,* (d) *parallel period,* (e) *contrasting period,* (f) *phrase group,* (g) *phrase chain.*

11. Describe two types of sections.

12. The two principal structures discussed in this chapter that are prevalent in virtually all Western style music are _____ and _____ .

13. Describe the *SDR principle.*

14. Describe the terms *verse, chorus,* and *bridge,* and indicate format(s) of various popular songs.

15. Define *extemporaneous composition.*

16. Define *cadenza*.
17. Describe the process of *modulation* and the three necessary conditions for it to occur.
18. Discuss the existence of nonharmonic tones in a musical passage and their implication for modulation.
19. Describe three broad types of modulation.

Exercises

1. Extend the motives into four-measure phrases and add chords. Label all chords, cadences, and nonharmonic tones.

(a)

(b)

(c)

2. Develop each cell into a motive, a phrase, and finally, a period. Add chords. Label all chords, cadences, and nonharmonic tones.

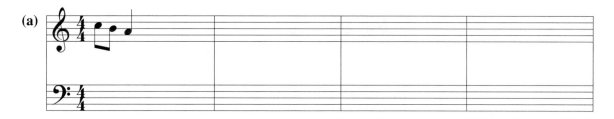

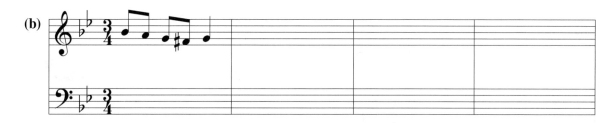

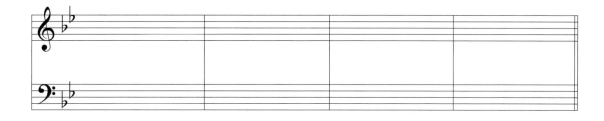

(c) (for solo instrument and piano accompaniment)

3. Compose cadences, as indicated.

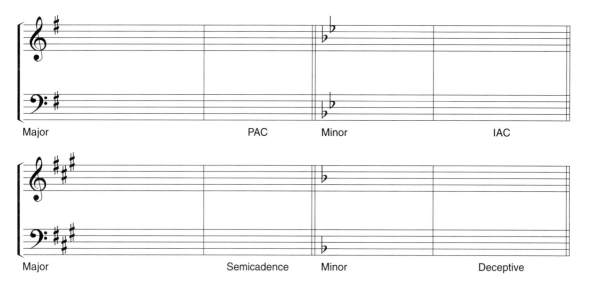

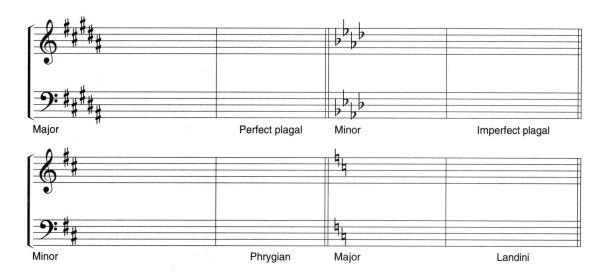

4. Compose V7-to-I, or V7-to-i cadences. Then substitute a tritone dominant for the V7. See the *example*.

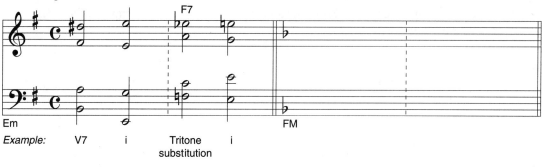

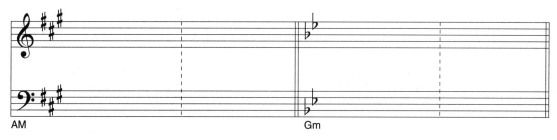

5. Compose modulations in which various emphasized pitches cause a modulation to the designated key.

(b)

DM to GM

(c)

CM to Am

(d)

FM to Am

6. All of the following begin in C major. From the added sharps and flats, determine a probable modulation. Complete each line appropriately.

(a)

(b)

(c)

(d)

7. Identify each type of modulation. Label all chords with Roman numerals and chord symbols.

12

SECONDARY DOMINANTS
AND
DOMINANT SEVENTHS

Chromaticism and Diatonicism

Chromaticism, from the Greek "chroma," means "color"; hence, *chromatic* implies colorful. Chromaticism is introduced into a melody or harmony by the addition of pitches foreign to the key in which the musical work is written.

Chromaticism is necessary because the available pitches and harmonic structures in a diatonic key, can, after time, become not only monotonous but even predictable. However, in defense of a diatonic format it must be pointed out that many successful "pop" hits and classical works have been written in a primarily diatonic framework, containing little, if any, chromaticism in either melody or harmony. *Example 12–1* is a strictly diatonic work of the common-practice period. Several other works that are essentially diatonic in either the melody or both in the melody and harmony include: "Who Am I," by Claude-Michel Schönberg and Herbert Kretzmer, from *Les Misérables*; "The Last One to Know," by Jane Mariash and Matraca Berg; "You Don't Bring Me Flowers," by Marilyn and Allan Bergman and Neil Diamond; "That's All," by Alan Brandy and Bob Haymes; the first theme from the first movement of Mozart's *Eine Kleine Nachtmusik*, K.525; and "Hallelujah," from Handel's *Messiah*.

Baletto

G. S. Löhlein

Example 12–1. A diatonic work. Although this short piece is strictly diatonic, interest is maintained through the use of contrasting rhythmic figures in the treble and bass parts, through textural changes (single vs. double notes) in the treble part, and through a melody that incorporates leaping and stepwise movement.

The addition of chromaticism into a musical work does not necessarily guarantee appeal. Moreover, since harmony and melody are certainly not the only factors present in a musical work, one must always consider the elements of rhythm, structure, and timbre in also providing appeal.

Secondary-Dominant Chords

◆ *Origin and Derivation*

With the introduction of secondary dominants, the dimension of chromaticism is extended. The origin of the secondary dominant is from chromatic passing tones; later, these passing tones became established as secondary harmonic functions.

Since a typical dominant chord is a major triad whose normal resolution lies a perfect 5th below or a perfect 4th above its root, it follows that *any triad in a key can be embellished by a major triad whose root lies a perfect 5th above or a perfect 4th below the embellishing chord*, thus creating a dominant-tonic function. However, it is not as common in traditional practice to embellish diminished and augmented triads as it is to embellish major and minor triads by dominant relationships since the former triads are not functional as tonics of major or minor keys.

To facilitate an understanding of the derivation of a secondary dominant, one should consider the resolution of the secondary dominant as *tonicizing* the resultant chord of resolution. The term **tonicize** means to *suggest* a new key center without actually establishing one. For example, in constructing the dominant of the ii chord in the key of F major, one considers the key of the ii chord (G minor) in order to locate and construct its dominant. In the key of G minor, the dominant is D major (D–F♯–A); the harmonic form of the minor is used. This D major triad is a secondary dominant in the key of F major and is labeled V/ii (V of ii). Likewise, in constructing the dominant of the V chord in the key of A minor, first consider the key of the dominant (E major). The dominant of E major, which is now being tonicized, is B major, spelled B–D♯–F♯. The dominant of E major in the key of A minor is thus labeled V/V. Four-part voice leading of secondary dominants is the same as for any dominant. Consider the secondary dominant as a dominant in the key of the chord that follows. Hence, double the root — never the leading tone. See *Example 12–2*.

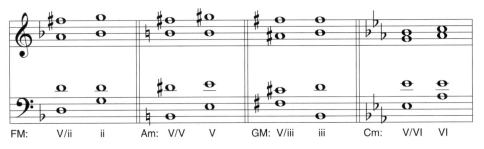

FM: V/ii   ii   Am: V/V   V   GM: V/iii   iii   Cm: V/VI   VI

Example 12–2. Secondary dominants in major and minor keys.

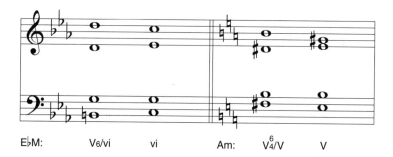

EbM: V6/vi   vi   Am: V$\overset{6}{4}$/V   V

Example 12–3. A $\overset{6}{4}$ inversion whose root is doubled. In fact, doubling the 5th (F♯) would be a duplication of a chromatically altered 5th. Doubling the D♯ would result in a doubled leading tone.

◆ Inversions

Secondary dominants can be constructed in any inversion. For example, in the key of E♭ major, the first inversion of the dominant of the vi triad would be indicated as V6/vi. This dominant (G–B–D) is taken from the tonicized key of C minor (vi in E♭ major) and written in its first inversion as B–D–G or V6/vi. Similarly, in the key of A minor, the second inversion of the dominant of the V triad would be indicated as V$\overset{6}{4}$/V. This dominant is taken from the tonicized key of E major (V in A major) and written in its second inversion as F♯–B–D♯. Except for the root, avoid doubling any chromatically altered pitch of the secondary triad. See *Example 12–3.*

◆ Assessment

Secondary dominants must be assessed within the context of the surrounding chord progression to determine if they are, in fact, embellishments or simply normal progressions within the harmonic content.

In measure 1 of *Example 12–4*, the V to I is not a secondary-dominant embellishment since the two chords, although related by a 5th, appear within the key of G major. In measures 2 and 3, both the B and A triads are *secondary dominants*; they are chromatic, and both precede a triad appearing in the key of G major.

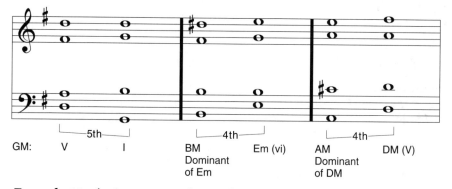

GM: V   I   BM   Em (vi)   AM   DM (V)
       └──5th──┘   Dominant   Dominant
                            of Em   of DM
                 └──4th──┘   └──4th──┘

Example 12–4. Assessment of secondary dominants. In measures 2 and 3, the B and A triads are secondary dominants.

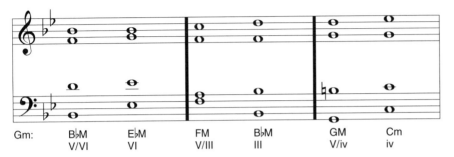

Gm: B♭M   E♭M   FM   B♭M   GM   Cm
        V/VI   VI   V/III   III   V/iv   iv

Example 12–5. Assessment of secondary dominants. Upon initial observation, it would appear that the B♭M in measure 1 and the FM in measure 2 are diatonic. This, of course, would depend upon the form of the minor scale considered. In Gm (natural form), these triads do appear. However, in the harmonic form, a B♭ triad is augmented and an F triad is F♯ diminished. Although composers occasionally use the augmented triad for B♭, it is most often used as B♭ major. Nevertheless, its secondary function must be examined.

In measures 1 and 2 of *Example 12–5*, both the B♭ and F secondary-dominant triads can appear within the key of G minor. In the G minor (harmonic) scale, the B triad is augmented (B♭–D–F♯), and the F triad is diminished (F♯–A–C). In measure 3, the G major triad is definitely a secondary dominant; it is chromatic and is in a dominant-tonic relationship.

Secondary-Dominant Seventh Chords

The secondary-dominant 7th contains an additional degree of tension in its secondary-dominant function. This structure, like any normally occurring dominant 7th, also contains the dissonant minor 7th interval. Secondary-dominant 7ths are derived in exactly the same manner as secondary dominants.

◆ Inversions and Introductory Remarks on Resolution

As in the dominant 7th, all inversions of the secondary-dominant 7th are available and are labeled according to function. For example, in the key of G major, the V7/iii infers that iii (the B minor triad) is to be tonicized. Therefore, in assuming the key of B minor, the dominant 7th consists of the pitches F♯–A♯–C♯–E (taken from the harmonic minor). The resultant chord yields V7/iii. This secondary-dominant 7th in its first inversion reads V^6_5/iii; in its second inversion it reads V^4_3/iii, and in its third inversion it reads V^4_2/iii. See *Example 12–6*.

The 7th of secondary-dominant 7ths is *prepared* and resolved in the same manner as a dominant 7th. That is, the 7th is usually prepared by step or common

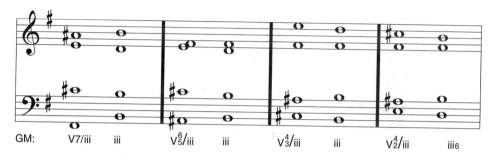

Example 12–6. *Root position and inversions of a secondary dominant seventh in G major.*
Notice that the normal resolution of the V_2^4/iii is to a first-inversion triad. This is because the seventh (bass) resolves downward by step.

tone, although leaps are possible; the dissonant 7th degree is usually resolved downward by step; the leading tone (the 3rd of the 7th chord) is resolved upward by step, and the remaining voices move smoothly, avoiding any parallels or incorrect doublings. Recall that in the $\frac{4}{3}$ inversion of the dominant 7th, as here in the $\frac{4}{3}$ inversion of the secondary-dominant 7th, if the bass moves upward by step, so can the seventh. See *Example 12–7.*

Resolutions of Secondary-Dominant Chords

◆ *Deceptive Resolutions*

Just as normal dominants and dominant 7ths can evade their intended resolutions, so too can secondary dominants, secondary-dominant 7ths in root position, and all

Example 12–7. *Preparation of the seventh and alternate resolution of the V_3^4 in the last two measures.*

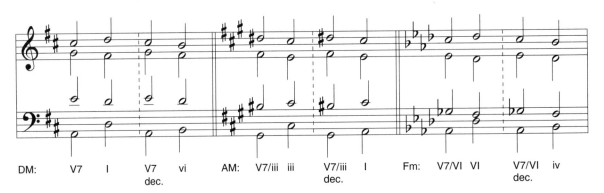

| DM: | V7 | I | V7 dec. | vi | AM: | V7/iii | iii | V7/iii dec. | I | Fm: | V7/VI | VI | V7/VI dec. | iv |

Example 12–8. Deceptive resolutions of the dominant and secondary dominant.

their inversions. Recall that in a deceptive resolution or deceptive cadence, the dominant or dominant 7th resolves to a chord whose root is a 6th above the intended chord of resolution. In the key of D major, for example, the dominant (A major, V), or dominant 7th (V7) usually resolves to I (D major) or to a chord whose root lies a 6th above D in the key of D major — thus, B minor (vi) — a deceptive resolution. Similarly, a secondary dominant or secondary-dominant 7th can also resolve in a deceptive fashion. The following demonstrates this concept: In the key of A major, the V7/iii is G♯–B♯–D♯–F♯ (iii is C♯ minor; its dominant 7th is therefore V7 in the key of C♯ minor). The normal resolution of V7/iii in A major would, of course, be to iii (C♯ minor). To effect a deceptive resolution, the V7/iii does not resolve to iii, but to a chord in the key of A major whose root lies a 6th above iii (C♯) — that is, to A.

As another example, consider the V7 of VI in the key of F minor. The VI in F minor is a D♭ major triad. The dominant 7th of D♭ is A♭ dominant 7th (a perfect 5th above D♭). In a deceptive resolution of the A♭ dominant 7th, the resultant chord of resolution is iv (a B♭ minor triad) in the key of F minor. This is because the B♭ minor triad lies a 6th above the D♭ triad within the key of F minor; hence, it is the resultant triad of a deceptive resolution. See *Example 12–8*.

This type of resolution is an extremely important one and should be thoroughly understood; it appears in all genres of music. *Example 12–9* illustrates two deceptive resolutions of secondary dominants and secondary-dominant 7ths, using root position and inversions. In the Beethoven Sonata, *Example 12-9(a)*, the B major triad in the third measure is a dominant of vi (E minor). The resolution, however, is to IV (a C major triad). The C is a 6th above the E and is therefore a deceptive resolution of the B major secondary dominant.

Example 12–9. Deceptive resolutions of secondary dominants and secondary-dominant sevenths.
(a) Deceptive resolution of a secondary dominant in first inversion. **(b)** Deceptive resolutions of the dominant 7th (in measures 1 and 2) and a secondary dominant in measure 7.

(a)

Sonata, **Op. 49, No. 2**
Minuet

L. v. Beethoven

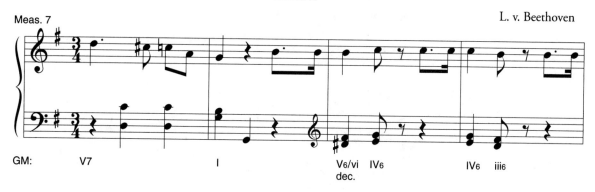

(b)

"Don't Ask Me Why"

Billy Joel

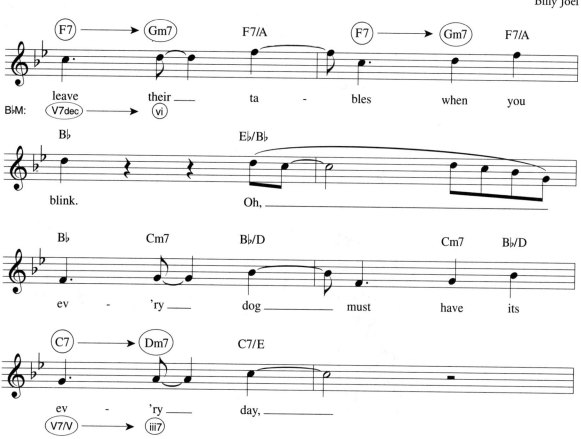

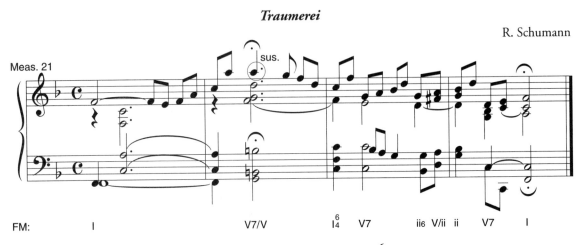

Example 12–10. *A secondary dominant seventh resolved to a tonic $^6_4$.*

In the Billy Joel piece, *Example 12–9(b)*, F7, the dominant 7th, is resolved deceptively to vi7 in the second and third measures. In the eighth measure, C7, the V7/V also resolves deceptively (to D minor), a 6th above the dominant F and is the iii in B♭ major.

◆ V/V and V7/V to the Tonic Six-Four

Another resolution of the secondary dominant and secondary-dominant 7th of V is to the tonic $^6_4$ at the cadence. The V/V and V7/V chords can resolve to the tonic $^6_4$ since the cadential $^6_4$ is a substitute for V. See *Example 12–10.*

◆ Circle Progressions

Secondary dominants and secondary-dominant 7ths in any inversion can resolve to other secondary dominants, to secondary-dominant 7ths, or to any other chord qualities in a cyclic pattern, usually by progression by 5ths. This is illustrated in *Example 12–11* on pages 293–94.

◆ The V7/IV

An important concept, one that is often misunderstood by students beginning their study of chromaticism, is the secondary-dominant 7th structured on the I triad. In the key of C major, for example, the harmonic structure C–E–G–B♭ is often incorrectly identified as I7. This is totally incorrect! The addition of the B♭ immediately suggests the occurrence of a tonicization to the key area of F (major or minor (IV)). The C–E–G–B♭ must be considered as an embellishment

Example 12–11. *Resolutions of secondary dominants and secondary-dominant sevenths in inversions.*

(a) Since the bass of the $\frac{4}{3}$ in measure 1 moves upward, so can the 7th (see Chapter 7). In the V6/ii in measure 2, the 5th (soprano) is doubled in this first inversion. Although leading tones most often resolve upward, they may resolve downward in a step approach to the 7th of the ensuing chord. This avoids a leap to the 7th, and assures smooth voice leading. See the D♯ to D♮ in measure 2, the G♯ to G♮ in measures 2 and 3, and the C♯ to C♮ in measure 3. (b) Notice the resolution of the leading tones (encircled). The leading tones appearing in the soprano on the second beat of measures 5 through 7 also ultimately resolve downward one half step on the first beat of each ensuing measure, as indicated by ⌒↘ . (c) A circle progression of secondary dominants. The key signature of this piece is C major, but the harmonic content is so chromatic that no particular key is fully established for any significant time.

(c)

"Ego"

Elton John, Bernie Taupin

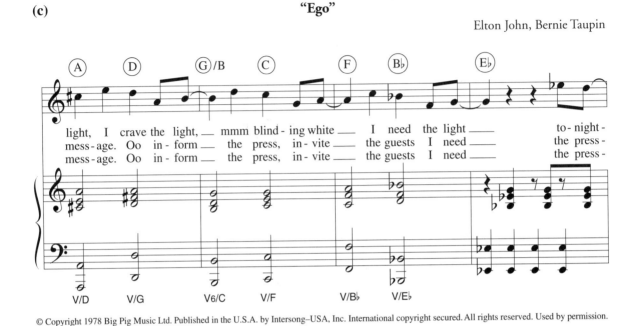

of IV and thus must be identified as V7/IV. Furthermore, this harmonic structure is not a I7 because I7 would be spelled C–E–G–B. Notice how Beethoven begins his First Symphony with this chromatic chord *(Example 12–12)*.

◆ *Unusual Resolutions*

Any dominant-function chord (typically of Mm7 quality) can resolve virtually anywhere. Although literally these are not always secondary dominants, they do occur in most styles of Western music and are considered secondary dominant functions. In any resolution of these chord structures and in any unusual resolution of a secondary dominant, proper treatment of chord factors should be applied whenever possible. Music of the common-practice period permits less freedom in the movement of the individual voices; more modern usage is not as restrictive. See *Example 12–13* on pages 296–98.

Example 12–12. Two secondary dominants and a deceptive resolution occurring in the first four measures of this work. Observe the resolutions of all 7ths and leading tones.

Symphony #1

L. v. Beethoven

(a)

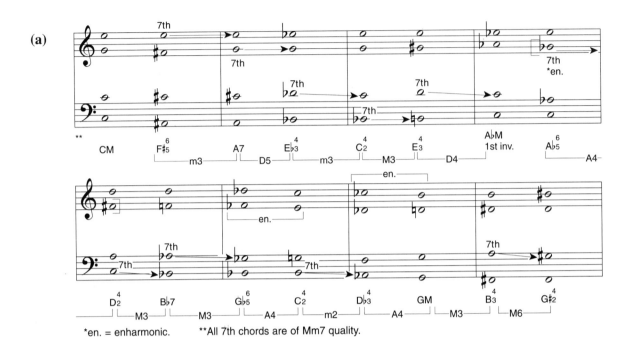

*en. = enharmonic.   **All 7th chords are of Mm7 quality.

(b)

Demand et Réponse

S. Coleridge-Taylor

(c)   *Fantasia in C Minor,* K. 475

W. A. Mozart

Meas. 10

BM: I   V$^6_5$

Common

V7/D   → Fm

V7/C   → E♭m

Example 12–13. *Resolutions of secondary dominant functions and unusual secondary-dominant seventh resolutions.* **(a)** This progression contains root movements of various types. Notice the treatment of chord factors.

(b) An unusual resolution of the secondary dominant 7th. The V$^4_3$/V would normally resolve to V(D). Here, it resolves to FMm7, the V7 of B♭. The additional note (G) is a 9th factor. The Cm triads in the fourth and fifth measures are referred to as *borrowed chords* (discussed in Chapter 14). **(c)** In measures 12 and 14, Mozart resolves the secondary chromatic function chords to a root that is a minor 3rd above the typical resolution. The seventh of the V$^6_5$ remains a common tone in the $\frac{\text{V7}}{\text{D}}$. The seventh of the $\frac{\text{V7}}{\text{D}}$ resolves downward to F in the Fm triad. The seventh of the $\frac{\text{V7}}{\text{C}}$ resolves downward to E♭. **(d)** In C major, D7 is a secondary dominant that would normally resolve to V(G). Here, it resolves to the subdominant, F.

(d)   **"Sgt. Pepper's Lonely Hearts Club Band"**

Words and Music by John Lennon and Paul McCartney

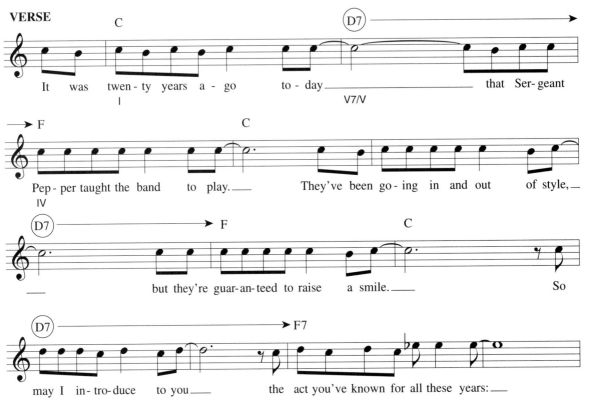

It was twen-ty years a - go to - day_____ that Ser- geant
I   V7/V

Pep- per taught the band to play.__ They've been go - ing in and out of style, _
IV

__ but they're guar-an-teed to raise a smile.__ So

may I in-tro-duce to you__ the act you've known for all these years: __

Chapter Review

Secondary dominants, which are derived from another key area, normally introduce the first occurrence of *chromatic* harmony. This adds an element of "color" to a musical work by utilizing notes foreign to the prevailing key. Secondary dominants are *embellishing chords* and often suggest movement to another key center.

Secondary dominants are major triads or major-minor 7th chords whose roots lie a perfect 5th above or a perfect 4th (inversion of the perfect 5th) below the embellished chord. Secondary dominants usually embellish major and minor triads within the key center when employed in a 5th relationship. When a secondary dominant functions in a 5th relationship to an embellished triad, *tonicization*, the momentary suggestion of a new key center, occurs.

Secondary dominants and secondary-dominant 7ths use the same labeling process to designate inversions as is used for any 7th chord. However, whenever the secondary-dominant root lies a perfect 5th above the embellished chord, the Roman numeral will be V since "dominant" implies fifth scale degree. Resolutions of the chord factors in secondary embellishments function as they do in any proper voice-leading operation; leading tones normally resolve upward by step and 7ths resolve downward by step.

Secondary dominants can also be deceptive and evade the expected resolution by resolving to a chord in the prevailing key whose root lies a 6th above the chord of intended resolution. Other resolutions of the secondary dominant include: the V/V, V7/V to the tonic $\overset{6}{4}$, secondary dominants within a cyclic pattern, such as E–A–D–G–C–F, etc., and secondary dominants to any chord outside a 5th relationship.

Anthology References

For additional usage and analysis, see the following examples in Distefano, Joseph P. and James A. Searle, *Music and Materials for Analysis: An Anthology.* New York, Ardsley House, Publishers, Inc., 1995.

deceptive resolutions of secondary dominants
Example 35.   *Album Leaves,* Op. 124, Waltz, Robert Schumann, pp. 193–200.
circle progressions
Example 58.   *Tar River Blues,* Joseph P. Distefano, pp. 341–48.
Example 59.   *A Little Duet (for Zoot and Chet),* Jack Montrose, pp. 349–54.
V7/IV (which is not I7)
Example 41.   *Waltz,* Op. 39, No. 15, Johannes Brahms, pp. 233–38.

Self-Test

1. Discuss the difference between *chromaticism* and *diatonicism.*
2. What does *embellish* mean?
3. What does *tonicize* mean?
4. The roots of secondary dominants normally lie an interval of a _____ above or an interval of a _____ below the chord of intended resolution.
5. The triad quality in the secondary dominant is typically _____ .

6. Secondary dominants belong to, and are derived from, the key of _____ .

7. Mention several functions of secondary dominants.

8. A deceptive resolution of a secondary-dominant chord resolves to a chord whose root lies a _____ above or a _____ below the normal chord of resolution.

9. The V/V or V7/V may resolve to the _____ .

10. Describe the movement of secondary dominants in a cyclic pattern.

11. (a) Spell the V7/IV in the major keys of C, F, B♭, E♭, and A♭.

    (b) Spell the V7/iv in the minor keys of B, E, A, D, and G.

12. In the major keys of D, C, and B♭, spell the secondary-dominant 7th of the ii chord upward from the bass in root position and in all inversions.

13. In the major keys of E, G, and B♭, spell the secondary-dominant 7th of the iii chord upward from the bass in root position and in all inversions.

14. In the minor keys of F♯, A, and C, spell the secondary-dominant 7ths of VI upward from the bass in root position and in all inversions.

15. The resultant chord root of a deceptive resolution of the V/IV in F major is _____ .

16. The resultant chord root of a deceptive resolution of the V7/vi in E♭ major is _____ .

17. The resultant chord root of a deceptive resolution of the V/iii in D major is _____ .

18. The resultant chord root of a deceptive resolution of the V7/V in G minor is _____ .

19. The resultant chord root of a deceptive resolution of the V/VI in A minor is _____ .

Exercises

1. Notate the secondary dominants. See the first measure of Part (a).

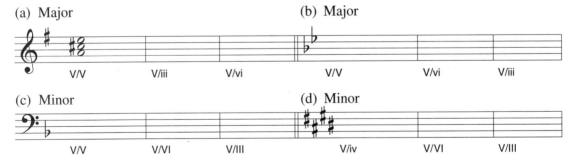

(a) Major (b) Major

    V/V   V/iii   V/vi   V/V   V/vi   V/iii

(c) Minor (d) Minor

    V/V   V/VI   V/III   V/iv   V/VI   V/III

2. Write and resolve. See the first measure of Part (a).

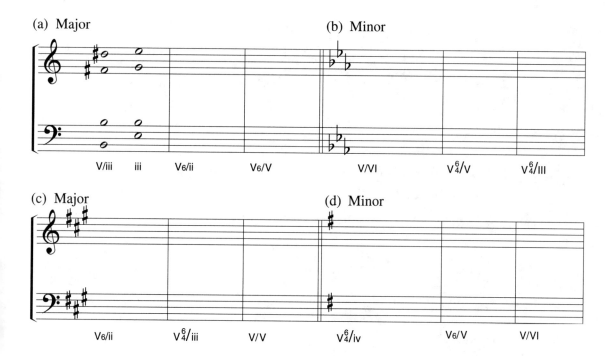

(a) Major   (b) Minor

V/iii   iii   V6/ii   V6/V   V/VI   V$^6_4$/V   V$^6_4$/III

(c) Major   (d) Minor

V6/ii   V$^6_4$/iii   V/V   V$^6_4$/iv   V6/V   V/VI

3. Write and resolve the secondary-dominant 7ths.

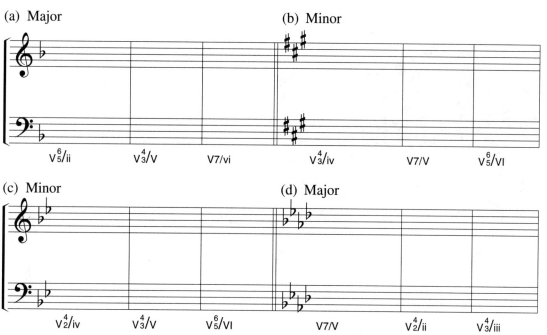

(a) Major   (b) Minor

V$^6_5$/ii   V$^4_3$/V   V7/vi   V$^4_3$/iv   V7/V   V$^6_5$/VI

(c) Minor   (d) Major

V$^4_2$/iv   V$^4_3$/V   V$^6_5$/VI   V7/V   V$^4_2$/ii   V$^4_3$/iii

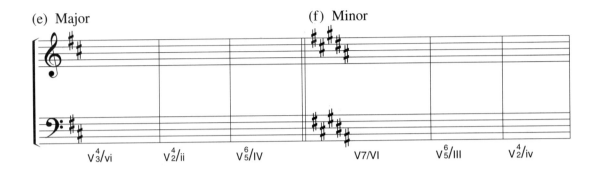

(e) Major   (f) Minor

$V\frac{4}{3}/vi$ $V\frac{4}{2}/ii$ $V\frac{6}{5}/IV$ V7/VI $V\frac{6}{5}/III$ $V\frac{4}{2}/iv$

4. Notate and label by Roman numeral the chords of deceptive resolution.

(a) Major   (b) Minor

Example   V7/iii   I   V7/IV $V\frac{6}{5}/V$ $V\frac{4}{3}/III$ $V\frac{4}{2}/V$ $V\frac{6}{5}$

(c) Minor   (d) Major

$V\frac{4}{3}/V$ $V\frac{4}{2}/III$ V7/VI   V7/iii $V\frac{4}{2}/IV$ $V\frac{6}{5}/vi$

(e) Major   (f) Minor

Example   V7/vi   IV $V\frac{4}{2}/iii$ $V\frac{6}{5}/IV$ V7 $V\frac{4}{3}/VI$ $V\frac{4}{2}/III$

(g) Major   (h) Minor

$V\frac{4}{2}/V$ $V\frac{4}{3}/vi$ $V\frac{6}{5}/IV$ $V\frac{6}{5}$ V7/III $V\frac{4}{3}/V$

5. Label all chords, as shown in the first and third measures. Also, in each blank measure, notate the dominant 7th of the ensuing triad as shown in the second measure.

(a) Major

(b) Major

(c) Major

(d) Minor

(e) Minor

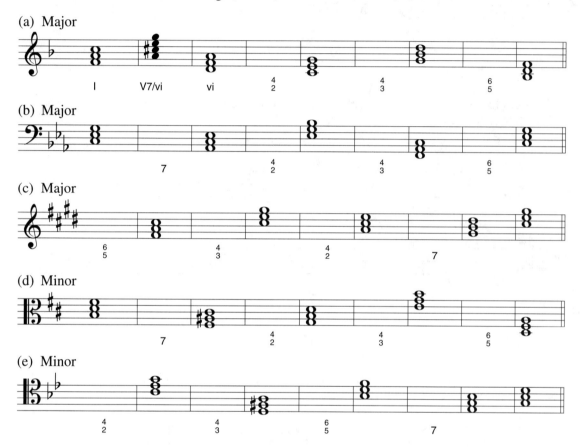

6. Label with Roman numeral and describe the function of each 7th chord and resolution. See the first measure of Part (a).

(a) Major

(b) Minor

(c) Minor

7. Write a circle progression using P5 related roots. Use triads and 7th chords. Label all chords. See the first measure of Part (a).

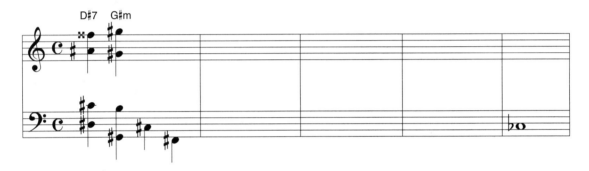

8. Resolve each 7th in an unconventional manner by avoiding resolution in a dominant-tonic relationship and deceptive resolution.

9. Compose a simple melody to each chord progression. Label all chords and nonharmonic tones.

(a)

(b)

(c)

(d)
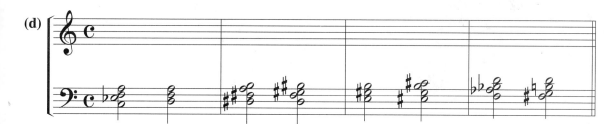

10. Complete in SATB format. Use triads, secondary dominants, secondary-dominant 7ths, and deceptive resolutions. Label all chords.

13

FUNCTIONS OF DIMINISHED CHORDS

Description and Location of Diatonic Diminished Chords

Of the various triads and 7th chords discussed earlier, diminished chords exhibit the greatest potential for generating motion in a musical work. Without exception, each diminished chord contains at least one tritone interval: the diminished 5th or its inversion, the augmented 4th. As was noted, the tritone is the most active of any interval. The fully diminished 7th chord, appearing as a vii°7 in the harmonic minor scale, contains not one, but two tritone intervals. Three types of diminished chords occur diatonically:

1. Diminished triads appear as vii° in a major key, as ii° and vii° in the harmonic minor, as ii° in the natural minor, and as vi° and vii° in the ascending melodic minor.

2. Fully diminished 7ths appear as vii°7 in the harmonic minor.

3. Half-diminished 7ths appear as viiø7 in a major key, as iiø7 in the harmonic and natural minor, and as viø7 and viiø7 in the melodic minor.

(See *Examples 5–4, 5–6,* and *5–7,* on pages 79–81, *Table 6–3,* on page 106, and *Example 6–16,* on page 119.)

Embellishing Function of Diminished Chords

◆ *Origin of Diminished Chords*

The diminished triad, fully diminished 7th chord, and half-diminished 7th chord function primarily as leading-tone chords. Their root of origin lies one *half step below* the intended chord of resolution. Whereas the dominant and secondary dominant are in a perfect 5th relationship above the root of the intended chord of resolution, the leading-tone diminished chords are in a minor 2nd relationship. Leading-tone chords other than those on viiº, as well as secondary dominants, are often referred to as **embellishing chords** because they enhance the chord of resolution.

◆ *The viiº and V7*

Like the secondary dominant and secondary-dominant 7th, the diminished triad, formed on the leading tone of a subsequent chord, functions as an embellishment of that chord. A review of the intervallic content of the two structures will facilitate the comprehension of their relationship. For example, in the key of C major, the viiº triad consists of the pitches B–D–F, with the diminished 5th interval occurring between B and F. If a major 3rd interval is added below the B, the root of the viiº triad, the resultant structure is a V7. Hence, the 3rd, 5th, and 7th of the V7 are actually identical with the pitches of the viiº triad. Notice the result when a minor 3rd is added below; a fully diminished 7th, whose chord of resolution lies a major 6th above the tonic, is formed. See *Example 13–1*.

◆ *The viiø7, viiº7, and V7*

Continuing within the key of C major, consider the viiø7 chord and the harmonic structure that results when a major 3rd interval is placed below the root, B, producing G–B–D–F–A. With the incorporation of the pitch G, an embedded V7 is created by the pitches G–B–D–F. The remaining note, A, forms a 9th interval above the G root. If the same process is applied to the viiº7 in C minor, the only difference is that A is now A♭. Remember that leading-tone diminished chords are constructed on leading tones that are a half step below the intended

CM: viiº   V7   viiº7/Am(vi)
                                     Major 3rd added   Minor 3rd added
                                     below viiº   below viiº

Example 13–1. A comparison of the viiº, V7, and viiº7/vi.

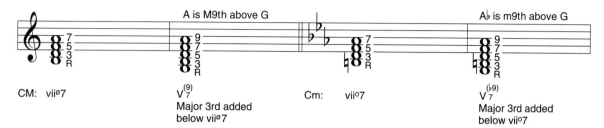

Example 13–2. *The vii*ø*7 and vii*º*7 with major 3rd added below.*

chord of resolution. It is therefore necessary to utilize the harmonic form of the minor scale; hence, B, not B♭, is used to achieve the leading tone. By examining this process one can understand why diminished structures are functionally similar to secondary dominants and secondary-dominant 7ths. See *Example 13–2.*

Applications

◆ *The Secondary vii*º

Virtually any chord structure appearing in major or minor keys can effectively be preceded by its leading-tone diminished triad, its fully diminished 7th, or its half-diminished 7th. However, it is uncommon to precede a diminished or augmented triad by its dominant.

The process of *tonicization* applies here as it did in determining secondary dominants. For example, if the vi triad in G major is preceded by its leading-tone diminished triad, consider vi (E minor) as being tonicized. The viiº triad in E minor is spelled D♯–F♯–A; consequently, this is the spelling of viiº/vi in G. Similarly, in the key of A♭ major, if IV (D♭ major) is tonicized, the viiº triad constructed on the leading tone of D♭ produces the pitches C–E♭–G♭ (viiº/IV). See *Example 13–3.*

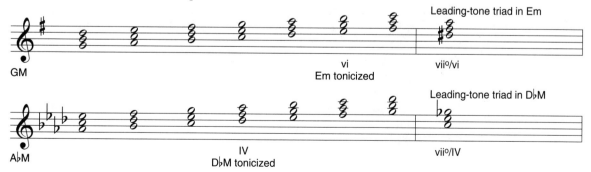

Example 13–3. *Triads tonicized by the leading-tone diminished triad.*

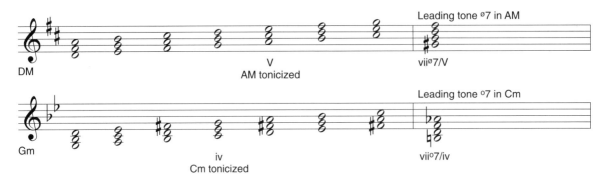

Example 13–4. *Secondary ø7 and º7 chords.*

◆ *Secondary Fully and Half-Diminished Sevenths*

The tonicization process for fully diminished 7ths and half-diminished 7ths is exactly the same as that for diminished triads. For example, in the viiø7 of V in the key of D major, V (A major) must be tonicized. The viiº triad in A major consists of G♯–B–D. In order to construct the viiø7, one additional pitch, F♯, the 7th above the root G♯, must be included. Therefore, the viiø7/V in D major consists of G♯–B–D–F♯. Similarly, if the iv chord in G minor is to be tonicized by its leading-tone diminished 7th, C minor (iv) must be tonicized. Constructing the viiº7 yields B–D–F–A♭ (viiº7/iv). Note that minor triads yield fully diminished 7ths and major triads yield half-diminished 7ths. This is due to the whole- and half-step configurations of the major and minor scales. However, it is also acceptable to use a fully diminished 7th when tonicizing major triads. See *Example 13–4.*

◆ *Deceptive Resolution of Diminished Chords*

Similar to the behavior of dominants, secondary dominants, and secondary-dominant 7ths, leading-tone diminished triads, fully diminished 7ths, and half-diminished 7ths can *evade* their resolutions. These *deceptive* resolutions are determined in exactly the same manner as are resolutions of dominants. Recall that in a deceptive resolution, an embellishing chord is resolved to a chord whose root lies a 6th above the intended chord of resolution within the prevailing key.

In effecting the resultant chord in the deceptive resolution of viiº7/vi in the key of B♭ major, for example, it is necessary to determine G minor as the vi chord. Tonicizing G minor yields the pitches F♯–A–C–E♭ as the viiº7. Remember that the harmonic form of the scale must be used to calculate the correct chord spelling. To evade the resolution of the viiº7, the chord root appearing a 6th above G within the key of B♭ will be the resultant chord; this chord root

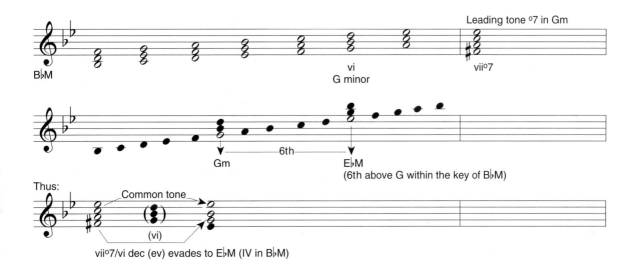

Example 13–5. *Deceptive resolutions of vii*ø*7 and vii*º*7: the seventh is common with the root of the resultant triad.*

is E♭. Therefore, the deceptive resolution of viiº7/vi in B♭ major is to an E♭ major triad. Roman and Arabic numerals indicating deceptive resolutions are followed by the abbreviation dec or ev, as in viiº7/videc or viiº7ev. See *Example 13–5.*

 Next, consider the resultant chord of resolution for the directive viiø7/Vdec in the key of D major. The V chord in D major is an A major triad. The viiø7 in A major is spelled upward from the bass: G♯–B–D–F♯. Since the resolution of this chord is to be evaded, it will resolve a 6th above A within the key of D major; hence, F♯ minor will be the resultant chord of resolution. This is illustrated in *Example 13–6* on page 312.

 As a final example, consider a directive of viiø7ev in the key of C♯ major. The leading tone of the C♯ major scale is B♯. Therefore, the viiø7 must be correctly spelled, beginning with the root, B♯, not its enharmonic equivalent, C. It must be remembered that leading tones are always one alphabetical half step below the root of the intended resolution. The correct spelling of the viiø7 produces the pitches B♯–D♯–F♯–A♯. Since the viiø7 in this case does not embellish a chord other than the tonic I, there is no need to tonicize any other chord. The viiø7 is simply as it appears in C♯ major. Therefore, the only necessary additional step is to determine the chord whose root lies a 6th above C♯. This root will be A♯, the resultant chord of the deceptive resolution of viiø7ev in C♯ major. Since the vi chord in a major key is always minor in quality, the resultant chord is A♯ minor. This is shown in *Example 13–7* on page 312.

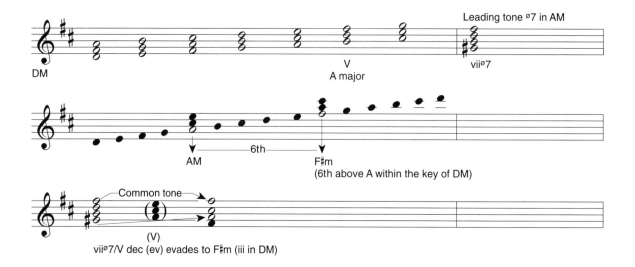

Example 13–6. *A deceptive resolution of the vii°7/V.*

◆ *Inversions of Diminished Chords*

Each of the aforementioned diminished triads, fully diminished 7ths, and half-diminished 7ths can appear in any inversion. Since the diminished triad consists of only three notes, its root position, first inversion, and second inversion are identified in exactly the same way as are those of any other triad; that is, root position — vii°; first inversion — vii°6; second inversion — vii°$^6_4$. Fully diminished 7ths and half-diminished 7ths follow the same Arabic numeral configuration as do other 7th chords.

Although this discussion mentions only those diminished chords appearing on the 7th degree of the scale, the same labeling process applies to any diminished chord — for example, ii° or vi°.

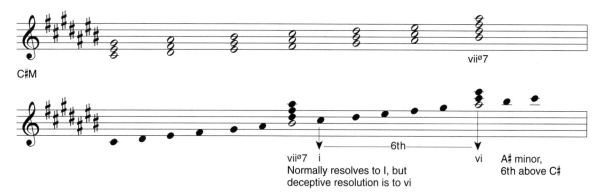

Example 13–7. *A deceptive resolution of the diatonic vii°7.*

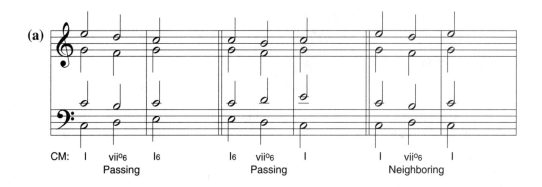

CM: I vii⁰6 I6   I6 vii⁰6 I   I vii⁰6 I
    Passing   Passing   Neighboring

(b)   **Chorale:** *Aus meines Herzens Grunde*

J. S. Bach

GM: I   IV6 V6   I   V   vi   IV vii⁰6 I   V
                                      Passing

Example 13–8. The vii⁰6. **(a)** Passing and neighboring vii⁰6. **(b)** Use of the passing vii⁰6 at the cadence.

♦ *vii⁰6, the Predominant Inversion*

In music of the common-practice period, the diminished triad occurs rather rarely in root position, but first inversions of the vii⁰6 triad are quite common. The vii⁰6 serves primarily as a passing chord in which the bass note moves in scalar motion stepwise between two chords or as a neighboring chord in which the bass note of the diminished triad moves in exactly the same manner as a lower neighboring tone. Most often, notes of the vii⁰6 are approached and left by step. See *Example 13–8.*

♦ *Preparation and Resolution of the Tritone and Seventh*

The preparation and resolution of fully diminished and half-diminished 7ths are similar in several ways to those of Mm7th chords. The two least stable intervals — the diminished 5th and diminished 7th — are best prepared by:

1. Common tone *(smoothest)*

2. Stepwise movement *(relatively smooth)*

3. Leap *(least smooth)*

Proper voice-leading procedures should be maintained when constructing a progression utilizing diminished chords. Under any circumstances, disregarding the practice of avoiding parallel fifths and octaves is incorrect. It is preferable to write an unusual doubling rather than an incorrect voice movement.

Additional Characteristics of Diminished Chords

Much more will be said of diminished chords in subsequent chapters. However, at this point it is necessary to discuss several characteristics of these harmonic structures, characteristics that make the diminished chord one of the most intriguing elements of the harmonic vocabulary.

◆ *Pitch Spellings of Fully Diminished Sevenths*

This chord contains a **symmetrical intervallic structure**; that is, all intervals are a *minor third* apart when the chord is viewed in tertian order. *Example 13–9* examines the viio7 in the key of G minor — F♯–A–C–E♭. Although the appearance of

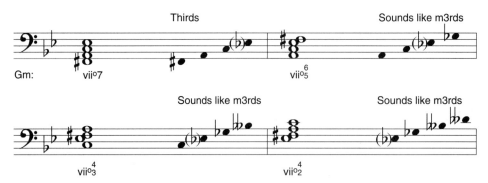

Example 13–9. Pitch spellings of the viio7 in G minor, with thirds spelled from each factor.

the tertian order changes upon inversion, the sound nevertheless remains that of superimposed minor 3rds. See *Example 13–9*.

If the vii°7 in the key of E minor, the vii°7 in the key of B♭ minor, and the vii°7 in the hypothetical key of D♭ minor are compared with the initial vii°7 in G minor, it will be apparent that all four fully diminished 7ths contain the same enharmonic pitches, though not the same note spellings. It will also be noticed that the tonics of the aforementioned keys, as well as the roots of the leading-tone fully diminished 7ths, align within minor 3rd symmetrical structures, that is, keys:

$$\overset{\displaystyle \overset{m3 \quad m3 \quad m3}{\wedge \ \ \wedge \ \ \wedge}}{E - G - B\flat - D\flat}$$

or leading-tone fully diminished 7th-chord roots:

$$\overset{\displaystyle \overset{m3 \quad m3 \quad m3}{\wedge \ \ \wedge \ \ \wedge}}{D\sharp - F\sharp - A - C}$$

This leads to the conclusion that any one of these diminished 7th chords can serve as the leading-tone diminished chord for any of the keys presented. However, this is only partially true. The "sound" of the chord can function in this way, but *the spelling must be determined by the leading-tone function of the fully diminished seventh*. For example, the vii°7 in the key of G minor must be spelled F♯–A–C–E♭ — not A–C–E♭–G♭, as it would be in the key of B♭ minor, or D♯–F♯–A–C, as it would be in the key of E minor, or C–E♭–G♭–B♭♭, as it would be in the key of D♭ minor. See *Example 13–10*.

Spelling the fully diminished 7th incorrectly is a common error. Unfortunately, many publishers of pop music use these incorrect spellings in lead sheets in a misguided attempt to facilitate chord reading. This is especially true when double flats are incurred in the correct spelling. Publishers of popular music tend to notate various melodic and harmonic structures by utilizing the most familiar symbols and spellings. Although this may facilitate the reading, it contributes to the musical illiteracy of the reader. However, the publisher should not receive the

Em: vii°7   B♭m: vii°7   D♭m*:   vii°7   Gm: vii°7

*D♭m is a hypothetical key (with 8 flats).

Example 13–10. *A comparison of the vii°7 in E minor, the vii°7 in B♭ minor, the vii°7 in D♭ minor, and the vii°7 in G minor.* All chords contain D♯ (E♭), F♯ (G♭), A (B♭♭), and C.

Often written:

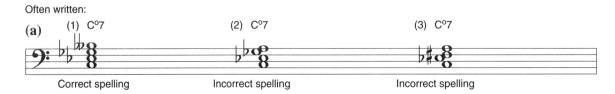

Example 13–11. Spellings of the fully diminished seventh. (a) (1) Correctly spelled as a vii°7 of a D♭m triad. (2) Incorrectly spelled C°7, but correctly spelled as a vii°7 of a B♭m triad. The actual root is A. (3) Incorrectly spelled C°7, but correctly spelled as a vii°7 of a Gm triad; the actual root is F♯. (b) The B♭°7 in m4 should be spelled from an A♯ root since the function of this chord is as a leading tone to B, the 5th of EM in m5. The E/B, a $^6_4$ inversion of EM, is a substitute for B, the dominant; hence, A♯°7 (A♯, C♯, E, G) is the leading tone °7 of B.

entire blame for this situation. Music practitioners who are not formally trained in theoretical application also help to perpetuate the practice of incorrect notation. See *Example 13–11*. Ultimately, the correct notation of any musical symbol depends upon the prevailing key and context. The musician must make every effort to use the correct form in a musical work, regardless of its style.

◆ *Alteration of Fully Diminished and Half-Diminished Seventh Chords*

Another interesting characteristic of the fully diminished 7th chord is its "dominant 7th" mutation. Any fully diminished 7th chord can be transformed into a dominant 7th by lowering any one pitch of the chord by one half step. Returning to the vii°7 in G minor, F♯–A–C–E♭, one can see that by lowering the F♯ to F, the resultant chord is an F-dominant 7th, the V7 of the relative key of B♭ major. Lowering the A to A♭ produces an incorrectly spelled dominant 7th in the key of D♭; the correct spelling of the V7 in D♭ is, of course, A♭–C–E♭–G♭. Lowering the C to C♭ produces a C♭ dominant 7th or an enharmonic B dominant (again incorrectly spelled). Finally, lowering the E♭ to D produces the correctly spelled dominant 7th in G minor or G major.

Raising any one pitch of a fully diminished 7th produces a half-diminished 7th. Thus, F♯–A–C–E♭ altered to G–A–C–E♭ produces a third inversion A half-diminished 7th; the spelling F♯–A♯–C–E♭ produces an incorrectly spelled C half-diminished 7th in the second inversion; F♯–A–C♯–E♭ produces an incorrectly spelled D♯ or E♭ half-diminished 7th in the first inversion; and F♯–A–C–E produces a correctly spelled F♯ half-diminished 7th in root position.

This concept will prove most beneficial in Chapter 20, which treats modulation. See *Example 13–12* on page 318.

(b)

"Stranded in a Limousine"

Paul Simon

Example 13–12. Alteration of a vii°7 in G minor. (a) Here, each pitch is lowered to produce a dominant 7th (Mm) quality. (b) Here, each pitch is raised to produce a half-diminished 7th (dim, m7) quality.

◆ The °7 and m7♭5

In many lead sheets, for "convenience," the half-diminished 7th is symbolically notated as a *minor 7th flat-five* chord (F♯m7♭5 or F♯m7–5, B♭m7♭5, Am7♭5, etc.) which is as a minor triad with a flatted 5th and the addition of a minor 7th interval above the root. Of course, a minor triad with a flatted 5th yields a diminished triad. The addition of the minor 7th interval above the root produces a half-diminished 7th chord. It is the belief and practice of many pop publishers and musicians that it is safer to write the m7♭5 symbol because most performers can readily construct the correct chord without a knowledge of the less commonly known half-diminished 7th. In popular styles, the m7♭5 usually precedes the dominant and functions as a ii°7. Fortunately, correct use of the °7 symbol as a representation of function is becoming more universal. See *Example 13–13.*

Several examples of diminished chords from the literature are presented in *Example 13–14* on pages 320–21. Notice the F♯m7–5 and the Bm7–5 chord symbols in "Moon River" *(Example 13–14(d)).* Both these chords can also be written as m7♭5; they are functions of the subsequent dominant 7ths and the minor triads that follow.

A **key region** is a brief section, often one to several measures long, in which a particular progression of chords, typically on the roots of the supertonic, dominant, and tonic, suggests, but does not establish, a completely new key center. Jazz musicians, particularly, rely on their sense of key regions, rather than on each individual chord change, to create continuity in their improvisations.

In "Moon River," Bm7–5 is, in effect, a ii°7 in A minor. The progression and, hence, the key region of this three-chord sequence is A minor, in which Bm7–5 is ii°7, E7 is V7, and Am is i. In the last three-chord sequence, F♯m7–5, B7, Em, the progression is ii°7, V7, i in the key region of E minor.

Example 13–13. Spellings and symbols of several seventh types.

(a)

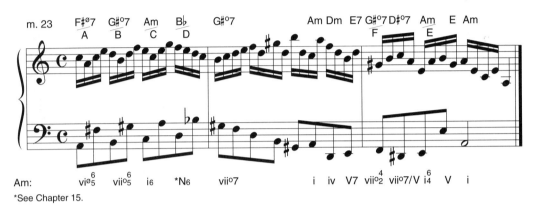

*See Chapter 15.

(b)

(c)

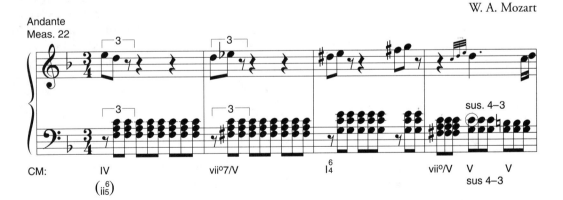

Example 13–14. Examples of diminished chords **(a)** The function of the vii°7/V is similar to that of the V/V to the tonic $\overset{6}{4}$. Compare this D♯°7 with B7, the V/V. The vii°7/V and the V/V have three pitches in common: D♯, F♯, and A. **(b)** The vii°/V to the tonic $\overset{6}{4}$. **(c)** The vii°7/V to the tonic $\overset{6}{4}$. The vii°/V to the V with a suspension. **(d)** Two key regions, Am and Em, are established through use of ii⌀7 and V7.

(d)

"Moon River"

Words by Johnny Mercer, Music by Henry Mancini

Chapter Review

Diminished-chord structures are perhaps the most active and unstable elements in the harmonic vocabulary. This is due primarily to the tritone interval in the diminished triad and in the half-diminished 7th chord, and to the two tritones in the fully diminished 7th chord. Because of their active nature and their location on the 7th degree of the scale, the resolution tendency of leading-tone diminished structures is normally to tonic chords. Diminished structures on the supertonic degree in the harmonic and natural minor can also function as leading tones to the III or become 3rd, 5th, and 7th factors of the vii°7. For example, the vii°7 in C minor, B–D–F–A♭, contains the diminished triad D–F–A♭, which is the ii° in C minor. Hence, these ii° triads move well as leading-tone chords to III, to V (as in a circle progression), and even to i. *Embellishing diminished chords* are derived from leading tones whose roots lie a minor 2nd below the chord of normal resolution.

Any triad can be preceded by its leading-tone diminished triad; any triad — major or minor — can be preceded by a fully diminished or a half-diminished 7th chord, although a ø7 to a minor triad is utilized least often.

As with secondary dominants and secondary-dominant 7ths, diminished chords can embellish any chord whose root lies a minor 2nd above the root of the diminished chord, or can evade the intended resolution. In most instances, the resultant chord of resolution is one whose root lies an interval of a 6th above the root of the diminished chord, within the prevailing key. For example, a deceptive resolution of a viiø7/IVev in C major yields E–G–B♭–D resolving to D–F–A, the ii in C major, which lies a 6th above IV (F–A–C). When embellishing a chord, the diminished structure must be extracted from the key of that chord (*tonicization*). In a deceptive resolution, after the diminished structure is extracted, the resultant chord of resolution is within the prevailing key.

Fully diminished and half-diminished 7ths utilize the same means of *identification* for inversions as do other 7ths: Root position requires a Roman numeral followed by 7; first inversion, $\frac{6}{5}$; second inversion, $\frac{4}{3}$; third inversion, $\frac{4}{2}$. Diminished triads, of course, follow the same labeling process as do any major or minor triad.

The most effective voice leading of diminished chords is achieved by approaching and resolving the chord by step. However, the approach is not as critical as the resolution. Smooth motion is obtained when the resolution is by step.

Since the fully diminished 7th contains a *symmetrical intervallic configuration* (all minor 3rds in close root position), modified spellings of certain notes can effectively place these chords within alternate key centers. The fully diminished chord B–D–F–A♭, which is the vii°7 in C minor, becomes a vii°$\frac{6}{5}$ when the A♭ is enharmonically changed to G♯, as in the key of A minor: B–D–F–G♯ (in root position, G♯–B–D–F). Fully diminished 7ths can also be altered to correctly spelled dominant 7ths when the root or 7th is lowered one half step. This is especially important in the process of modulation, presented in Chapter 20. Raising the pitch of any note in a fully diminished 7th by one half step produces a resultant half-diminished 7th sound. Spellings must always be assessed and adjusted where necessary.

Anthology References

For additional usage and analysis, see the following examples in Distefano, Joseph P. and James A. Searle, *Music and Materials for Analysis: An Anthology.* New York, Ardsley House, Publishers, Inc., 1995.

diminished sevenths, secondary diminished chords
   Example 30.   *Rondo,* Wolfgang Amadeus Mozart, pp. 135–40.
   Example 33.   *Waltz,* Franz Schubert, pp. 179–84.
deceptive resolutions of °7 chords
   Example 26.   *Larghetto,* Wolfgang Amadeus Mozart, pp. 109–14.
vii°6
   Example 18.   *O Lord! How Many Miseries,* Johann Sebastian Bach, pp. 69–73, 77.

Self-Test

1. Why do diminished chords exude a strong tendency toward motion?
2. On which scale degrees do diminished structures appear in the major and the three forms of the minor scales?
3. What is the intervallic structure of a fully diminished 7th chord and of a half-diminished 7th chord from the root upward in close position?
4. Secondary leading-tone chords are constructed an interval of a _____ below their normal resolution.
5. What is meant by *symmetrical intervallic configuration*?
6. Describe *tonicization*.
7. Explain the concept of deceptive resolution of diminished-chord structures.
8. In consideration of the fully diminished 7th chord C♯–E–G–B♭, explain:
   (a) where the chord originates;
   (b) what it has in common with E, G, and B♭ fully diminished 7ths;
   (c) how its resultant resolution is related to the keys of D, F, A♭, and C♭;
   (d) how the keys of B♭M, D♭M, and the hypothetical keys of F♭M and A♭♭M are related.
9. (a) By lowering each note of an F fully diminished 7th chord, determine the resultant dominant-7th sound.
   (b) Respell any pitches necessary to produce a correct spelling.
   (c) Determine the keys from which each resultant dominant 7th appears.
10. (a) Identify the resultant chord structure when any one pitch of the C fully diminished chord is raised one half step.
   (b) Respell any pitches necessary to product a correct spelling.

(c) Perform the same procedure with each pitch of the C fully diminished 7th.

(d) Determine the keys in which the resultant structures appear.

Exercises

1. Determine a °7 or ø7 from each of the given tritones. Complete the chord and resolve to a tonic; also resolve as a deceptive function.

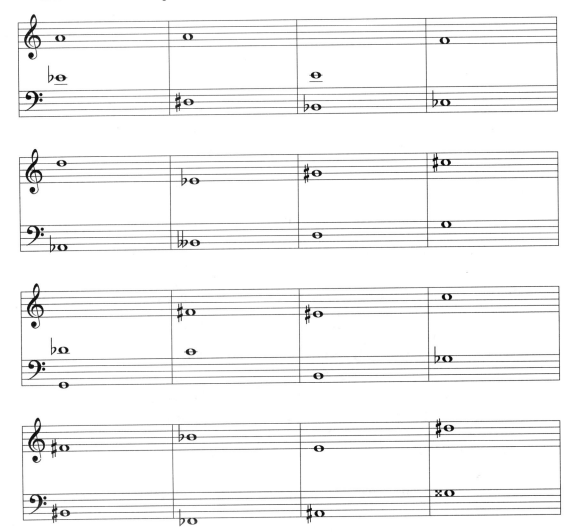

2. Determine a key in which each diminished structure can be found, as in the first measure.

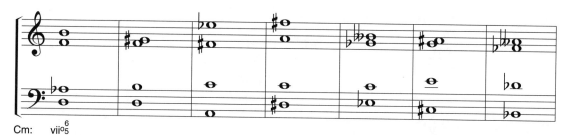

Cm: vii°$_5^6$

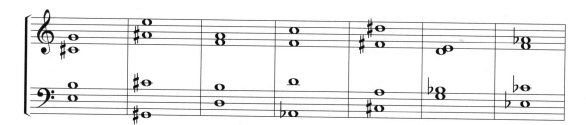

3. Determine a secondary function for each diminished structure, as in the first measure.

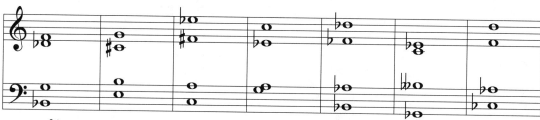

D♭:   vii∅$_5^6$/V

4. Add major and minor thirds below each root. Identify the result. Determine a key in which each appears diatonically. See the example.

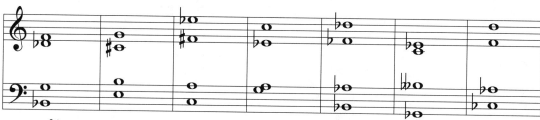

Ex.	E°	CMm7	C#°7
Key:	FM	FM	Dm
	Fm	Fm	
As:	vii°	V7	vii°7

5. Place the leading-tone diminished chord before each of the following. Label all chords.

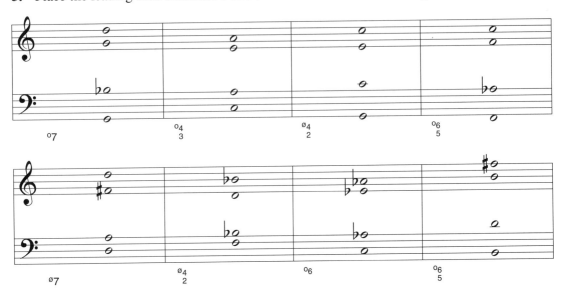

6. Write and resolve each diminished chord in SATB format, as in the example.

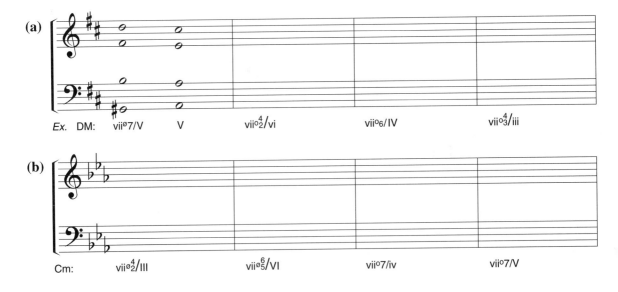

7. Resolve each diminished chord deceptively. Label all chords. See the example.

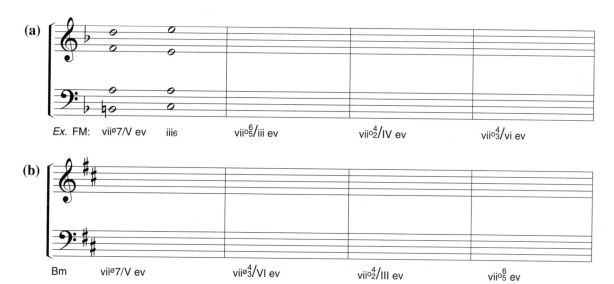

8. Respell each °7 chord three ways and determine the key in which each appears as vii°7. See the example.

9. Correctly respell according to the chord symbol.

10. Lower one note by a half step. Identify the result and label as a secondary dominant. See the example.

Ex.   B°7   F: V⁶₅/V

11. Notate each chord and apply traditional SATB voice distribution, as in the first measure.

C#m7♭5	C7	F°7/A♭	B♭7	E♭m7	A♭7/E♭	D♭M7	B⌀7/D

C+7	F#m7♭5/C	B+7	E°/B♭	A7♭5	DM7	G7+5	Cm+7

Fm7♭5   B♭M7   E♭°/B♭♭   A♭m7   D♭7/A♭   G♭M7

12. Complete in SATB format (add alto and tenor), as in the first measure.

FM: V$^6_5$ I   V$^4_2$/V   V6   vii°$^6_5$/vi   IV6   vii°7/vi   vi   I   V7/IV   IV   vii°7/V   I$^6_4$ V7   I

I   V$^6_5$/ii   ii   vii°$^4_3$/V   V6   V7/ii   ii   V$^6_5$/iii   iii   vii°7/iii   I6   ii$^6_5$ I$^6_4$ V7   I

14

BORROWED FUNCTIONS: MOVEMENTS AND REGIONS

Chromaticism

The many varieties of music offer melodies, harmonies, rhythms, shapes, structures, sounds, and personal meanings that seem to be limitless. For example, although only four basic triads exist, their *contextual* use and progression are perhaps infinite. The possible combinations of the seven pitches of a major or minor scale can be mathematically calculated, and it would seem that there is a finite number of possible melodic ideas. But when the multitude of rhythmic possibilities is applied to the pitches of these melodic ideas, the possibilities are, really, incalculable. Add harmony, orchestration, tempo, and dynamics to this stew and the results become staggering. Surely, music is limitless in its creative content and ideally, there should be some element of uncertainty as to what comes next in every musical statement. Thus, there is always more to be learned about the syntactical content and workings of music.

The chords presented in this chapter are structurally no different than any previously studied. What is different is their use and context. *Borrowed chords* and *change-of-quality chords* are chromatic, and in many cases their progression results in remote movement or relationships. Frequently, a series of these chromatic chords establishes a key region other than the prevailing key center.

Borrowed Chords

A **borrowed chord** (BC) is a chord that is taken from the *parallel key* of the prevailing music. Many students make the error of confusing the parallel key with the relative key. The distinction, however, is simple: parallel keys possess the identical tonic pitch; but unlike relative key relationships, they do not possess the same key signature. The parallel key of D major, for example, is D minor; the parallel key of E♭ minor is E♭ major. Borrowed chords can be taken from a *hypothetical* key such as D♭ minor — the parallel key of D♭ major — with eight flats. It is therefore necessary to be familiar with all possibilities, as outlined in *Table 14–1*.

◆ *Function*

Borrowed chords can be utilized at any time in order to provide an additional element of color and variety to a progression. It is more common to see borrowing done while in major keys because minor keys offer a more diverse variety of borrowed chords due to the availability of the three forms of the minor scale. Borrowed chords function in essentially the same way as do diatonic chords. The

TONIC	RELATIVE KEY AND SIGNATURE	PARALLEL KEY AND SIGNATURE
CM	Am – no ♯s or ♭s	Cm – B♭, E♭, A♭
C♯M	A♯m – F♯, C♯, G♯, D♯, A♯, E♯, B♯	C♯m – F♯, C♯, G♯, D♯
D♭M	B♭m – B♭, E♭, A♭, D♭, G♭	*D♭m – B♭♭, E♭, A♭, D♭, G♭, C♭, F♭
DM	Bm – F♯, C♯	Dm – B♭
E♭M	Cm – B♭, A♭, E♭,	E♭m – B♭, E♭, A♭, D♭, G♭, C♭
EM	C♯m – F♯, C♯, G♯, D♯	Em – F♯
FM	Dm – B♭	Fm – B♭, E♭, A♭, D♭
F♯M	D♯m – F♯, C♯, G♯, D♯, A♯, E♯	F♯m – F♯, C♯, G♯
G♭M	E♭m – B♭, E♭, A♭, D♭, G♭, C♭	*G♭m – B♭♭, E♭, A♭, D♭, G♭, C♭, F♭
GM	Em – F♯	Gm – B♭, E♭
A♭M	Fm – B♭, E♭, A♭, D♭	A♭m – B♭, E♭, A♭, D♭, G♭, C♭, F♭
AM	F♯m – F♯, C♯, G♯	Am – no ♯s or ♭s
B♭M	Gm – B♭, E♭	B♭m – B♭, E♭, A♭, D♭, G♭
BM	G♯m – F♯, C♯, G♯, D♯, A♯	Bm – F♯, C♯
C♭M	A♭m – B♭, E♭, A♭, D♭, G♭, C♭, E♭	*C♭m – B♭♭, E♭, A♭♭, D♭, G♭, C♭, F♭

*For practical purposes these key signatures are not utilized. Enharmonic equivalents are substituted. However, borrowed chords usually incorporate the correct spellings of the pitches as they appear in the hypothetical key.

Table 14–1. Borrowed chords.

use of borrowed chords creates a condition known as **modal mixture** because of the interchanging of major and minor keys.

In both traditional and contemporary practice, the Picardy third is often utilized; here, a work written in a minor key is frequently closed with a final (borrowed) major tonic chord.

◆ Borrowed Chords and Secondary Chords

When analyzing chord function, a point to remember is the difference between a borrowed chord and a secondary chord. In fact, any chromatic chord appearing in a musical work must initially be assessed as a possible embellishment. A case in point is the use of a dominant of iv in a minor key. For example, in C minor, in order to identify the use of a C major triad progressing to the iv chord, F minor, one must question whether the C major triad is borrowed from C major or whether it is an embellishment of F minor. Here, the C major triad is most likely functioning as a secondary chord rather than as a borrowed chord. This is because borrowing the tonic triad from the parallel key creates a sense of *tonal ambiguity* since it is the tonic triad that most firmly establishes the sense of major or minor key. This is not to deny that there are many situations in which the tonic triad is borrowed; however, an initial assessment must question the possibility of a secondary embellishment.

◆ Qualities

Table 14–2 illustrates resultant borrowed chords from a selection in F major, the parallel key from which the chords are borrowed. Clearly, borrowing from a minor key offers many more choices than does borrowing from the major.

When embellishing a major triad, the vii°7 is often chosen over the viiø7 for use as a borrowed chord. Although it is the viiø7 that appears as the leading-tone diminished 7th chord to a major triad, this half-diminished quality is often substituted with a fully diminished 7th; the result is smoother voice movement because of the closer proximity of the root and 7th of the fully diminished 7th to the root and 5th of the ensuing triad. See *Example 14–3*.

F MAJOR	I	ii	iii	IV	V	vi	vii°
	F–A–C	G–B♭–D	A–C–E	B♭–D–F	C–E–G	D–F–A	E–G–B♭
F MINOR (harmonic)	i	ii°	III+	iv	V	VI	vii°
	F–A♭–C	G–B♭–D♭	A♭–C–E	B♭–D♭–F	C–E–G	D♭–F–A♭	E–G–B♭
F MINOR (melodic)	i	ii	III+	IV	V	vi°	vii°
	F–A♭–C	G–B♭–D	A♭–C–E	B♭–D–F	C–E–G	D–F–A♭	E–G–B♭
F MINOR (natural)	i	ii°	III	iv	v	VI	VII
	F–A♭–C	G–B♭–D♭	A♭–C–E♭	B♭–D♭–F	C–E♭–G	D♭–F–A♭	E♭–G–B♭

Table 14–2. Resultant borrowed chords in F major from the three forms of the parallel minor scales.

Example 14–3. The vii°7 borrowed from G minor.

Sonata, Op. 26

L. v. Beethoven

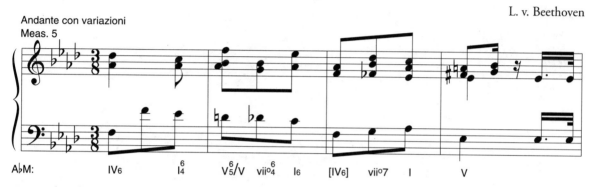

Example 14–4. The bracketed Roman numeral indicating an implied chord.

In the excerpt from Beethoven's piano sonata in *Example 14–4*, the vii°7 in the third measure is a fully diminished 7th. This chord does not occur as a fully diminished 7th in A♭ major. The vii7 is half diminished in a major key; a vii fully diminished 7th on a G root, which this chord is, appears in the key of A♭ minor. It is, therefore, a borrowed chord, and is taken from the parallel key of A♭ minor.

◆ *Part Writing*

In part writing of borrowed chords it is beneficial to keep in mind that **altered notes** — those notes appearing only in the parallel key — are seldom doubled. Otherwise, the usual voice-leading practices are observed. Altered notes are usually prepared stepwise and resolve stepwise in the direction of the alteration. See *Example 14–5* on page 334.

Change-of-Quality Chords

Change-of-quality (CQ) chords are nondiatonic, nonembellishing chords that are not derived from the parallel key. Essentially, they can be considered as the

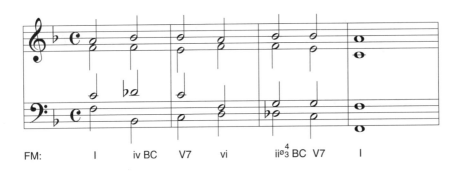

FM: I   iv BC   V7   vi   ii°3⁴ BC V7   I

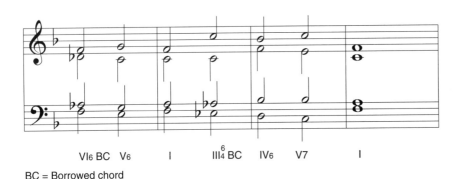

VI6 BC V6   I   III4⁶ BC IV6   V7   I

BC = Borrowed chord

Example 14–5. Borrowed chords from the parallel key of F minor.

free use of a harmonic structure. While not new in structural content, CQ chords contribute immensely to the chromatic dimension of harmony. Also, like nearly all harmonic structures, CQ chords are the result of placing one melodic line against another.

The study of counterpoint, which in its most elementary connotation is the study of note against note and, hence, melody against melody, will not be discussed here. Suffice it to say that harmony, both in its vertical aspect and in its forward progressive thrust, is the result of two or more melodic lines moving simultaneously. As harmonic structures become more complex both in vertical dimension and in progressive movement through the use of more chromaticism and, inevitably, more dissonance, melodic harmony must be considered as a developmental process behind those resultant vertical structures. Melodic harmony, then, is harmony created primarily for the purpose of accommodating melody. Chords, therefore, are not the fundamental musical foundations of harmony. It is ultimately melody that determines vertical harmonic structure.

As it becomes increasingly difficult to assess chords as functions of consecutive chords because of the introduction of chromaticism in melody, it becomes more important to determine harmonic content as a result of melodic movement. This should not suggest an abandonment of functional harmony —

or, worse yet, a "free for all" in the use and analysis of harmony. It is only after one is able to comprehend those harmonic motions that were refined during hundreds of years of musical practice utilizing the technique of melodic interplay that one should feel qualified to expand on his or her creative impulses.

◆ *Characteristics*

In the key of A major, for example, a progression reads: AM(I)–DM (IV), B7 (V7/V), E7 (V7), Am (i BC), B♭m (?), Bm (ii), E7 (V7), AM (I). Every chord except the B♭m can be explained as being either diatonic, a borrowed chord (Am), or a secondary embellishment (B7). Certainly, B♭ minor is not diatonic nor is it a secondary chord. Its use is most likely in the accommodation of a chromatic melody note, perhaps the note F. To determine whether a chord in question is a change-of-quality chord, it is necessary to consider the following steps *in order*:

1. Investigate the possibility of a diatonic function.

2. Investigate the possibility of a secondary function.

3. Investigate the possibility of a borrowed-chord function.

Step 2 requires two possibilities:

i. that of a secondary function as a dominant or leading-tone diminished chord and

ii. that of the deceptive resolution, whereby the resultant chord is not readily apparent as a typical resolution, but its root is a 6th above the intended chord of resolution.

The process of inserting CQ chords is simply an expansion of a diatonic key center, employing remote chromaticism.

In *Example 14–6* the key signature indicates B♭ major. The B7 and E7 chords in measure 2 are not from the key of B♭ major *(Step 1)*. The B7 chord

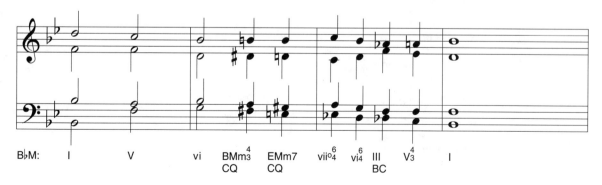

Example 14–6. CQ-chords and borrowed chords in a passage in B♭ major.

does not tonicize a subsequent triad that appears in B♭ major; E7 does not appear in B♭ major *(Step 2)*. The B7 chord is not borrowed from the parallel key of B♭ minor *(Step 3)*. It is, then, a CQ chord. Similarly, the E7 chord is not borrowed from the parallel key of B♭ minor. However, B7 and E7 can be considered secondary chromatic functions (see page 294) whereby B7 is V$^4_3$/E and E7 is V7/A.

The third chord in measure 3 is a D♭ major triad. This chord appears as a III in B♭ minor, the parallel of B♭ major, and is therefore a borrowed chord.

Related and Remote Movement

The key areas related to a tonic are the relative major or minor of the tonic as well as the subdominant and the dominant and their relative majors or minors. In the key of E major, for example, E major is the tonic; C♯ minor (vi) is the relative minor; A major is the subdominant IV; F♯ minor (ii) is the relative key of A major; B major (V) is the dominant, and G♯ minor (iii) is the relative key of B major. These relationships are shown in *Table 14–7*.

Closely related keys are keys that are separated by no more than one sharp or flat. The keys surrounding E major are all considered to be closely related keys. Any key area other than the ones indicated in *Table 14–7* are considered to be **remotely related** (separated by more than one sharp or flat) to the key of E major. The movement of chords and progressions into unrelated key areas is referred to as **remote movement**.

SUBDOMINANT	TONIC	DOMINANT
A major ——	E major ——	B major
IV	I	V
F♯ minor ——	C♯ minor —	G♯ minor
ii	vi	iii

Table 14–7. The tonic, subdominant, and dominant in E major with relative minor keys.

Key Regionalizing

Recall that the *firm* establishment of a new key center is referred to as *modulation*. Frequently, however, composers temporarily leave a key center without firmly establishing a new key, a practice called **key regionalizing**. This means that several chord structures from a related or remote key are interpolated into the existing key, but the actual tonic has not been replaced by a new tonic. This often occurs with the introduction of borrowed chords and change-of-quality chords. Several questions now arise:

1. How many chord structures in the new region constitute "several"?

2. For what length of time can the interpolated progression last before a new key becomes established in the listener's ear?

3. How is the establishment of a new key avoided?

There are many factors that have bearing on these questions — for example, style, tempo, rhythm, melodic implications, and perhaps most importantly, subjective evaluation. What one person might think is the establishment of a new key may not sound like a convincing modulation to another. There is no specific chord progression, no predetermined length of time, and no rule that mandates that certain conditions must be met before a musical passage is interpreted as either key regionalized or modulated. However, certain practices should be avoided in order to prevent actual modulation from occurring and thus affecting regionalization:

1. Avoid an extended series of chords in the regionalized key.

2. Avoid the reiteration of those accidentals foreign to the tonic key.

3. Avoid reiteration of the leading tone of the regionalized key.

4. Avoid wholly new melodic material in the regionalized key.

5. Avoid all strong cadence patterns, especially the perfect authentic cadence (PAC) and the prolonged use of the progression ii, V, I in the regionalized key. Although ii and V are quite frequently employed in regionalization, the avoidance of a prolonged tonic (I) is recommended.

6. Avoid more than two consecutive regionalizations, as this tends to destroy the tonic center.

These practices should be employed both in the composition of musical works and in their analysis. Every passage must be evaluated from the proper perspective. Initially, think of progressions as being diatonically related. Next, evaluate those chord structures that are foreign to the diatonic center as possible tonicizations. Further along in the assessment of chromatic content, consider the

"Unforgettable"

Words and Music by Irving Gordon

Example 14–8. Borrowed chords, change-of-quality chords, and key region. Notice the key signature of G major and the final tonic of C major. Tonal ambiguity persists throughout this song. A tonal region of C major is established beginning in measure 5; hence, the Fm7 in measure 10 is a borrowed chord from C minor. The D♭7 in measure 14 is a CQ-chord resulting from the harmonization of the F♮ (melodic harmony). The Em7♭5 as ii∅7 and the A7 as V7 suggest D minor as a region, but, of course, they resolve to D7, the V7 in G. Notice also the E♭ in measure 10 (the 7th of Fm7) and the E♮ in measure 26. One may interpret this latter melodic motive as the climax of the song; lyrically, this assumption is also justified. It is no wonder that this song has remained a gem in the repertoire.

possible use of borrowed chords, followed by change-of-quality chords, and finally, by key regionalizing.

Example 14–8 demonstrates borrowed chords, change-of-quality chords, and key region.

Chapter Review

Borrowed chords (BCs) and change-of-quality (CQ) chords are not uniquely structured harmonies. The terms given these chords are a result of derivation and function. *Borrowed chords* are taken from the parallel key of the prevailing key center of a musical work; *change-of-quality* chords are neither borrowed nor are they within an embellishing function, such as secondary dominants. Although the tonality of the key is not disturbed by the use of BCs and CQ chords, these chords sometimes suggest *remote movement. Tonal region* is the term employed to identify the temporary appearance of a musical segment in a key area other than the prevailing tonic key.

BCs and CQ chords function in essentially the same way as do other diatonic chords. The use of BCs in a work is often referred to as *modal mixture;* in this context, *modal* refers to major and minor. A common use of modal mixture utilizing a borrowed chord is in the Picardy third, whereby a work in a minor key is closed with a borrowed major triad.

Part writing of borrowed chords is quite similar to part writing of other diatonic chords. It must be remembered, though, that if possible, chords containing notes that appear only in the parallel key should not be doubled. For example, if the iv triad F minor is borrowed from C minor (assuming the prevailing key is C major), the A♭ should not be doubled since A♭ does not appear in C major. Too frequent doubling of nondiatonic notes causes the key center to gravitate toward the "mode" of the borrowed chord.

In the assessment of whether a chord is a CQ chord, one must question its function. CQ chords are neither diatonic nor borrowed; they are also not typical secondary functions. They are simply harmonic structures that are incorporated for the purpose of coloring melody notes. Harmony, after all, is a result of melody.

Related key areas include: the tonic, subdominant, dominant, and their relative keys. Any other movement of chords and keys is considered *remote*. The movement of chords in a remote key area does not necessarily establish *modulation*, which is the firm establishment of a new key center. The practice of entering a key area without firmly establishing a new key center is called *key regionalizing*. In the assessment of chord and key movement, one must follow the correct procedures as discussed in this chapter; for it is tempting in many analytical situations to designate a particular chord as "borrowed," rather than searching for its linear embellishing function.

Anthology References

For additional usage and analysis, see the following examples in Distefano, Joseph P. and James A. Searle, *Music and Materials for Analysis: An Anthology.* New York, Ardsley House, Publishers, Inc., 1995.

borrowed chords
Example 28.   *Sonatina,* First Movement (Allegro), Franz Joseph Haydn, pp. 121–24.
Example 29.   *Variations on a Swiss Song,* Ludwig van Beethoven, pp. 125–34.
Example 34.   *Die Winterreise,* Op. 89, "Muth," Franz Schubert, pp. 185–92.
change-of-quality chords
Example 53.   *Music for Children,* Op. 65, March, Sergei Prokofiev, pp. 301–4.
key regions
Example 59.   *A Little Duet (for Zoot and Chet),* Jack Montrose, pp. 349–54.

Self-Test

1. Why are the creative components of music considered limitless?
2. From where are borrowed chords derived?
3. What is meant by *change-of-quality chords?*
4. Define *remote movement.*
5. Define *key regionalizing.*
6. Define *parallel key* and *relative key.*
7. What is meant by *modal mixture?*
8. How is the Picardy third used in the context of modal mixture?
9. Which notes of a borrowed chord should not be doubled too frequently?
10. Explain why fully diminished 7ths can resolve to a major triad.
11. Discuss the steps necessary in the determination of change-of-quality chords.
12. List the related key centers for a work in the following keys: (a) A♭ major, (b) B major, (c) E♭ minor, and (d) F♯ minor.
13. Discuss the necessary steps in evaluating harmonic function in the assessment of (a) diatonicism, (b) tonicization, (c) borrowed chords, (d) change-of-quality chords, and (e) key regionalizing.
14. In the following progressions which begin on the tonic, identify those chords that are *i.* diatonic, *ii.* secondary, *iii.* borrowed, *iv.* change-of-quality.

    (a) FM, D7, Gm, C7, Fm, B♭m, GM, Dm, G♯o7, FM

    (b) Am, Cm, E7, FM, F♯m, B°, A7, Dm, DM, Am.

Exercises

1. Write in SATB format.

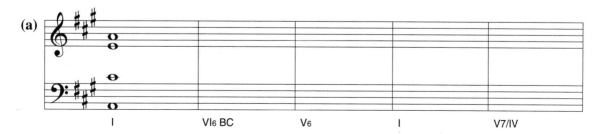

(a)

| I | VI6 BC | V6 | I | V7/IV |

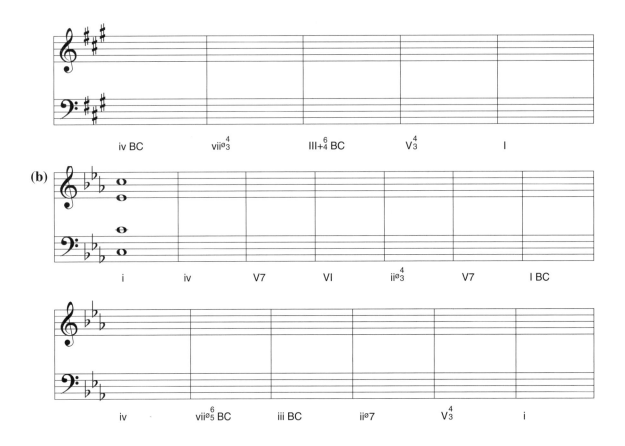

2. Provide a chord accompaniment in the style indicated. Use diatonic chords, chromatic chords, embellishing chords, BCs, and CQ-chords. Label all chords.

3. Complete in SATB format.

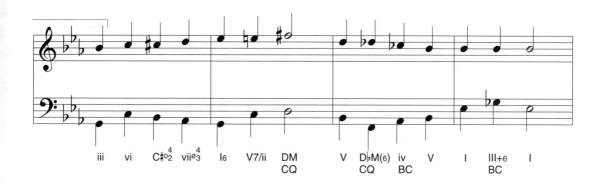

4. Label each chord with Roman numerals and chord symbols. Locate tonal regions and describe chord functions.

5. Write several eight-measure progressions in SATB format. Use diatonic chords, secondary chords, BCs, CQ-chords, and tonal regions. End in tonic keys.

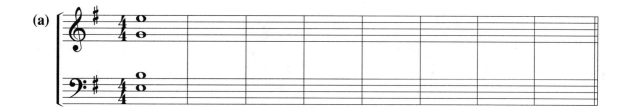

15

THE NEAPOLITAN CHORD

The Neapolitan chord, which has been in use for several hundred years, extends the concept of chromaticism. The origin of the term *Neapolitan* is unknown.

The basic idea in constructing this rather simple chord structure is not a wholly new one in chord construction; however, a heretofore unusual chromatic function is utilized. The Neapolitan chord (N) is a major triad constructed on the lowered second degree of a major or minor scale. Its most common appearance is in first inversion; hence, it is denoted by N6.[1]

Spelling of the N6

In the key of G major or G minor, the Neapolitan chord is spelled A♭–C–E♭ (as a major triad constructed on the lowered second degree of the G scale). In its first inversion, N6, the chord reads upward from the bass: C–E♭–A♭. The N6 in

---

1. Some discussions of the N6 refer to the chord as the *Neapolitan sixth* (N6th). It is this author's contention that the label "6th" is incorrect. The Arabic numeral 6 refers to first inversion, and no other first-inversion chords are referred to as "6th." (We do not say "I6th," "ii6th," "iii6th," etc.)

F major or minor reads: Bb–Db–Gb (as a Gb major triad in first inversion). In the keys of Bb major or minor, the N6 spelled upward from the bass reads: Eb–Gb–Cb. The chord must be spelled correctly; thus, in the case of the Neapolitan in Bb major or minor, it would be incorrect to construct the chord on B, the enharmonic of Cb. Note that B is not the lowered second of Bb; rather, B is the augmented unison of Bb. See *Example 15–1(a)*.

In the *Requiem: Lacrymosa (Example 15–1(b)* on page 348), the first chord is an N6 in A minor. Its derivation is from the flat second degree of the A minor scale. It appears in typical voicing and resolves to the tonic $\overset{6}{4}$. For review, notice the voice (part) movement in measures 4 through 6 in this circle progression and the deceptive resolution of the dominant 7th in measure 8. The N6 appears again in measure 9.

Characteristics of the Neapolitan

1. In a four-voice context, the third (bass) of the N6 is doubled, as illustrated in *Example 15–2* on page 349.

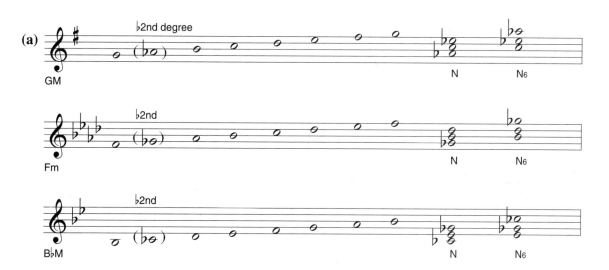

Example 15–1. Construction of the Neapolitan from the flat second degree. In part **(b)** on page 348, the movement begins with the N6. The piece is in A minor; the flat second degree is Bb.

(b) *Requiem: Lacrymosa*

R. Sorce

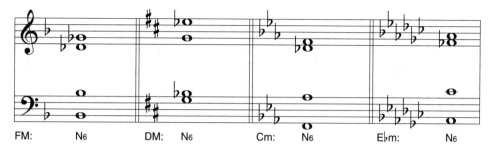

| FM: | N6 | DM: | N6 | Cm: | N6 | E♭m: | N6 |

Example 15–2. Doubling the third of the N6 in a four-voice context.

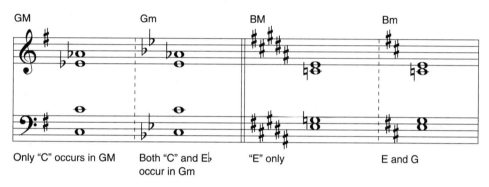

Only "C" occurs in GM | Both "C" and E♭ occur in Gm | "E" only | E and G

Example 15–3. The N6 in major and minor keys. Observe the common tones.

2. The N6 is used somewhat more frequently in the minor key than in the major. The movement is smoother in the minor key since the N6 contains two pitches from the minor key as opposed to only one pitch from the major. This is shown in *Example 15–3*.

3. The N6 normally progresses to V, V7, I$\overset{6}{4}$, or i$\overset{6}{4}$ because it functions as a preparatory chord to the dominant. See *Example 15–4*.

Example 15–4. The progression of N6 to V, V7, and i$\overset{6}{4}$.

| Am: | N6 | V | N6 | V7 | N6 | i$\overset{6}{4}$ |

Prelude in C Minor, Op. 28, No. 20

F. Chopin

Example 15–5. Root-position Neapolitan.

(a) Popular usage

(b)

Prelude in C♯ Minor

S. Rachmaninoff

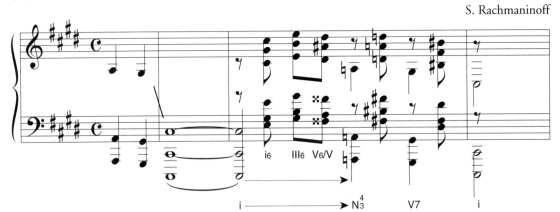

4. In the music of the later periods, in particular, in Romantic, Impressionist, contemporary, and popular music, the Neapolitan often occurs in root position. *Example 15–5* shows this use of the Neapolitan in a piece from the Romantic period.

5. The Neapolitan may contain a 7th. In certain styles of later common-practice works as well as in popular music, the Neapolitan with an added minor 7th interval above the root, and quite frequently, with additional upper partials, can be viewed as a tritone substitution for the dominant 7th.[2] See *Example 15–6(a)*. The Rachmaninoff *Prelude in C♯ Minor (Example 15–6(b))* illustrates a Neapolitan with an enharmonically spelled minor 7th (in this case, an augmented 6th) in second inversion, $^4_3$.

6. Resolution of the N6 may be interrupted by the interpolation of the I6, i6, or vii°/V, as illustrated in *Example 15–7* on pages 351-52.

Example 15–6. Alternate uses of the Neapolitan. (a) The Neapolitan relationship as a tritone substitution. In (1), E♭7 substitutes for the dominant A7; in (2), A♭7 substitutes for D7; in (3), D♭7 substitutes for G7. (b) The N in C♯ minor is D♮–F♯–A. Here, the composer added an enharmonically spelled 7th (B♯) and wrote the chord in second inversion. See Chapter 16 for a discussion of this particular intervallic spelling.

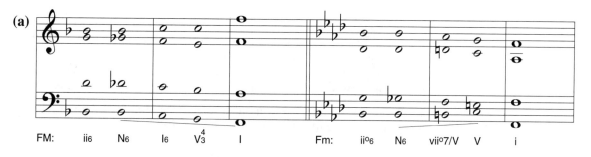

Example 15–7. Interpolations interrupting the resolution of the N6. (a) Notice the stepwise bass movement as a result of the interpolated I6, and the half-step bass movement created by the vii°7/V. (b) Interpolation of the vii°7/V between N6 and i$^6_4$.

<hr />

2. A detailed discussion appears in Chapters 17 and 19.

(b)

Fantasia in C Minor, K. 475

W. A. Mozart

7. On rare occasions, the Neapolitan is preceded by its dominant, thus suggesting a key region. See *Example 15–8(a)*. In the Chopin prelude (*Example 15–8(b)*), it may be said that the 5th, 6th, 7th, and 8th chords — VI, N, V7/VI, and VI, respectively, suggest a key region of A♭ major, in which VI is viewed as I, N is viewed as IV, and V7/VI is viewed as V7.

8. The Neapolitan is considered a substitute for the ii, ii°, IV, or iv chords. Notice the many similarities, as illustrated in *Example 15–9*.

Part Writing of the N6

Although the Neapolitan chord is a major triad occurring most often in first inversion (N6), its treatment is somewhat different than that of other major triads. Generally, first-inversion major and minor triads appear with the soprano

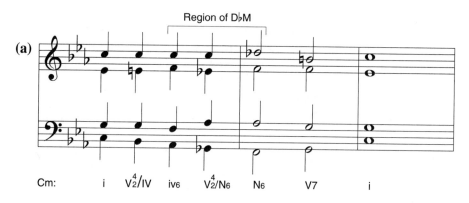

(b)

Prelude in C Minor, Op. 28, No. 20

F. Chopin

Cm: i   iv7   V7   i   VI   N   V7/VI   VI

or: i   iv7   V7   i   ⌊ I   IV   V7   I ⌋

Region of A♭ major

Example 15–8. Key regions resulting from the use of the Neapolitan.
(a) The N6 preceded by its dominant. Notice the smooth bass movement caused
by the V2⁴ inversion. (b) The key region of A♭ major resulting from the use of
the Neapolitan.

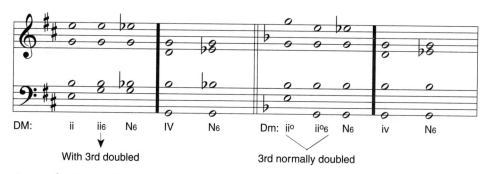

Example 15–9. Similarities among the Neapolitan, ii, ii°, IV, and iv.

doubled. This is not the case with the N6. The Neapolitan is a subdominant function, and, as such, normally progresses to the tonic or dominant. Its treatment must be handled carefully, since it is its preparation, resolution, and most importantly, its relationship to the tonic (flat second degree) that distinguishes the N6 from other major triads.

The following lists the procedures in correct part writing of the N6.

1. Double the bass (3rd) of the chord in four-part texture, as shown in *Example 15–10.*

2. N6 to V: Move the three highest voices down to the nearest notes of V; move the bass contrary to the three upper voices. *See Example 15–11.*

3. N6 to V7: Move the two upper voices to the nearest notes of the V7; move the bass contrary to the upper voices; leave the 3rd of the N6 as a common tone (it becomes the 7th of V7). See *Example 15–12.*

4. N6 to I$^6_4$ or i$^6_4$: Avoid placing the 5th above the root of the N6; invert the interval to a perfect 4th to avoid parallel fifths in resolution to the tonic $^6_4$. Move the three highest voices downward by step; move the bass contrary to the three highest voices. See *Example 15–13.*

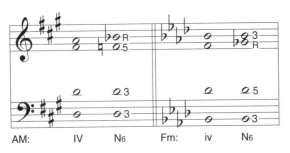

Example 15–10. Doubling the bass of the chord in four-part texture.

Example 15–11. N6 to V.

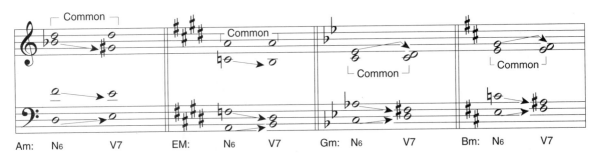

Example 15–12. N6 to V7.

Example 15–13. N6 to i$^6_4$.

The Neapolitan as a Tritone Substitution

Whereas it may seem that the use of the Neapolitan chord is almost exclusively a classical technique, it may also be observed in somewhat obscure fashion in more contemporary popular works. The purely triadic use of the Neapolitan chord is not usually a device of contemporary practice; but a derivative of it may be seen in several examples of cadential formulas.

In a popular work, the typical progression of V or V7 to I or i often contains a substitute chord for the V or V7. The chord structure whose root lies a tritone interval from the dominant, or a half step above the tonic, is among several possible substitutes for the dominant. This half step above the tonic is most often spelled as a lowered second degree. In the key of F major, for example, a substitute for the dominant C would be the chord whose root lies a tritone from C — hence, G♭. Although a tritone interval from C can be spelled as either F♯ or G♭, it is the spelling G♭ that is used most frequently since it is a minor 2nd (lowered second degree) above the tonic, F. This lowered second degree is, of course, the root of the Neapolitan.

Although it is rare that a pure N6 appears in popular style, the relationship is nevertheless retained. The Neapolitan chord that often results is of a major-minor 7th quality, and in many instances the result contains additional upper partials of the chord — for example, 9ths, 11ths, and 13ths. For the dominant substitution discussed, the G♭ substitute may read "G♭7" (G♭–B♭–D♭–F♭). Notice the complete Neapolitan (G♭–B♭–D♭) contained within the G♭7 chord. Almost any variant of the G♭ dominant structure is possible in this substitute formula. In popular practice the term that is normally used for the function of the Neapolitan is **tritone substitution**. For any chord, most often one of a dominant quality (major-minor 7th), a chord whose root lies a tritone apart may be substituted. The tritone substitution offers an additional element of color to virtually any chord progression.

Ornithology

Charlie Parker and Benny Harris

Example 15–14. *A♭7 in a Neapolitan relationship with G major and also functioning as a tritone substitution for the dominant, D.*

In the penultimate measure of "Ornithology" *(Example 15–14)*, the A♭7 is in a Neapolitan relationship with the tonic, GM7. The A♭7 is a major-minor 7th on the lowered second degree of the G major scale. This quality, of course, is not traditional triadic form, in which case the Neapolitan would have read simply as A♭–C–E♭. Notice that the root of the Neapolitan is a tritone apart from the root of the dominant, D.

Chapter Review

The *Neapolitan chord* is a major triad whose root lies a minor 2nd above the tonic of the prevailing key. It most often occurs in first inversion — hence, the "6" in its notation, N6.

The Neapolitan normally progresses to I and V in major and minor keys. In most instances, the 3rd of the Neapolitan is doubled in four-part texture; this 3rd factor is the subdominant degree of the prevailing key. In more recent music periods it is not uncommon to see the Neapolitan in root and even in second inversion.

The Neapolitan chord is also employed in popular-style works, although its use and function are often obscured by resolution and additional chord factors. It often appears as a *tritone* substitution for the dominant. The root of the tritone interval from the dominant is a half step above the tonic of the prevailing key. For example, in G major, the dominant is D. The tritone interval above D is A♭, and A♭, the root of the Neapolitan, is a minor 2nd above G. Even though G♯ is also a tritone from D, G♯ does not yield a minor 2nd above the tonic; hence, using G♯ would result in an incorrect root spelling of the Neapolitan.

Anthology References

For additional usage and analysis, see the following examples in Distefano, Joseph P. and James A. Searle, *Music and Materials for Analysis: An Anthology*. New York, Ardsley House, Publishers, Inc., 1995.

N6

    Example 35.   *Album Leaves,* Op. 124, Waltz, Robert Schumann, pp. 193–200.

N7

    Example 33.   *Waltz,* Franz Schubert, pp. 179–84.

Neapolitans in root position

    Example 39.   *Prelude,* Op. 28, No. 20, Frédéric Chopin, pp. 219–24.

Self-Test

1. The root of the Neapolitan chord is the _____ degree of the scale in the prevailing key.
2. The Neapolitan most often appears in _____ inversion.
3. In traditional practice the Neapolitan is a substitute for _____ .
4. In popular styles the Neapolitan often functions as a _____ for the dominant.
5. In traditional practice the Neapolitan usually progresses to _____ .
6. In four-voice texture, which factor of the Neapolitan is normally doubled?
7. How can the Neapolitan suggest key region?
8. How is the Neapolitan often obscured in popular-style works?
9. Spell the Neapolitan in close position upward from the bass in all twelve major and relative minor keys. Be sure to use first inversion and to spell the notes correctly as they appear in tertian relationship in a root-position major triad.

Exercises

1. The given notes are flat second degrees. Determine each tonic, as in the first measure.

2. Construct the N6 in each of the following keys. The key signature represents major and minor keys. See Part (a).

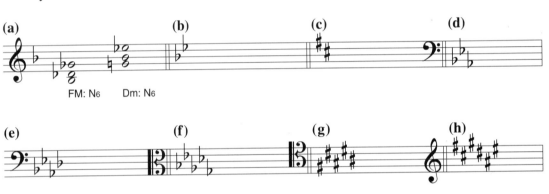

3. Label with both a Roman numeral and a chord symbol, as in the first measure of Part (a).

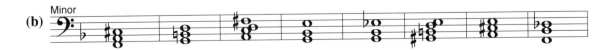

Major

(c)

Minor

(d)

4. Resolve the N6 chords to I, i, V, or V7. Label all chords.

Am:　　　V7　　　B♭M:　　　I$^6_4$　　　DM:　　　V7　　　FM:　　　V

C♯m:　　　i$^6_4$　　　D♭M　　　I$^6_4$　　　G♯m:　　　V7　　　Em:　　　V7

5. Write and resolve the chords in SATB format.

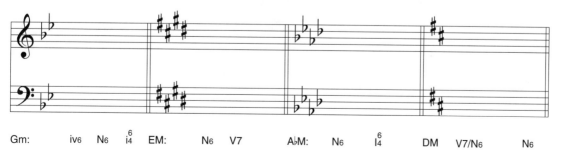

Gm:　　　iv6　　N6　　I$^6_4$　　EM:　　　N6　　V7　　A♭M:　　N6　　I$^6_4$　　DM　　V7/N6　　　N6

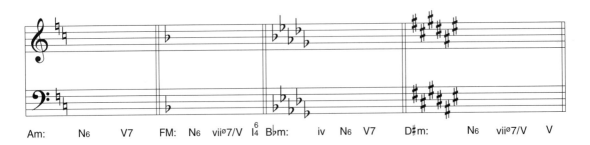

Am: N6 V7 FM: N6 vii°7/V I⁶₄ B♭m: iv N6 V7 D♯m: N6 vii°7/V V

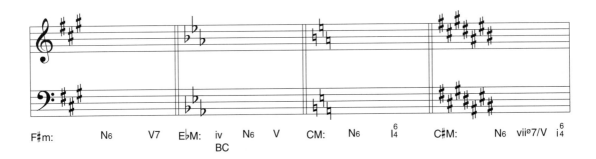

F♯m: N6 V7 E♭M: iv N6 V CM: N6 I⁶₄ C♯M: N6 vii°7/V i⁶₄
                    BC

6. Write a chord progression in C major in which the N6 is regionalized. Label all chords.

7. Write a chord progression in E minor in which the N is regionalized.

8. For each dominant 7th and secondary-dominant chord, write the tritone substitution. Label all chords. See the example.

Ex.   I   V⁶₅   Tritone substitution

9. Add alto and tenor. Label all chords with symbols.

10. Add the soprano, alto, and tenor as in the first chord of the first measure. Label all chords.

(a)
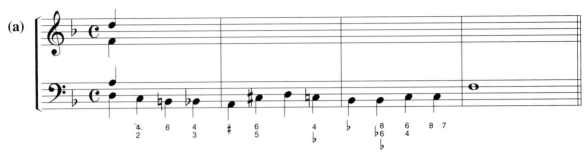

(b)
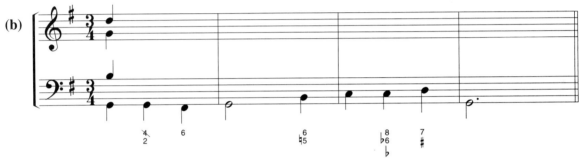

16

GERMAN, FRENCH, AND ITALIAN AUGMENTED SIXTH CHORDS

Augmented Sixths

The three types of augmented 6th chords — *German*, *French*, and *Italian* — can be identified by the presence of an *augmented 6th interval* above the root.[1]

The interval of an augmented 6th is indistinguishable in sound from a minor 7th interval. However, the augmented 6th interval contained in each of the augmented 6th chords resolves outward by half step without exception. (Recall that in the interval of the minor 7th contained in a major-minor 7th chord, the 7th resolves downward by step in virtually every resolution, although in the $\frac{4}{3}$ inversion, the 7th may resolve upward by step.)

◆ Root Origin

An augmented 6th chord is constructed on a root originating on the lowered sixth degree of a major scale or on the normally occurring sixth degree of the harmonic and natural-minor scales — hence, a minor 6th above the tonic.

---

1. Alternative origins of the augmented 6th root are discussed later in this chapter.

In the key of C major or C minor, for example, the root of any augmented 6th is A♭; in F major or F minor, the root is D♭; in G major or G minor, the root is E♭. Every augmented 6th chord will contain the interval of an augmented 6th above the prescribed root. Therefore, in C major or C minor, an F♯ will appear above A♭; in F major or F minor, a B will appear above D♭; and in G major or G minor, a C♯ will appear above E♭.

◆ *Implications of Intrinsic Augmented Sixths*

This characteristic interval of the augmented 6th chord requires investigation concerning its relationship to the prevailing key. In C major and C minor, for example, what is the rationale for the use of the two pitches A♭ and F♯? What relationship and function do these two pitches have to the keys of C major and C minor? Since the augmented 6th interval invariably resolves outward by half step, as has been discussed, what better way to reinforce and embellish the note of resolution (the dominant) than by a half-step resolution? In fact, the note F♯ of the augmented 6th interval above the root, A♭, is the leading tone of the dominant; in the hierarchical appearance of chromaticism, it is typically the first chromatic pitch to be introduced out of the diatonic system. Conversely, the root, A♭, is not a leading tone to the dominant, but its resolution tendency as it appears in the minor key is descending to the dominant G. Other possibilities for its relationship to the dominant exist. It is the lowered second degree of the dominant, and hence, a Neapolitan relationship between it and the dominant exists. If the dominant, G, is considered to be temporarily tonicized, as is the case with resultant chords of resolution of chromatic dominants and leading-tone diminished chords, it would seem that reinforcing a temporary tonic by the use of its leading tone (F♯ in this case) and Neapolitan root (A♭) is a logical explanation.

◆ *Passing-Tone Motion and Approach*

Perhaps the smoothest approach to the augmented 6th interval and the augmented 6th chord is through the IV6 or iv6. In the case of the IV6 in the key of

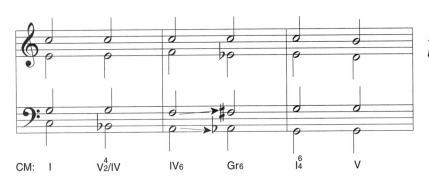

Example 16–1. Approach to the German sixth.

CM: I   V$^4_2$/IV   IV6   Gr6   I$^6_4$ V

C major, for example, A, the bass note, resolves downward to A♭ while F, the root, resolves upward to F♯. Thus, A♭ and F♯ can be considered chromatic passing tones on their way to the dominant, G. It is reasonable to assume this linear function of the augmented 6th when one is considering harmony as the result of melodic movement. As with all harmonic structure, it is linear melodic movement that must be scrutinized; for in the final analysis, it is melodic movement that determines harmonic structure. See *Example 16–1*.

Structure and Function of German Sixths

◆ *Intervallic Structure*

The **German sixth** (Gr6) consists of the following intervallic configuration above its root: a major 3rd; a perfect 5th, which is occasionally spelled as a DA4 when the resolution of the 5th is outward by one half step, as in the case of the German 6th to the major tonic $^6_4$; and an augmented 6th. See *Example 16–2*.

◆ *Resolution*

Resolution of the German 6th is most often to the I^6_4 or i^6_4. Resolving the German 6th to V would create parallel fifths, which should be avoided. It should be mentioned that whereas a German 6th sounds exactly like a dominant 7th, it contains no interval of a 7th; thus, in conventional usage, it resolves to the I^6_4 or i^6_4 of the prevailing key. Other resolutions and functions will be discussed later.

Although the smoothest approach to any augmented 6th chord is either by stepwise or common-tone motion, occasionally, one or more of its pitches are

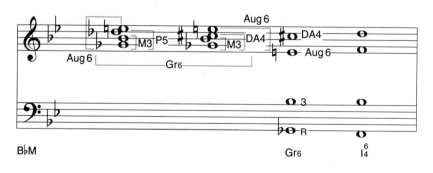

Example 16–2. Spellings of the German sixth in B♭ major. The intervals can be simple or compound.

approached by leap. Correct traditional resolution of the augmented 6th interval (simple or compound), which is outward by half step to the octave (simple or compound), assures correct voice leading of the remaining pitches. Similarly, correct resolution of the simple or compound inverted augmented 6th interval (diminished 3rd), which is inward to a unison or compound unison (octave or compound octave), assures correct voice leading. Both types assume the presence of the remaining notes of the tonic $^6_4$.

As in inversions of the dominant 7th and of leading-tone diminished and half-diminished 7ths, any inversion of the German 6th is usable, although most appear in root position. Inversions of the German 6th include the Gr$^6_5$ — first inversion, the Gr$^4_3$ — second inversion, and the Gr$^4_2$ — third inversion, as shown in *Example 16–3*.

Examples of German 6ths from the literature of the common-practice period are illustrated in *Example 16–4* on pages 367– 68. In measure 19 of the Mozart Sonata, (which is the fifth measure shown in *Example 16–4(a)*), the augmented 6th does not appear to be complete in a vertical configuration;

*Inversion of the P5 (C–G to a P4 (G–C) eliminates parallel fifths.

Example 16–3. Resolutions of the German sixth and its inversions.

rather, it is the combination of the notes F–A–C–D♯ of beat 1 that comprise the German 6th. Interestingly, and wholly by melodic design, it will be seen that the first half of beat 2 in combination with the initial bass note F in beat 1 comprise an Italian 6th with the usual doubling; this same process of incorporating the bass note F comprises a French 6th on the last half of the second beat.

In the Tchaikovsky excerpt *(Example 16–4(b))*, a German 6th appears in the 3rd inversion in G minor.

The *Waltz* by Brahms *(Example 16–4(c), page 368)* suggests an impending augmented 6th in measure 11 (third measure, first line of the example). In measures 13 and 14, a densely textured German 6th is illustrated.

(a)

Sonata, **K. 331**

W. A. Mozart

(b)

Chanson Triste

P. I. Tchaikovsky

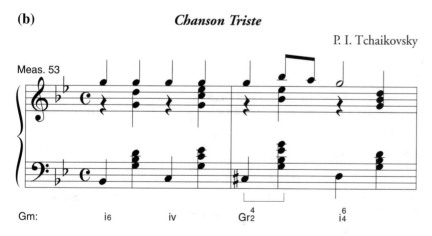

Example 16–4. Use of the German sixth in common-practice works. **(a)** Other types of augmented 6ths are formed in measure 5 by melodic design. (See French and Italian 6ths, pages 368–71.) **(b)** The German $\frac{4}{2}$ in G minor. The upper note of the augmented 6th interval is in the bass. **(c)** An impending augmented 6th appears in measure 3. The chord is realized in measures 5 and 6 and resolves directly to a V.

(c)   *Waltz*, Op. 39, No. 2

J. Brahms

Structure and Function of French Sixths

◆ *Intervallic Structure*

The structure of the **French sixth** (Fr6) differs from that of the German 6th in only one respect. Whereas the German 6th contains a perfect 5th interval above the root (or the enharmonic DA4), *the French 6th contains an augmented 4th interval above the root.*

◆ *Resolution*

The root and augmented 6th interval resolve outward by half step to the dominant note in any traditional resolution of an augmented 6th chord. In the

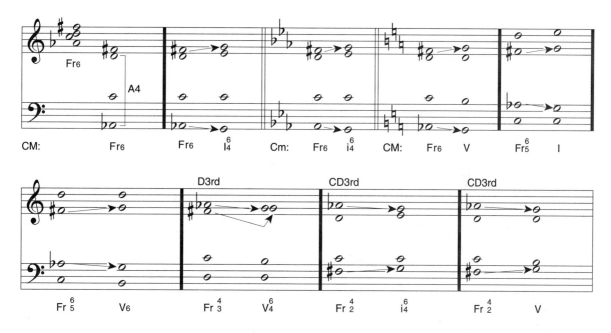

Example 16–5. *Inversions and resolutions of the French sixth identified with seventh-chord numerals.*

resolution of the French 6th to the $\overset{6}{4}$, the 3rd remains as a common tone and the augmented 4th resolves upward by step to the 3rd of the $\overset{6}{4}$. In the resolution of the French 6th to V, the 3rd resolves downward by step to the 3rd of the dominant and the augmented 4th remains as a common tone.

Like the German 6th, the French 6th appears most often in root position, but inversions are possible. Inversions are identified by Arabic numerals: Fr $\overset{6}{5}$ — first inversion, Fr $\overset{4}{3}$ — second inversion, Fr $\overset{4}{2}$ — third inversion. As in the German 6th, care must be taken in resolution of the augmented 6th interval and its inversion, the diminished 3rd. See *Example 16–5.*

◆ French Sixths and Supertonics

If any augmented 6th appears to be derived from an *alternative* scale degree, surely it is the French 6th. In the construction of the French 6th in the key of C major or C minor, for example, the spelling in close position reads: A♭–C–D–F♯. Note the similarity between this structure and the pitch content of the V7/V (D–F♯–A–C) — a dominant 7th on the supertonic. The only difference, of course, is the note A♭, which when incorporated into the V7/V creates a V7♭5/V. See *Example 16–6 on page 370.*

CM: Fr6   V7/V   Fr6   V3♭5/V

Example 16–6. A comparison of the French sixth with the supertonic major-minor seventh chord.

Example 16–7 illustrates a French 6th in E♭ major. Notice the intervallic configuration of this close-voiced French 6th. Here, C♭ is the root, E♭ is the 3rd, F is the augmented 4th above the root, and A is the augmented 6th above the root. Considering the supertonic, F, as a root derivation produces F–A–C♭–E♭, the V7♭5/V.

◆ Seventh Flat-Five Chords and French Sixths

Not all dominant 7th flat-five (♭5) chords are considered French 6ths, as illustrated in *Example 16–8*. A dominant 7th flat-five chord can appear as any dominant or chromatic secondary dominant — for example, as a V7♭5/vi. If this embellishment were to be considered in G major, the V7♭5 would be spelled B–D♯–F–A, which is the spelling of the dominant 7th flat-five of the E minor triad. Augmented 6th chords are defined as such because of their relationship to the prevailing tonic.

Sonata Pathétique

L. v. Beethoven

Rondo, meas. 43

E♭M: I   V2   I6   IV6   Fr6   V

Example 16–7. A French sixth in E♭ major. Compare the pitches of this chord with the supertonic, F7♭5 (V3♭5/V).

GM: V7♭5/vi   vi

Example 16–8. A dominant seventh flat 5 that is not a French sixth chord. A French sixth or any augmented sixth chord constructed from the root B, as in this example, would appear in the key of D♯M, a hypothetical key containing nine sharps, or in D♯m. Futhermore, F♮ would be spelled as E♯ in the French sixth.

Structure and Function of Italian Sixths

◆ *Intervallic Structure*

The **Italian sixth** (It6) contains no type of 4th or 5th above the root; its structure consists of a root, a major 3rd, and the interval of the augmented 6th. Its sound is less dense than that of the German 6th.

◆ *Resolution*

The resolution of the Italian 6th is to V. In a four-voice texture, the factor to be doubled is the 3rd, the tonic of the key. Therefore, in this resolution the augmented 6th interval again must be resolved outward by half step to the doubled dominant degree; each note of the doubled 3rd resolves by step in contrary motion, one to the 3rd of the dominant and the other to the 5th of the dominant. Since the Italian 6th contains no type of 4th or 5th above the root, only a root position and two inversions are possible: the It$\frac{6}{5}$ — first inversion — and the It$\frac{4}{2}$ — third inversion. (The $\frac{4}{3}$ does not exist.) This is illustrated in *Example 16–9.*

A use of the Italian 6th, from Beethoven's *Sonata Pathétique*, is illustrated in *Example 16–10* on page 372 . Notice the lack of a 4th or 5th from the root, C♭.

More on Augmented Sixths

Although augmented 6ths appear in both major and minor keys, their linear movement is significantly *smoother* in minor keys because of the common-tone

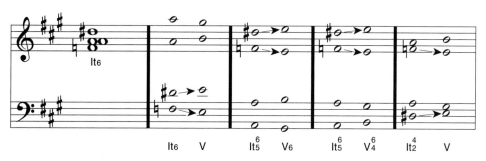

Example 16–9. Inversions and resolutions of the Italian sixth identified by seventh-chord numerals.

Sonata Pathétique

L. v. Beethoven

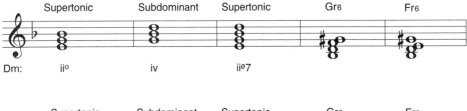

Example 16–10. *An Italian sixth in E♭ minor.*

factor inherent in the root, which is the sixth degree of the harmonic and nat-ural-minor scales. The close relationship of augmented 6ths to supertonics and subdominants is also rather conspicuous. Compare any of the augmented 6th structures to the supertonics and subdominants in the keys in which they appear, and several pitches will be seen to be in common. It will also be appar-ent that more pitches are in common in minor keys. See *Example 16–11.*

◆ *Popular Genres*

As a result of incorrect pitch spellings, augmented 6th chords in popular music are rather inconspicuous. It is rare, indeed, to find the authentic spelling of an augmented 6th in these genres. For example, the German 6th in G is properly

Example 16–11. *A comparison of the German and French chords with the super-tonic and subdominant triads in major and minor keys.* The Italian sixth is omitted because it contains one less factor than the German sixth or French sixth.

spelled: E♭–G–B♭–C♯. A German 6th function in popular music (preceding I or V) in G most certainly would be spelled: E♭–G–B♭–D♭ — the correct spelling of an E♭ major-minor 7th. Although the spelling of the augmented 6th may be obscured in the composer's or publisher's interpretation, the function and effect are nevertheless preserved.

To locate these characteristic sounds in popular works, one need only search the cadential areas of phrases and sections. In popular literature, the functional augmented 6th normally appears as a half-step embellishment above the dominant, with the root normally spelled as a minor 2nd (as in common-practice literature), rather than as an augmented unison. However, it is *uncommon* in popular music for the "augmented 6th" to resolve to the $^6_4$ inversion of the tonic. The most likely resolution is to I, V, or V7, or to a derivative of the dominant. These augmented 6ths are also frequently expanded to incorporate other chord factors, such as 9ths, 11ths, and 13ths, and may also exhibit alterations of these factors. Regardless of their spellings, alterations, often unusual voice leadings, and resolutions, the unmistakable thrust toward the tonic or dominant, is omnipresent.

In *Example 16–12*, B7, the augmented 6th, is structured from the *enharmonic* lowered sixth degree of the E♭ major scale, B, instead of C♭, and in this example is an augmented unison rather than a minor 2nd above the dominant, B♭. Its resolution is to I7. However, evidence of its function as an augmented 6th can be seen in the treatment of the melody note, A. This note is the 7th of the B7 chord. Sevenths normally resolve downward. But this 7th, in actuality, is the augmented 6th interval above the root, C♭, of the obscured German 6th, and hence resolves upward.

"I Remember Duke"

Music by Woody Herman

Example 16–12. Use of the B7 penultimate chord, which is enharmonically C♭, the root of the augmented sixth in E♭.

Example 16–13. The German sixth in which #4 is considered the root.

◆ Alternative Origin: the #4

Many theorists believe that the actual root of the augmented 6th is the raised fourth degree of the scale and that construction and identification should be from this root.

Using the key of D major or D minor as an example, the root of any augmented 6th is derived from the lowered sixth degree of D major or from the normally occurring sixth degree in D harmonic or natural minor, as has been described earlier in this chapter. The resultant root is, therefore, B♭. In the alternative method, G♯, the raised fourth degree of the scale supplies the root. Construction of the German 6th, as an example, would consist of the following intervallic configuration from G♯: diminished 3rd (B♭), major 3rd (D), minor 3rd (F). The resultant configuration yields G♯–B♭–D–F as the root position of the chord. As a consequence, the figured-bass numerals are modified to adapt to this procedure and the resulting G♯–B♭–D–F yields the root position Gr6. Similarly, B♭–D–F–G♯ yields the first inversion, or Gr $\overset{6}{5}$; D–F–G♯–B♭ yields the second inversion, or Gr $\overset{4}{3}$; and F–G♯–B♭–D yields the third inversion, or Gr $\overset{4}{2}$. This system is logical since the alphabetical appearance of the pitches is consistent with the Arabic numerals. Either method yields the same results, the difference being merely in the interpretation of the position of the chord. The reader should be familiar with both procedures. See *Example 16–13.*

Chapter Review

The *French, German,* and *Italian 6th* chords provide another process of embellishment occurring at cadences and at other strategic locations in musical passages. The root of the augmented 6th is derived from the lowered sixth degree of the major scale or from the naturally occurring sixth degree of the harmonic and nat-ural-minor scales. Alternative root origins are from the supertonic and raised fourth degree of the scale.

The characteristic interval of the augment-ed 6th chord is the augmented 6th interval, which occurs between the root (taken from the lowered sixth degree) and the 6th above the root. This augmented 6th interval invariably resolves outward by step. Inversion of the aug-mented 6th interval (the diminished 3rd) resolves inward by step.

Augmented 6th chords are normally employed in root position, although any inver-sion is possible. Root positions of these chords are identified by type — Gr, Fr, It; inversions follow the same procedure as for any other 7th chord, even though no interval of a 7th occurs.

The sound of the augmented 6th is that of a 7th chord containing a minor 7th interval; there-fore, the labeling process is maintained.

Although each type of augmented 6th contains an augmented 6th interval, the differ-ence among the chords lies in the 3rd factor — the 5th, which is either alternately spelled or, as in the Italian 6th, omitted.

Augmented 6ths tend to resolve to I and V chords, as well as to inversions of these chords. It will be seen in subsequent chapters how aug-mented 6ths can resolve in other ways.

The augmented 6th does not appear as such in popular genres; however, its function can still be present as a half-step major-minor 7th-chord (dominant 7th) embellishment above the dominant.

Anthology References

For additional usage and analysis, see the following examples in Distefano, Joseph P. and James A. Searle, *Music and Materials for Analysis: An Anthology.* New York, Ardsley House, Publishers, Inc., 1995.

German sixths
  Example 31.   *Sonata,* Hob. XVI, No. 27, First Movement, Franz Joseph Haydn, pp. 141–48.
  Example 32.   *Sonata,* K. 333, Wolfgang Amadeus Mozart, pp. 149–78.
  Example 35.   *Album Leaves,* Op. 124, Waltz, Robert Schumann, pp. 193–200.
French sixths
  Example 33.   *Waltz,* Franz Schubert, pp. 179–84.
  Example 39.   *Prelude,* Op. 28, No. 20, Frédéric Chopin, pp. 219–24.
Italian sixths
  Example 29.   *Variations on a Swiss Song,* Ludwig van Beethoven, pp. 125–34.

Self-Test

1. The augmented 6th interval in the augmented 6th chord resolves _____ .
2. The diminished 3rd interval (the inversion of the augmented 6th interval) in the augmented 6th chord resolves _____ .

3. Discuss three derivations of the augmented 6th chord.

4. Explain the linear function of the notes of the augmented 6th interval in their resolution to the dominant note.

5. Describe the intervallic configurations of (a) the German 6th, (b) the French 6th, and (c) the Italian 6th.

6. Why do augmented 6th chords often utilize the same inversion labels as major-minor 7th chords?

7. Why is a $\frac{4}{3}$ inversion of the Italian 6th impossible when the root is derived from the lowered sixth degree of the major scale?

8. How do dominant 7th flat-five chords compare with French 6th chords? In what respects are they different?

9. Which note in the Italian 6th is doubled in four-part texture?

10. Explain how the presence of an augmented 6th chord in popular music can be detected.

11. How can an augmented 6th chord be viewed as a tritone substitution of the V/V?

12. How might a German 6th chord in the key of E major tonicize F major?

13. How might a German 6th chord in the key of F minor tonicize F♯ minor?

14. How might a German 6th chord in the key of D minor tonicize C minor?

15. Spell (a) the German 6th chord, (b) the French 6th chord, and (c) the Italian 6th chord in all the major and minor keys.

Exercises

1. Write an augmented 6th interval above each note.

2. Write a diminished 3rd interval above each note.

3. Determine a key in which each augmented 6th and diminished 3rd interval appears in an augmented 6th chord.

4. Write the German, French, and Italian 6th chords in B, A, G, F, E♭, and D♭. Use various voicings. Write key signatures.

(a) German

(b) French

(c) Italian

5. Write and resolve to I, V, or inversions of these. Use SATB format.

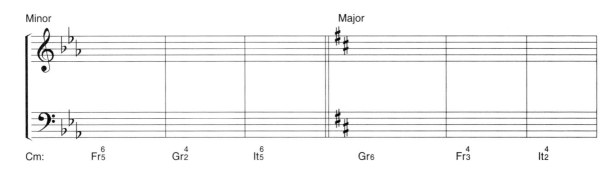

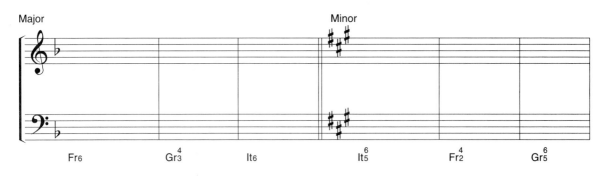

6. Determine a key in which the dominant 7♭5 chords would appear as French 6ths with enharmonically spelled A4ths. Label the inversions. See the first measure.

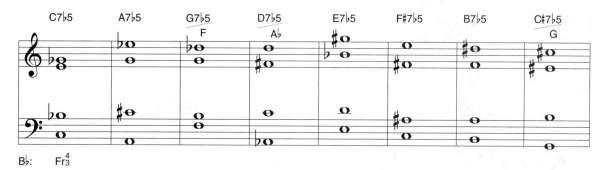

7. Using the given bass note as a raised fourth degree of a scale, construct the required augmented 6th chord. Indicate the keys in which each appears.

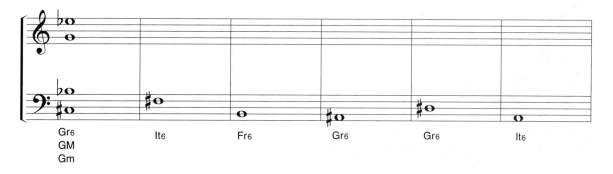

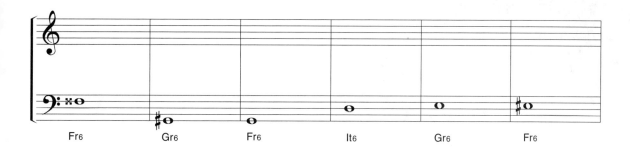

8. Write the correct inversion, considering ♯4 as the root.

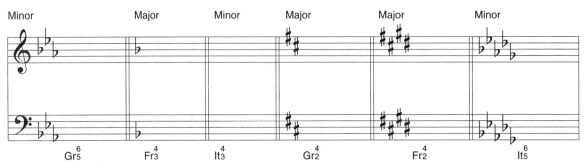

9. Complete in SATB format. Label all chords and modulations.

(a)

(b)

(c)

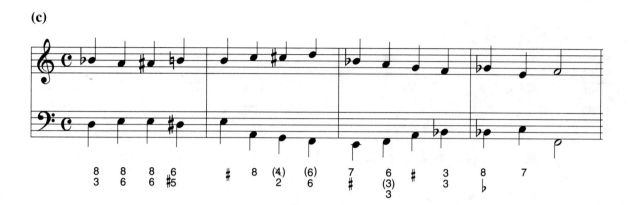

17

UPPER-PARTIAL CHORDS: NINTHS, ELEVENTHS, AND THIRTEENTHS

Until now, the discussion has been focused on those chords that are constructed within an *octave*. Although brief mention has been made of 9ths, 11ths, and 13ths, no details concerning these structures have been presented. The tertian ordering of chord construction has been limited to chords extending only through the major 7th.

Since the chord structures discussed have been constructed with superimposed 3rds, it is a logical assumption that this process can be continued in the construction of upper-partial chords. For practical purposes, however, the extension of tertian construction terminates with the 13th chord. A chord of the 15th would duplicate the octave in a diatonic environment, and chords of the 17th, 19th, etc. would duplicate the 3rd, 5th, etc., respectively. Although alterations of scale degrees permit chord structures beyond the 13th, the concern here is to limit the discussion of harmonic construction to the most prevalent chords in both common-practice and popular composition. See *Example 17–1.*

Characteristics of Upper-Partial Chords

Ninths, 11ths, and 13ths substantially increase the problems as well as the possibilities involved in usage, voice leading, and identification. In chord structures previously discussed, the primary concerns were with progression, doublings, and

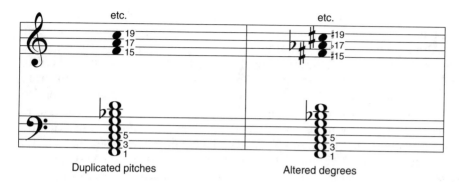

etc.   etc.

Duplicated pitches   Altered degrees

Example 17–1. Extension of tertian stacking by chromatic alteration from an F root. Note that in the second measure, ♯15, ♭17, and ♯19 are chromatic alterations of 15, 17, and 19 in the first measure.

voice leading. Upper-partial chords are *extensions* of chords previously examined; *they are not new in function.* Whereas certain factors of the chords must be treated carefully and alterations of some chord factors possess particular resolution tendencies, the fact remains that these upper-partial chords are extensions of simpler chords and the functions of these upper partials *imitate* those of these simpler structures. What is achieved by the construction of upper-partial chords is added dissonance, color, and tension.

Ninth Chords

◆ Diatonic Ninths

The discussion of 9ths begins with the various types available. Their qualities, Roman-numeral identifications, and popular-use chord symbols are listed in *Table 17–2* on page 384, in which the keys of C major and C minor serve as key centers. Although the chord structures marked with asterisks are possible as ninths, they are infrequently used in common practice and in popular genres. A cursory examination will reveal reasons for avoidance. In the first structure, E–G–B–D–F, isolation of the last four pitches, G–B–D–F, produces a complete V7. The presence of the E in the chord anticipates the 3rd of the chord of resolution, which is, of course, also the note of typical resolution of the 7th, F. In the structure B–D–F–A–C, a similar situation arises. Isolating the first four pitches, B–D–F–A, produces a complete viiø7. The usual chord of resolution is the I, whose root is now contained as the 9th factor of the viiø9 and thus is destructive of the resolution tendency of the leading tone, B. In the structure E♭–G–B–D–F, the condition is similar to that of the iii9 in C major;

here it appears in C minor. The use of the structure A♭–C–E♭–G–B is uncommon, but does occur occasionally. The problem arises in the major-minor conflict. Although it is not apparent from the spelling, a conflict nevertheless exists between the third, C, and the augmented 9th, B. The B, when considered enharmonically as C♭, produces the minor 3rd required to form an A♭ minor triad. One important issue should be discussed here. Although the major, minor 7th, augmented 9th does not appear in *Table 17–2*, it is a 9th chord that is used extensively, especially in jazz and in certain styles of popular music. Had the structure in question, that is, A♭–C–E♭–G–B, contained a G♭ instead of a G, the chord would be rather common. Finally, the structure B–D–F–A♭–C presents the same situation as the B–D–F–A–C in C major discussed previously.

C MAJOR

PITCHES	QUALITY	ROMAN NUMERAL	CHORD SYMBOL
C–E–G–B–D	M, M7, M9	I9	CM9
D–F–A–C–E	m, m7, M9	ii$\overset{9}{7}$	Dm9
E–G–B–D–F*	m, m7, m9	iii9	Em7♭9, Em7–9
F–A–C–E–G	M, M7, M9	IV$\overset{9}{7}$	FM9
G–B–D–F–A	M, m7, M9	V$\overset{9}{7}$	G9
A–C–E–G–B	m, m7, M9	vi$\overset{9}{7}$	Am9
B–D–F–A–C*	dim, m7, m9	vii$ø\overset{9}{7}$	Bm7♭5♭9, Bm7$\overset{-5}{-9}$

C MINOR (HARMONIC)

PITCHES	QUALITY	ROMAN NUMERAL	CHORD SYMBOL
C–E♭–G–B–D	m, M7, M9	i$\overset{9}{7}$	Cm9+7, Cm9M7
D–F–A♭–C–E♭	dim, m7, m9	ii$ø\overset{♭9}{7}$	Dm7♭5♭9, Dm7$\overset{-5}{-9}$
E♭–G–B–D–F*	Aug, M7, M9	III+$\overset{9}{7}$	E♭M9+5
F–A♭–C–E♭–G	m, m7, M9	iv$\overset{9}{7}$	Fm9
G–B–D–F–A♭	M, m7, m9	V$\overset{♭9}{7}$	G7♭9
A♭–C–E♭–G–B*	M, M7, Aug9	VI$\overset{♯9}{7}$	A♭M7+9, A♭M7♯9
B–D–F–A♭–C*	dim, dim7, m9	vii°$\overset{♭9}{7}$	Bdim7♭9, B°7♭9

* These pitches are discussed in the text.

Table 17–2. Diatonic ninths. Chord symbols are not standardized. For example, +, ♯, or Aug indicates that the factor is raised one half step; −, ♭, or dim indicates that the factor is lowered one half step.

Example 17–3. *The dominant 9, ♭9, and ♯9.*

◆ Ninth Factors

Essentially, only three possible 9th additions to a chord root exist — the *natural ninth*, the *lowered ninth*, and the *raised ninth*. From G, for example, the natural-appearing 9th is A, the lowered 9th is A♭, and the raised 9th is A♯. Care must be taken when considering 9ths that normally appear as sharp or flat notes. For example, the natural-occurring 9th above B is C♯; lowering the 9th produces C, and raising the 9th produces C𝄪 — not the enharmonic note D. Similarly, a natural-occurring 9th above D♭ is E♭; lowering the 9th produces E♭♭; raising the 9th produces E. In another situation involving the root E♭, the natural-occurring 9th is F. Lowering the 9th produces F♭, rather than the more common pitch of E. Raising the 9th produces F♯. A normally occurring 9th is labeled simply by the numeral 9, a lowered 9th by either ♭9 or −9, and a raised 9th by either ♯9 or +9. See *Example 17–3*.

◆ Major Ninths and Dominant Ninths

Most 9th chords require the presence of a 7th in order to generate the 9th factor as an extension. A *major 9th chord* (M9), for example, requires the presence of the major 7th interval above the root since a major 9th chord consists of a major triad with major 7th and major 9th intervals added. (Refer to *Table 17–2.*) A *dominant 9th chord* (9) requires the presence of a minor 7th interval above the root because the chord consists of a major-minor 7th and a major 9th.

◆ Hybrid Structures

Ninth chords that do not normally appear in the major or harmonic minor are considered *hybrid* and require further investigation.

The chordal structure C–E–G–B♭–D♯ does not appear in any major or minor scale as a tertian arrangement; yet the chord is used quite extensively, especially in certain popular formats. It is referred to as a **major-minor seventh, raised ninth** (C7♯9). The chord is dominant in quality, and it is a logical conclusion that it appears in some type of F tonality. However, D♯ is present neither in F major nor in F minor. If the D♯ were considered as an enharmonic E♭, then C, the root, could be seen as generating a major and a minor quality. (See *Example 17–4.*) But D♯ is not E♭; it is the raised 9th above the C root and must be spelled accordingly. This harmonic structure is not a naturally occurring chord in F major or F minor and must be considered a hybrid. Any chord that does not naturally occur in the major or minor key is considered an **altered chord**.

◆ Add 9 Chords

Another ninth chord that appears most often in popular formats is the **add 9 chord** (add9), occasionally referred to as the *add 2* or *sus 2* (*suspended 2*). This chord consists of a major or minor triad with the addition of the 9th factor. *No 7th is present.* See *Example 17–5.*

The symbol "G add 9" indicates that the note A, which is the 9th above G, is added to the G major triad. The 9th can be imbedded within the triad or placed above the triad, but it cannot be put below it. The use of the symbol "add 2," however, means that the A should literally be placed next to the note G. Other 9ths and additions to upper partials will be discussed later in the chapter.

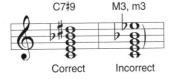

Example 17–4. *The dominant ♯9 with correct and incorrect spellings.*

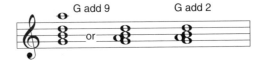

Example 17–5. *Symbols for the major triad with added 9 and 2.*

Eleventh Chords

This tertian extension exists in only two types: the *natural-occurring eleventh* and the *raised eleventh*. Lowering the 11th produces an enharmonic 3rd; it is therefore rendered useless as a chord factor. See *Example 17–6*.

◆ *Dominant Elevenths and 4–3 Suspensions*

Traditional and modern usage of the 11th requires investigation and evaluation of the implications of the presence of the chord factors in the lower supporting structure. In particular, the dominant 11th requires special attention since it is the most common 11th structure in tertian harmony. The *dominant eleventh* (V11) contains a minor 7th interval above the root and, hence, a tritone interval between the 3rd and 7th factors. The chord is extremely active and normally requires resolution to I, i, VI, or vi; other resolutions are possible, but these are the most common.

The dominant 11th in C major will be used as an example. A complete dominant 11th in C major consists of the pitches G–B–D–F–(A)–C (the inclusion of the 9th factor, A, is optional). However, in the strictly classical common-practice sense, the dominant 11th in its complete form does not exist. The tendency of the V7 is a resolution to the tonic, with the chord factor most directed toward the tonic being the 3rd of the V7 — in this case, B. The presence of the C as the 11th of the V7 creates an immediate conflict in the function of the V11. The note C is the intended root of resolution of the tension-laden V11. There is no problem with that, as C could be interpreted as an anticipation. The problem is with the presence of the 3rd factor, B, in the V11. Of course, B is the leading tone to C, but C is already present as the 11th in the V11. This conflict of function causes a reconsideration of the chord factors necessary to create a functionally correct dominant 11th. Since it is not possible to eliminate the 11th in an 11th chord, the factor to be omitted in the major-minor 7th, perfect 11th (V11) is the 3rd, B.

Example 17–6. Eleventh chords, also containing ninths.

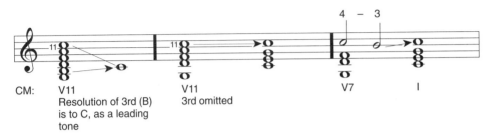

CM: V11   V11   V7   I

Resolution of 3rd (B)   3rd omitted
is to C, as a leading
tone

Example 17–7. Characteristics and derivation of the eleventh.

The presence of the 11th factor in a dominant-7th structure in common-practice literature was considered and employed as a 4–3 suspension; the 4, as a nonharmonic tone, resolves downward to the 3rd. This suspension device and the omission of the 3rd in conjunction with the dissonant 4th in the dominant structure explains the absence of the complete dominant 11th in traditional practice. See *Example 17–7.*

◆ *The "Sus 4" Symbol in Popular Music*

Inherent in the symbolic representation of 11th chords in popular music is the ambiguity presented by the chord symbols: sus, sus 4, and 7 sus 4. "Sus" represents the term *suspension*, and the implication of the "sus" refers to the fourth degree above the root of the chord. Thus, "F sus" means that a perfect 4th above the root F is to be included in the chord. The symbol "sus 4" means exactly the same as "sus." The symbol "7 sus 4" as in F7 sus 4, indicates that a perfect 4th is to be added to an F7 (F major-minor seventh); this results in an F11 chord or the structure : F–(A)–C–E♭–B♭. Since the resultant chord is an 11th, the 3rd factor, A, must be omitted, as has been previously discussed. Whenever the term "sus" appears in popular notation, the 3rd factor must be replaced by the perfect 4th — simple or compound — above the bass. See *Example 17–8.*

Stephen Sondheim's use of the sus 4 (indicated there by "sus") in "Send in the Clowns," *Example 9–8(b)* on page 206, is an excellent example of how this unique harmonic structure is utilized.

F sus   F sus 4   F7 sus 4   F11

Example 17–8. B♭, the fourth degree of the F major scale, when considered as a compound fourth, produces the eleventh.

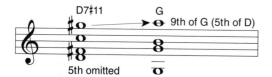

Example 17–9. Resolution tendency of the #11.

Example 17–10. F♭, the ♭5, tends to resolve downward; E, the #11, tends to resolve upward.

◆ Augmented Eleventh Chords

It has been shown that an 11th can appear as a compound perfect 4th above the root and that an 11th cannot be lowered, since the flatting of an 11th would produce an enharmonic 3rd, which would render the 11th useless. However, 11ths can be augmented. In the augmented 11th, the compound perfect 4th interval above the bass is raised to create a compound augmented 4th. Used primarily with a supporting major-minor 7th structure (V7), the augmented 11th does not require the omission of the 3rd factor of the lower structure. Instead, it is most common to omit the 5th of the supporting structure since the tendency of the augmented 11th factor is to resolve upward by a half step. This upward resolution is to the pitch that would be the 5th factor in the lower supporting structure of the #11 chord, as is illustrated in *Example 17–9*.

For symbolic representation of the augmented 11th, a common indication is "♭5." A lowered 5th is essentially the same as a raised or augmented 11th. Hence, the symbol "B♭7♭5" or "B♭7−5" represents a chord structure of a major, minor 7th, augmented 11th. Flatting the 5th results in an M♭5 triad (a hybrid); F, the perfect 5th interval above the B♭, is replaced with F♭, the lowered 5th. In most cases, the ♭5 factor tends to resolve downward. See *Example 17–10*.

◆ Minor Eleventh Chords

The *minor eleventh chord* (minor-minor 7th, perfect 11th) presents no problem with the inclusion of the minor 3rd factor; it must be present in order to render the triad minor. Extracting the four upper factors of the 11th structure produces a minor, minor 7th chord; since no tritone interval is present, as in the upper structure of the V11, the chord poses no problems in either structure or resolution. See *Example 17–11*.

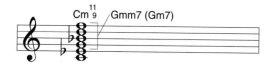

Example 17–11. An embedded Gm7 chord produced by the four upper factors.

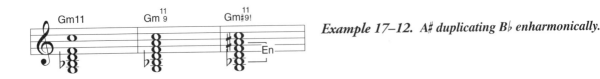

Example 17–12. A♯ duplicating B♭ enharmonically.

♦ *9,11 Chords*

Eleventh chords do not require the addition of the 9th factor, although the 9th may be included for color and reinforcement. Again, care must be taken in the choice of additional chord factors. A minor 11th chord with the addition of a raised 9th is redundant because the raised 9th is the enharmonic 3rd of the lower supporting structure. See *Example 17–12.*

♦ *Elevenths on Other Scale Degrees*

As demonstrated previously, the use of 11th chords on various scale degrees and as upper partials of various types of 7ths and 9ths requires consideration of the lower supporting structure. Elevenths may be used with any supporting structure provided that this does not result in a conflict of function. Since upper partials are actually extensions of the prevailing function of the supporting structures (usually 7th chords), the function of the supporting structure must be clear and must not be violated.

Thirteenth Chords

This last of the applicable upper partials incorporates the remaining diatonic 3rd in the tertian system. *Thirteenth chords* are formed by the addition of the compound major or minor 6th interval above the root. An augmented 13th chord is not available since the augmented 6th interval enharmonically duplicates the minor 7th. Thirteenth chords normally appear as *dominant functions;* that is, they are extensions of the dominant 7th, as are many of the 9ths and 11ths. They require a supporting structure of a major-minor 7th chord. The use of a 9th or an 11th within a 13th structure only adds color and density to the chord, and is optional. Dominant-quality 13th chords derived from the major mode and containing the compound major 6th are identified by V13; dominant-

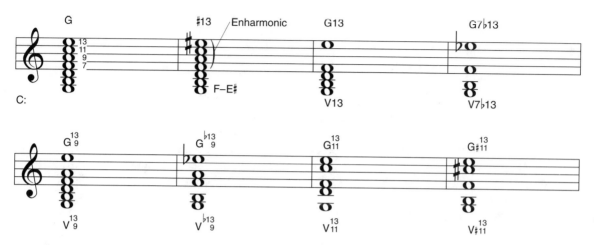

Example 17–13. *Several types of thirteenth chords, including some which include ninths and elevenths.* The ♯13 does not exist because it is an enharmonic duplication of the m7.

quality 13th chords derived from the minor mode and containing the compound minor 6th are denoted by V♭13 or V–13. It is quite common to see ♭13 chords symbolized by 7♯5, in which the ♯5 is actually the "simple" enharmonic interval of the compound m6 (♭13). The 5th is frequently omitted in the ♭13 chord.

In all identifying symbols of 9ths, 11ths, and 13ths, the larger the numeral, the higher it is placed; for example, $V_{-9}^{-13}{}_{11}$ indicates a dominant-quality supporting structure with the addition of a lowered 13th, an 11th, and a lowered 9th; $V_{+11}^{13}{}_{9}$ indicates a dominant-quality supporting structure with the addition of a 13th, an augmented 11th, and a 9th. See *Example 17–13*.

◆ Add 9, Sus 4, and Add 6 Chords

In 9th chords, as discussed previously, the addition of a 9th usually requires a supporting 7th structure. An exception to this is the add 9 chord. In 11th chords, the addition of an 11th also requires the supporting structure of a 7th. An exception to this is the sus or sus 4. With 13ths the situation is the same; 13ths require the supporting structure of a 7th, most often, the major-minor 7th chord. When a major 6th or compound major 6th is added to a major-major 7th supporting structure, the chord is no longer a 13th; it is a *major seventh add 6*, written M7add 6 or $M\overset{7}{6}$. Minor 6ths or compound minor 6ths added to a major-major 7th structure are nonfunctional because the minor 6th is the equivalent of an enharmonic augmented 5th. The resultant chord is a *major seventh, raised fifth*, written M7♯5 or M7+5.

General Remarks on Upper-Partial Chords

◆ Other Scale Degrees

An investigation of upper-partial chords constructed on supporting structures other than dominant 7ths is in order. To begin, 9ths, 11ths, and 13ths in their diatonic appearance will be constructed on each scale degree of a G major and G harmonic minor scale; later, they will be discussed as functional or nonfunctional structures. *Table 17–14* lists upper-partial chords on every scale degree.

◆ Symbols in Popular Music

In *Example 17–15*, popular chord-symbol notation is illustrated for several types of upper-partial chords. These symbols are frequently used to facilitate quick interpretation of these often complex structures and, in many cases, to assure correct pitch content. It must be agreed that the appearance of a symbol such as Bb7/C is easier, quicker, and less likely to produce incorrect pitches than the symbol C7$^{b13}_{11}{}_{9}$, especially in the course of sight-reading.

G MAJOR

	NINTH	ELEVENTH	THIRTEENTH
I	G–B–D–F♯–A	G–B–D–F♯–A–C	G–B–D–F♯–A–C–E
ii	A–C–E–G–B	A–C–E–G–B–D	A–C–E–G–B–D–F♯
iii	B–D–F♯–A–C	B–D–F♯–A–C–E	B–D–F♯–A–C–E–G
IV	C–E–G–B–D	C–E–G–B–D–F♯	C–E–G–B–D–F♯–A
V	D–F♯–A–C–E	D–F♯–A–C–E–G	D–F♯–A–C–E–G–B
vi	E–G–B–D–F♯	E–G–B–D–F♯–A	E–G–B–D–F♯–A–C
vii°	F♯–A–C–E–G	F♯–A–C–E–G–B	F♯–A–C–E–G–B–D

G MINOR (HARMONIC)

	NINTH	ELEVENTH	THIRTEENTH
i	G–Bb–D–F♯–A	G–Bb–D–F♯–A–C	G–Bb–D–F♯–A–C–Eb
ii°	A–C–Eb–G–Bb	A–C–Eb–G–Bb–D	A–C–Eb–G–Bb–D–F♯
III+	Bb–D–F♯–A–C	Bb–D–F♯–A–C–Eb	Bb–D–F♯–A–C–Eb–G
iv	C–Eb–G–Bb–D	C–Eb–G–Bb–D–F♯	C–Eb–G–Bb–D–F♯–A
V	D–F♯–A–C–Eb	D–F♯–A–C–Eb–G	D–F♯–A–C–Eb–G–Bb
VI	Eb–G–Bb–D–F♯	Eb–G–Bb–D–F♯–A	Eb–G–Bb–D–F♯–A–C
vii°	F♯–A–C–Eb–G	F♯–A–C–Eb–G–Bb	F♯–A–C–Eb–G–Bb–D

Table 17–14. Upper partials on every scale degree.

Embedded Harmonic Structures

◆ *Triads*

Perhaps the most revealing aspect of an upper-partial chord is seen when one deletes the factors that appear at the beginning of the structure but retains at least the last three factors. For example, in the first row of *Table 17–14,* for the

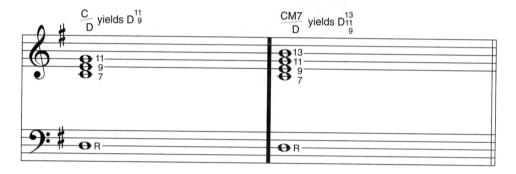

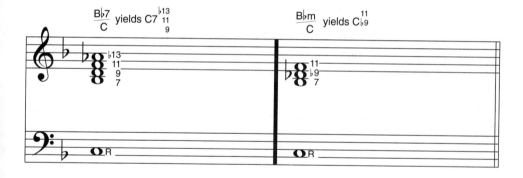

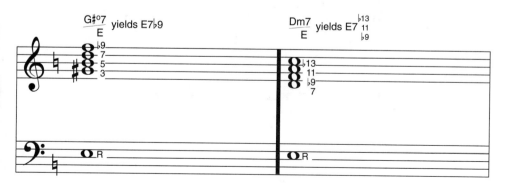

Example 17–15. Alternate upper-partial chord symbols in popular music.

thirteenth G–B–D–F♯–A–C–E, one could consider any of the following *embedded* chords:

B–D–F♯–A–C–E, D–F♯–A–C–E, F♯–A–C–E, A–C–E

Clearly, more than one chord structure is contained in each of the upper-partial configurations listed in *Table 17–14*. Without exception, every *triad* consisting of the last three factors of any of these upper-partial chords can be considered an autonomous triad of the major, minor, diminished, or augmented quality. For example, extracting the last three pitches of the G major, major 7th, major 9th, or the I9, produces the V triad (D–F♯–A). Performing the same procedure on the i9 in G minor also produces the V triad. The same process involving the ii9 in G major yields the notes E–G–B, the 5th, 7th, and 9th, thus producing the identical pitches contained in the vi triad (E minor) in G major. The ii°9 in G minor produces the pitches E♭–G–B♭, an E♭ major triad, which is also the VI in G minor. Familiarity with this concept will serve to demonstrate the interrelationships among these complex structures. A similar remark will apply to the ensuing discussion of 7ths. See *Example 17–16*.

◆ *Sevenths*

The reversal procedure can be extended further by configuring a four-note 7th chord. For example, forming a 7th structure consisting of the last four factors of the IV11 in G major produces a G major, major 7th, or a I7 (G–B–D–F♯). The same procedure applied to the iv11 in G minor also produces a i7, but in this case, the quality is minor-major 7th. This procedure of extracting embedded harmonic structures from upper-partial chords results in a comprehensive understanding of the true nature of the structures.

It is beneficial to examine the potential structures available when one or more upper partial is altered to contain a pitch other than one of the available diatonic

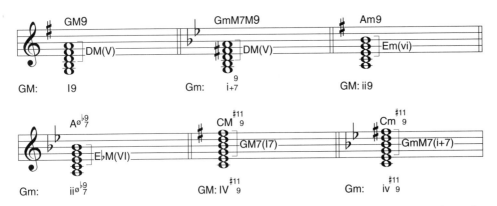

Example 17–16. Embedded harmonic structures extracted as other qualities from the scale.

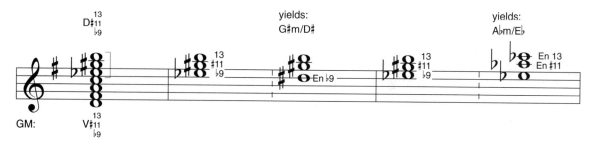

Example 17–17. Enharmonic embedded structures.

pitches. For example, assuming that all the pitches are actually included, $V{+11}^{13}$ in G major contains the pitch structure: D–F♯–A–C–E♭(–9)–G♯(+11)–B. Extracting the last three pitches, E♭–G♯–B, the –9, +11, and 13, does not produce any available root-position diatonic triad. However, a *respelling* of one or more of these pitches might reveal the presence of an embedded structure. If E♭ is respelled enharmonically as D♯, a second-inversion G♯ minor triad is produced: D♯–G♯–B. If the G♯ is respelled as A♭ and the B as C♭, a second-inversion A♭ minor triad, E♭–A♭–C♭, is produced. Of course, G♯ minor and A♭ minor are enharmonic equivalents. See *Example 17–17*.

◆ *Implications*

Two more examples of the aforementioned concept will now be presented. First, consider a $V{+11}^{-13}$ in F minor. The F minor key signature contains four flats: B♭, E♭, A♭, and D♭. The pitches of the $V{+11}^{-13}$ include: C–E♮–B♭–D♯(+9)–F♯(+11)–A♭(–13); since the structure contains an augmented 11th (compound augmented 4th — F♯), the 5th, G, is omitted. Also, D♯ is the correct spelling of the +9, even though it is an enharmonic E♭, a note of the key signature. Two factors justify the spelling of the +9 as D♯: D♯ is the +9 interval above the root, C, and E is the seventh degree of the F minor harmonic scale from which the dominant is extracted. But the concern here is with the embedded harmonic structure created by the +9, +11, and –13, D♯, F♯, and A♭, respectively. Obviously, the arrangement of the notes and the spelling do not yield a simple triadic structure; in fact, no respelling or rearrangement of the pitches will produce a simple triad. However, the resultant structure may very well yield a type of chord that can be rendered incomplete by the spelling D♯–F♯–A♭. Respelling the D♯ as E♭ and the F♯ as G♭ produces a potential A♭Mm7 or A♭mm7 as well as other possibilities. Similarly, respelling the A♭ as G♯ produces a potential implied EMM7M9 or BM add 6 as well as other possibilities. See *Example 17–18* on page 396.

As a second example, consider a $ii{+11}^{13}_{9}$ in the key of G major. The pitches are: A–C–E–G–B–D♯–F♯. The embedded upper triad, B–D♯–F♯, produces a B

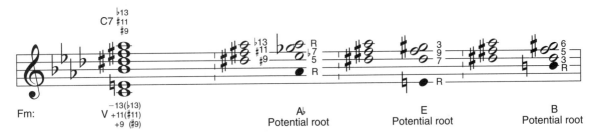

Example 17–18. An embedded structure with root implications resulting from enharmonic spellings.

major triad; inclusion of the G produces a G augmented major 7th; inclusion of the E produces an E minor, major 7th, major 9th; inclusion of the C produces a C major, major 7th, augmented 9th, augmented 11th. None of the resultant embedded structures fulfill the original intended function of a ii triad. That does not mean, however, that the chord should be avoided. It does mean that the complete embedded sound, function, and purpose of the chord must be considered when assessing the degree of tension present in a progression. See *Example 17–19.*

Inversions of Ninths, Elevenths, and Thirteenths

Although it is most common to see 9ths, 11ths, and 13ths in root position, inversions are also possible. However, inversions of these structures are *used with discretion.* The critical decision to be made in the use of inversions is the *retention of character* of the upper partials; that is, does the resultant configuration maintain the character, quality, and function of the chord?

Those inversions most often employed include: the $\frac{6}{5}$ (first inversion); the $\frac{4}{3}$ (second inversion); and the $\frac{4}{2}$ (third inversion). Symbolic representation of upper-partial structures is, understandably, more complex because other factors must be considered. For example, a dominant −9 in first inversion is written $V \frac{-9}{\frac{6}{5}}$; a

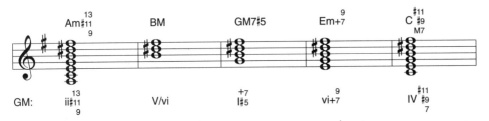

Example 17–19. Embedded structures in the extended ii chord.

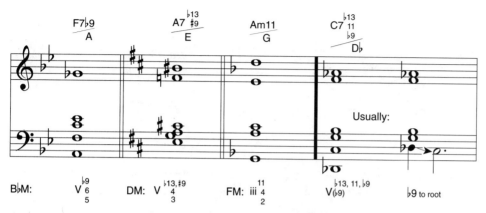

Example 17–20. Inversions of several upper-partial chords.

dominant -13, 11, $+9$ in second inversion is written: $V\,{}^{-13,11,+9}_{4}_{3}$; a iii11 in third inversion is written: iii $\,{}^{11}_{4}_{2}$. Although it is possible to see an upper-partial factor in the bass, these pitches are usually *nonharmonic melodic devices* and are not considered authentic upper-partial functions. Such inversions, if they are to be identified as chord factors, are indicated by parenthesizing the upper-partial numeral in the lower part of the symbol. The dominant -13, 11, -9, with the 9th in the bass, is indicated by $V\,{}^{-13,11,-9}_{(-9)}$. No extension of the Arabic numeral system, such as $\,{}^{6}_{5}$, $\,{}^{4}_{3}$, $\,{}^{4}_{2}$, which is used in the identification of 7th chords, is available.

Popular symbol notation for inversions of 9ths, 11ths, and 13ths utilizes the same conventions used in triads and 7ths — for example, $\frac{D9}{F\sharp}$. See *Example 17–20*.

◆ Rerooting and Root Ambiguity

In inversions of 9th, 11ths, and 13ths in which one of the upper partials is in the bass, the original chord is often rerooted to avoid an ambiguity in the tertian function of the chord.

Consider a D minor, minor 7th, perfect 11th, D–F–A–C–E–G. If the 11th, G, were placed in the bass, yielding G–D–F–A–C–E, a correctly spelled G major, minor 7th, major 9th, perfect 11th, major 13th chord would result — $G\,{}^{13}_{11}_{9}$. The use of D as a root would be completely ineffective in this inversion. Similarly, a C major, minor 7th, major 9th, perfect 11th, major 13th, C–G–B♭–D–F–A, with the 11th, F, in the bass, would completely void C as a root. The consecutive perfect 5ths, F–C–G, reinforce F as a root; the addition of the B♭ creates a suspended 4th, which would ultimately resolve to the 3rd, A, that is already present. The D is an added 6th; neither B♭ nor D can be considered upper partials to F, that is, an 11th and a 13th, since no 7th (E♭) is present to generate them. Would the bass note, F, then be considered a pedal tone to the C root or just an intervallic structure? In

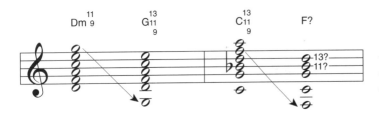

Example 17–21. A G rooted chord resulting from placing the eleventh in the bass. A similar situation occurs in measure 2.

this type of situation every note of the prevailing chord must be considered as a potential root; ultimately, perhaps, no apparent rooted triadic structure exists. See *Example 17–21.*

In most styles of music that utilize upper-partial chords, the character of the chord is maintained; hence, any ambiguity as to root identity is avoided. It is possible, however, that in certain situations, a composer may knowingly incorporate all the factors of a chord, such as a $\sharp 11 \atop \flat 9$ with a 13, in such a way that the actual root is obscured in a mass of sound. This may very well be the composer's style or a technique that he or she favors. However, it is also quite possible that the composer was not considering any typical tertian vertical structure, but chose those pitches which, in the process of analysis, suggest an ambiguous harmonic structure.

Voice Leading of Upper-Partial Chords

An important fact to remember is that upper-partial chords, as they are constructed and used in contemporary and popular practice, were not part of the harmonic vocabulary of the common-practice period. Whereas it is certainly true that the factors of upper-partial chords did appear in common-practice works, they were considered nonharmonic tones and were treated as such. Therefore, the practice of voice leading of upper-partial chords is for the sake of maintaining the character, quality, and integrity of the chords, and for achieving coherent musical lines among the voices of an upper-partial chord and of the chords that precede and follow it.

◆ *Necessary Chord Factors*

To formulate a list of rules or practices for all the possibilities for voice leading of upper-partial chords, their inversions, and their voicings would be a monumental task and one that would prove to be fruitless. For each such rule there

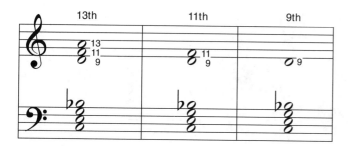

Example 17–22. Upper-partial chords with every factor included.

Example 17–23. A skeletal, but effective, dominant thirteenth.

is an exception; for each voicing there is an alternative. What must be considered in this aspect of these harmonies is the pitch content necessary to establish a particular sonority and the tendencies of particular partials to resolve; but it must be remembered that musicality and stylistic considerations are the final decisive factors.

Most upper-partial chords can be constructed with *three, four, or five pitches* so as to retain their identity. It is unnecessary to include every note of the tertian construction in the formation of a 13th, for example. A 13th chord, if constructed in full complement, contains seven notes; an 11th contains six notes; a 9th contains five notes. See *Example 17–22*.

In discussing the various upper-partial chord structures, it was demonstrated how certain factors may be omitted in some chords, and yet these chords will still maintain their character and quality. Virtually every upper-partial chord requires the *presence of a seventh*, major or minor. The exception to this is the add9. Dominant 11th chords require the *omission* of the 3rd; dominant *raised* 11ths require the *omission* of the 5th. In any upper-partial dominant-function chord of the 9th, 11th, or 13th, the minimum requirement for securing the character and integrity of the chord is the presence of a *root*, a *minor seventh*, and the *pitch representing that upper partial*. For example, an F♯ dominant 13th (F♯13) requires only the root, F♯, the minor 7th, E, and the 13th, D♯, as shown in *Example 17–23*. Of course, the chord will sound sparse; but it will retain the quality of a dominant 13th. Any notes added to this 13th structure will only serve to enhance its color and density.

An upper-partial chord of minor quality, such as a minor 11th, must contain the *minor third* as well as the *minor seventh*. In this structure, then, it is necessary to incorporate the root, the minor 3rd, the minor 7th, and the 11th. Any alteration of the intrinsic pitches of an upper-partial chord must obviously be contained in the structure. A raised 9th must include the raised 9th, as well as a major 3rd, since the raised 9th is the same pitch as the enharmonic minor 3rd. It is the *tension* caused by the raised 9th against the major 3rd that characterizes the sound of the raised 9th chord. It is a matter of musical judgment as to which factors should be included with any of these structures. *Example 17–24* on page 400 illustrates several voicings of upper-partial chords.

Example 17–24. *Several voicings of upper-partial chords.*

Pitch Tendency

◆ *Ninths*

The reader is already familiar with pitch tendencies in 7th chords. With upper-partial chords, resolution tendency is a matter of awareness of the *spelling* and *implied direction* of each upper-partial pitch. Generally speaking, as shown in *Example 17–25,* a lowered 9th tends to resolve downward by a half step; a diatonic 9th tends to resolve downward by a whole step or remain as a common tone; and a raised 9th tends to resolve upward by a half step. Other movements are possible.

◆ *Elevenths*

With 11th chords, the diatonic 11th can gravitate downward by a half step, as in the 4–3 suspension; it can also resolve downward by a whole step, or remain as a common tone. The raised 11th moves upward by a half step as a resolution of its leading-tone spelling. Other movements are possible. See *Example 17–26.*

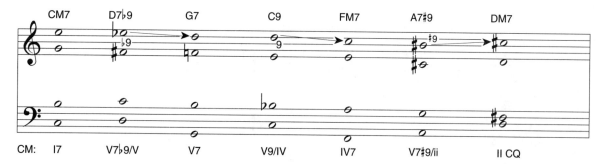

Example 17–25. Pitch tendency in ninth chords.

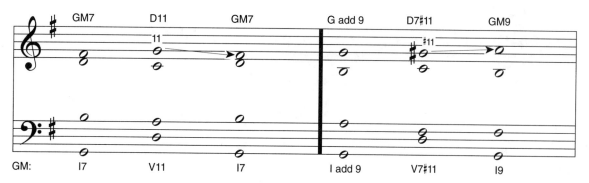

Example 17–26. Pitch tendency in eleventh chords.

◆ Thirteenths

The diatonic 13th can resolve downward by a major 3rd, downward by a major 2nd, or remain as a common tone. Lowered 13ths tend to move downward by a half step. The enharmonic ♯5 in the 7♯5 tends to resolve outward by step. Other movements are possible. See *Example 17–27* on page 402.

◆ Adapting the Rules

An important point to remember is that chord-factor resolution ultimately depends on the style, context, and period of a musical work. No composer or songwriter will abandon his or her inclination to resolve chord factors based solely on accepted practice and naturally occurring resolution tendencies. The experienced writer senses the best ways of creating a musical work by adapting the rules.

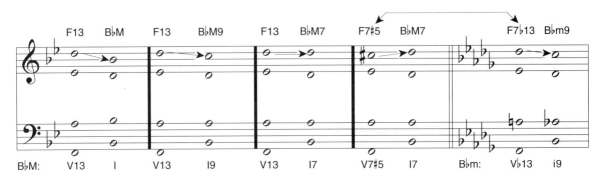

Example 17–27. Pitch tendency in thirteenth chords. In the tenor part of the last chord, if A were natural, the chord would have been i+7 (Bbm9M7).

Authentic and Appoggiatura Upper-Partial Chords

Upper-partial chords are essentially of two types; *authentic* and *appoggiatura*. An **authentic** upper-partial chord *resolves directly* to a chord of a different root.

Example 17–28. The two types of upper-partial chords. **(a)** Authentic upper-partial chords. **(b)** Appoggiatura upper-partial chords formed by nonharmonic tones.

With an **appoggiatura** chord, one or more upper partial contained in the structure will first resolve to a pitch of the supporting triad before progressing to a chord of a different root. In other words, an *appoggiatura* chord first *resolves within itself* before resolving to the next harmony. Care must be taken in determining whether or not the upper partials in question are simply nonharmonic tones or actual upper partials. This can only be confirmed by an assessment of the *rhythmic stress* placed on the partials and the manner in which they resolve. See *Example 17–28*.

The excerpts in *Example 17–29* on pages 404–8 illustrate various types of upper-partial chords in common-practice as well as popular works. See also *Example 16–12,* "I Remember Duke," on page 373.

(a)

Prelude, Op. 28, No. 9

F. Chopin

(b)

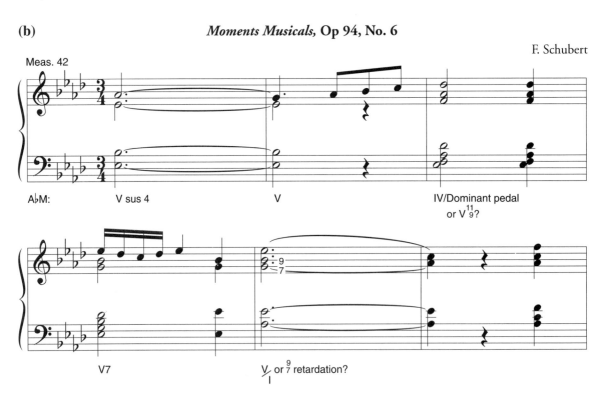

Moments Musicals, Op 94, No. 6

F. Schubert

(c) *Sonata No. 2, Violin and Piano,* **Op. 100**

J. Brahms

Example 17–29. Upper-partial chords in common-practice and popular works. **(a)** An appoggiatura upper-partial chord resulting from a suspended tone. **(b)** The progression of V to IV in the second and third measures (mm. 43–44) is unlikely. However, if the third measure is V^{11}_9, it is an appoggiatura chord. The 3rd (G) is omitted because the chord contains the 11th. **(c)** The $\frac{V7}{N}$ in measure 4 might at first sound like a German 6th in A. **(d)** Notice the unconventional movement of the nonharmonic tones in this excerpt. **(e)** An authentic upper-partial 9th, A9 (V9/V), resolving directly to DM(V). **(f)** Of the several 9th chords in this excerpt, D9/C is the least common. However, observation of the surrounding progression reveals that this chord probably has a bass-line function, that is, D–C–B. The D9 does not normally resolve to B minor. **(g)** In the last chord the correct spelling is A♯ (♯9), instead of B♭ (m3). **(h)** Notice the 9th (A) placed adjacent to the 3rd (B♭).

(d)

Valses Poeticos #3

E. Granados

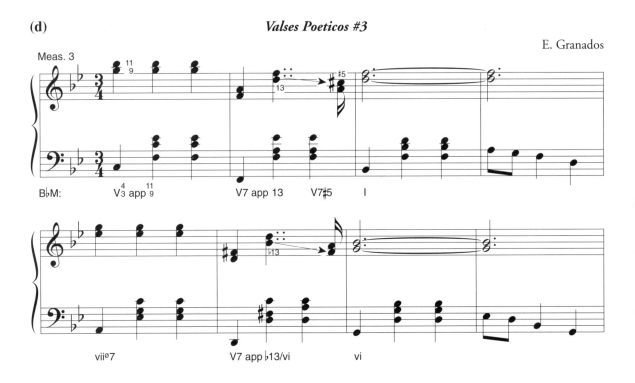

(e)

Grandmother's Minuet

E. Grieg

(f)

"Love Is Here to Stay"

Words by Ira Gershwin, Music by George Gershwin

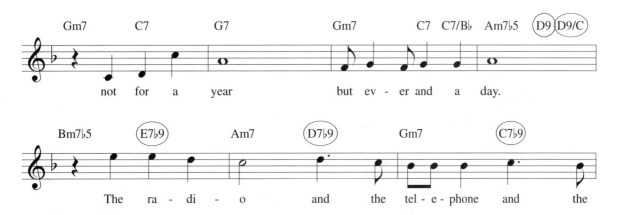

(g)

"Fake Your Way to the Top"

Words by Tom Eyen, Music by Henry Krieger

(h)   **"Sorry Seems to Be the Hardest Word"**

Elton John, Bernie Taupin

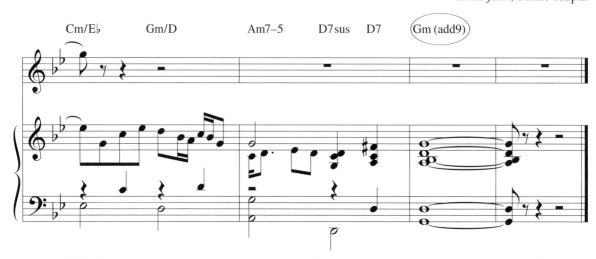

Chapter Review

Continuing chord construction by the process of tertian stacking, this chapter examined the types of *ninths, elevenths,* and *thirteenths* available in the major and minor scales as well as those upper-partial harmonies considered to be hybrid types. *Hybrids* are those chord structures that do not appear as a result of the available pitches in a scale, but are structured as a result of pitch alteration.

Ninths appear as normally occurring, both lowered and raised; 11ths as normally occurring and raised; and 13ths as normally occurring and lowered. Alterations of the lower supporting structure of these chords are, of course, numerous. Ninths, 11ths, and 13ths are the upper-partial chords most employed in common-practice and popular genres, although higher-numbered partials are also possible.

It is essential that one consider the intrinsic impact of each particular pitch in an upper-partial chord. By understanding the function of these chords, logical conclusions can be made pertaining to the inclusion or omission of certain notes. A case in point is the dominant 11th chord. The tendency of a dominant structure is toward the tonic chord. The 11th, being the fourth degree of the scale, has a tendency toward the third degree. Therefore, including the major 3rd in a dominant-11th chord structure is antithetic in conventional practice. However, in the pursuit of certain musical effects and in specific styles, pitches that fulfill a particular need for sonority, regardless of acoustical principles, are utilized.

In most cases, chords of upper-partial designation can be constructed with a minimum of pitches. Most 9th, 11th, and 13ths are generated and supported by the root and seventh; hence, it is possible to construct an effective dominant 13th chord by the use of the root, minor 7th interval, and 13th. Additional pitches, such as 3rds, 5ths, and certain types of 9ths and 11ths, add additional colors and tensions to the 13th, but do not affect its function. Similar conditions pertain to most other types of upper-partial chords.

Observation of upper-partial chords containing all tertian degree factors in their construction reveals the presence of embedded triads, 7ths, etc., depending upon the complexity of the upper-partial

structure. When viewed from the top downward, an $E\flat\overset{13}{\underset{9}{\sharp11}}$ (E♭–G–(B♭ omitted)–D♭–F–A–C) contains an F major triad (F–A–C, the 9th, raised 11th, and 13th of E♭) and a D♭M7♯5 (D♭–F–A–C, the 7th, 9th, ♯11th, and 13th of E♭). A recognition of these embedded structures provides a better comprehension of the harmonic relationships within and among complex harmonic structures and the relatedness inherent in remote chromaticism.

Inversions of upper-partial chords must be handled with discretion. It is most important that the character and function of the chord be maintained in any inversion. Inversions containing the 9th, 11th, or 13th in the bass do not function well. An upper partial appearing in the bass is most often a nonharmonic tone function.

In the broadest sense, there exist essentially two types of upper-partial chords: the authentic and the appoggiatura. *Authentic* types resolve directly to a chord of a different root; *appoggiatura* types are those in which one or more upper partials resolve within the prevailing chord itself before progressing to a different root.

Anthology References

For additional usage and analysis, see the following examples in Distefano, Joseph P. and James A. Searle, *Music and Materials for Analysis: An Anthology.* New York, Ardsley House, Publishers, Inc., 1995.

ninth chords

Example 38.   *Prelude,* Op. 28, No. 7, Frédéric Chopin, pp. 213–18.

Example 42.   *Morgen,* Richard Strauss, pp. 239–46.

appoggiatura elevenths

Example 42.   *Morgen,* Richard Strauss, pp. 239–46.

appoggiatura sharp elevenths including the ♭5, 9, ♭13

Example 56.   *Sonata for Violin,* No. 2, Third Movement, "The Revival," Charles Ives, pp. 325–34.

m9, M9

Example 57.   *Divertimento for Band,* Prologue, Vincent Persichetti, pp. 335–40.

enharmonically spelled sharp ninths
>   *Example 58.*   *Tar River Blues,* Joseph P. Distefano, pp. 341–48.

upper-partial chords resulting from the pentatonic scale
>   *Example 45.*   *Preludes,* Book I, No. 2, "Voiles" ("Sails"), Claude Achille Debussy, pp. 259–66.

flat thirteenths
>   *Example 55.*   *Twelve Poems of Emily Dickinson,* No. 3, "Why Do They Shut Me Out of Heaven?,"
>   Aaron Copland, pp. 317–24.

ninths, elevenths, thirteenths
>   *Example 44.*   *Poème,* Op. 69, No.1, Alexander Scriabin, pp. 253–58.

Self-Test

1. List the three types of 9th chords, the two types of 11th chords, and the two types of 13th chords.

2. Upper-partial chords that utilize altered scale degrees are referred to as _____ types.

3. Most upper-partial chords require a 7th in the supporting structure. One particular chord used extensively in popular style that does not require the 7th is the _____ .

4. Explain the reasoning concerning the omission of the 3rd in a dominant 11th chord.

5. Explain the chord symbol "7sus4."

6. Explain the chord symbols "add2," "add9," and "sus2."

7. Explain what is meant by "embedded harmonic structures."

8. What decisions must be made in the use of upper-partial-chord inversions?

9. What is the result of upper-partial-chord factors used in the bass?

10. What are some necessary considerations in effective voice leading of upper-partial chords?

11. Explain the terms *authentic* and *appoggiatura* as they pertain to upper-partial chords.

12. Based on musical logic, how can upper-partial chords of the 15th, 17th, 19th, etc. be constructed?

Exercises

1. Construct diatonic 9th chords on each note. Identify by Roman numeral and quality.

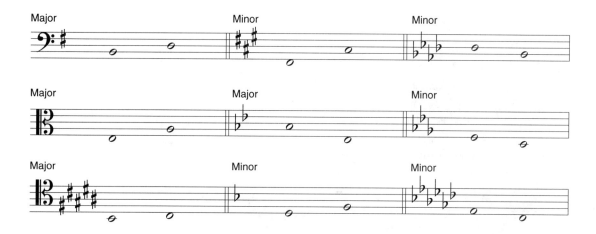

2. Construct dominant 9th chords on each note, as in the first measure.

3. Construct dominant ♭9 chords on each note.

4. Construct dominant ♯9 chords on each note.

5. Construct "add 9" chords on each note.

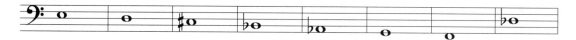

6. Construct "add 2" chords on each note.

7. Construct dominant 11th chords on each note, as in the first measure.

8. Construct minor 11th chords on each note.

9. Construct dominant ♯11 chords on each note.

10. Construct the indicated chords.

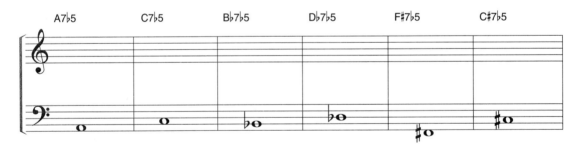

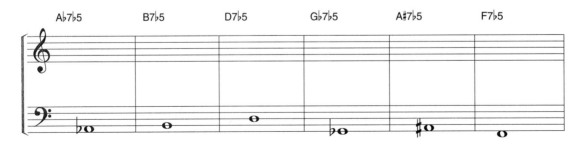

11. Construct dominant 13th chords on each note, as in the first measure.

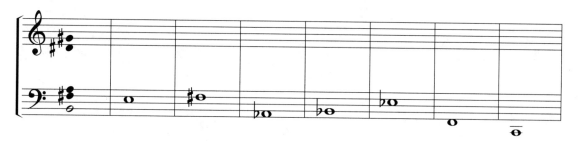

12. Construct dominant ♭13th chords on each note.

13. Identify each chord by letter and quality and also as a possible key function, as in the first measure.

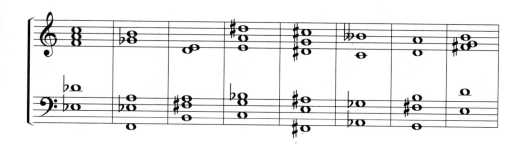

14. Identify each upper embedded triad and seventh chord. Label each complete structure. See the first measure.

15. Construct in several voicings, as in the first measure.

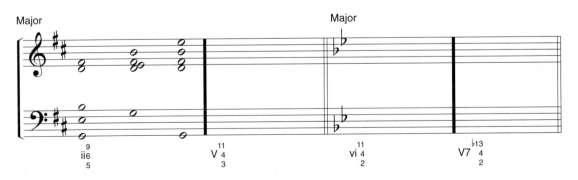

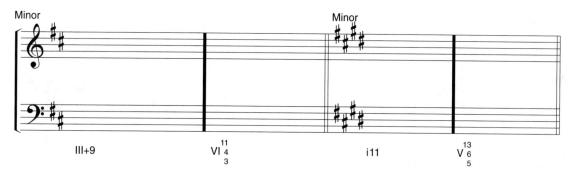

16. Complete the SATB.

(a)

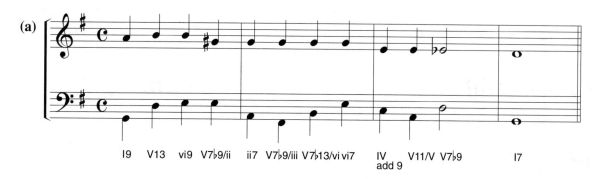

(b)

(c)

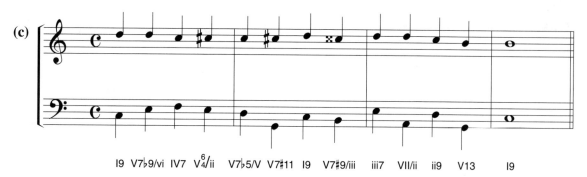

17. Label as upper-partial chords, as in the first measure.

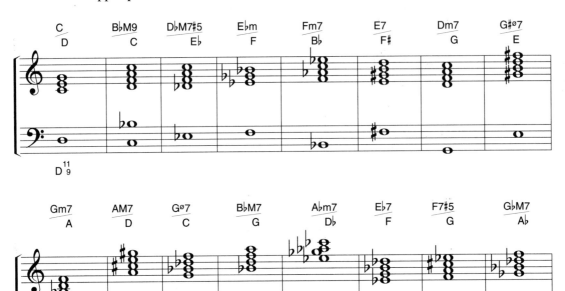

STEPWISE, MEDIANT, AND TRITONE RELATIONSHIPS

Cyclic Movement

In tonal music, chord movement occurs for the most part in cyclic patterns of 4ths and 5ths. Progressions that appear to be chord movements in 2nds and 3rds are usually substitute, embellishing, or nonstructural chords, and quite often, result from melodic harmony.

It is apparent in the Mendelssohn excerpt *(Example 18–1* on pages 418–19)* that the composer was more concerned with linear melodic movement than with vertical harmonic results. Nevertheless, it is still possible to detect a progression suggesting cyclic movement. (See the encircled chord symbols.)

Noncyclic Movement

In a diatonic environment, chromaticism can be introduced without actual movement to a new key center. This was investigated in the discussions concerning embellishments, Neapolitans, augmented 6ths, and altered and extended chords

The Adieu, Op 85, No. 2

F. Mendelssohn

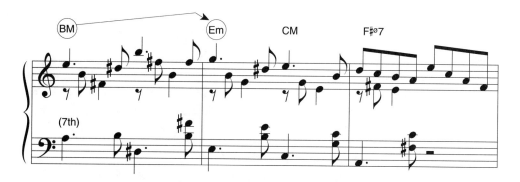

Example 18–1. Cyclic movement. The encircled symbols indicate cyclic movement. The last chord in measure 4 is an Italian 6th. Notice the similarity between the Italian 6th and B7♭5, the dominant ♭5 of V(E). A tritone root relationship occurs between FM and BM in measures 13 and 14 and between CM and F♯ø7 in the last two measures.

(nondiatonic partials of the 9ths, 11ths, and 13ths). But what about chromatic chords not included in the preceding? How are they accounted for in essentially diatonic progressions? What is their role, their derivation, and their implication?

Stepwise movement means root movement by whole step, half step, or possibly both intermittently. **Mediant movement** is chromatic movement by a 3rd, major or minor, ascending or descending, and is occasionally enharmonic. Consecutive mediant movement in major 3rds ceases to offer any difference in roots after the third root; and consecutive movement in minor 3rds ceases to offer a new root after the appearance of the 4th root. **Tritone movement** is root movement separated by an augmented 4th or a diminished 5th. See *Example 18–1*. Consecutive tritone movement of more than two roots is not feasible since the tritone duplicates itself by the second appearance. These tritone and mediant, major and minor 3rd configurations are referred to as *symmetrical (intervallic) movements,* meaning that the consecutive-root intervals are of the same quality. However, whereas chords structured on these intervals are limited in number, *alternate root spellings* produce additional symmetrical structures of the same quality. See *Example 18–2*.

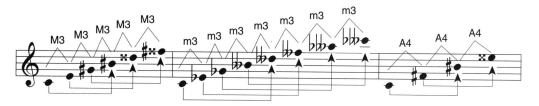

Example 18–2. Enharmonically duplicated pitches. The pointers indicate the pitches.

Stepwise Movement

Stepwise movement describes those series of chords that are not explained by "conventional" function. *Conventional functions* include: diatonic chords that move by whole or half step to another diatonic chord; deceptive resolutions of the dominant, secondary dominant, dominant 7th, and secondary-dominant 7th; the leading-tone diminished triad, the secondary leading-tone diminished triad, the leading-tone diminished 7th, the secondary leading-tone diminished 7th, the leading-tone half-diminished 7th, and the secondary leading-tone half-diminished 7th; the Neapolitans to $^6_4$ inversions; and the French and Italian 6ths to the V. The same holds true for upper-partial chords. See *Example 18–3*.

Stepwise movement occurs between two or more chordal structures, one of which can include a diatonic harmony. The progression of a C major triad in the key of C major to a B♭ major triad is considered stepwise root movement provided that the key of F major is not suggested as a possible key center. Similarly, a C major triad to a D major triad is considered stepwise provided that D major does not tonicize a G triad or a G dominant 7th as a secondary dominant. See *Example 18–4*.

Stepwise root relationships often establish a technique of **harmonic sequence**, whereby the stepwise movement temporarily tonicizes a key region. Although a complete key change is not realized, the regionalized key can be

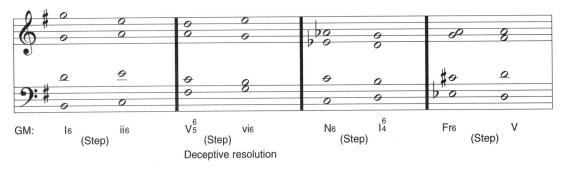

Example 18–3. Stepwise root movement in conventional functions.

Example 18–4. In measure 1, stepwise movement; in measure 2, the second chord is not a functional V/V. Note that ♭VII indicates a major triad on the lowered seventh degree of the scale. See page 431.

established by the introduction of the initial stepwise chord or else the initial stepwise chord can become a structural secondary chord, such as a dominant, dominant 7th, in the regionalized key. See *Example 18–5.*

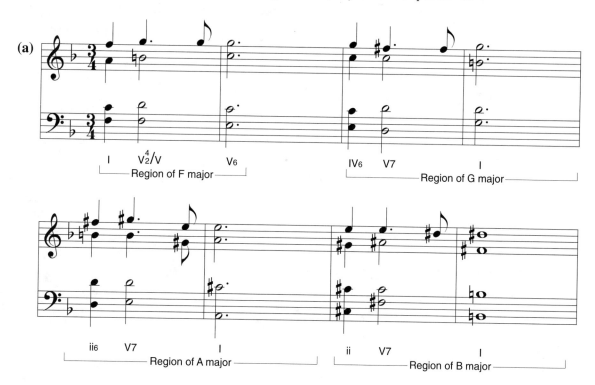

Example 18–5. Harmonic sequence. (a) A sequence of whole-step key relationships. (b) The chord indicated by the asterisk is a result of bass and melodic motion. Notice the stepwise descending bass and stepwise ascending melody in measures 2, 3, and 4.

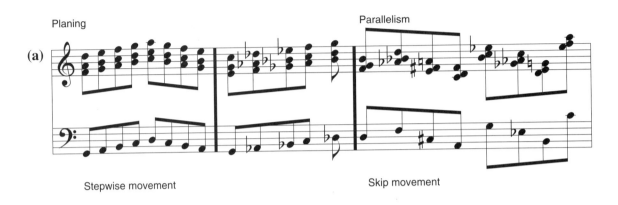

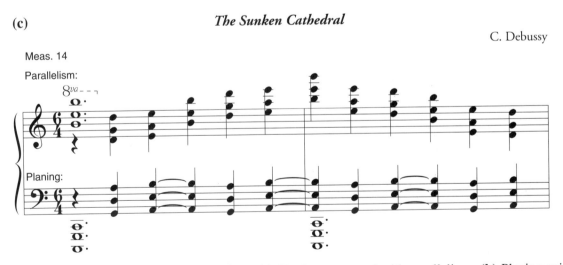

Example 18–6. Planing and parallelism. **(a)** Planing compared with parallelism. **(b)** Planing using 7th and 9th chords. **(c)** Simultaneous use of parallelism and planing.

◆ *Planing and Parallelism*

Although stepwise root movement can include as few as two chords, it can also be protracted to include several consecutive chords. A technique of chords of the *same voicing* moving in whole- and/or half-step fashion for an extended period (more than two chords) is called **planing**. Planing should not be confused with **parallelism**, which is similar to planing in that it maintains the voicing of the chords; however, its pattern of movement is not restricted to whole and/or half steps. These concepts are illustrated in *Example 18–6*.

Mediant Movement

Mediant root movement describes any chromatic movement in major or minor 3rds, allowing for *enharmonic equivalents*. For example, a movement of an E root chord to an A♭ root chord is mediant, although it appears as a diminished 4th. Mediant movement within a diatonic framework is quite common: for example, I to iii or I to vi. See *Example 18–1* on page 419. However, it is *chromatic mediant movement* to nonembellishing chords that differentiates mediant relationships from typical conventional movements in 3rds. The movement of I to V/vi is a mediant type of root movement that is often used. However, in G major, for example, I (GM) to B♭m — a minor 3rd — is not common, nor is I to E♭m or to E♭7, a major 3rd lower. Determination of chromatic mediant movement, then, is made with consideration given first to the possibility of diatonic progression, then to the possibility of a secondary function, and finally to the likeliness of an actual chromatic mediant relationship. See *Example 18–7* on pages 423–24.

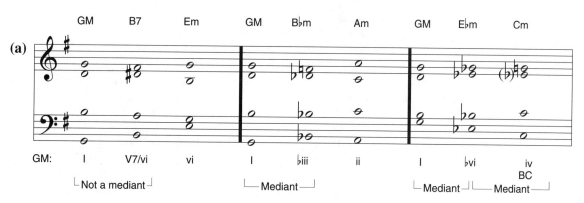

Example 18–7. Mediant root movement. **(a)** Although the roots are mediant-related in measure 1, B7 is a secondary dominant. In measures 2 and 3, no embellishing function exists. **(b)** The interval from A♭ down to E is a diminished 4th as well as an enharmonic major 3rd. The key movement is a mediant relationship (see Chapter 19); the A♭ minor is treated as G♯ minor; the iii in E major.

(b)

Sonata Pathétique

L. v. Beethoven

Second movement, meas. 41

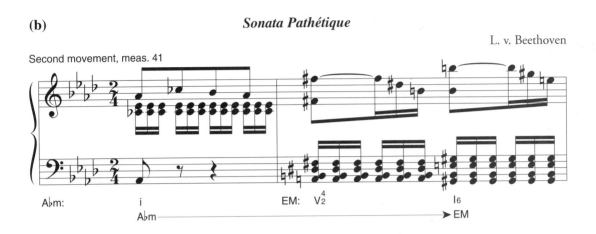

A♭m: i

EM: V$_2^4$

I6

A♭m ──────────────────────────────────► EM

Tritone Relationship and Movement

It is not the prolonged freedom of movement that is characterized by the tritone relationship, but rather, the relatedness of the tritone interval to other chord structures. This was illustrated briefly in previous discussions on chord substitution.

In the key of F major, an example of the tritone relationship that exists between the dominant-7th chord and the same-quality chord whose root lies a tritone apart from the dominant 7th will be examined. The dominant 7th in the key of F major as well as in the key of F minor is C major, minor 7th (C–E–G–B♭). The major, minor 7th structure whose root lies a tritone apart from a C root is G♭ major, minor 7th, the dominant 7th of C♭. (G♭ is the root of choice since it, rather than F♯, is more closely related to F, as in a Neapolitan relationship.) The G♭ major, minor 7th consists of the pitches G♭–B♭–D♭–F♭. The relationship between the C major, minor 7th and the G♭ major, minor 7th can be observed by comparing the 3rd and 7th factors of each chord. The 3rd in the C7th is the note E; the 7th is B♭. In the G♭7th, the 3rd is B♭ and the 7th is F♭ (the enharmonic of E). The two chords, C7 and G♭7, share the same tritone although one pitch is enharmonically spelled (E as F♭), as illustrated in *Example 18–8.*

The relationship does not end there. If C7 and G♭7 are extended to include upper partials (diatonic and chromatic), many more similarities are revealed. A C7♭9 incorporates the note of D♭, the 5th of G♭; the addition of a raised 11th (F♯) yields an enharmonic G♭, the root of the G♭7; and the addition of the lowered 13th (A♭) produces the 9th of G♭. If the raised 11th (F♯), 7th (B♭), lowered 9th

Example 18–8. Tritone-related roots.

(D♭), and 3rd (E) are extracted, respectively, from the C dominant structure, the resulting chord is G♭7. (Enharmonic spellings, of course, exist.)

By reversing the process and examining the G♭7th structure, the addition of a lowered 9th, A♭♭ (enharmonic G), produces the 5th of the C7; the raised 11th, C, produces the root of C7, and the lowered 13th, E♭♭ (enharmonic D), produces the 9th of the C7.

Other common-chord factors may also be generated by alterations of the upper partials. By incorporating the diatonic 9th of C7, a raised 5th, D, will be created on the G♭ root; the addition of the diatonic 13th, A, into the C dominant chord will produce the raised 9th on the G♭ dominant chord, as shown in *Example 18–9.*

The interpretations and mutations of the tritone roots can be continued. If the enharmonic root of F♯ is substituted for G♭, the spelling of the intrinsic pitches becomes F♯–A♯–C♯–E. Again, comparison of the 3rds and 7ths yields common pitches. The 7th of C7, B♭, is enharmonically the 3rd, A♯, of the F♯7,

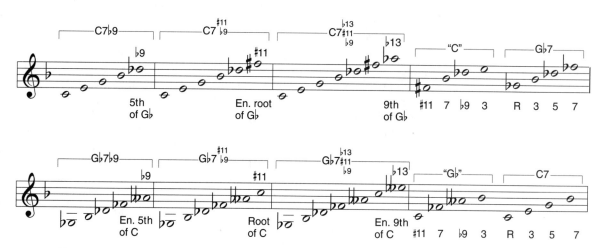

Example 18–9. The C and G♭ tritone-related roots and upper-partial relationships.

Example 18–10. Tritone-related C7 and F♯7 chords.

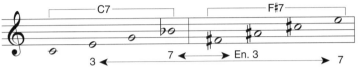

and the 3rd of the C7, E, is the 7th of the F♯7. Whereas the substitute function of the G♭ dominant for the C dominant can facilitate a key movement to C♭ (G♭7 is the V7 of C♭ — major or minor), the substitution function of the F♯7 suggests key movement to B major or B minor. Interestingly, both C♭ and B are a tritone root from the initial key of F major, and, of course, C♭ and B are enharmonic equivalents. See *Example 18–10.*

Tritones and Augmented Sixths

◆ *German Sixths*

In our discussion of the tritone relationship, we consider another function of the major, minor 7th structure. When considering augmented 6th chords in Chapter 16, similarities between the augmented 6ths and the major, minor 7th were illustrated. The German 6th, for example, sounds exactly like a major, minor 7th chord. A French 6th has the sound of a major, minor 7th with a lowered 5th, and the Italian 6th is comparable to an incomplete major, minor 7th, that is, with the 5th omitted. If the C major, minor 7th in the preceding discussion were considered a partially enharmonically spelled German 6th, C–E–G–A♯, the root, C, would be considered as the lowered sixth degree of E major or as the normally occurring sixth degree of E minor. In either key, C is the root of the German 6th. By respelling B♭, the 7th of the C major, minor 7th chord as A♯, this structure is no longer diatonically related to the key center of F, but to the key center of E. Similarly, if F♭, the 7th of the tritone-related G♭ major, minor 7th is enharmonically spelled as E, G♭ major, minor 7th is no longer related to the key center of C♭. A German 6th whose root originates on G♭ is indicative of the key center of B♭ — major or minor. The relationship of the key centers explicated between the C German 6th and the G♭ German 6th is also a tritone relationship: E–B♭. See *Example 18–11.*

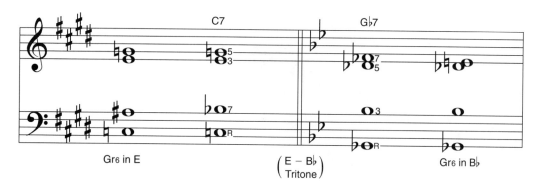

Example 18–11. Tritone-root and chord-factor relationships in the dominant seventh and German sixth.

◆ *French Sixths*

Investigation of the French 6th produces interesting similarities. A French 6th emanating from a C root produces the pitches C–E–F♯–A♯. This French 6th appears in the key of E major or E minor. Respelling the French 6th from a tritone-related root of G♭ produces the pitches G♭–B♭–C–E, and the French 6th is, of course, related to the key of B♭ major or B♭ minor. Since the roots are separated by a tritone, the related keys are also separated by a tritone (E–B♭), as in the discussion of the German 6th. See *Example 18–12.*

Though normally inclusive of the interval of an augmented 4th above the root, the French 6th is *exactly the same in sound quality* as a major, minor 7th with a lowered 5th — for example, C7♭5 and G♭7♭5. In these structures the spellings are C–E–G♭–B♭ and G♭–B♭–D♭♭–F♭, respectively. But even though the sound is the same, the function is not. The major, minor 7th with lowered 5th is viewed as a dominant function, that is, G♭7♭5 is the dominant 7th of a C♭ root. Whereas the resolution of the G♭7♭5 may be to another chord, as in a deceptive resolution, it is still initially a 5th relationship. In the C7♭5 structure, the implied relationship of the dominant quality is to an F root chord, and, of course, this too may be evaded. See *Example 18–13* on page 428.

Although it is the spelling that in most instances determines the function of augmented 6ths, these chords may be used, as has been discussed, to suggest other keys either by respelling certain pitches, or simply by resolving in

Example 18–12. The tritone-related French sixth.

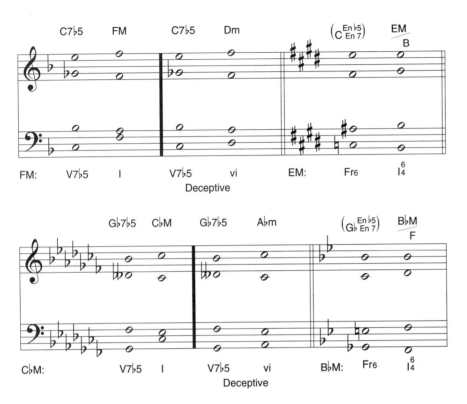

Example 18–13. *Comparison of the French sixth and seventh flat five.*

unconventional ways. In the case of the French 6th chord, the remote relationship of alternate resolution is more obvious.

Returning to the French 6th on C will aid in clarification of this concept. It was determined that the augmented 6th constructed on a C root is derived from the key center of E major or E minor. The pitches of the C French 6th are C–E–F♯–A♯. Looking at this structure from the tritone root above C — the F♯ — and constructing an F♯7♭5 produces F♯–A♯–C–E, the exact pitches of the C French 6th. The preceding demonstrates the relationship between the C French 6th and a tritone-related root (F♯) of a major, minor 7th with flatted 5th.

The C French 6th resolves most commonly to E$^6_4$ or to the dominant of E. In either resolution the bass note is B. The F♯7♭5 is a dominant function; it resolves most commonly to B, but also frequently to E$^6_4$ as a secondary-dominant embellishment. Recall that the V/V often resolves to a tonic $^6_4$. Thus, a resolution of F♯ dominant to E is not uncommon. This demonstration is yet another example of seemingly *remote relationships* that, upon investigation, are rather closely related. (These types of relationships will be further examined in the next chapter.) See *Example 18–14.*

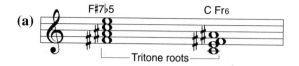

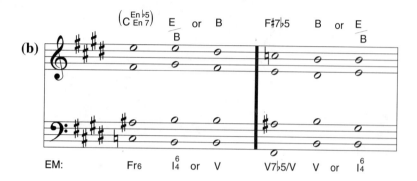

Example 18–14. Comparison of the F♯7♭5 and the C French sixth. **(a)** The F♯7♭5 contains the same pitches as the C French 6th. **(b)** Resolution of the French 6th and the V7♭5/V.

◆ Implied Roots

Further examination of the French 6th may clarify the concept of possible root derivation originating on the *second degree* of the scale. (See Chapter 16.) The C French 6th, C–E–F♯–A♯, was shown to be closely related to F♯7♭5, and, of course, to C7♭5 by chromatic alteration. But is there another root implied in the observation of these pitches? What is being sought is a chord whose root is not present in the French 6th.

The search for a so-called missing root of the aforementioned French 6th, C–E–F♯–A♯, and the related F♯7♭5, F♯–A♯–C–E, brings us once again to the issue of *chord substitution,* a concept discussed in previous chapters. The attempt to locate a possible implied root supports, in part, the principle of conceptualizing augmented 6ths as a derivation of the raised 4th (♯4) and of the supertonic degree of the scale.

Substitute chords are located in many ways, one of which is to compare the pitches of the initial chord with pitches of the possible substitute. Often, chords that contain certain numbers of common pitches are suitable as substitutes. Another method for attaining a suitable substitute is to extend the initial chord either upward or downward in diatonic or chromatic 3rds. For example, the G major triad G–B–D extended *downward a minor third* to E–G–B–D (Emm7) yields a possible substitute; further extension by a major 3rd produces C–E–G–B–D (CMM7M9). Extension *upward a major third* produces G–B–D–F♯ (GMM7). Applying this technique to the C French 6th can produce:

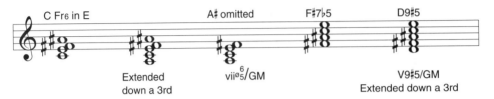

Example 18–15. *E and G associated as "relative" keys.*

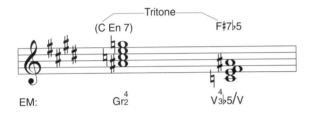

Example 18–16. *Support of an E root by the tritone-related C and F♯.*

A–[C–E–F♯–A♯] (Am add 6, en♭9? or F♯7♭5, en♯9?, etc.)[1]

A♭–[C–E–F♯–A♯] (A♭+en 7, en 9?)

Both solutions offer a paucity of support for ♯4 and supertonic-degree origina-tions of the augmented 6th. However, applying the same technique to the tri-tone-related F♯7♭5 produces quite different results. By extending a major 3rd downward, the more common harmonic structure, D–[F♯–A♯–C–E], is pro-duced. This chord is appropriately labeled D9♯5, or D major, minor 7th, major 9th, raised 5th (DMm7M9♯5). It is at once revealed that D9♯5 is rather closely related to the relative major key of G. Looking back for a moment at the down-ward extended C French 6th does, in fact, reveal a relatedness, not to E at first, but to the relative major of G. By omitting the A♯ and retaining the A–C–E–F♯, a vii⌀$^6_5$ is produced, also known in more modern terms as an Am add6 or Am6. What about the omitted A♯? Perhaps it is the leading tone of the dominant B in E major or E minor? See *Example 18–15*.

Upward extension of the ♯4 using A♯ as a potential root from the French 6th produces A♯–C–E–G (C en7 $^4_2$, a Gr 2^4 in E). *Downward* extension from A♯ produces A♯–F♯–E–C (F♯7♭5) — a secondary dominant of V. Support of an E key center is revealed from both results.

If this all seems rather esoteric and perhaps even somewhat bizarre, it sug-gests that certain relationships in music that initially appear to be rather remote, actually reveal, upon careful investigation, diatonic mutations. See *Example 18–16*.

---

1. En = enharmonic

Applications

Although this chapter has focused on stepwise, mediant, and tritone root relationships and movement, it is necessary for the reader to apply these concepts in musical examples through voice-leading practice. Once again, it is part-movement consideration that is of greatest importance. Chromaticism is, of course, extended by the incorporation of nondiatonic harmonies that surface in these alternate chord movements. In a progression of chords and types of chords whose movement is other than conventional, choices of part movement must be made from a strictly musical stance. Logic dictates that unconventional chord movement cannot be totally guided by conventional voice-leading practice.

However, some general practices do prevail. Parallel motion should be treated carefully. It is still the independence of voices that is of importance. Conventional doublings should always be considered to avoid jeopardizing the character of the chord. Resolutions of leading tones, tritones, 7ths, etc., must be handled in a musical way; since conventional resolution is not always possible, *smooth voice leading* usually is. The practitioner must remember that as chromaticism and movement become more complex, the style deviates more from the traditional, and hence, *strict application of the rules is not possible.* It is here that the familiar adage about "breaking the rules" presents itself. The rules are never broken; they are simply adapted to the evolving styles.

◆ *Chord Identification in Unconventional Root Movements*

Traditional functional Roman numerals will obviously not be applicable in situations in which chord movement and relationship is unconventional. Where harmony is not a function in conventional terms, chords can be labeled by alternative methods. The first method involves a description of the altered scale degree by a Roman numeral adjusted to accommodate that particular scale degree. For example, an F♯ minor triad in second inversion in the key of C major can be labeled as ♯iv$^6_4$; a B♭ major triad in first inversion can be labeled as ♭VII6. Care must be taken not to label every chord that appears to be remote in this fashion. A G♯° triad in the key of C major must not be labeled as ♯v° if it is a function of vi (vii°/vi) or if it evades to IV.

The second method of identification involves a description similar to popular symbolism. An E♭ minor triad in second inversion in any key, for example, is simply labeled as E♭m$^6_4$; an A♭7 in first inversion is labeled as A♭7$^6_5$. Again, it is imperative that function be assessed first. Thus, B7 progressing to E minor in the key of C major is V7/iii; if B7 resolves to C, it is a deceptive resolution — hence, V7/iii ev or V7/iii dec.

In *Example 18–17* on page 432, unconventional harmonic content and movement are illustrated in four- and five-part textures. As in any other chorale style, many possible harmonizations can be performed.

Example 18–17. Unconventional harmonic content. (**a**) In a four-part texture. (**b**) In a five-part texture. S=stepwise movement, M=mediant movement, T=tritone movement.

Chapter Review

The salient point of discussion in this chapter was unconventional harmonic movement. Most traditional harmonic function involves progression by 4ths and 5ths; what appear to be alternative movements are in many cases substitute harmonies.

The *stepwise, mediant,* and *tritone* harmonic movements incorporate those chord-to-chord movements that are not conventional in the sense of diatonic, chromatic, and embellishing functions.

Two additional types of movements discussed are planing and parallelism. These two terms are often considered synonymous, but they are, in fact, different. *Planing* is the movement of chords in whole or half steps while maintaining a particular voicing. *Parallelism,* on the other hand, maintains chord voicing, but is not restricted to whole- and half-step movement.

A feature of this chapter was the demonstration of similarities among chords in a tritone root relationship and in symmetrical chord construction. An ability to see an F♯ major triad, for example, as related to a C dominant triad is essential. On a C root, F♯ is ♯11; A♯ is the enharmonic minor 7th; C♯ is the enharmonic ♭9. The entire structure can be viewed as C7♯11♭9, a dominant of F. (Of course, G, the fifth, would most likely be omitted in the ♯11.) Moreover, C is also in a Neapolitan relationship with B, a tonic relationship of F♯. This type of thought process is necessary in gaining a comprehensive understanding of the workings of music.

With unconventional harmonic content and movement, the problem of voice leading becomes apparent. A point to remember is that the decision to move from one chord to another should always be based upon a sense of musical pragmatism. Although conventional rules may not be applicable, adaptations of these rules will lead to musical results.

Chord identification other than by conventional function, as provided by Roman numerals, was also introduced. *Altered Roman numeral identifications* accommodate chromatic scale degrees, and an *adaptation of popular symbols* expresses the chord root by letter, quality, and inversion in conventional nomenclature.

Anthology References

For additional usage and analysis, see the following examples in Distefano, Joseph P. and James A. Searle, *Music and Materials for Analysis: An Anthology.* New York, Ardsley House, Publishers, Inc., 1995.

planing; stepwise movement
   Example 56.   *Sonata for Violin,* No. 2, Third Movement, "The Revival," Charles Ives, pp. 325–34.
noncyclic movement
   Example 44.   *Poème,* Op. 69, No. 1, Alexander Scriabin, pp. 253–58.
7♭5

   Example 53.   *Music for Children,* Op. 65, March, Sergei Prokofiev, pp. 301–4.

Self-Test

1. Explain *stepwise harmonic movement*. Differentiate between diatonic and chromatic relationships.
2. Explain *mediant root movement*. Differentiate between diatonic and chromatic relationships.
3. What is meant by "symmetrical movement" as it applies to the intervallic root movements of certain chords?
4. Explain the technique of *planing*.
5. Explain the technique of *parallelism*.
6. Discuss the similarities and differences between the major, minor 7th and the German 6th of the same root; also discuss the key relationships that may be derived from them.
7. Discuss the similarities and differences between the 7♭5 and the French 6th of the same root; also discuss the key relationships that may be derived from them.
8. A French 6th can be seen as derived from the _____ scale.
9. How does the adage concerning "breaking the rules" apply to this chapter?
10. List and explain two alternative methods for the identification of nonconventional chord content and movement.
11. Discuss, explain, and label the following progression in F major:

    FM, AM, Gm, D♭7, Am, B♭m, E7, FM, Fm, G7, B♭M, FM
12. Discuss, explain, and label the following progression in E minor:

    F♯7, B7, CM, DM, Em, B♭7, Am, FM, Em, Am, C7, BM
13. Spell the following chords in B♭M:

    (a) I BC   (b) ♯IVM7   (c) viim7   (d) III7   (e) ♭VIM7   (f) ♭III7   (g) V♭5

Exercises

1. Determine the type of movement between the roots. Label all chords as illustrated in the first three measures.

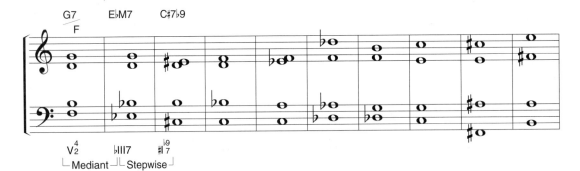

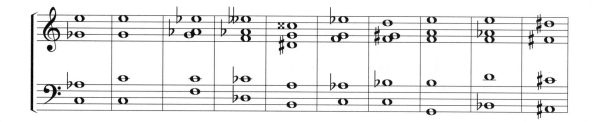

2. Write tritone substitutions. Use D5 and A4 roots, wherever possible. See the first measure.

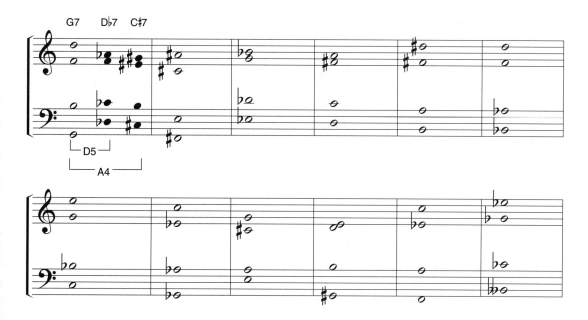

3. Alter by respelling the dominant structures as augmented 6ths. Determine a key center. Label all chords. See the first measure.

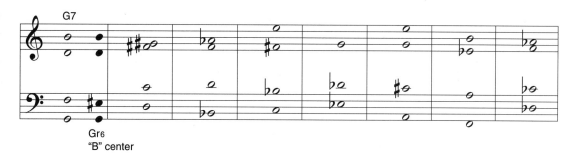

4. Alter by respelling the augmented 6ths as dominant structures. Determine a key center. Label all chords. See the first measure.

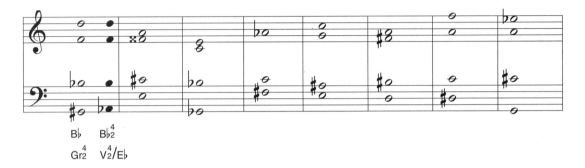

B♭   B♭²₄
Gr⁴₂   V⁴₂/E♭

5. Extend each chord downward by the addition of a major or minor third. Analyze the result and label. See the first measure.

F♯°7   D7♭9

6. Complete in SATB format. Label all chords Use stepwise, mediant, and tritone movement and upper-partial chords.

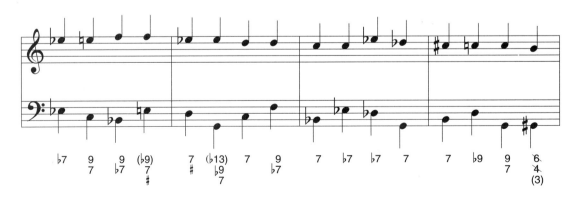

♭7   9   9   (♭9)   7   (♭13)   7   9   7   ♭7   ♭7   7   7   ♭9   9   6
      7   ♭7   7   ♯   ♭9   ♭7   7   4
                   ♯   7   (3)

7. **(a)** Continue the planing:

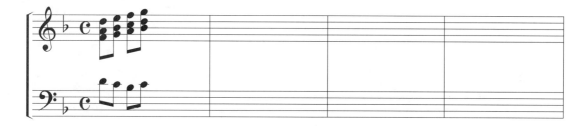

(b) Continue the parallelism:

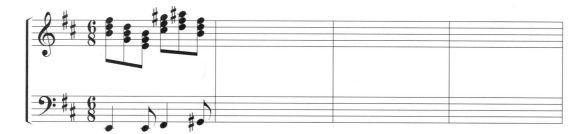

8. Harmonize using stepwise-, mediant-, and tritone-related chord movement. Label all chords.

(a)

19

MODULATION

The term *modulation* is derived from the Latin, *modulari,* which means to change, fluctuate, or vary. In music, **modulation** is the technique by which the key of a musical work is changed. The process of modulation can range from quite simple techniques that involve elementary harmonic and melodic manipulations to procedures that are complex, protracted, and even ambiguous. Key relationships can be closely related or remote, and added to this are the many types of modulatory procedures.

At various places in this book, modulation has been mentioned but never fully examined, and there was good reason for this. Although in many instances modulation can be a rather simple process, it could not be thoroughly explored until a substantial knowledge of chromatic harmony had been gained. At this point, the reader should possess a sufficient understanding of diatonicism and chromaticism for this purpose.

Establishing a New Key Center

A *key region* emphasizes a particular key other than the tonic, but a new key center is not fully established. *Tonicization* was stressed in the discussion of

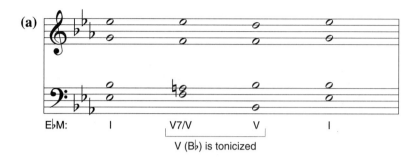

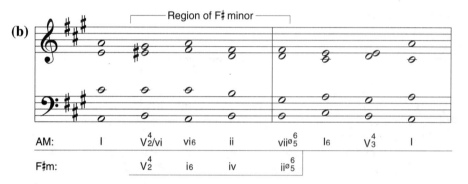

Example 19–1. Tonicizations within key centers. (a) Tonicization of the V. (b) A chord progression in A major in which a segment can be viewed as the region of F♯ minor. Although F♯ minor is not established as a key center, it can provide convincing preparation for an ensuing modulation.

secondary chords (Chapters 12 and 13) whereby the tonicized chord is considered as a momentary tonic. A tonicization is briefer than a key region, which, in turn, is briefer than a modulation — at least in principle. A *modulation* is the convincing establishment of a totally new key center. See *Example 19–1.*

Perhaps the most confounding aspect of modulation is the *subjectiveness factor,* that is, the degree to which the listener is convinced of the establishment of a new key center. In many tests conducted on theory students by this author, not once was a class in total agreement on a modulation that was anything but extraordinarily obvious. True, these students were aware that movement to a new key area was in progress. However, there was a question as to whether the key did, in fact, change and whether a new key had been established. Or was the newly arrived-at key merely temporary and the movement incomplete; must there be further establishment of a more convincing closure?

What, then, is required to convince a listener that a modulation has been realized? Is it the length of the passage in the new key, the number of chords in the new key, the melodic design, the tempo, the rhythm, the harmonic rhythm, the structure; or is it the brevity of the modulation itself? Is quick movement to a new key area the most convincing modulatory technique? There is no guaranteed formula for creating a convincing modulation. Only one aspect will ultimately be agreed upon — the protracted temporal dimension. If a musical segment in a new key center is extended for a long-enough duration, the listener will eventually accept this new key center as established. Further discussion of this mental process will not be investigated in this book; it belongs ultimately to the disciplines of psychology, sociology, and ethnomusicology.

Why Modulate?

A protracted musical segment, regardless of its melodic, rhythmic, dynamic, and structural content, and even its *production,*[1] can eventually become harmonically stagnant. This is not to suggest that every musical work must modulate at some time. Stylistically, it may not be appropriate to effect a modulation in certain genres. However, extended works usually contain at least one modulation. Popular songs, folk songs, many jazz compositions, and short works normally do not contain extensive modulation, although some do.

There are many effects of modulation. These include: a variety of harmonic content, a contrast of mood, a delineation of structural divisions, and dramatic effect. Beginning with the advent of simple chromaticism as far back as the fourteenth century, modulation has continued to evolve. Now even key identification can become ambiguous due largely to continuous and rapidly changing key centers.

There are various types of modulations, including:

1. common-chord modulation,

2. pivot-chord modulation,

3. chromatic modulation,

4. enharmonic modulation,

5. implied modulation,

6. static modulation, and

7. common-tone modulation.

---

1. **Production** refers to a work as it is prepared and presented to an audience — either live or recorded.

Common-Chord Modulation

A **common chord** is one that is present in both the prevailing key and the **target key** (or new key). Keys that are closely related to the tonic, for example, the dominant, subdominant, and their relative keys, as well as the relative key of the tonic, contain more common chords than do remotely related keys. As an example of this, G major and its closely related keys will be examined for common-chord content in *Table 19–2*. Since qualities of triads differ according to the type of minor scale used — harmonic, melodic, or natural — the Roman numerals in this table are for location purposes only, not for qualities.

As can be seen in *Table 19–2*, closely related keys contain a substantial number of common chords. However, in comparing the number of common chords among remotely related keys — those separated by more than one sharp or flat — the number of common chords decreases. A comparison of G major and A major, for example, reveals only two common chords: the iii (B minor) in G major is also the ii in A major and the V (D major) in G major is also the IV in A major. In a comparison of the keys of G major and E major, no common chords are available. Descending in fifths beyond the subdominant key of C major brings us to the key of F major. It is readily seen that F major and G major share two common chords: the iii (A minor) in F major is common with the ii in G major, and the V (C major) in F major is common with the IV in G major. The next key in the circle, B♭ major, does not share any common chord with G major. It can thus be seen that the further one moves from the tonic, the fewer the common chords that are available; this is illustrated in *Example 19–3* on page 444.

SCALE DEGREES	I	II	III	IV	V	VI	VII
GM Tonic	GM	Am	Bm	CM	DM	Em	F♯ dim
DM Dominant	DM	Em		GM		Bm	
CM Subdominant	CM		Em		GM	Am	
Em Relative to Tonic	Em	F♯ dim	GM (natural)	Am	Bm (natural)	CM	DM (natural)
Bm Relative to Dominant	Bm		DM (natural)	Em		GM	
Am Relative to Subdominant	Am	Bm (melodic)	CM (natural)	DM (melodic)	Em (natural)		GM (natural)

Table 19–2. Common chords in G major and closely related keys.

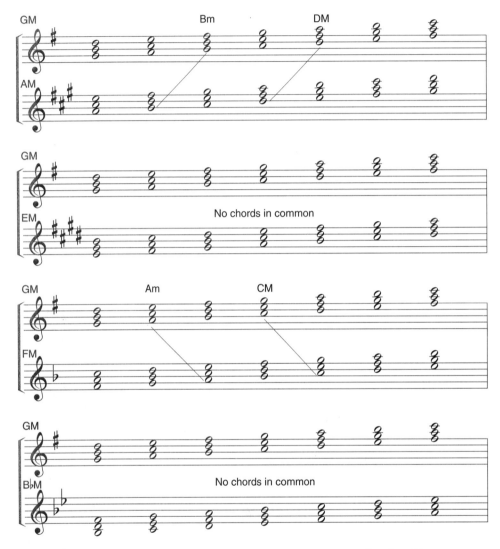

Example 19–3. Common chords in G major and several remotely related keys.

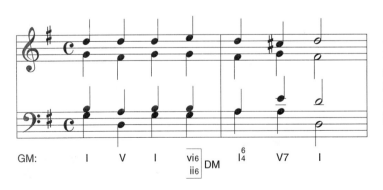

Example 19–4. **Common chord at the cadence.** In measure 2, even though every chord prior to the V7 appears both in G major and in D major, it is the ii6 that is closest to the cadential progression in D major.

The use of a common chord in the modulation process delineates the point at which the chord serves a *dual function:* first, its place or function — I, ii, iii, etc. — in the prevailing key, and second, what it becomes in the target key. If a musical work in the key of G major is modulating to D major and the vi chord (E minor) in G major is to be used as the common chord, the E minor chord becomes a ii chord in the key of D major. In the case of more than one chord in common, the best choice is that common chord closest to the cadence or appearance of accidentals in the new key. The use of a bracket, as demonstrated in *Example 19–4,* defines the common chord.

If, in the musical work, a modulation from G major to C major is initiated through the use of the common chord, A minor, then Am (ii) in G major becomes vi in C major. See *Example 19–5.* Several other common-chord modulations are illustrated in *Example 19–6* on pages 446–47.

Pivot-Chord Modulation

In a **pivot-chord modulation**, any chord with a relationship to both keys can be employed. Suppose, for example, a remote modulation from G major to B♭ major were to be performed. No common chords exist among the two keys. However, if in the G major harmonic progression of a musical work there appears a C minor triad, this triad can be considered a *borrowed chord,* that is, borrowed from the parallel key of G minor. This borrowed iv is clearly present in B♭ major; it is the ii. The C minor triad cannot be considered *common,* but it definitely can be used as a *pivot.* See *Example 19–7* on page 448. (Sometimes, *common chords* are also referred to as *pivot chords.*)

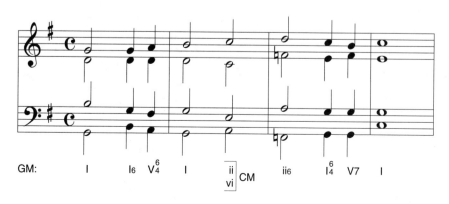

Example 19–5. The use of ii becoming vi in the new key.

(a)

Fantasia in D Minor

W. A. Mozart

(b)

Waltz in A♭

J. Brahms

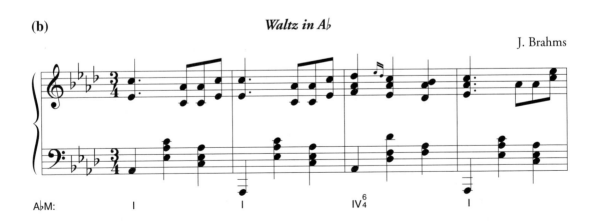

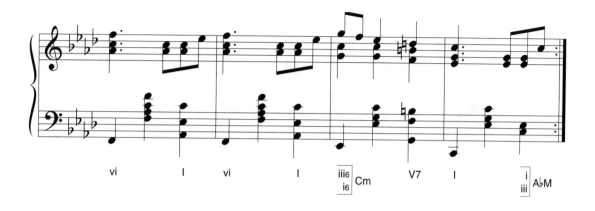

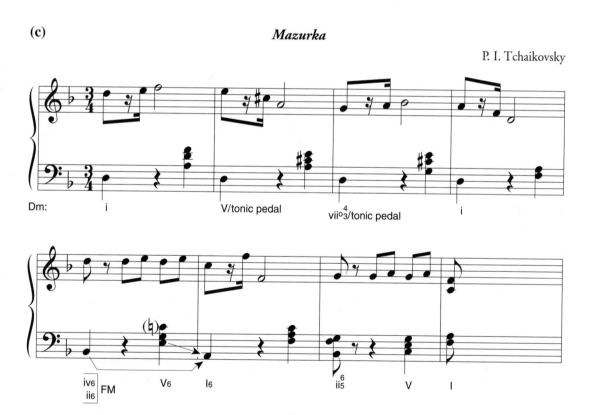

Example 19–6. **Common chords in modulation.** (a) The use of I becoming IV. (b) The use of iii becoming i. (c) The V6 normally resolves to a root position I. However, the B♭ bass note on the first beat, even though it is the third of $\frac{\text{iv6}}{\text{ii6}}$ FM, endures as a 7th of the subsequent V6 and is resolved downward to A in the I6.

Example 19–7. Borrowed chords as pivots. **(a)** Note that this example does not illustrate a complete modulatory process. The key of G major has not been firmly established; nor has the key of B♭ major. The point of the example is to demonstrate the pivot chord. **(b)** Schubert effects a mediant modulation through use of a borrowed i (B♭ minor in B♭ major), which functions as a vi in D♭ major.

Chromatic Modulation

Change-of-quality (CQ) chords can also be used as pivot chords. Modulations employing these CQs are more accurately referred to as *chromatic modulations*. A **chromatic modulation** involves the use of at least one pitch of the prevailing chord that is *chromatically altered* to propel the ensuing passage into the new key. See *Example 19–8*.

If, in our musical work in G major, a modulation to F♯ major is desired, it becomes apparent that again, no common chords exist. Suppose, however, that in the G major chord progression a B major triad is present that is not embellishing; that is, this B major triad does not function as a secondary dominant to vi (E minor) and it is not deceptive in its resolution (to C major, IV in G major). Can this B major triad be utilized in any way in a modulation to F♯ major? A search through the available triads in the key of F♯ major reveals that the B major triad is the IV chord. See *Example 19– 9* on page 450.

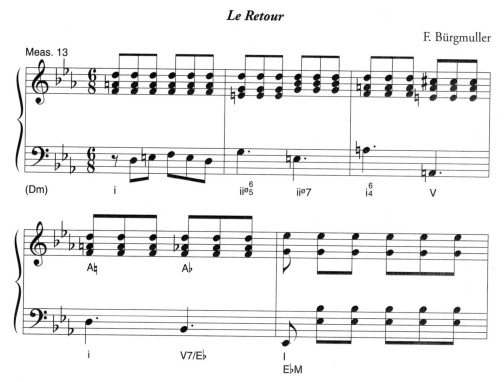

Le Retour

F. Bürgmuller

Example 19–8. A chromatic modulation in which the pivot has no functional relationship to the ensuing tonic.

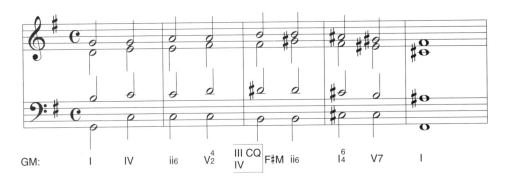

GM: I IV ii6 V$_2^4$ III CQ / IV F#M ii6 I$_4^6$ V7 I

Example 19–9. The CQ-chord as a pivot.

◆ *Neapolitan Chords*

Pivot chords can also be derived from Neapolitan chords. The appearance of an N6 that does not resolve in normal fashion (to a tonic $\overset{6}{4}$ or V) may be indicative of a modulation whereby the Neapolitan is considered a pivot in the target key.

The appearance of the Neapolitan in G major resolving in a remote area, such as E♭ major, A♭ major, or D♭ major, indicates that the A♭ major triad (the Neapolitan in G major) serves to effect a modulation to one of these remote key areas. Its function in the target key can be as a tonic in A♭ major, a subdominant in E♭ major, or a dominant in D♭ major.

Example 19–10 illustrates how a Neapolitan can be considered a pivot. In part (d), the D♭ major triad, which is a Neapolitan in C minor (or C major) functions as a I chord in the key of D♭ major. The ensuing progression of Cdim (first inversion), D♭M(first inversion), G♭M, D♭M (second inversion), and A♭M supports a key movement to D♭M.

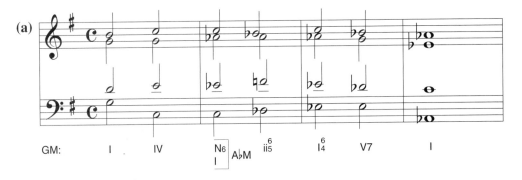

(a)

GM: I IV N6 / I A♭M ii$_5^6$ I$_4^6$ V7 I

Example 19–10. The Neapolitan as a pivot. (a) The N6 as a pivot resulting in a modulation to the tonic of its root. *(b)* The N6 as a pivot to a key in which the N6 is the subdominant. *(c)* The N6 as a pivot to a key in which the N6 is the dominant. *(d)* The Neapolitan as a pivot to the tonic of its root.

(d) **Sonata Pathétique**

L. v. Beethoven

◆ Borrowed Pivots in Target Keys

Remote relationships of chord functions are further confounded by the fact that *pivot chords can also be borrowed in the target key.* In the preceding discussion, the A♭ major triad that was initially the Neapolitan in G major may very well become the borrowed IV chord from E♭ minor, instead of simply the IV chord in E♭ major. One should always look further into the target key area to be certain that a modulation to that key area is, in fact, correctly assumed. The A♭ major triad may not resolve in a typical fashion in any of the remote key areas of A♭ major, E♭ major, or D♭ major. The Neapolitan chord in G major that shifts

Example 19–11. Regions resulting from the use of the Neapolitan as a pivot. (a) Here it is preferable to view the entire segment as a key movement to D♭, since E♭ minor has not been firmly established as a key center. (b) A♭ major has not been firmly established as a key center specifically because an E♭ minor triad (measure 3) would not function as its dominant.

the tonal center to what appears to be A♭ major may, in fact, be a modulation to D♭ major. In the progression from A♭ major to B♭ minor, what appears to be a movement of I to ii in A♭ major may, in fact, be V to vi in D♭ major. It is always necessary to look further into the new key area and, preferably, to locate the closest ensuing cadence. This often aids in determining the correct key center. Note the possible explanations for chord function in *Example 19–11.*

Enharmonic Modulation

An **enharmonic modulation** involves the *enharmonic alteration* of a melodic tone or of one or more of the chord tones of the modulatory pivot chord, as illustrated in *Example 19–12.*

Example 19–12. Enharmonic modulation occuring between the fourth and fifth measures shown. The F♭7 in the fourth measure is respelled as E7 in the fifth measure, thus effecting a modulation to AM. Notice also the Fr6 derivation of the E7♭5 from the relative key of A♭M. Chord structures result from the chromatic descending movement in measure 14.

◆ *Augmented Sixths as Pivots*

An excellent example of enharmonic modulation involves the *alternative function* of the augmented 6th chord used as a pivot. The augmented 6th chord in G major, for example, is constructed on the root of the lowered sixth degree (E♭). A German 6th is spelled E♭–G–B♭–C♯; the resolution of this chord is normally to I$^6_4$. If the harmonic structure of the German 6th is considered as a dominant 7th function, E♭–G–B♭–D♭, a potential key center is that of A♭ major or A♭ minor. This resulting E♭7th chord can even function as a secondary chord or in a deceptive resolution to an F minor chord. Either of these functions can serve to effect a modulation to a key other than A♭ major or A♭ minor. See *Example 19–13*.

◆ *Major-Minor Sevenths*

A *dominant seventh* can be respelled to form an *augmented sixth*. The dominant 7th in G major, D–F♯–A–C can be respelled as D–F♯–A–B♯, in which the D is now the root of the German 6th in either F♯ major or F♯ minor.

In the *Fantasia* by Mozart *(Example 19–14)*, the initial aural effect of the G-to-E♯ harmonic dyad in the second measure suggests a V7 of IV (G7 (G–B–D–F) to CM). However, Mozart spells this sound of the minor 7th interval (G to F) as G to E♯ and proceeds to use the harmonic structure as an augmented 6th chord to establish a modulation to B minor. (Note that G–B–D–E♯ is a German 6th in either B major or B minor.)

Similar alterations of the French and Italian 6ths are also available. Since all augmented 6ths are essentially the same in structure and function, differences occur only in the 3rd factor of each such chord. (An augmented 4th is present in the French 6th; no 5th is present in the Italian 6th.) See *Example 19–15*.

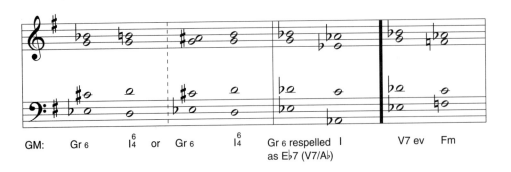

| GM: | Gr 6 | I$^6_4$ | or | Gr 6 | I$^6_4$ | Gr 6 respelled | I | | V7 ev | Fm |
| | | | | | | as E♭7 (V7/A♭) | | | | |

Example 19–13. The augmented sixth as a pivot.

Fantasia

W. A. Mozart

Meas. 20

GM: I

Bm: Gr 6 (initially, this interval sounds like a V7/IV function)

Bm: V   i   V

Example 19–14. *The initial effect of the G-to-E♯ dyad suggesting a V7/V.* The spelling of the dyad is clearly that of an augmented 6th in B.

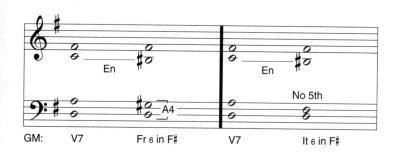

GM: V7   Fr 6 in F♯   V7   It 6 in F♯

Example 19–15. *The V7 in G and its alterations to a French sixth (measure 1) and an Italian sixth (measure 2) in F♯.*

◆ *Fully Diminished Sevenths*

One of the most confusing chord manipulations regarding function occurs in the alternate use of fully diminished 7th chords. As discussed in Chapter 18, diminished chords are spelled according to their leading-tone function. In many publications of popular music and even in some editions of classical works, these diminished chords are often spelled in a convenient way, rather than in the musically correct way. Necessary sharps and flats are often replaced with their enharmonic equivalents. This is shown in *Example 19–16.*

The use of fully diminished 7ths as pivot chords in modulation is both efficient and intriguing. The vii°7 in G minor is spelled F♯–A–C–E♭. This is the *only* correct spelling of the leading-tone fully diminished 7th chord in G minor. However, since this chord has a symmetrical structure (all minor thirds), any note of the chord or its *enharmonic spelling* can serve as a leading tone provided that the remaining notes are spelled correctly according to the newly established leading tone. If, for example, the note A is chosen as the new root of this fully diminished 7th, the remaining notes are correctly spelled (A)–C–E♭–G♭.

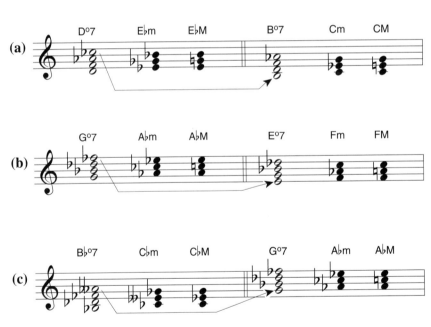

Example 19–16. Alternate spellings of fully diminished seventh chords.
(a) B°7 is often written instead of D°7 in order to eliminate the less common pitch, C♭. **(b)** E°7 is often written to eliminate the less common pitch, F♭. **(c)** G°7 is often written to eliminate the less common pitch, A♭♭. Nevertheless, the embellished chord should be preceded by its correct leading-tone diminished chord, that is, D°7 to E♭, *not* to C; G°7 to A♭, *not* to F; B♭°7 to C♭, *not* to A♭.

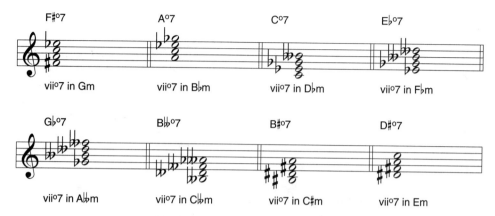

Example 19–17. Correct spellings of fully diminished seventh chords. It is highly unlikely that A♭ minor and C♭ minor will ever appear in the literature, but hypothetically, they do exist.

Although all the pitches are the same as those of the vii°7 in G minor, it is the spelling with G♭ rather than F♯ that is used, since the chord is now A diminished and is no longer F♯ diminished. Similarly, with C as the root, the remaining notes are (C)–E♭–G♭–B♭♭; and with E♭ as the root, the remaining notes are (E♭)–G♭–B♭♭–D♭♭. These are the *only* correct spellings from each of the given roots. Additionally, enharmonic equivalent roots are possible. Fully diminished 7ths can be constructed on G♭ (enharmonic to F♯), on B♭♭ (enharmonic to A), on B♯ (enharmonic to C), and on D♯ (enharmonic to E♭). In each case, the remaining 3rd, 5th, and 7th must be spelled correctly. See *Example 19–17.*

The use of fully diminished 7ths in modulation becomes obvious when enharmonic spelling is applied. Since the chord is a symmetrical intervallic structure, any note can become a leading tone to a target key. Hence, from the original F♯–A–C–E♭, A can become a leading tone to B♭, C a leading tone to D♭, and E♭ a leading tone to F♭. Enharmonic equivalents are also available: B♯, the enharmonic of C, becomes a leading tone to C♯, and D♯, the enharmonic of E♭, becomes a leading tone to E. In every instance, the targeted area can be major or minor. Thus, a D♯ fully diminished 7th can lead to either E major or E minor. See *Example 19–18* on page 458.

It is apparent that remote as well as closely related keys are available with the use of this respelling technique, as are impractical key centers, such as F♭ major or minor. It is also possible to consider the enharmonic of F♯ (G♭) a leading-tone fully diminished 7th to A♭♭ major or A♭♭ minor.

◆ *Augmented Triads as Pivots*

The augmented triad, which consists of two major 3rd intervals, is also in the category of symmetrical structures. This chord is normally considered a *dominant*

(a)

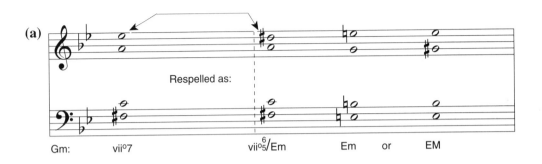

(b)

Sonata Pathétique

L. v. Beethoven

Example 19–18. Enharmonic spelling of fully diminished seventh chords. **(a)** The respelling of the vii°7 in G minor to a vii°7 in E. **(b)** The vii°7 in G minor (F♯–A–C–E♭) is respelled as vii°7 in E minor (D♯–F♯–A–C).

function and must be spelled accordingly. As illustrated in *Example 19–19(a),* the chord of C+ (C–E–G♯), also referred to as C aug or C+5, is a dominant function of F. Respelling the G♯ as A♭ creates an A♭–C–E structure, which is a dominant function of D♭; and respelling the E as F♭ creates an F♭–A♭–C structure, which is a dominant function in B♭♭. Thus, it becomes obvious that by spelling the G♯ enharmoni-

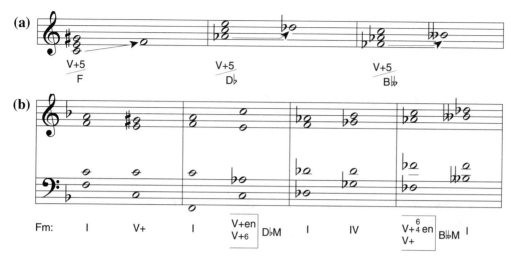

Example 19–19. The use of augmented triads in modulation. (a) Several spellings of the C+ augmented triad. (b) Extending the process of augmented triad pivots produces a modulation to B♭♭ in the last measure.

cally as A♭, a modulation to D♭ is possible, in spite of the fact that C+ was initially a dominant function of F. Notice that by retaining the doubled root (C) of the V chord in F, the resultant V (A♭) in D♭ contains two 3rds; this produces a doubled leading tone in D♭, in which case a wiser doubling would have been of the root A♭. Care must be taken to avoid any movement of parallel octaves. The 4th to 5th chords in *Example 19–19(b)* avoid the parallel octave by a leap resolution of C to A♭ in the soprano voice. Also, extending the process of augmented triad pivots produces a modulation to B♭♭ in the last measure.

Implied Modulation

A modulation without the use of accidentals in the melody itself is known as an **implied modulation**. Although a requirement of an implied modulation is the absence of accidentals in the melody, it is acceptable to have accidentals appear in the supporting harmony; but here too, it is possible for none to appear. An implied modulation in which no accidentals are employed is accomplished by the *prolongation of structural pitches* within the new key area, achieved by the *rhythmic stress* of these pitches. Special care must be taken in the interpretation

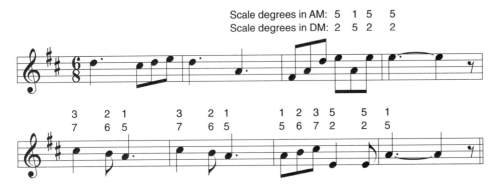

Example 19–20. An implied modulation to A major. Notice the absence of the leading tone. The implied cadence is V–I.

***Nachtstücke,* Op. 23, No. 3**

R. Schumann

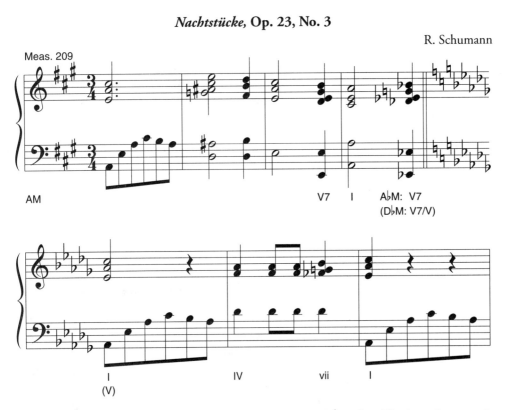

Example 19–21. Static modulation from A major to D♭ major. The key signature in measure 5 is correct because of a subsequent modulation to D♭.

of an implied modulation. In *Example 19–20,* which contains a key signature of D major, certain notes are emphasized by recurrence and intervallic relationship in order to establish key movement to A major without the use of the leading tone, G♯.

Static Modulation

A modulation that occurs *abruptly,* that is, with no apparent common or pivot chord — simply a change to a new key center — is known as a **static modulation**. Static modulation is utilized quite frequently in popular music, especially in ballads; but its use can be found in classical literature as well. Static modulation provides a sense of immediate urgency; it is meant to be dramatically and often emotionally effective, and it is not disguised in a protracted chord progression. It is an immediate change from one key directly into a new one. In popular terminology, static modulation is most often referred to as **key change**. Other terms used to identify this type of modulation are **phrase modulation** and **direct modulation**. See *Example 19–21.*

Common-Tone Modulation

Common-tone modulation involves the use of a *single note,* usually a melodic note, that is employed as a pivot. Assume for the moment a dominant 7th in the key of F major: C–E–G–B♭. The pitch B♭, as the 7th of the dominant 7th, has a tendency to resolve downward by step (see Chapter 7). However, B♭ can be *temporally manipulated* by repetition, reiteration, or any number of techniques so that its function becomes something other than the 7th of the dominant 7th — perhaps the major 3rd of a G♭ major triad, or the 5th of E♭ major or minor, or the (enharmonically spelled) augmented 6th of the German, French, or Italian 6th in E major or minor. The possibilities are enormous since each given note can become any one of the factors of a root. See *Example 19–22(a)* on page 462. In *Example 19–22(b),* the F♯ (measure 2), which is the fifth degree of the B major scale and the 5th of the B major triad, is treated as the third degree of D major; thus, it serves to establish a common-tone modulation to D major.

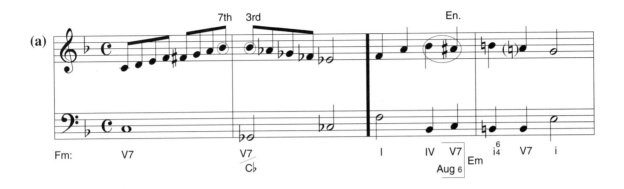

Example 19–22. Common-tone modulation. **(a)** By enharmonically spelling B♭ as A♯, an augmented 6th is created in measure 3. The implication is an augmented 6th in E. **(b)** Note that the F♯ in measure 2 is treated as the third degree of D major.

Further Remarks on Modulation

◆ Extensive Chromaticism

A desirable result in many types of modulations, especially those of the Baroque and Classical periods, was the graceful movement from one key to another. These modulations were primarily to closely related keys; hence, modulatory transitions were not difficult procedures since closely related keys contain several common chords. As music became more chromatic in the Romantic, post-Romantic, Impressionist, and contemporary periods, the practice of traditional methods of modulation became less stringent. Modulations to remote or foreign keys became symbolic of the various styles. There were many procedures for accomplishing these modulations; but one important new factor was now appearing in the music with increasing regularity — the extensive use of chromaticism.

Extensive chromaticism facilitates key movement, and the reason for this is simple. Diatonicism reinforces a prevalent key; chromaticism, especially extensive chromaticism, injects a certain amount of ambiguity concerning an established key center. Pitches and harmonies foreign to a key center do not normally contribute to the reinforcement of a tonal center. Rather, they draw attention away from the tonic key.

◆ Embedded Structures

Introducing pitches and harmonies foreign to the prevailing key is certainly one method of effecting a modulation. However, these pitches and harmonies are not restricted to the use of triads and sevenths, and herein lies the impact and enchantment of upper-partial chords in modulation. As described in Chapter 17, these chords often contain what can be interpreted as *embedded harmonic structures*. For example, a D major, minor 7th, major 9th, perfect 11th, major 13th, D–A–C–E–G–B (F♯ is omitted due to the presence of the 11th), when viewed as containing embedded chords, yields A minor; A minor, minor 7th; A minor, minor 7th, major 9th; C major; C major, major 7th; and E minor. See *Example 19–23*.

Altering the 13th, B, to a lowered 13th, B♭, yields another set of harmonic possibilities; altering the 11th, G, to a raised 11th, G♯, yields still other possibilities. It is the extraction, interpretation, and use of these *consequential chords* that permit movement with relative ease into remote or foreign keys. Possibilities for key movement using several consequential chords obtained as a result of manipulation of a D dominant structure are examined in *Example 19–24* on page 464. It is not necessary to limit this technique to dominant structures. Any upper-partial structure will yield comparable results.

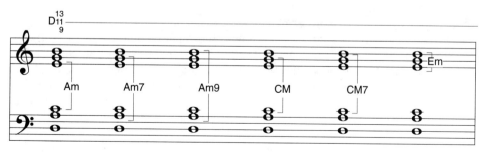

Example 19–23. Embedded structures in a $D^{13}_{11 \, 9}$ chord.

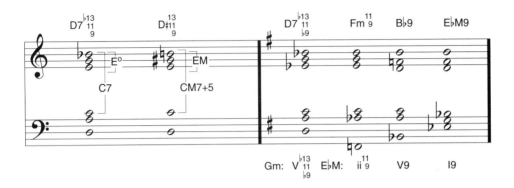

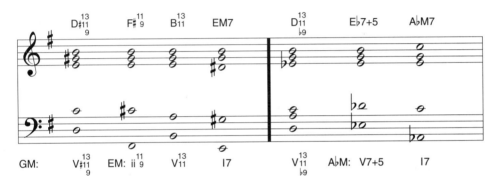

Example 19–24. Alterations to a D-dominant structure resulting in a smooth movement to remote keys.

◆ *Harmonic Structures Generated from Melodies*

The ensuing discussion moves toward the realm of contemporary classical-music practice; its presentation is warranted in view of the investigation of remote modulation. The generation of harmonies as a result of upper-partial manipulations extends to the perception of melodic tones other than their apparent chord-factor relationship. A melodic line, such as the one in *Example 19–25*, can appear with no indication of chord content. Nevertheless, its intervallic content and hence, harmonic implication can suggest a likely chord progression resulting in a modulation. This is determined by considering the key signature, by noting a tendency to remain diatonic in the choice of possible chords, and by recognizing that no related or remote chromaticism occurs in the melody.

Several possibilities for reharmonization of the melody are illustrated in Example 19–26. The second and third harmonizations result in modulation.

Example 19–25. Chords implied by a melodic line.

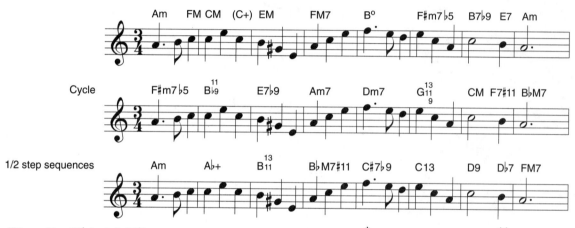

*F is considered E♯, the 3rd of C♯7.
**B is considered C♭, the 7th of D♭7.

Example 19–26. Possibilities for reharmonization.

◆ Unimplied Roots

Justification for these harmonizations lies in the fact that any pitch whatsoever, correctly respelled if necessary, can be a factor of any given chord root. The pitch E♭, for example, can be viewed as a root of E♭ major or minor, a major 3rd of C♭ major, a minor 3rd of C minor, a perfect 5th of A♭ major or minor, a diminished 5th of A diminished, a minor 7th of F7, a minor 7th of Fm7, a lowered 9th of D7♭9, a major 9th of D♭9, a perfect 11th of B♭11, an enharmonic raised 11th of A7♯11, a major 13th of G♭13, a lowered 13th of G13, etc. The fact that these and many other roots are available presents a host of possibilities for modulation to any key center. *Example 19–27* on page 466 presents several melodic pitches with potential roots and resultant harmonies.

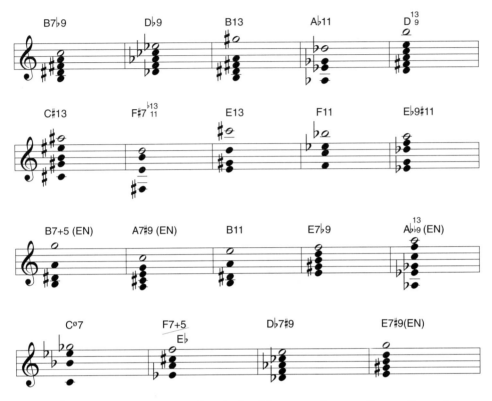

Example 19–27. The soprano of each chord interpreted as any factor of an arbitrary chord, even with enharmonic spelling. Note the following:

In B7+5, the tertian + 5 is F𝄪;

in A7♯9, the tertian ♯9 is B♯;

in A♭♭9 (with 13), the tertian ♭9 is B♭♭;

in E7♯9, the tertian ♯9 is F𝄪.

Chapter Review

In the context of music, *modulation* means a change of key center. In contrast with key regionalization and tonicization, a modulation is the firm establishment of a new key center. These key centers can be either closely related or remote.

In assessing whether a work has convincingly modulated, an element of subjectiveness is often a determining factor. Perception of modulation is frequently a personal phenomenon that can be based upon several factors, foremost of which are listening experiences and knowledge of musical practices and elements.

Modulation is not inherent in all genres of music. Certain stylistic practices do, however, require that pieces modulate, even to particular key centers.

The various types of modulations discussed in this chapter were: *common chord, pivot chord, chromatic, enharmonic, implied, static,* and *common tone.* To understand modulatory technique fully and to apply it correctly, a substantial familiarity with chromaticism is necessary.

In the establishment of pivot chords, an important procedure is the respelling of one or more pitches of a particular chord in order that the chord become a functional harmony in the ensuing key. Two particularly important chord structures demonstrated in this procedure were the augmented 6th and the fully diminished 7th.

The presence of embedded chords contained in upper-partial chords facilitates modulatory movement to remote key centers due simply to the complexity of chromaticism that may exist in the entire upper-partial structure. For example, assume a C♯$^{13}_{♯11}$$_{♭9}$: C–E–(G)–B♭–D♭–F♯–A. Notice the partially enharmonically spelled F♯ minor triad: D♭–F♯–A; the D♭ is an enharmonic C♯. Notice also the partially enharmonically spelled G♭ major triad, B♭–D♭–F♯; the F♯ is an enharmonic G♭. This structure can also be considered an F♯ major triad. The issue here is that these upper-partial notes can facilitate a smoother movement between two remotely related keys.

Anthology References

For additional usage and analysis, see the following examples in Distefano, Joseph P. and James A. Searle, *Music and Materials for Analysis: An Anthology.* New York, Ardsley House, Publishers, Inc., 1995.

various types of modulation

Example 22.   *Invention No. 4,* Johann Sebastian Bach, pp. 81–88.
Example 23.   *Invention No. 8,* Johann Sebastian Bach, pp. 81–86, 89–90.
Example 30.   *Rondo,* Wolfgang Amadeus Mozart, pp. 135–40.
Example 31.   *Sonata,* Hob. XVI, No. 27, First Movement. Franz Joseph Haydn. pp. 141–48.
Example 35.   *Album Leaves,* Op. 124, Waltz, Robert Schumann, pp. 193–200.
Example 41.   *Waltz,* Op. 39, No. 15, Johannes Brahms, pp. 233–38.

Self-Test

1. Discuss the difference between *modulation, key regionalization,* and *tonicization.*
2. Discuss what is meant by *remotely related* and *closely related keys.*

3. Discuss the subjectiveness factor in the assessment and perception of modulation.

4. A change of key must be _____ in order to be an unquestionably obvious modulation.

5. Why do musical works modulate? What are the function and results of modulation? What does it provide?

6. List the seven types of modulations discussed in this chapter and describe each.

7. Describe the *prevailing key* and the *target key*.

8. Describe what is meant by the *dual function* of a common chord used in modulation.

9. How are augmented 6th chords, major, minor 7th (dominant function) chords, and fully diminished 7ths alternatively utilized in modulation?

10. What is meant by the convenient spelling of a chord?

11. In what styles of music is key change commonly employed?

12. How does extensive chromaticism contained in certain upper-partial chord constructions facilitate the movement between remotely related keys?

Exercises

1. Write several common triads in the specified keys and label each with a Roman numeral, as shown in Part (a).

(a)

FM   I

B♭M   V

(b)

DM

AM

(c)

Am

GM

(d)

DM

CM

2. Write a chord progression of several measures and provide a common chord as a pivot to modulate to the following:

(a) Dominant

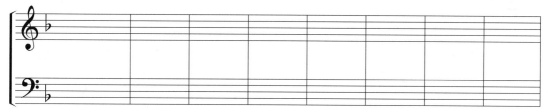

(b) Subdominant

(c) Relative minor

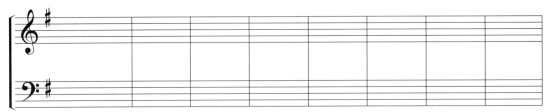

(d) Supertonic

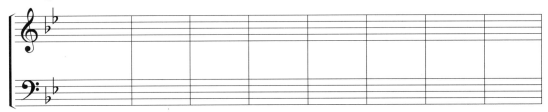

(e) Mediant

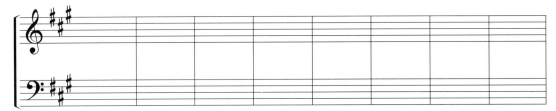

3. Establish modulations by use of a borrowed chord.

(a) to DM

(b) to FM

(c) to E♭M

4. Establish modulations by use of a CQ-chord.

(a) to EM

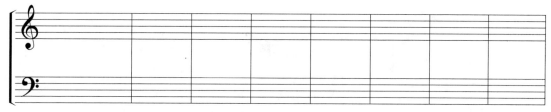

(b) to AM

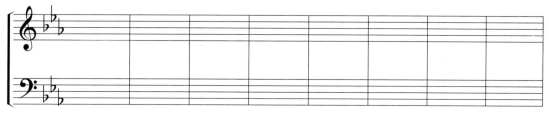

(c) to B♭M

5. Establish modulations by use of the Neapolitan chord.

(a) to B♭M

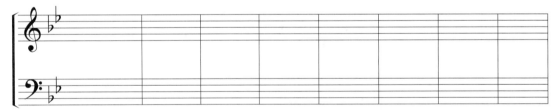

(b) to G♭M

(c) to GM

6. Establish enharmonic modulations by use of the German, French, and Italian 6th chords.

(a) to B♭m

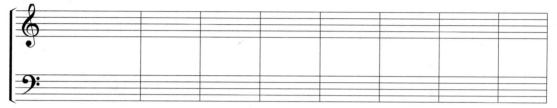

(b) to C♭M

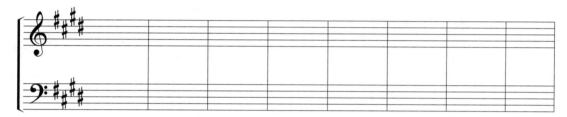

(c) to A♭M

7. Respell the dominant 7th of each key as an augmented 6th chord, and modulate to the appropriate key.

(a)

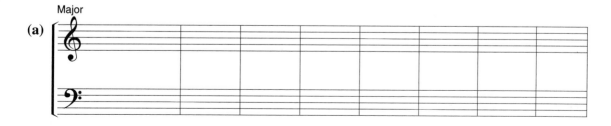

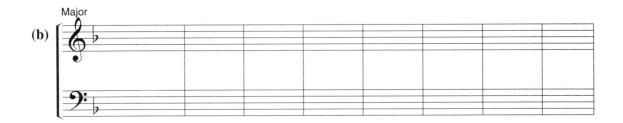

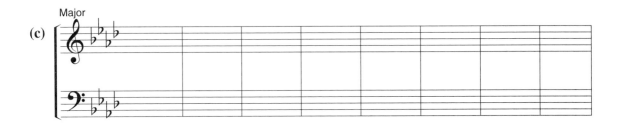

8. Respell the °7 of each key, and establish a modulation to a remote key center.

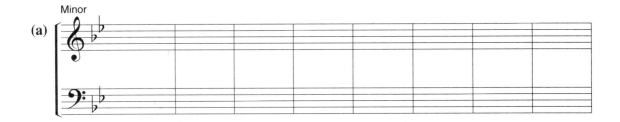

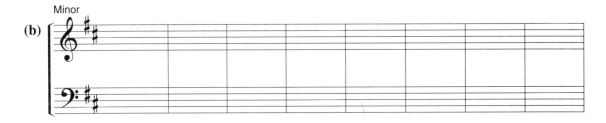

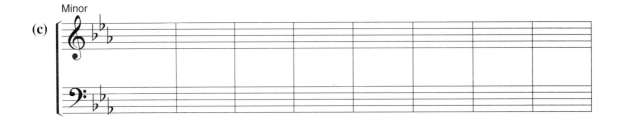

9. Compose a melody containing an implied modulation.

10. Compose an accompanied melody and provide a common-tone modulation.

11. Using upper-partial chords, modulate from CM to AM to B♭m to C♯M to G♭M to Fm to DM to E♭m to Cm. Label all chords, and describe their manipulation and functions.

12. Write the correct chord symbol above each designated pitch. See the first measure. Consider some of these pitches enharmonically.

20

SECUNDAL, QUARTAL,
AND
QUINTAL HARMONY

The tertian system of harmony *(Example 20–1)* — utilizing triads, 7ths, and also 9ths, 11ths, and 13ths in various disguises — had virtually been exhausted by the late 1800s. The rise of dissonance during the post-Romantic and Impressionist periods began with further manipulation of the tertian system — for example, authentic upper-partial chords, added-note chords of the 2nd or 9th, added 6ths, and altered chords. However, all these structures were derived from the tertian system and the resultant harmonic structures were essentially triads, either extended or colored by the addition of unconventional dissonances.

Example 20–1.** **The tertian system. ⨯ = deleted factors.

The Secundal System

◆ Chords in Seconds

Chords in seconds, or **secundal chords**, (not to be confused with added-note chords, such as add2, add9, or add6) are literally structures that are primarily comprised of intervals of major and/or minor 2nds. A simple chord requires at least three pitches; three-note secundal chords can contain four intervallic configurations of 2nds: minor-minor, minor-major, major-minor, and major-major, as illustrated in *Example 20–2.*

◆ Inversions

As with tertian triads, a *root position* and two inversions of secundal triads are possible, although the use of inversions is not as common with secundal chords as it is with tertian chords. It becomes apparent that upon inversion, the major-major, major-minor, and minor-major structures bear a close resemblance to various chords in the tertian system. The major-major is essentially an add 2 or add 9 on a major triad without the 5th; the major-minor, an add 2 or add 9 on a minor triad; and the minor-major, a major-major 7th, major 9th, without the 3rd and 5th. But these are not to be considered derivations and manipulations of tertian structures; used in proper context, they are chords in 2nds. See *Example 20–3.*

Example 20–2. Various intervallic configurations of secundal chords.

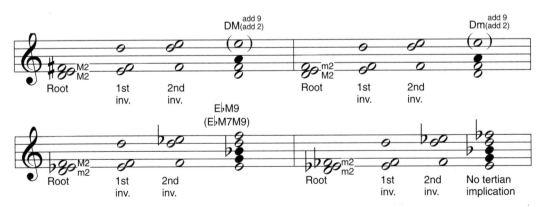

Example 20–3. Inversions of secundal chords with and without tertian implications.

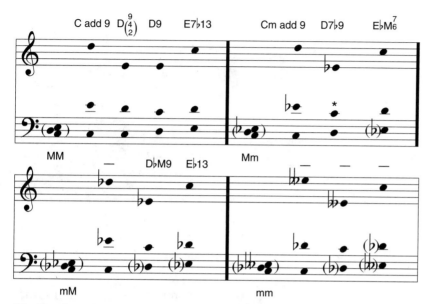

Example 20–4. Voicings of secundal chords with tertian implications.

*The third, F♯, of the root, D, is presumed, as this is more likely than F♮.
Dash indicates no tertian implications.

◆ Voicings

As with tertian chords, chords in 2nds can be voiced (spaced) in various configurations. Notice the tertian implications caused by certain voicings of three-note secundal chords, as illustrated in *Example 20–4*.

◆ Multinote Secundal Chords

As secundal chords become denser in structure by the addition of other 2nds, the **sound mass** (density) becomes thicker and more independent of possible tertian implications. These secundal chords — no longer simply three-note structures — are referred to as **multinote secundal chords**. Identification of inversions of any secundal chord is best achieved by first determining the root note of the chord — for example, C, E♭, F, etc — (by close arrangement of the inclusive notes) followed by the parenthesized Arabic numeral that identifies the chord factor in the bass. See *Example 20–5*.

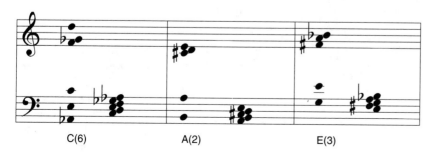

Example 20–5. Multinote secundal chords. Identification of inversions of secundal chords is best achieved by determining the root note of the chord.

Sonata, No. 3

B. Bartók

Example 20–6. Multinote secundal-chord clusters.

◆ *Clusters*

Multinote secundal chords in close voicing are referred to as **clusters**. (See *Example 20–6.*) Although it is not imperative that every two notes be separated by a 2nd, most secundal chords are in a cluster formation. Continuous use and movement of clusters negate authentic secundal harmonic identity because they relegate inner-voice movement to a coloristic function. In this situation only the bass and soprano voices are considered in voice-leading principles.

The use of secundal chords and cluster harmony is virtually nonexistent in popular-music styles. Their use is usually found in contemporary classical works. Although suggestions of secundal chords can be found in interpretations of certain jazz compositions, in most cases these chords are derived by manipulation of tertian-constructed chords. Secundal harmony is rarely extended beyond the use of a few chords; it is usually reserved as a percussive effect, and not as an authentic application of secundal voice-leading technique. In the style of "pop" song writing, current practice maintains chordal construction in the tertian system. It must be remembered that added-note chords, even when they appear in skeletal form, do not constitute secundal chords. Ultimately, it is the use of primarily 2nd intervals that renders any possible tertian root ambiguous and that, in turn, reinforces the existence of an actual secundal chord. See *Example 20–7.*

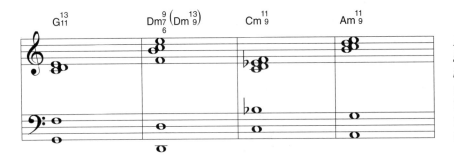

Example 20–7. Not secundal-chord structures. None of these are secundal-chord structures because they may easily be structured into common tertian chords.

The Quartal System

◆ Chords in Fourths

Essentially, **chords in fourths**, or **quartal chords**, are generated from nonharmonic ornamentation of triads and even from medieval contrapuntal practice. A triad in second inversion containing a suspension of a 4th, as in the 4–3 suspension, resembles the sound of a quartal chord in tertian harmony. The 4 in a 4–3 suspension normally resolves downward to the 3rd of the triad; in a quartal chord consisting solely of perfect 4ths, all 4ths are distinctive to the structure of the harmony. These inclusive pitches should not be considered as dependent upon their tertian implications, but rather, as independent chord factors. See *Example 20–8.*

There are three types of three-note quartal chords: *perfect-perfect, perfect-augmented, and augmented-perfect.*

◆ Perfect-Perfect Fourths

In the autonomous structure of a **perfect-perfect fourth**, any factor can be considered a root because *all intervals are equidistant.* As with augmented triads and fully diminished 7th chords, the perfect-perfect 4th chord is, intervallically, a symmetrical structure. Any perfect-perfect 4th chord containing two, three, or four superimposed perfect 4ths falls into the category of consonant 4th chords. A five-note perfect 4th chord contains all the degrees of the *pentatonic scale*; all perfect 4th chords of three and four factors evoke the essence of the pentatonic scale. (In jazz harmony and improvisation and in many melodies in jazz, folk, and popular idioms, the pentatonic scale is widely used.) See *Example 20–9* on page 482.

◆ Perfect-Augmented Fourths

The three-note **perfect-augmented quartal chord** falls into the category of *dissonant quartal harmonies.* The interval of a major 7th is present between the

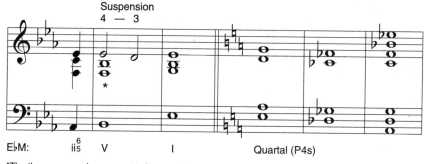

Example 20–8. Generation of a quartal chord from a 4–3 suspension.

*The three upper voices are not to be considered a quartal chord.

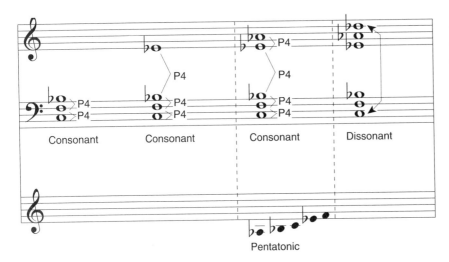

Example 20–9. Consonant and dissonant perfect fourth chords.

bass and soprano in root position. Unlike the root ambiguity present in the perfect-perfect quartal chord, with its symmetrical structure, the presence of an augmented 4th *tritone* creates a familiar tension that must be considered in resolution and progression. Whereas root implication remains ambiguous in the perfect-augmented quartal chord, movement is guided by melody, and in most situations either ascending or descending stepwise resolutions are preferred.

In a quartal structure containing the pitches C–F–B, *tertian implication* is difficult to ignore; the tonal center is clearly either major or minor C. The presence of the tritone F–B suggests an implied vii° triad (B–D–F), a viiø7 chord (B–D–F–A), a vii°7 chord (B–D–F–A♭), or a V7 chord (G–B–D–F). Hence, the note C, as the *implied tonic,* is present in conjunction with one of these possible chords. Should C be considered a tonic pedal tone under a diminished or dominant tension and thus be treated in that fashion? The answer is clearly no. In a quartal context, quartal chords are not considered as manipulations of tertian structures, just as secundal chords are not considered as added-note chords in tertian context. See *Example 20–10.*

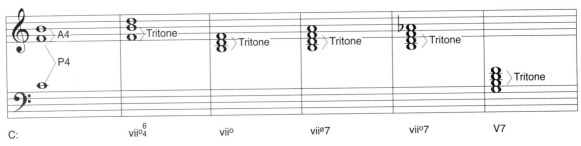

Example 20–10. The F–B, B–F tritone present in each dominant-function chord.

◆ Augmented-Perfect Fourths

With the **augmented-perfect fourth chord**, tertian implication can become even more pronounced and obvious. Again, as with perfect-augmented quartal chords, progression is guided by melody, and stepwise movement is preferred. An examination of this quartal structure reveals close similarities with tertian harmony.

In an augmented quartal chord containing the pitches F–B–E, a C major center is implied. Also implied by these three pitches is a rootless dominant 13th: [G]–B–[D]–F–E. Recall that in upper-partial chord structures in the tertian system, a root, 7th, and upper partial are all that are required for a dominant structure. The presence of the F (7th of G), B (3rd of G), and E (13th of G) strongly suggests G as an implied root. Moreover, the presence of the tritone F–B again suggests C as a tonal center, or at least as the chord of intended resolution.[1] Is it necessary to treat and resolve this structure as a tertian device? No. Can this structure be treated and resolved as a tertian device? Yes. Actually, all quartal chords can be incorporated within a tertian context, and vice versa. It is only when a quartal passage in a musical work is to be primarily quartal that any inference to tertian manipulation should be avoided. Quartal chords may remain autonomously quartal in a quartal context or be incorporated as color, extension, substitution, or contrast in tertian formats. See *Example 20–11.*

◆ Nonfunctional Augmented-Augmented Quartal Chords

Although an augmented-augmented 4th is possible as a correctly spelled chord, it is not usable because the second 4th enharmonically duplicates the initial pitch, as illustrated in *Example 20–12* on page 484.

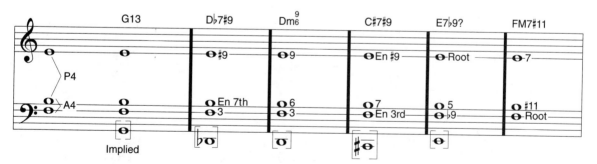

Example 20–11. Implied roots in the augmented-perfect 4th chord.

---

1. An implied G root chord is not the only possibility. The tritone substitution D♭ may also be implied by the pitches F–B–E, in which F is the 3rd, B is the enharmonic lowered 7th, and E is the raised 9th. The augmented-perfect 4th structure, though skeletal in nature, also lends itself to other less obvious possibilities and in many situations satisfies a harmonic implication—for example, Dm add6, 9; C♯, the enharmonic of D♭; E7♭9; FM7♯11, etc.

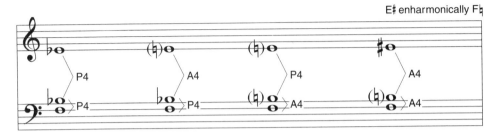

Example 20–12. **An augmented-augmented fourth chord (last structure): unusable.**

◆ Voicings

In order to avoid confusion with added-note chords and with chords of the 11th and 13th, as well as to preserve the quartal-chord quality, various voicings of the notes in quartal chords must contain *primarily fourth intervals.* Spacings containing a *perfect fifth* in the lower voices must be handled carefully and should be used only occasionally since the perfect 5th interval is virtually impossible to mask as a root 5th relationship in the tertian system. See *Example 20–13.*

◆ Consonance and Dissonance

Multinote quartal chords containing up to four perfect 4ths are considered *consonant.* The addition of a sixth factor, also a perfect 4th above the fifth note,

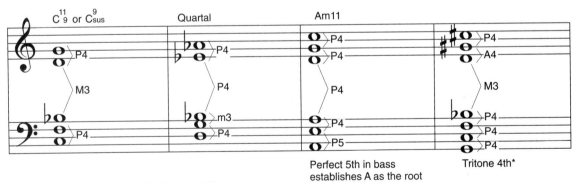

*See discussion of the tritone 4th chord on page 485.

Example 20–13. **A comparison of an upper-partial chord and quartal chords containing primarily 4th intervals.**

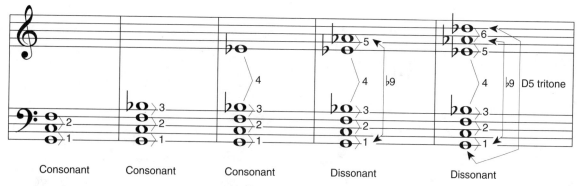

| Consonant | Consonant | Consonant | Dissonant | Dissonant |

Example 20–14. *Consonant and dissonant multinote quartal chords.*

creates a *dissonant* compound minor 9th with the bass. Therefore, a quartal chord containing five or more perfect 4ths is a dissonant perfect 4th chord. See *Example 20–14.*

Multinote quartal chords containing perfect 4ths and tritones must always be evaluated according to their consonant/dissonant content since these may contain more than one tritone. As with exclusively perfect 4th chords, **tritone 4th chords** — those containing at least one tritone — are ambiguous in their root implications, as shown in *Example 20–15,* and their harmonic movement (progression) is guided by melody and individual pitch tendency.

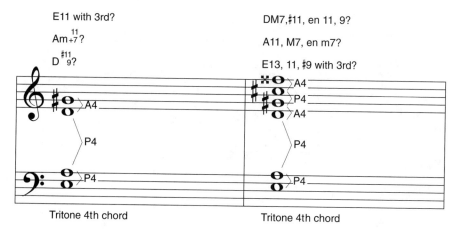

Example 20–15. *Root ambiguity created in tritone 4th chords.*

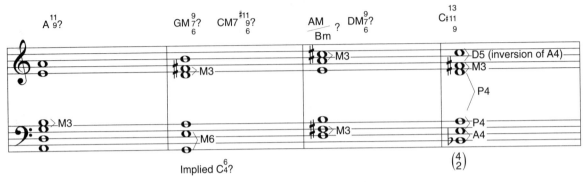

Example 20–16. Compound quartal chords with tertian implications.

◆ Compound Quartal Chords

Perfect 4th chords and tritone 4th chords that contain intervals other than 4ths are referred to as **compound**. The decision as to whether a chord is quartal or tertian depends upon the character of the chord as it is affected by the number and location of the additional nonquartal intervals. The decision is essentially an aural one. Multiple 4ths suggest a quartal structure, whereas multiple 3rds suggest a tertian structure. Placement, intensity, and timbre are also decisive factors. See *Example 20–16*.

◆ Inversions

Inversions and the resultant voicings of quartal chords must be handled carefully in order to preserve the character of the quartal structure. As an example,

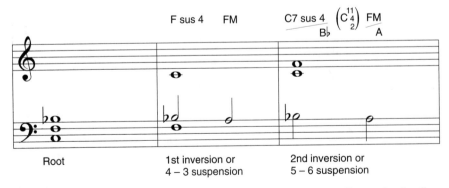

Example 20–17. Assessment of quartal character. In actuality, only the first chord fully preserves the quartal character.

the perfect 4th quartal structure beginning with C will be examined. Here, C–F–B♭ in first inversion becomes F–B♭–C. Is this quartal or it it an F sus 4? The second inversion, B♭–C–F, loses even more of the quartal character since the perfect 4th is now contained in the two upper voices and the chord is no longer grounded on a perfect 4th. Does this perhaps sound more like a C7 sus 4 or even a C11? Or, does it sound like F major with the suspension in the lowest voice? The decision is often determined by style and context. A single quartal chord rarely appears without other quartal chords. A suspension is used freely in tertian harmony. See *Example 20–17*.

Extending the C perfect 4th quartal chord further produces the structure C–F–B♭–E♭. The first inversion produces F–B♭–E♭–C. If there were any doubt that perfect 4th chords contain ambiguous roots, this inversion would justify that ambiguity. The interval of a major 6th, E♭–C, negates any possibility that C is a defined root. The predominant perfect 4th structure very definitely commences with the note F.

The second inversion produces B♭–E♭–C–F. Here, the perfect 4ths are contained between the two lower voices and between the two upper voices. With the major 6th contained between the two inner voices, the entire structure is less resonant as a perfect 4th quartal chord than is the root position. See *Example 20–18*.

◆ *Implied Roots*

The third inversion of C–F–B♭–E♭ yields E♭–C–F–B♭. In this inversion, the major 6th, E♭–C, is contained in the two lower voices. A three-note perfect 4th

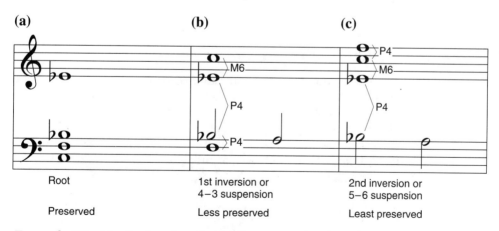

Example 20–18. Perfect fourth distributions in various voicings. (a) The chord consists entirely of perfect 4ths. (b) The two lower intervals are perfect 4ths and reinforce a potential perfect 4th chord. (c) The perfect 4ths are in the outer voices and do not provide as much support for a perfect 4th chord as do consecutive perfect 4ths.

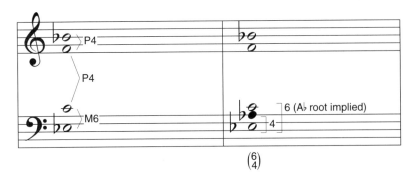

Example 20–19. A♭, the implied root in this major sixth interval.

quartal chord, C–F–B♭, is present in the three upper voices. While the interval of the major 6th grounds the chord on an interval other than a perfect 4th, the three upper voices establish a quartal sound. But is the entire structure, perhaps, an **implied root chord** — a root that is not present in the conglomeration of these pitches? The interval of a major 6th often implies a root that lies a perfect 4th above the bass — in this case, the root, A♭. The result of the addition of this implied root is a second-inversion A♭ major triad: E♭–A♭–C. If the remaining pitches, F and B♭, are superimposed on the A♭ major triad, the result is an A♭M add6, add9 chord. This is not to say that third-inversion perfect 4th quartal chords are to be considered in this manner — only that harmonic implications and ambiguities are inherent factors in progressive possibilities for these chordal structures. See *Example 20–19.*

◆ Identification of Inversions

Provided that the quartal chord under discussion is, in fact, an authentic quartal chord and not an 11th or 13th suspension, the arrangement of the inclusive notes into a hierarchy of 4th intervals will produce the root of the chord. The letter followed by the Arabic numeral that identifies the existing lower note, followed by the type of quartal chord that is present will serve to identify the quartal structure. For example, E2T4 indicates a tritone 4th quartal chord with a root of E and with the second note of the chord, A, in the bass. See *Example 20–20.*

◆ Analysis of Fourth Chords

Observe the chordal structure in measure 31 of *Example 20–21* on page 490. In the three upper parts (soprano 1, soprano 2, and alto), the notes are G♯, C♯, and G. Here, G♯ to C♯ produces a perfect 4th, whereas C♯ to G produces a diminished 5th tritone. Had the G been spelled F𝄪, an apparent quartal chord would have

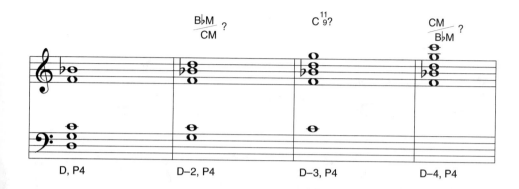

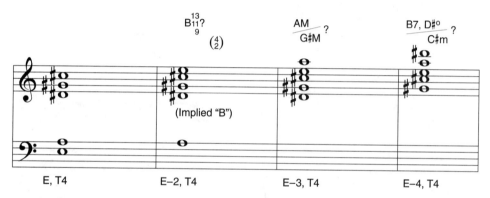

Example 20–20. Possible inversions of quartal chords (here, D and E). Quartal chords are identified by root, bass factor, and type.

resulted; as such, it would have been a tritone 4th chord since C♯ to F× is an augmented 4th. Nevertheless, the harmony does produce a tritone 4th chord.

In consideration of the lower supporting harmony in the piano part, the D♯ is also a perfect 4th below the G♯. However, B is a major 3rd below the D♯. Can the entire vertical structure be considered one harmony? It is not likely because although the B and the D♯ suggest a root of B and the G♯ and the C♯ can be considered the 13th and 9th, respectively, of B, there exists no 7th to support these upper partials. Even the G can be considered an enharmonic ♯5 (F×) or ♭13; but it is highly unlikely that a 13th and a ♭13th would appear in the same vertical structure. Even when the piano part moves to A and C♯, a conflict is present. If the root were now considered A, the G♯ and G♮ would be in conflict as major 7th and minor 7th, respectively. Chord factors of these types that are in conflict are referred to as **double inflections**.

Spring and Fall: To a Young Child

R. Sorce

Example 20–21. *Analysis of a quartal structure.*

The Quintal System

◆ *Chords in Fifths*

Chords in fifths, or **quintal chords,** are assumed to contain only perfect 5ths because a diminished 5th is enharmonically equivalent to an augmented 4th (quartal harmony), and an augmented 5th is enharmonically equivalent to a minor 6th (tertian harmony).

Undoubtedly, the lower perfect 5th of a quintal chord structure anchors the remaining structure in a tonic-dominant relationship. Regardless of the remaining intervallic configurations contained in the chord, the lowest note of the lower perfect 5th is firmly established as the root of the chord. Although a conglomeration of seemingly unrelated intervals above the lower perfect 5th might visually appear to be nonsupportive of the root, these intervals produce, at the very extreme, **polychordal structures**. That is, they are two or more simultaneously sounding chord structures with distinctly different roots. The lower perfect 5th, then, is harmonically stable as a root-5th relationship.

Unlike the ambiguity of a root in a quartal chord, a simple perfect 5th chord (three factors) or a multinote perfect 5th chord retains its root identity regardless of the number of superimposed 5ths or the superimposition of any number and type of interval above the lower 5th. See *Example 20–22*.

◆ *Perfect Fifth Dyads*

Perfect 5th chords must be observed and evaluated in the proper context. In popular music, it is not uncommon for perfect 5th sonorities to be incorporated into the harmonic content of songs. These 5ths are more commonly in the form of a *dyad* — a two-note harmonic interval — and consist of the root and 5th of a particular (possible) chord. By omitting the 3rd, the chord may be ambiguous as to its quality (major, minor); this also provides a desirable primordial tertian effect in the harmony. Perfect 4th chords are also occasionally employed in this

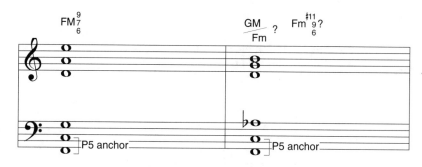

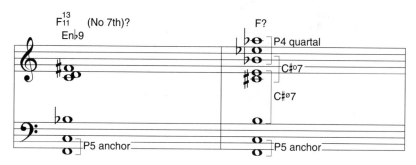

Example 20–22. The perfect fifth anchor-and-root support.

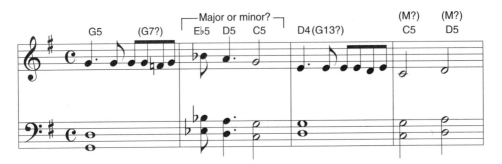

Example 20–23. The ambiguity of quality resulting from perfect fifth dyads and a perfect fourth dyad in measure 3.

manner. Notice the effect in *Example 20–23*. Compare the "open" sound of this with **organa** (the harmonization of chants in perfect 4ths and 5ths) of the early Middle Ages. (Perfect 5th dyads are also known as **open fifth chords**.)

◆ *Superimposed Fifths*

Extending the perfect 5th anchor to include three factors yields a root, a 5th, and a major 9th above the root. This structure is similar to the add9 chord, but contains no 3rd. The addition of the next-occurring 5th produces a major 13th interval above the root and might be interpreted as similar to an add6, add9 chord. Finally, with the addition of the next 5th, the 3rd of the chord root appears.

In a perfect 5th structure beginning on D, the five factors appearing in ascending fashion, as described in the preceding paragraph, include D–A–E–B–F♯. Is the chord a DMadd6, add9 or a perfect 5th? A perfect 5th voicing of this type of chord is not typical of most popular styles. Add6, add9 chords are typically voiced in closer position. See *Example 20–24*.

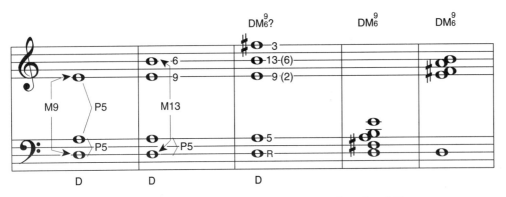

Example 20–24. A D structure resulting from superimposed perfect fifths.

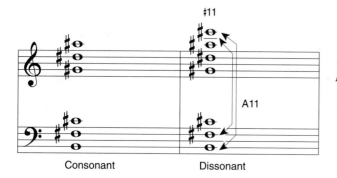

Example 20–25. Consonant and dissonant perfect fifth chords. Enharmonically, the #11 is a ♭5 (F♮), thus causing a double inflection. (See the discussion of 11th chords in Chapter 17.)

◆ *Consonant and Dissonant Perfect Fifths*

Perfect 5th chords remain consonant through the superimposition of *five* additional factors above the bass. A six-note perfect 5th structure may be heard as an M9, 7, 6 chord. The addition of the next-occurring 5th produces the compound augmented 11th; it is between the 5th above the root and the #11 that dissonance is generated, thus causing what can be considered an enharmonic double inflection.

Multinote perfect 5th chords as well as multinote perfect 4th chords very often contain the same pitches as upper-partial tertian chords. One must remember, however, that the coincidence is theoretical; in most instances, it is the *aural effect* that determines the type of sonority. See *Example 20–25.*

◆ *Perfect Fifths and Perfect Fifth Anchors*

The term **perfect fifth chord** implies a chord built *exclusively* of perfect fifths. However, these chords are used only occasionally and only first appear in contemporary classical works, particularly with the rise of greater dissonance in harmonic material.

Ludmila Ulehla employs the term **perfect fifth anchor** for harmonic structures constructed on a perfect 5th interval in which those pitches appearing above the initial perfect 5th often comprise an array of *various intervals,* only some of which are supported by the lower perfect 5th.[2] Quintal harmony, then, is *rooted on a perfect fifth;* it most likely contains other perfect 5ths in its structure, but it always contains various other intervals and is not a compound structure of a tertian chord. Notice the perfect 4ths in the treble part of *Example 18–6(c)* on page 422. These perfect 4ths do not negate the perfect 5th character established by the remaining intervals. Do quintal chords exist as autonomous entities? The decision is certainly contingent upon *aural evaluation.* See *Example 20–26.*

---

2. Ludmila Ulehla, *Contemporary Harmony* (New York: Free Press, 1966), p. 383.

(a)

String Quartet No. 5

B. Bartók

*P5s or F with add 9 and add 6?

**P5 or Dm$\overset{9}{6}$?

***P4?

(b)

Etchings

R. Sorce

*indicates a different voicing of G♯–C♯–F♯ (perfect 5ths).

Example 20–26. Compound perfect fourth and perfect fifth chords. **(a)** Perfect 5th and perfect 4th chords with root ambiguity. Notice the overlap of violin 2 and viola in conjunction with the cello in the first and fifth measures, thus affecting the quality of what may first appear to be multiple perfect fifths. **(b)** The harmonic content in this excerpt is comprised primarily of perfect 5th chords. However, other intervals are also present in many of these chord structures.

Chapter Review

The tertian system of harmonic construction has been, and continues to be, the predominant method for chord construction. However, other systems exist, and include *secundal, quartal,* and *quintal harmonies.* In the traditional system of harmonic construction, 2nds are considered dissonant; in most cases 4ths are also considered dissonant. Perfect 5ths, on the other hand, are consonants.

However, many intervallic structures become dissonant as multiple intervals of the same size and quality are superimposed. Notably, this does not occur with multiple superimpositions of major or minor 3rds. The perfect 5th creates a dissonance upon the use of a 3rd factor — for example, C–G–D. The D is dissonant with C as a major 9th.

There are four types of *chords in seconds,* or *secundal chords*: *major-major, major-minor, minor-major,* and *minor-minor. Multinote secundal chords* contain more than three different pitches. Multinote secundal chords in close voicing are referred to as *clusters;* because of voice-leading practice, it is the soprano and bass that are considered most carefully. Inner-voice content is a matter of tension and color considerations.

Three types of *chords in fourths,* or *quartal chords* exist; *perfect-perfect, perfect-augmented,* and *augmented-perfect. Consonant perfect fourth chords* include those chords containing anywhere between two and four superimposed perfect 4th intervals. With the addition of the next perfect 4th interval, the perfect 4th chord becomes dissonant. The *perfect-augmented fourth chord* and the *augmented-perfect fourth chord* are considered dissonant 4th chords. In all quartal chords containing a tritone, the resultant structure is considered a dissonant quartal chord. Progression of quartal chords is guided by melody and bass movement, with the inner voices treated as colors. However, in any quartal chord containing a tritone, this tritone interval must be examined and considered for its resolution tendency; in a uniquely quartal context, it should not be treated in resolution with any regularity as a traditional tritone. A perfect 4th chord and a tritone 4th chord containing additional intervals other than 4ths are considered compound 4th chords.

Chords in fifths, or *quintal chords,* contain perfect 5ths. The lower perfect 5th interval of a perfect 5th chord serves as an *anchor* and supports the remaining upper pitches. Hence, it is difficult, if not impossible, to destroy the root implication of the lowest pitch of a perfect 5th chord no matter what the remaining superimposed intervals may be. Perfect 5th chords remain consonant through the superimposition of five perfect 5ths above the bass note. With the addition of the 6th interval, creating a compound augmented 11th above the bass, the quintal chord becomes dissonant. Quintal harmony must be viewed as harmony that is rooted on perfect 5th intervals; it most likely contains other perfect 5ths in the structure; it may contain various other intervals; and it is not a compound structure of a tertian chord. The authenticity of secundal, quartal, and quintal chords is ultimately one of context and aural evaluation because all of these structures, in one way or another, depending on their complexity, might be viewed as tertian derivatives and even modifications of tertian chords.

Anthology References

For additional usage and analysis, see the following examples in Distefano, Joseph P. and James A. Searle, *Music and Materials for Analysis: An Anthology.* New York, Ardsley House, Publishers, Inc., 1995.

added-note chords
>   ***Example 55.***   *Twelve Poems of Emily Dickinson,* No. 3, "Why Do They Shut Me Out of Heaven?,"
>   Aaron Copland, pp. 317–24.

quartal chords
>   ***Example 56.***   *Sonata for Violin,* No. 2, Third Movement, "The Revival," Charles Ives, pp. 325–34.
>   ***Example 60.***   *Six Short Pieces for Piano,* Op. 19, No. 5, Arnold Schoenberg, pp. 355–61.

secundal chords, clusters, compound-quartal and quintal chords
>   ***Example 56.***   *Sonata for Violin,* No. 2, Third Movement, "The Revival," Charles Ives, pp. 325–34.

Self-Test

1. Define *tension* and *resolution* in harmony, as they are affected by consonance and dissonance.
2. Three-note secundal chords are of four types; they are _____ , _____ , _____ , and _____ .
3. How would a three-note secundal chord consisting of two major 2nds differ from the close voicing of the root, 7th, and 9th of a dominant 9th chord?
4. Describe *sound mass.*
5. Describe the method for identifying a secundal chord in inversion.
6. Describe what is meant by a *cluster.*
7. Quartal chords are of three types; they are _____ , _____ , and _____ .
8. What is meant by *symmetrical structure* in chordal construction?
9. Define *consonant* and *dissonant perfect 4th chords.*
10. Discuss tertian implication in the augmented perfect 4th chord.
11. How is a *tritone fourth chord* defined?
12. Describe a *compound perfect fourth chord.*
13. Discuss the process of identifying inversions of quartal chords.
14. Discuss the concept of the *perfect fifth anchor.*
15. Discuss the meaning of chords labeled as C5, B♭5, F♯5, D5, etc.
16. Upon the addition of which factor does a quintal chord become dissonant?

Exercises

1. Construct three-note secundal chords from each pitch.

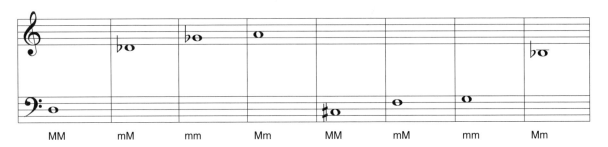

2. Arrange each harmonic structure as a secundal chord. Identify by letter and by numeral. See the first measure.

3. Invert the secundal chords. Determine, if possible, the tertian implication of each. See the first measure.

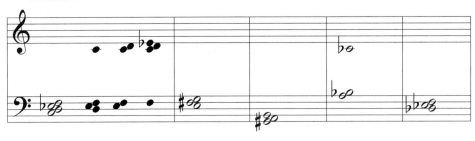

4. Determine whether each harmonic structure is tertian or secundal.

5. Construct three-note quartal chords.

PP   PA   AP   PP   PA   AP   PP   PA

6. Determine the key, if any, implied by the quartal chords.

7. Determine several possible tertian-implied roots for each quartal chord.

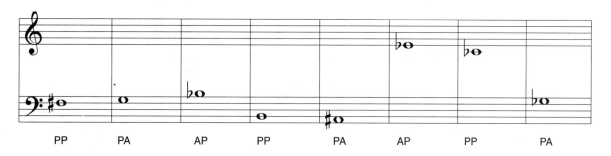

8. Determine whether the following are quintal chords or tertian chords with added notes.

9. Determine whether each chord is secundal, tertian, quartal, or quintal.

10. In the perfect 5th anchor chords, identify each factor. See the first measure.

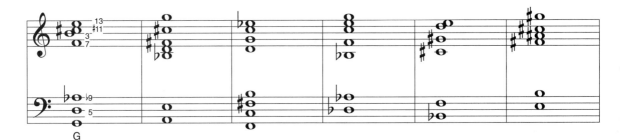

11. Compose several terse diatonic and chromatic melodies, and harmonize with secundal, quartal, and quintal harmony. Label all chords and melody notes as harmonic factors.

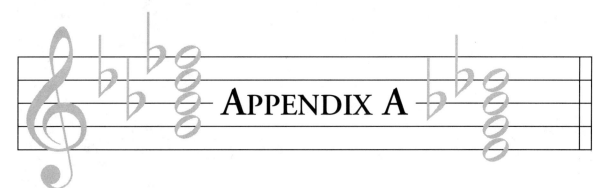

APPENDIX A

Several Scale Constructions from C

The scale structures in *Example A* are those used in the majority of classical, popular, and contemporary Western practice musical works. Although the list is not exhaustive, it does represent, to a large degree, those formations from which secundal, tertian, quartal, and quintal harmony, as well as melody, have been developed over the past several hundred years.

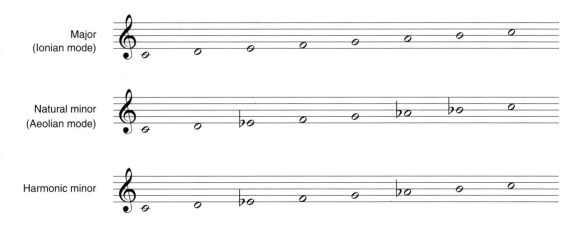

Major
(Ionian mode)

Natural minor
(Aeolian mode)

Harmonic minor

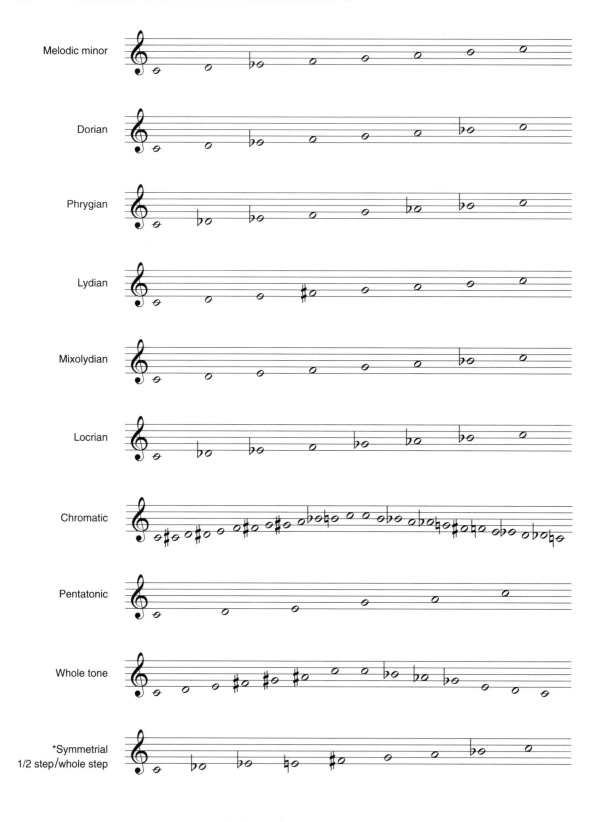

*Symmetrial
Whole step/1/2 step

Blues

*Also referred to as diminished scale (or octatonic).

Example A. ***Scale constructions.***

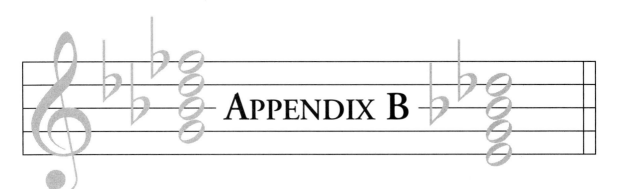

APPENDIX B

More on Chord Construction and Function

The following is a presentation of several available chord structures on a C root in tertian construction. Of course, all of these structures can be transposed to any root — just be sure that the spellings are correct. In certain cases notes have been deleted; this is in agreement with the construction of certain upper-partial chords. Additionally, several other harmonic structures are illustrated — for example, B♭/C, C5, etc. See *Example B.*

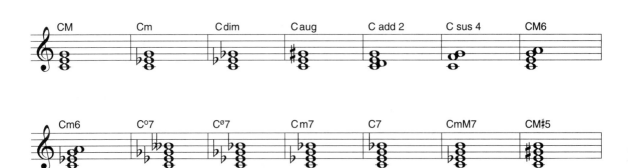

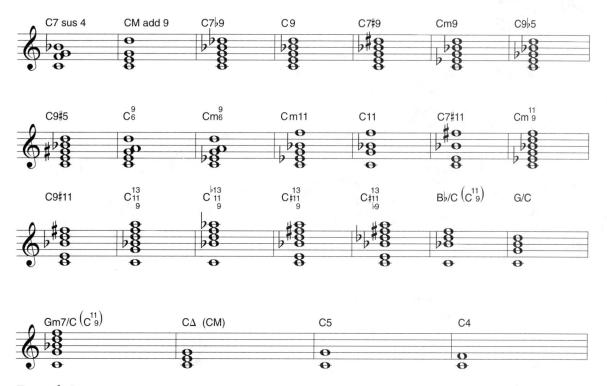

Example B. Chord constructions.

Harmonic Construction and Progression Revisited

Many of the chord structures presented here have been discussed within the text. After an initial review, additional features are now presented.

Symmetrical intervallic chords are those constructed by the vertical stacking of same-quality intervals — for example, all minor 3rds or all major 3rds. These include fully diminished 7th chords (all minor 3rds) and augmented triads (all major 3rds).

A fully diminished 7th chord can have as its root any pitch class contained in the chord provided that the remaining pitches are spelled correctly, according to tertian construction. Therefore, if a D°7 (D–F–A♭–C♭) were to be considered as an F♭7, the spelling must read: F–A♭–C♭–E♭♭. Similarly, E♭♭ must be used instead of D; otherwise, the tertian spelling, F–A♭–C♭–D, would be incorrect. In this spelling D lies an alphabetical 2nd above C♭. The root note of any fully diminished 7th serves as a leading tone. Thus, D°7 is a leading tone to E♭; F°7 is a leading tone to G♭.

The D°7 spelling can be altered to accommodate any inclusive pitch as a leading tone and, also, any pitch altered enharmonically. Therefore, D can become C𝄪, a leading tone to D♯; F can become E♯, a leading tone to F♯; A♭ can become G♯, a leading tone to A; C♭ can become B, a leading tone to C. This readily demonstrates the mobility afforded by this unique chord structure in the movement to remote chords and keys.

Another feature of fully diminished 7th chords is their dominant function. A major 3rd interval added below the root of any fully diminished 7th chord produces a dominant 7♭9 structure on that added pitch. (By the same process, the addition of a major 3rd interval below the root of a half-diminished 7th chord produces a dominant 9th chord.)

Any note of a fully diminished 7th chord lowered by a half step produces a dominant-7th-chord sound. The word "sound" is used because the resultant dominant 7th is not always correctly spelled. Consider the notes of a B°7 (B–D–F–A♭). In the alteration to a dominant 7th, the following chords result: B–D–F–G (A♭ has been lowered), a correctly spelled first inversion of a G dominant seventh; B–D–E–A♭ (F has been lowered), an incorrectly spelled E dominant 7th (E–G♯–B–D); B–D♭–F–A♭ (D has been lowered), an incorrectly spelled D♭ dominant 7th (D♭–F–A♭–C♭), or a correctly spelled D♭ German augmented 6th chord; B♭–D–F–A♭ (B has been lowered), a correctly spelled B♭ dominant 7th.

The B fully diminished 7th also lends itself well to a rootless C♯7♭9 (C♯–E♯–G♯–B–D), in which F and A♭ are enharmonically spelled, or a D♭7♭9 (D♭–F–A♭–C♭–E♭♭), in which B and D are enharmonically spelled. Another root that can be implied by the B fully diminished 7th is E: E–G♯–B–D–F as E7♭9, in which A♭ is enharmonically spelled. It is worthwhile to experiment with other possible roots.

The half-diminished 7th is often referred to as an m7♭5 chord in popular formats. For example, the C half-diminished 7th, C–E♭–G♭–B♭, is a Cm7 with the 5th, G, lowered. Another modern chord structure is the m6. Thus, E♭m6 (E♭–G♭–B♭–C) contains exactly the same pitches as C∅7 and, of course, Cm7♭5. Akin to the m6 is the M6. This major triad with the added sixth degree of the major scale is actually a first-inversion minor 7th: G–B–D–E (GM6 = E–G–B–D, an m7 chord). In common practice, an m7 in first inversion was used for this structure.

The chord symbols used in popular music are in certain cases rather crude and in other cases quite precise and foolproof. For example, take the symbol $\frac{C}{D}$, or $\frac{C}{D}$. This indicates that a C major triad is to be sounded over a D bass. The result of this is a D$^{11}_{9}$, which is quite precise. With D as the root, C produces the 7th; E, the 9th; and G, the eleventh. No F♯ is present; this is correct since the chord is an 11th. Furthermore, the 5th, A, is omitted, which is also acceptable because a 5th may be omitted at any time, provided that it is not altered, as in a ♭5 or ♯5.

Consider the symbol $\dfrac{\text{Bm7♭5}}{\text{E}}$, or $\dfrac{\text{Bm7♭5}}{\text{E}}$. Here, the resultant structure from the bass upward produces E–B–D–F–A, an E11♭9, in which E is the root; B, the 5th; D, the 7th; F, the ♭9; and A, the 11th. The 3rd, G♯, is correctly and conveniently omitted in this 11th chord. Upper-partial chords are often best symbolized by this process, rather than by the complete description of the desired harmony. In many instances the process of placing a simpler chord over a bass note alleviates the possibility of the inclusion in the harmony of an undesired chord tone, such as the 3rd in a natural 11th chord.

Popular chords symbols do not indicate voicing of chords or doubling of certain notes. This is done at the discretion of the performer and is dependent on musicianship, sensitivity to style, concern for the melody line, and texture.

Whereas chord progression and voice leading were presented at length, some highly inventive chord movement — especially at cadences and in the embellishing process — is witnessed in all styles of music and is frequently quite adventuresome in certain popular works.

Most embellishments can be viewed as common-practice derivatives — for example, secondary dominants, secondary diminished chords, augmented 6ths, the Neapolitan 6, deceptive resolutions, alternative resolutions, etc. But observation of music often reveals cadences that do not employ the typical cadential chord progressions. For instance, what is one to make of a cadence in C major that incorporates a B♭7 as the penultimate chord? Although B♭7 is only a whole step from C, it appears to be nowhere in the vicinity of the key of C. Some thought, however, may reveal otherwise. By dropping the root of the B♭7, the remaining notes are D–F–A♭. This is a ii° in C minor; D, F, and A♭ are also the 3rd, 5th, and 7th, respectively, of a B fully diminished 7th, the leading-tone diminished 7th in C minor, or the 5th, 7th, and ♭9, respectively, of G7♭9, the dominant 9th in C minor. Furthermore, B♭7 is also the V7 of E♭ major or minor, and is not a C root the relative minor of E♭ major? Observe that C is also the root note of a deceptive resolution of a B♭7 in E♭ major. It can be seen, then, that the use of a B♭7 at a cadence in C major is not such a remote idea after all.

In many situations, remotely related cadential chords and embellishing chords are explainable if one searches deeply enough into key and substitute-chord relationships and derivations. But chords are often chosen as a result of melodic and rhythmic stress, and remotely related harmonies are frequently "smoothed" by the addition of diatonic and chromatic upper partials. For example, is an E rooted chord a likely penultimate cadence chord in C major? Clearly, E–G♯–B progressing to C–E–G is not a common movement. However, E–[G♯]–B–D–F–A (E♭9) is not such a far-fetched idea. Notice the G♯–B–D–F. Are these pitches not those of a viii°7 in C minor (B–D–F–A♭), the four upper pitches of a G dominant

♭9th, the dominant in C? Examine B–D–F–A; this produces a vii°7 in C major, which includes the four upper notes of a G-dominant 9th, the dominant in C. If the E♭9^{11} is used, the G♯ (third) will most likely be omitted. If the chord is extended to its ♭13th (C), the tonic of C is then included and can be viewed as either reinforcing the tonic C or as the 11th of a G11th chord, the dominant 11th in C. Incidentally, E is the dominant of A, the relative minor of C.

There are many processes for discovering remotely related implied roots. For example, an A-minor triad in first inversion reads C–E–A upward from the bass. Can this structure in any way be related to an A♭ root? The question is how are C–E–A related to A♭? The addition of an A♭ root below this structure establishes C as the 3rd, E as the augmented 5th, and A as the enharmonically flatted 9th (B♭♭). If the pitch G♭ is added above the A♭, the resultant structure reads, from the bass upward: A♭–G♭–[C–E–A]. An A♭7♭9♯5 is produced (A, of course, is the enharmonic of B♭♭). Can D° (D–F–A♭) be incorporated in a C rooted chord? Note that D° supported by a lower minor 7th interval on C (C–B♭) produces C7$^{♭13}_{11}$. Can an F♯ triad be incorporated in a C rooted chord? With C as the root, F♯ is the raised 11th, A♯ is the enharmonic minor 7th (B♭), and C♯ is the enharmonic lowered 9th (D♭). The result is a C7$^{♯11}_{♭9}$.

This kind of thinking must be part of every musician's creative process, for it allows even the most abstract musical works to be analyzed and explained, and it enables one to produce new and interesting sounds from the twelve pitch classes.

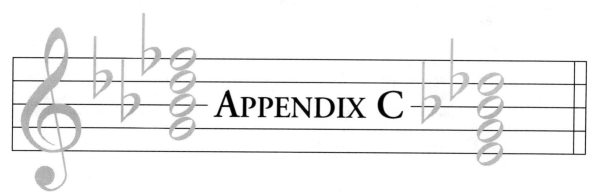

APPENDIX C

Instruments and Voices

Transposing Instruments

The sophisticated engineering involved in instrument manufacturing in modern times was not available when certain instruments were invented and developed. As a result, many of these early instruments contain peculiarities with regard to their tunings. Hence, they are *transposing instruments;* that is, the pitch that appears in the score of these instruments is not the pitch that they produce.

This appendix is not a discussion of orchestration or arranging. Its purpose, rather, is to enable the reader to understand those notes that appear in scores intended for transposing instruments.

Regardless of the style of music one practices, every musician should possess the ability to follow and read a chamber work as well as an orchestral work; for it is not only orchestral music that utilizes transposing instruments, but other genres as well.

Essentially, there are four broad categories of instruments. These include: the woodwinds (the modern ones are not necessarily made from wood), the brasses, the percussion instruments, and the strings.

The *woodwinds* include: piccolos, flutes, oboes, English horns, clarinets, bassoons, and saxophones. *Brasses* include: French horns, trumpets, cornets, flugelhorns, trombones, euphoniums, baritone horns, and tubas. *Percussion instruments* include: all types of drums; triangles, claves, cymbals, wind machines, bells, chimes, marimbas, xylophones, vibraphones, celestes, harpsichords, pianos, organs, and other keyboards — generally speaking, any instrument that is struck. *Strings* are stringed instruments that are not struck; they include: violins, violas, cellos, and basses, which are bowed, and harps, guitars, and mandolins, which are plucked. (Although an acoustic piano is a stringed instrument, its strings are struck by a hammer, thus rendering it a percussion instrument.)

In *Table C,* each instrument is followed by its correctly written intervallic placement, which is necessary to produce the required (concert) pitch, followed by the clef(s) used. For example, *P4 higher* means that the written pitch must be a perfect 4th higher than the sounding pitch.

INSTRUMENT	WRITTEN INTERVAL FOR SOUNDING PITCH	CLEF(S) USED
Piccolo	One octave lower	Treble
Soprano flute	As written	Treble
Alto flute	P4 higher	Treble
Bass flute	One octave higher	Treble
English horn	P5 higher	Treble
B♭ clarinet	M2 higher	Treble
A clarinet	m3 higher	Treble
E♭ clarinet	m3 lower	Treble
B♭ bass clarinet	M9 higher	Treble
Bassoon	As written	Bass and tenor
Contrabassoon	One octave higher	Bass and tenor
B♭ soprano saxophone	M2 higher	Treble
E♭ alto saxophone	M6 higher	Treble
B♭ tenor saxophone	M9 higher	Treble
E♭ baritone saxophone	M13 higher	Treble
B♭ bass saxophone	Two octaves and M2 higher	Treble
French horn in B♭	M2 higher	Treble and bass
French horn in A	m3 higher	Treble and bass
French horn in A♭	M3 higher	Treble and bass
French horn in G	P4 higher	Treble and bass
French horn in F	P5 higher	Treble and bass
French horn in E	m6 higher	Treble and bass
French horn in E♭	M6 higher	Treble and bass
French horn in D	m7 higher	Treble and bass
French horn in C	One octave higher	Treble and bass
Trumpet in F	P4 lower	Treble
Trumpet in E	M3 lower	Treble
Trumpet in E♭	m3 lower	Treble

Trumpet in D	M2 lower	Treble
Trumpet in C	As written	Treble
Trumpet in B	m2 higher	Treble
Trumpet in B♭	M2 higher	Treble
Trumpet in A	m3 higher	Treble
Cornet	M2 higher	Treble
Trombone	As written	Bass and tenor
Euphonium (bass clef)	As written	Bass
Euphonium (treble clef)	M9 higher	Treble
Tuba	As written	Bass
Timpani	As written	Bass
Xylophone	One octave lower	Treble
Marimba	As written	Treble and bass
Vibraphone	As written	Treble
Celeste	One octave lower	Treble and bass
Piano	As written	Treble and bass
Orchestra bells	Two octaves lower	Treble
Violin	As written	Treble
Viola	As written	Alto and treble
Cello	As written	Bass, tenor, and treble
Bass	One octave higher	Bass, tenor, and treble
Guitar	One octave higher	Treble
Harp	As written	Treble and bass

Table C. Instruments, transpositions, and clefs.

Instrument and Voice Ranges

Ranges are approximate for voices and for many instruments. Although for voices this is self-explanatory, for instruments this is due to their characteristic constructions. For example, the lowest practical note for a tenor trombone is the E that is located one ledger line below the bass-clef staff. However, other lower notes (pedal notes) are available, depending upon the ability of the performer. Similarly, the practical upper limit of the soprano flute is one octave above high C, the note appearing just above the fifth ledger line above the treble staff. But again, other higher notes are available. However, with the violin, the lowest possible note is the G below the treble staff. This G is the lowest open string available on the violin.

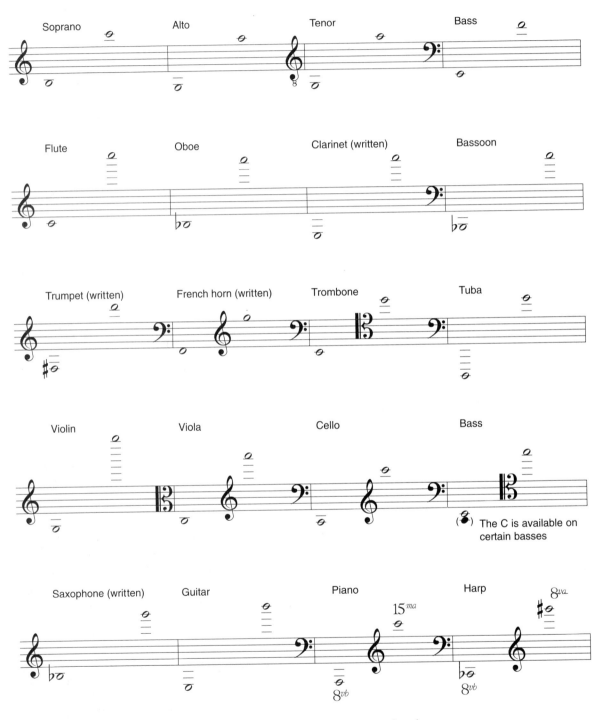

Example D. Voice and instrument ranges. Several of these are approximations.

The soprano voices include the soprano and mezzo-soprano categories. In the soprano category are coloraturas (highest), lyric, dramatic, choral, and child. Mezzo-sopranos (characterized by a darker quality and slightly lower in range than sopranos) include coloraturas, lyric, dramatic, and choral. Alto voices are the lowest female voices and include altos and choral altos. Tenor voices include the countertenor (highest), lyric tenor, dramatic tenor, and choral tenor. Baritones include the lyric baritone, dramatic baritone, bass baritone, and choral baritone. Bass voices include the bass, basso profundo, and choral bass. See *Example D.*

APPENDIX D

The Major Scales
and the
Three Forms of the Minor Scales

MAJOR SCALES

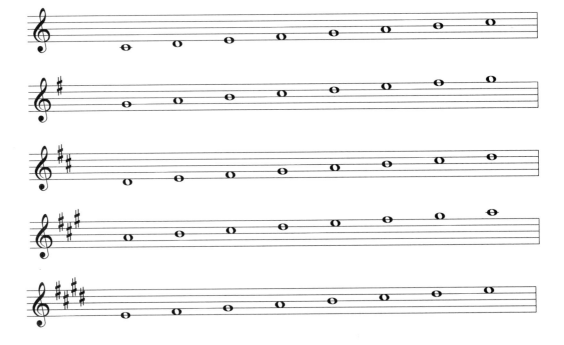

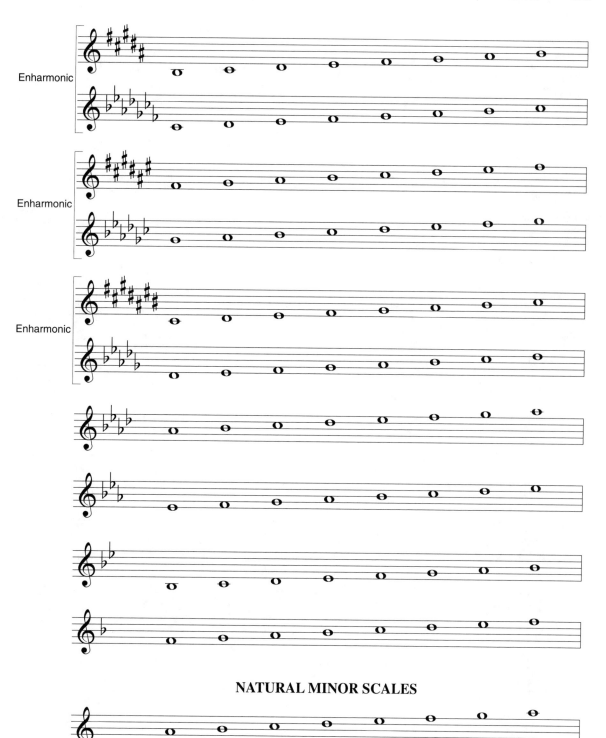

NATURAL MINOR SCALES

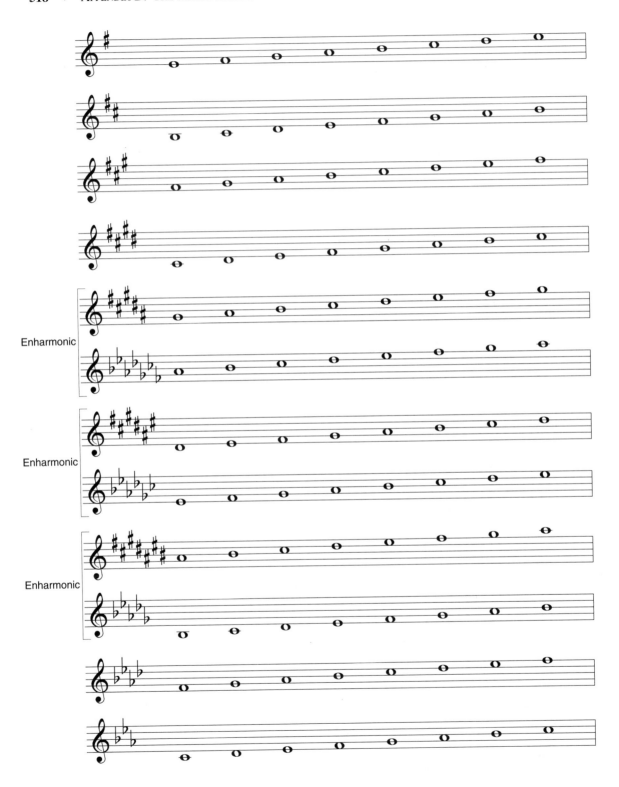

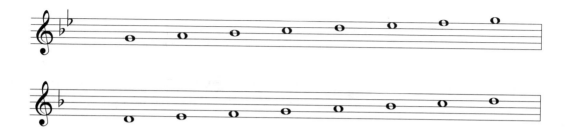

HARMONIC MINOR SCALES

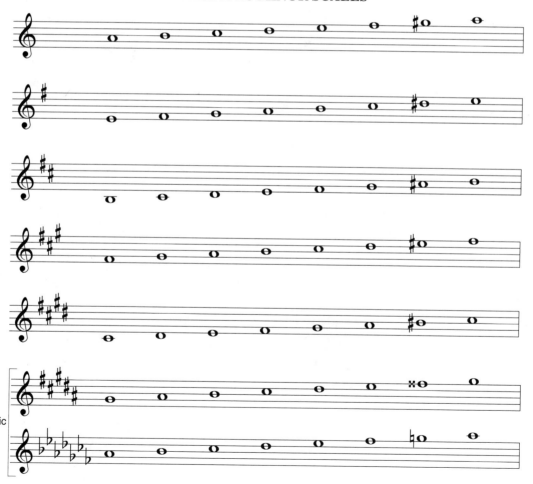

Enharmonic

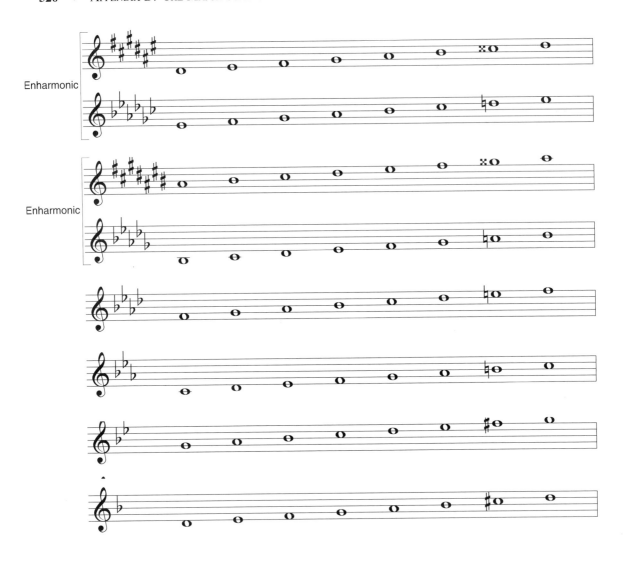

MELODIC MINOR SCALES

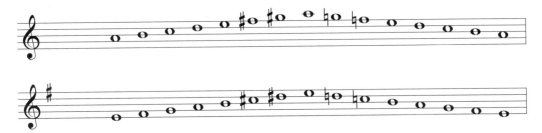

Enharmonic

Enharmonic

Enharmonic

Example D. *The major, natural minor, harmonic minor, and melodic minor scales.*

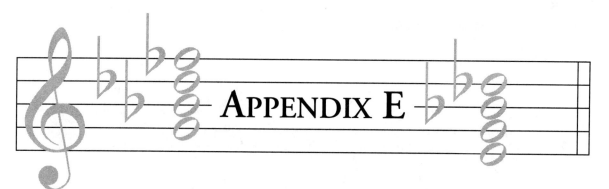

APPENDIX E

Historical Perspective

Throughout the course of this book, mention has been made of style character-istics relating to syntactical usage in the employment of the melodic, harmon-ic, rhythmic, and structural components of music. If one general trend can be observed, it is the increase of complexity in all of these components over the centuries. The development of Western music is sometimes viewed as begin-ning in the Renaissance period and continuing through the current period. But music had its beginnings thousands of years ago. Before A.D. 800 , however, music was in its early formative stage and relatively little is known about it.

The major periods in Western classical music are generally considered to be:[1]

Early Middle Ages	c. 600 – 1150
Gothic	c. 1150 – 1400
Renaissance	c. 1400 – 1600
Baroque	c. 1600 – 1750
Classical	c. 1770 – 1830
Romantic	c. 1790 – 1910

---

1. These dates are by no means universally agreed upon. Note that there is a gap between the Baroque and Classical periods and there is also some overlapping of periods.

Post-Romantic/Impressionist   c. 1875 – 1920

Contemporary   c. 1920 – present

Music of the early Middle Ages, which was primarily music of the Catholic Church, exemplified the use of chant, parallel fourths, fifths, and octaves, modes, and later, the use of the independent vocal line as an embellishment of the underlying chant.[2]

Music of the Gothic period introduced triple meter, rhythmic notation, multiple vocal parts, and rhythmic variety, including syncopation. During the latter part of the Gothic period, vocal lines became more melismatic, the secular motet was developed, imitation was incorporated, resulting in more melodic independence, and the intervals of 3rds and 6ths were employed. However, triads were not yet recognized.

The Renaissance witnessed the development of ad hoc instrumentation, dynamics, polyphonic texture, triads, tonality, weak cadential patterns, irregular meters, and vocal-type melodies in conjunct motion in a rather limited tessitura. The element of contrast characterized instrumental and vocal texture. Vocal genres included the Mass, motet, hymn, chorale, madrigal, and solo song. Instrumental genres included dance suites, toccatas, variations, ricercari, and canzoni.

Music of the Baroque period produced imitative counterpoint within a harmonic framework, major and minor tonality, more vertical dissonance, strong cadences, regular meters, active rhythmic figures of shorter note durations, and motivically derived melodies in a wider tessitura; in general, there occurred highly complex and decorative fashioning of the musical elements. Types included the suite, trio sonata, solo sonata, concerto grosso, sinfonia, overture, fugue, song, opera, oratorio, and cantata.

The late Baroque period is often called the Rococo period (c. 1720 – 50). The music of this period was in Style Galant, which was characterized by consistent dynamic balance, a triadic-based accompaniment, usually in Alberti bass style, major keys, active rhythmic configurations, decorated and arpeggiated melodies, and symmetrical designs. Genres included keyboard music, chamber music, the concerto, symphony, opera, Mass, and oratorios.

Within the Classical period, the Style Bourgeois (c. 1730 – 1803), or *Sturm und Drang* (Storm and Stress), is exemplified by more dynamic change and contrast, sudden changes in texture, more dissonance (nonharmonic tones), chromaticism through key change, more rhythmic contrast, and fragmentation. The term *Sturm und Drang* defines the content of raw human emotion in this style.

In the Classical period sonata structure was developed into its compound-ternary design of exposition, development, and recapitulation. The orchestra became moderately large and could be classified into four primary groups: woodwinds, brasses, percussion instruments, and strings. The music was generally

---

2. For definitions of terms used in this appendix, see the Glossary.

homophonic, with migrant movement to remote keys. Seventh chords became acceptable dissonances. Regular duple and triple meters were abundant and heterorhythmic patterns were the norm. Melody was usually quite symmetrical in phrase length, triadic (in structural terms), and within a moderate range. Genres included the sonata, concerto, minuet and trio, rondo, theme and variations, suite, overture, symphony, Mass, and opera.

The Romantic period fostered the idea of creativity through inspiration, rather than through predescribed expectations and Classical restraints. Hence, the music of this period exemplified bold excursions from the norm in its use of melody, rhythm, harmony, structure, and dynamics. This was the age of the virtuoso and the nonconformist composer. A larger orchestra and greater dynamic range were characteristics of Romantic sound. Harmony was tonal, mainly homophonic and migrant. Tempo was varied, often ad lib, rubato, and often extreme in fast and slow passages. Melody was quite lyrical, not as symmetrical as in Classical style, and was wide in range. Genres included program music, the sonata, fantasia, symphony, overture, suite, theme and variations, symphonic poem (tone poem), concerto, opera, Mass, oratorio, and art song, as well as character (titled) instrumental works, especially for piano.

Post-Romantic and Impressionist music expanded the horizon of the composer by the effects of extramusical stimuli. Musical elements were employed to express emotions evoked from nature as well as themes derived from literary and fine-art works. It was music inspired by impressions. Extended harmony, sweeping melodic lines, and rich textures within asymmetrical designs were characteristic of this period. Timbres were used to convey mood, instead of employing perfectly sonorous resonant sounds. Traditional Classical and Romantic style compositional devices, such as major and minor scales, triads and 7th chords, cadential formulae, and textures, were either modified or abandoned in exchange for more complex harmonies, modern use of modes, atypical harmonic progressions, nonfunctional chord relationships, and freer structures.

The contemporary period may well be considered the age of experimentation in a pluralistic environment. Observation of works created in this century reveals styles that retain and even develop all the elements of earlier periods. This is due to the multitude of new uses of music in this century, as is exemplified by the roles of popular music, film music, jazz, and radio and television scores, as well as the various types of concert music. Each of these genres requires for its success certain parameters necessary to appeal to a wide variety of musical tastes. Hence, contemporary music ranges from the freest aleatoric style to the most structured popular style. Melody can range from being highly disjunct and angular to the opposite extreme of imitating chant, the latter often heard in popular songs. Harmony can be completely devoid of any resemblance to tertian structure and may consist of basic 4th and 5th dyad accompaniments. Rhythm can be highly complex, nearly indecipherable; there are also simple rhythmic figures, such as those appearing in elementary works. Instrumental combinations and textures are often ad hoc, except for the more established ensembles, such as orchestras, string quartets, brass quintets, and jazz trios. No particular stylistic trend can be identified; current contemporary music continues to be created in a multicultural environment, the results of which may never again be unidirectional.

Common Structures in Common-Practice and Popular Music

A comparison of common-practice and popular-style works reveals little, if any, difference in fundamental musical syntax. Of course, this is not to infer that music has remained entirely static over the past several centuries. In fact, we can say that, generally, music has evolved chromatically. When viewed chronologically, musical works clearly become increasingly chromatic in their melodic and harmonic content.

Nevertheless, the structural harmonic content of music, that is, those structures that contribute most to the establishment and reinforcement of the key center, have remained largely unchanged. It is still the tonic-dominant relationship that is prevalent in Western music composition. And although chromatic embellishment appears more frequently in popular works, much of it can be traced to common-practice syntax and technique. A case in point is the tritone substitution. Observation of the tritone substitution of a V7 and its variants — the V7b5b9, for example, which is prevalent in modern works — reveals a similarity to the Neapolitan chord, which is used in common-practice works. Another example is the V7b5b9/V, which is also prevalent in modern works, but which can easily be viewed as a rootless Gr6: both behave as secondary-dominant functions.

The symbolic representation of pitch and rhythm has also changed only minimally since the thirteenth century. More complex rhythmic figures have evolved, but the representation of time duration has essentially remained the same.

In addition, Western music is still based on the same system of scale constructions as those used over the past several hundred years; that is, the major scale, the three forms of the minor scale, and the modern modes. Although modal usage was more prevalent prior to the Baroque period, modes are still incorporated into modern works of any style. The other types of scales that are used in modern music, such as the pentatonic scale and the whole-tone scale, are generally variants of the more common major, minor, or modal scale structures, although they may be borrowed from other cultures or may even be composer-created.

Tertian harmony, or harmony based on the system of superimposed 3rds, has consistently been the predominant method of chord construction. Although upper-partial chords (9ths, 11ths, and 13ths) are more common in modern music, their lower supporting triad and 7th structures are still generally the same as those used in prior centuries. Triads have also remained unchanged. Only four basic triads exist: major, minor, diminished, and augmented, and unless one adapts another scale system or considers construction in intervals other than thirds, triads will remain as they are.

Seventh chords in past centuries consisted primarily of Mm7ths, mm7ths, °7ths, and ø7ths; however, in modern works it is not uncommon to see other types of 7ths, such as the +M7, mM7, and M7♭5. But whereas many of these "alterations" are modern creations, they are nonetheless still in the tertian system.

Upper-partial chords of the 9th, 11th, and 13th are nothing more than decorated triads and 7ths, with these upper-partial factors now utilized as chord tones, rather than as nonharmonic tones, as they were used in the past. The discussion of embedded triads revealed that most upper-partial chords exhibit a type of polychordal character whereby an Mm7, M9, P11, M13 chord, for example, was viewed as a superimposed supertonic triad over an Mm7th chord, two conventional harmonic structures in common-practice works.

Perhaps the most unconventional use of harmony in modern music is the application of secundal, quartal, and quintal chords. Although these chords are not directly based on the tertian system, much in their character, when employed in certain styles, is not radically different from conventional tertian chord construction. For example, it was demonstrated how a three-note quartal chord resembled a 4-3 suspension, how a secundal chord might be viewed as an added-note chord, and how a quintal chord related to the organ point or pedal tone. Also not to be overlooked is the 5 chord, a "triad" with its 3rd omitted, which is quite popular in many rock tunes but has its origin in thirteenth century Gregorian chant. These "new" structures are only new in their presentation, their interpretation, and their use. They may all still be viewed as derived from common-practice syntax.

Of course, not all structures in modern music have such clear ties to their counterparts in common-practice music. For example, intervals, the building blocks of vertical structured harmony and linear resolution tendencies, do reveal a certain amount of modification, due primarily to the complexities of modern tertian harmony. Harmonic structures have become more complex in certain modern chordal structures, exhibiting a greater level of dissonance, and interval designations have been adjusted to accommodate these pitch considerations. Thus, a ♭9, ♯11, 13th vertical structure is a relatively modern creation and contains an interval of an augmented 3rd between the ♭9 and ♯11; augmented 3rds are not typical occurrences in common-practice and earlier works.

Chord progression has also changed quite a bit since the earlier common-practice works. Chord movement in common-practice works is generally characterized as movement in 4ths and 5ths, although in much music of this period, movement is certainly not limited to this type of progression. Modern works in the popular genre may also be characterized similarly; however, stepwise and mediant progression and key movement are quite common, as are traditionally unrelated chromatic harmonies, such as change-of-quality chords.

Despite these two examples, however, it is still clear that the similarities between the structures of common-practice and popular music far outnumber the differences. For example, the simultaneous sounding of complex dissonance in contemporary chordal construction is a modern musical technique, but these dissonances have appeared in works of the past as nonharmonic tones.

The uses of voice leading in the two styles of music are also quite similar. Modern application of voice leading may not appear to be as rigid as that in earlier works; but the result of a well-constructed work based on careful reflection of its voice-leading content will still unquestionably be more effective than had it not been considered. Although modern melody and accompaniment may generally be viewed as less undulating than melody of the common-practice style, a good sense of voice leading has always been necessary to construct musically coherent works.

We have attempted to bridge the styles of common-practice and popular music by demonstrating the similarities of musical syntax between them. Nevertheless, these styles are clearly quite different in their overall effect. Thus, if it is not the syntax that is different, then it must be the assemblage of musical components that enables the listener to recognize that which is "classical" and that which is popular. And the way that musical elements are put together is often defined by the culture from which a musical work emerges. Melody, rhythm, harmony, structure, and instrumentation all fulfill particular cultural conventions and reflect the tastes of the times. Language, or lyrical content, must also be considered in the determination of style; for it is language that reflects the era, or more specifically, the culture.

But regardless of the differences which may place separate pieces of music into distinct genres, the musical structures that the pieces are based upon are often quite similar. It is therefore important for a musician practicing in any style to gain a firm hold on the theoretical background that serves as a foundation for all musical genres.

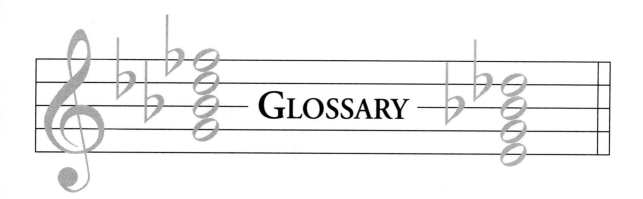

GLOSSARY

absolute music: music composed with no direct reference to nonmusical associations.

AC (adult contemporary): popular music appealing to an older audience.

a capella music: vocal music performed without accompaniment.

accelerando: to increase the tempo of a musical work.

accent: emphasis given to a particular note or chord.

acciaccatura: an accented grace note struck simultaneously with the ensuing note or chord.

accidental: a sharp, flat, double sharp, double flat, or natural sign occurring in a segment of music that is not indicated in the key signature.

adagio: slow.

adagio assai: very slow.

adagio cantabile: slow and in a sustained, flowing singing style.

add-note chord: a triad that includes an add 6th, an add 9th (2nd), or both.

ad libitum (ad lib): literally, "at will," indicating that performance parameters are at the discretion of the performer.

affettuoso: to be performed with an expression of tenderness.

agitato: in an agitated, restive manner.

agogic accent: an accent achieved by an increase in the durational value of a note.

Alberti bass: a style of accompaniment consisting of broken-chord figures.

aleatoric: synonymous with indeterminate, referring to the interpretation and performance of a work beyond the control of the composer.

al fine: to the end.

alla breve: $\frac{2}{2}$ meter, or cut time, indicated by ¢.

alla marcia: performed in the style of a march.

allargando: gradually becoming slower and broader.

allegretto: slower than *allegro;* moderately fast.

allegro: lively, brisk.

all' ottava (8va): depending on placement, indicates those notes to be played an octave higher or lower than shown on the staff.

altered chord: any diatonic chord that has been altered by raising or lowering one or several of its factors.

amoroso: lovingly.

anacrusis: represents any incomplete measure at the beginning of a work or a section of a work. Also called *upbeat.*

andante: a slow and even tempo.

andantino: not quite as slow as *andante.*

anima, animato: animated, spirited.

antecedent phrase: the first phrase in a period form.

anticipation: a nonharmonic tone that is sounded before the chord in which it is contained is sounded.

antiphony: the singing of alternate verses of a hymn by a double or divided choir.

appassionato: passionately.

appoggiatura: a nonharmonic tone usually placed on a stressed portion of the beat and often approached by leap and left by step. It may appear, with omission of the leap, as an accented neighbor.

appoggiatura chord: a chord consisting of one or more upper-partial factors of the ninth, eleventh, and thirteenth that first resolve to other factors of the prevailing triad before moving to a chord of a different root.

aria: a song, usually a solo in an opera.

arpeggio: the various notes of a chord written and/or performed individually in succession.

arsis: upbeat or anacrusis.

articulation: the distinctiveness with which a note is performed.

art song: a term used to define a song for a single voice that is different in character from a folk song. Art songs are considered to be of a more serious nature.

assai: very.

asymmetric meter: a meter in which the normal division is neither by 2 nor by 3. Common examples include $\frac{5}{8}$, $\frac{5}{4}$, $\frac{7}{8}$, $\frac{7}{4}$, and $\frac{11}{8}$.

asymmetric structure: a phrase consisting of an odd number of measures.

a tempo: a directive to return to the original speed of the work.

atonality: literally, the absence of a tonal or key center.

attaca, attaca subito: a directive to begin immediately without pause or hesitation.

augmentation: a process by which the notes of a repeated melodic idea are durationally increased by the same proportion.

augmented sixth chord: the German, French, or Italian sixth, each of which contains the interval of an augmented sixth.

authentic upper-partial chord: any upper-partial chord of the ninth, eleventh, or thirteenth in which the chord resolves directly to a new chord.

avant-garde music: music characterized by experimental, nonconforming practice.

bar line: a vertical line used to divide music into measures containing a specific number of beats.

Baroque: the period of Western art music between 1600 and 1750. Baroque music is characterized by expressive multiple melodic lines (polyphony), intricate rhythmic design, and a highly elaborate and embellished texture.

basso continuo: the bass line and harmonic content in certain Baroque compositions performed by the keyboard and bass instrument, often containing a figured bass.

basso ostinato: a repeated bass figure or pattern supporting variations of a melody.

beam: a horizontal line used to connect and group particular notes into rhythmic figures. The longest value note employing a single beam is the eighth note.

beat: the regular recurring pulse in a measure; the method by which note and rest values are counted.

bellicoso: indicates music to be performed in an aggressive manner.

ben, bene: done well and in a deliberate manner.

ben marcato: well-marked.

bitonality: the simultaneous occurrence of two tonal centers.

blues: a style of American popular music having its roots in black spirituals.

blues progression: a twelve-bar period incorporating the tonic, subdominant, and dominant chords.

blues scale: a major scale with lowered third and seventh (Dorian mode). The blues scale often contains the flatted fifth.

boogie woogie: a style developed from the blues in which a blues progression is reiterated over a distinct recurring bass-line figure.

borrowed chord: a chord taken from the parallel key.

break, breakdown: in popular dance music, the process of systematically eliminating instrumental parts, resulting in the skeletal content of the ensemble.

bridge: in popular music, that section linking the verse with the chorus and/or a section following the chorus, which leads back to the verse. In a fugue, a bridge serves as a transition to the original key of the subject. Essentially, bridges are transitional passages.

brillante: brilliant.

brio: spirited, energetic.

cadence: delineates a closure at the end of a phrase, period, section, movement, or entire work. Cadences include perfect authentic, imperfect authentic, semicadences or half cadences, perfect plagal, imperfect plagal, deceptive, Phrygian, Landini, and linear.

cadenza: an ornamental passage sometimes written by the composer, but often improvised by the performer. A cadenza normally appears after the $^6_4$ cadential chord near the close of the first and/or last movement of a concerto. Based on material introduced in the movement and in the style of a fantasia, it is a solo effort demonstrating the skill of the performer.

caesura: a point of division of melodic and/or rhythmic material within a phrase or period, characterized by a strong or weak beat and marked with the symbol (//).

calando: gradually becoming softer and slower.

calmato: in a tranquil and quiet manner.

cambiata: a three- or four-note figure consisting of a nonharmonic second note followed by the downward leap of a third and resolution by step to a harmonic tone. Also called *nota cambiata* and *changing tone.*

canon: the strictest form of imitation among two or more parts in a musical work.

cantabile: songlike and flowing in style.

cantata: an extended vocal work with accompaniment, consisting of solo and chorus section, recitatives, and duets. Cantatas can be sacred or secular.

canzona: a lyrical song of the eighteenth and nineteenth centuries in sectional structure, containing secular lyrics. Canzoni were also written as instrumental works in homophonic and polyphonic textures.

capo: the beginning, head, or top.

capriccio: a free form of instrumental music.

cesura: *see* caesura.

chamber music: music performed by a group smaller than a full orchestra, such as a trio, quartet, or quintet, and originally presented in venues smaller than concert halls.

chance music: some or all elements of a composition, the performance of which is left to the discretion of the performer. Also called *indeterminacy.*

change-of-quality chord: a chromatic chord that is neither borrowed nor secondary.

changing tone: *see* cambiata.

chant: music, usually of a liturgical nature, that is monophonic, unaccompanied, and without strict rhythm.

chorale: a hymn or sacred piece performed by a chorus.

chorale-hymn: a tune of the Protestant Church performed by a chorus.

chord: the simultaneous sounding of at least three pitches, usually in a particular intervallic configuration.

chorus: 1. a group of singers.   2. the main section of a popular song or instrumental piece.

chromatic pitch: any pitch that does not appear in the scale of the prevailing key.

circle of fifths: a cycle that begins with any pitch and proceeds in intervals of descending perfect fifths until all twelve pitches are exhausted. Also called *cycle of fifths.*

circle progression: a chord progression in which the root relationship is a descending fifth.

Classical: the period of Western art music between 1770 and 1830. Music of this period exudes a concern for gracefulness, symmetry, balance, clarity, and objectivity.

clef: a symbol placed at the beginning of a staff designating the location of a particular pitch from which the locations of all other pitches are calculated.

closely related keys: the relative key of the tonic, the subdominant and its relative key, and the dominant and its relative key.

cluster: a chord consisting of at least three notes with no more than a whole step between any two notes.

coda: a concluding passage to a movement or entire work. Codas can be quite extended in length.

codetta: a short coda.

col., colla, etc: with the....

common chord: in the construction of a modulation, a chord appearing diatonically in the prevailing key and in the target key.

common time: $\frac{4}{4}$ meter, often indicated by c.

comp: literally, meaning *to complement*. In practice, this jazz term means *to accompany* — usually in an extemporaneous manner.

compound interval: any interval exceeding the span of an octave.

compound meter: a meter in which the beat unit divides into three parts.

con: with.

concerto: a work for one or more solo instruments and orchestral accompaniment.

concerto grosso: a work for a small group of instruments accompanied by full orchestra.

conjunct: a melodic movement characterized by stepwise motion.

consequent phrase: the phrase following the antecedent phrase. It normally satisfies the need for completion and closure.

consonance: an acoustical phenomenon in which the vibrations of two sounding bodies are in complement, thus resulting in a stable effect.

con sordino: with mute.

contrary motion: the motion between two lines or parts that progress linearly in opposition.

corde: string, as in *una corda:* one string; *tre corde:* three strings.

counterpoint: from the Latin *punctus contra punctum,* which literally means *note against note.* In the broader sense it refers to the technique of writing melody against melody, and in the most general sense, counterpoint indicates any note against any other note.

crescendo: an increase in intensity.

cut time: $\frac{2}{2}$ meter or alla breve; indicated by ₵.

da, dal, dalle: from.

Da Capo (D.C.): from the top, head, or beginning.

dance suite: a Baroque instrumental genre consisting of several movements, each in the style of a dance. These can include the allemande, courante, sarabande, gigue, minuet, gavotte, bouree, and polonaise.

decrescendo: a decrease in intensity.

degree: a scale pitch.

diatonic pitch: a pitch within the prevailing key.

diminuendo: diminishing in volume.

diminution: a process in which the notes of a repeated melodic idea are durationally decreased proportionally.

direct fifth: the approach to a perfect or compound perfect fifth by similar motion.

direct octaves: the approach to a perfect or compound perfect octave by similar motion.

dissonance: an acoustical phenomenon in which the vibrations of two sounding bodies are in opposition, thus resulting in a kinetic effect.

divisi: divided.

dodecaphonic: a general term used to describe twelve-tone music.

dolce: sweetly, tenderly.

doloroso: in a sad and sorrowful manner.

dominant: the fifth degree of the scale.

double flat: the symbol ♭♭ which indicates that a note is to be lowered one whole step.

double sharp: the symbol x which indicates that a note is to be raised one whole step.

duple meter: a meter characterized by two beats in a measure.

duplets: a group of two notes and/or played in the time of three.

dyad: a harmonic interval of two notes.

dynamics: the various degrees of volume or intensity applied to either pitches or entire passages of music.

échappée: a nonharmonic tone usually approached by a harmonic tone one step below and left by a leap to a third below. Also called *escape tone.*

electronic music: music composed and processed by electronic means.

eleventh chord: a seventh chord, usually mm7 or Mm7, incorporating the eleventh degree of the scale.

elision: an overlap, whereby the end of one pattern or figure also functions as the beginning of the next.

embellishment: decoration or ornamentation.

energico: with energy, vigor.

enharmonic spellings: alternate spellings of the same pitch.

ensemble: a group of performers.

equal temperament: the modern and most widely used system of tuning in Western music in which the octave is divided into twelve equal divisions.

escape tone: see échappée.

espressione: with expression

espressivo: expressively.

etude: a solo piece meant to emphasize a particular technique.

extended chord: any chord that utilizes factors above the seventh.

facile: lightly, in an easy manner.

fake: a term used to describe the process of playing "by ear."

fakebook: an illegal duplication of popular songs consisting only of the melody, lyrics, and chord changes indicated by symbols.

fantasia: a comparatively free-form work in the style of an improvisation.

fermata: the symbol ⌒ which indicates that a note or rest is to be sustained.

feroce: in a wild, frenzied manner.

figured bass: a shorthand for indicating the notes to be incorporated above a written bass note.

finale: the closing or last movement of an extended work.

forte (f): loud.

forte piano (fp): loud, then soft.

fortissimo (ff): very loud.

forza: force.

fugue: literally, *chase.* Fugues are usually in two or more voices and represent the most developed style of imitative counterpoint.

fundamental tone: the initial sounding pitch in the production of a sound.

funk: a term used to describe a style of popular music characterized by heavily accented and punctuated beats, often in highly intricate rhythmic patterns.

fuoco: with fire and passion.

furioso: furiously, passionately.

giocoso: in a humorous, playful manner.

giusto: in a strict, correct, and exact manner.

glissando: a rapid-scale effect attained by sliding across the notes.

grace note: a note of short duration, usually borrowing time from the ensuing note.

grandioso: majestically, grandly, pompously.

grand staff: two separated five-line staves bracketed on the left side, on which pitches are notated. Used in piano, organ, and harp music. Also called *great staff.*

grave: very slow and heavy.

grazia: gracefully, elegantly.

groove: used in popular music to denote the easy, natural, and flowing feel of a musical work.

grosso: great, large, heavy.

ground bass: a reiterating bass-line figure. *See* basso ostinato.

gruppetto: a four-note ornament characterized by a principal note that is first approached by its upper neighbor, followed by a step down to the principal note, a step down to the lower neighbor, and a return to the principal note.

half step: the distance from one note to an adjacent note.

harmonic: 1. characterizing the simultaneous sounding of two or more pitches. 2. synonymous with "overtone," in reference to the overtone series. Harmonics are inclusive pitches in a fundamental tone.

harmonic minor scale: a minor scale with raised seventh degree.

harmonic movement: the progression of chords in a musical work.

harmonic rhythm: the rhythmic rate at which chords change in a piece.

harmony: the simultaneous sounding of two or more notes.

head: a term used primarily in jazz to denote the top or beginning of a piece.

hemiola: literally, a 3:2 ratio whereby two measures of triple meter are performed as three measures of duple meter. In modern use, this technique can be applied over shorter distances.

hidden fifth: see direct fifth.

hidden octave: see direct octave.

homophonic music: music consisting of a single melody line supported by a harmonic accompaniment.

hook: a term used in popular music to define that section of a song or piece that is the most memorable. Often synonymous with "chorus" when used in reference to musical structure.

hymn: a sacred ballad or hymn of praise.

imitation: the repetition and overlapping of a melodic idea at a prescribed durational interval.

Impressionism: a movement in the arts begun during the late nineteenth century in which creative artists, through their mode of creativity, attempted to convey the essence of objects. In Western music, this was the period between 1875 and 1920, chacterized by extended harmony, sweeping melodic lines, and rich textures within asymetrical designs.

impromptu: a musical work of extemporaneous character, slight development, and in the manner of a fantasia.

improvisation: extemporaneous composition.

indeterminacy: see chance music.

interlude: an intermezzo or section of music inserted between the main sections of a work.

interval: the numerically and qualitatively measured distance between two notes.

intonation: the degree of accuracy with which a musical pitch is executed.

inversion (chord): any position of a chord other than root position.

inversion (interval): the exchange of position of the inclusive notes of a harmonic or melodic interval.

inversion (melodic): the intervallic inversion of the notes of a melody.

inverted mordent: an ornament consisting of a single rapid alternation of the principal note and the note a step above.

jazz: a distinctly American style of music characterized by colorful harmony, improvisation, unique rhythmic content, and instrumentation.

key: the pitch relationships that establish a tonal center.

key signature: the necessary sharps, flats, or lack of these, placed at the beginning of a musical passage or work indicating the scale from which the majority of the ensuing notes are derived.

largamente: in a broad manner.

largo: a slow, broad tempo; the slowest of the tempo markings.

leading tone: the seventh degree of the scale.

ledger lines: lines added above or below a staff to accommodate pitches too high or too low for placement on the staff.

legato: smoothly.

leggiero: lightly.

leitmotif: a theme in a dramatic musical work that identifies a character, situation, or idea.

lento: slow tempo.

letter class: all pitches represented by a particular letter.

libretto: the words of an opera or other dramatic work in book form or more specifically, without the presence of the music.

lick: in popular music, a very distinct, short, and appealing improvisatory melodic figure.

lied: a song with a German text.

linear harmony: harmonic content suggested or implied by particular melody notes, either by their rhythmic stress, duration, or recurrence.

linear movement: horizontal, melodic, or harmonic movement.

linear tonality: the tonal area implied by melodic content and motion.

l'istesso tempo: in the same tempo as the previous section.

loco: designates a return to the same "place," usually seen after an indication of octave transposition.

lungo: long, prolonged.

madrigal: a style of vocal music dating from the fourteenth century, consisting of lyrics of an amorous or peaceful nature and written in two- or three-part texture.

maestoso: majestically.

major: a reference to the quality of a scale, interval, or chord. Literally, greater or larger than minor.

marcato: marked, emphasized, accented.

marcia: march.

Mass: The text of the Roman Catholic service set to music. The various sections include the Ordinary, Kyrie, Gloria, Credo, Sanctus, Agnus Dei, and Benedictus.

measure: the metrical unit or space between two bar lines. A measure is often referred to as a "bar."

mediant: the third degree of the scale.

mediant relationship: any intervallic relationship of a third.

melisma: two or more notes sung to a syllable of text.

melody: a succession of pitches in a linearly and temporally controlled parameter.

meno: less.

meno mosso: less movement, slower.

meter: the prescribed values of notes and rests and the groupings of these values into measures.

mezzo: middle.

minimalism: simple motivic idea reiterated and developed gradually over an extended period.

minuet: an early French courtly dance in triple meter.

M.M.: the Maelzel metronome, invented by Johann Maelzel in 1815. This is a mechanical sound device which consistently and regularly beats time, and is used as an aid in the practice of musical works.

modal mixture: the alternating use of parallel keys in a musical work.

mode: an early octave scale. The modes are Ionian, Dorian, Phrygian, Lydian, Mixolydian, Aeolian, and Locrian.

moderato: moderate in tempo.

molto: much.

monody: a predominantly single-line melody for a solo or group in unison.

monophony: a single-line unaccompanied vocal melody.

MOR: "Middle Of the Road," referring to a "soft" popular rock style, appealing to an older audience.

mordent: an ornament, consisting of a single rapid alternation of the principal note and the note a step below.

morendo: gradually dying away.

mosso: movement, motion.

motet: originally, an unaccompanied contrapuntal vocal work on a sacred text. The motet dates from the thirteenth century.

moto: motion, movement, tempo.

musique concrete: music using the natural sounds of the environment and processed with various types of tape and/or electronic manipulations.

natural: the symbol ♮ which indicates the restoration of a note after a sharp or flat.

natural minor scale: the minor scale with no alterations to any degrees. It retains the key signature of its relative major.

Neapolitan chord: a major triad constructed on the lowered second degree of a scale, most often appearing in first inversion (N6).

neighboring tone: a nonharmonic tone intervallically separated by a step either above or below the principal harmonic note.

Neoclassicism: a return to the stricter style of Classical composition after the freedoms employed during the Romantic period.

New-Age music: a style of popular music utilizing the elements of jazz and electronic instruments.

ninth chord: a chord that includes the ninth degree (second or compound second) of the scale of its root added to at least a triad and most often to a seventh chord.

nondominant seventh: a seventh chord of any quality other than that of Mm7.

nonharmonic tone: any note or notes that are not factors in the supporting harmony.

non troppo: not too much.

obbligato: an indispensable passage or instrumental part.

oblique motion: motion between two parts whereby one part is static and the other moves either toward it or away from it.

octave: an interval consisting of the distance of eight notes.

opera: a drama set to music for voices and instruments.

opus: the numbered grouping of written compositions.

oratorio: an extended dramatic vocal composition for soloists and chorus with orchestral accompaniment, based on a sacred text.

organ point: often considered synonymous with *pedal point* or *pedal tone,* the organ point differs from these in that it is a nonharmonic-tone entity consisting of a perfect fifth interval, usually the tonic and fifth of the prevailing key.

organum: early Christian church music in which most of the harmony consisted of two parts in parallel fourths and fifths.

ornamentation: either written or improvised, ornamentation is essentially a decorative process in which a note is preceded and/or followed by flourishes.

ostinato: a short reiterated musical pattern or figure.

overtone: the additional pitches generated by a fundamental pitch. They are fainter and much weaker than the fundamental pitch, but add to it the characteristic timbre.

overture: an introductory movement to a large-scale work, such as an opera.

palindrome: a word, phrase, or sentence that reads the same backwards and forwards. Applied to a melodic line, the segment would sound exactly the same in reverse. Palindromes are obviously nonretrogradable.

pandiatonicism: a diatonically harmonic content in which no particular scale degree is of primary importance and typical chord function is avoided.

parallel fifths: simple or compound perfect fifths approached or left by the same interval.

parallelism: chord structures, usually of the same inversion, moving in parallel fashion at any melodic interval.

parallel motion: the movement of two or more voices (parts) in the same direction and at the same interval.

parallel octaves: simple or compound perfect octaves approached or left by the same interval.

parlando: in a speaking style.

partita: a series of pieces (suite) in various dance forms of the Baroque period.

passing tone: a nonharmonic tone moving in scalewise fashion between two chord tones.

passione: passionately.

pedal point, pedal tone: a nonharmonic tone — usually the tonic or fifth — either sustained, repeated, or reiterated under, between (internal pedal), or above (inverted pedal) a series of chords, producing both dissonance and consonance with these chords.

pentatonic scale: a five-tone scale that can be considered as the first, second, third, fifth, and sixth degrees of a major scale.

perdendosi: dying away.

period: the smallest section of music evoking completeness through a beginning and a musically satisfying ending. Periods can consist of two phrases — an antecedent and a consequent — but can also consist of more than two phrases. A period structure in the broadest sense is a complete musical statement ending with a conclusive cadence.

pesante: heavy, ponderous.

piacere: at pleasure, according to the performer's discretion.

pianissimo (pp): very soft.

piano (p): soft.

Picardy third (tierce de Picardie): the use of a major-quality triad to end a piece written in a minor key.

piu: more.

piu mosso: more motion.

pizzicato: plucked, such as a plucked string.

planing: often considered synonymous with parallelism, planing actually differs from parallelism in that harmonic structures move in stepwise fashion only.

poco: little.

poco a poco: little by little.

pointillism: a style of melodic writing in which the notes are severely disjunct.

polychord: the simultaneous sounding of at least two different chords. Care must be taken that the upper chord is not an extension (upper partial) of the lower.

polyphony, polyphonic: the simultaneous use of two or more complementary melodic lines.

polyrhythm: the simultaneous use of at least two distinctly different rhythmic ideas. Also called *cross rhythm.*

polytonality: the simultaneous use of two or more different key centers.

pomposo: pompous.

portamento: a smooth gliding of one note to another.

post-Romanticism: the period of Western music between 1875 and 1920, immediately following the Romantic era and overlapping Impressionism.

prelude: an introductory piece of music used to prepare a more extended movement or composition.

prestissimo: extremely fast.

presto: fast.

prime: an interval that begins and ends at the same pitch. Also called *unison.*

program(matic) music: music composed in response to an extramusical idea, for example, a fine-art work, story, poem, or play.

pulse: the regular and recurrent underlying beat of a musical work.

quadruple meter: the regular grouping of rhythmic units by four.

quartal harmony: chords structured primarily on intervals of fourths.

quintal harmony: chords structured primarily on intervals of fifths.

rallentando: a gradual slowing of the tempo.

recitative: a style of declamatory singing usually performed *ad libitum,* unless otherwise marked. In such singing, musical accompaniment is minimal.

retardation: a suspension in which the nonharmonic tone is resolved upward.

retrograde: in reverse order.

retrograde inversion: in reverse order and with inverted intervals.

rhythm: the temporal placement of sounds against a regularly recurring pulse.

ricercare: a style of instrumental music during the sixteenth and seventeenth centuries characterized by the imitative treatment of one or more of the inclusive melodies.

riff: in jazz, a distinctive melodic variation of the melody, usually performed by more than one player.

rinforzando: reinforced, accented.

ritardando, rit.: a slowing of the tempo.

ritenuto: held back in slower tempo.

rock: since the 1960s, the general term used to describe popular music characterized by a "heavy" beat.

Rococo: the late Baroque period of music, particularly in France (c. 1720–50). Music of the Rococo is referred to as *Style Galant* and is characterized by its appeal to the masses through its pleasantness and charm.

Romanticism: the period of Western art music from 1790 to 1910. Music of this period portrays the freedom of the human spirit, a concern for human emotion, and a reaction against the formalism of the Classical period.

rondo: a musical work structured on a returning main section after each new thematic section.

rubato: literally, "robbed." The deliberate borrowing of time from one or more note or rest values to express other values. With rubato, the inclusive time duration of the entire passage must be the same as if no rubato were employed.

sans: without.

scale: a series of notes within an octave.

scat: a type of singing, utilized particularly in jazz, wherein the vocalist improvises a melismatic style on particular syllables or individual sounds.

scherzando: playfully, in a toying manner.

secondary dominant: a chromatic chord of major

quality, often an m7 (Mm7) in a P5 relationship to chords in a key.

secondary embellishing chord: a general term indicating both secondary dominants and secondary leading-tone chords.

secondary leading-tone chord: a chromatic chord of diminished, diminished seventh, or half-diminished seventh quality whose root lies a half step below the chord of intended resolution.

secular music: any music other than that of a sacred nature.

secundal harmony: chords structured in major and minor seconds.

segno: sign.

segue: to follow without hesitation.

semplice: in a simple manner.

sempre: always, continually.

senza: without.

sequence: a transposition of a melodic segment to a different scale degree.

serialism: twelve-tone music in which the parameters of rhythm, pitch order, dynamics, etc. are precisely predetermined by the composer.

seventh chord: any chord structure consisting of a tertian stacking of four notes.

sforzando: accented, forced, special stress.

similar motion: two parts moving in the same direction but not at the same interval.

simile: to continue in a like manner.

simple meter: a meter in which the beat divides into two parts.

slentando: becoming slower.

slur: a curved line placed over or under two or more (usually different) notes indicating a smooth execution.

smorzando: dying away, fading away.

solfeggio: a vocal exercise that utilizes the syllables of solmization (do, re, mi, etc.)

solo song: a relatively short work based on a text and scored for a solo voice. Solo songs are most often accompanied by one or more instruments.

sonata: an instrumental composition, usually for a solo instrument, in three or four movements incorporating a particular general structure.

sonata allegro: a structure utilized in a great majority of sonatas, consisting of an exposition, development, and recapitulation.

song: a musical work that usually consists of words set to a musical accompaniment.

sordino: mute.

sostenuto: sustaining note and rest values for their full duration.

sotto voce: softly; under; with restrained sound.

sound mass: a texture of complex density in which the inclusive elements cannot be identified individually.

spacing: the distances between voices in a harmonic structure.

spirito: with spirit, fire.

staccato: detached, separate.

staff: the five lines and four spaces upon which notes and other music symbols are written.

stepwise movement: linear movement in whole and/or half steps.

stretto: the overlapping of melodic lines.

stringendo: accelerating, quickening.

strophic: using the same music in each successive verse.

structural harmony: chords of significant importance necessary for the establishment and maintenance of a tonal center.

Sturm and Drang: Storm and Stress. A style of music in the early Classical period representing emotion, rather than entertainment.

Style Bourgeois: a style of music prominent during the years 1730–1803, exemplifying pronounced dynamic changes and contrast, sudden changes in texture and keys, little melodic continuity, considerable rhythmic contrast, a variety of articulation, and generally, an overall freedom from the confines of the Style Galant.

Style Galant: a style of music during the late Baroque (Rococo) period that separated from the polyphonic texture prevalent in Baroque style. It consisted of accompanied melody, rather than contrapuntal texture.

subdominant: the fourth degree of a scale.

subito: suddenly, quickly.

submediant: the sixth degree of a scale.

suite: a single extended musical work consisting of several autonomous movements, usually used to accompany various dance forms.

supertonic: the second degree of a scale.

suspension: a nonharmonic-tone configuration consisting of three steps: preparation (consonance), suspension (dissonance), and resolution (consonance). The ultimate resolution of the suspension is downward by step.

swing: a style of jazz execution.

symphonic poem: orchestral music of the nineteenth and twentieth centuries, which is inspired by an extramusical idea, such as a literary work.

symphony: a composition for orchestra that normally consists of four movements. Typically, these comprise: an allegro (1st movement), an adagio (2nd movement), a scherzo (3rd movement) and another allegro (4th movement).

syncopation: the shifting of normal rhythmic stress, accomplished by either accent or note-value modification.

tacet: silence.

tempo: the rate of speed of a musical work.

tempo primo: the original tempo.

tempus imperfectum: in medieval times, duple meter, represented by C, in which the breve (double whole note) was equal to two semibreves (whole notes).

tempus perfectum: in medieval times, triple meter, represented by O, in which the breve (double whole note) was equal to three semibreves (whole notes).

teneramente: tenderly, delicately.

tenuto: held for full value.

ternary structure: music consisting of three distinct sections.

tertian harmony: harmony (chords) constructed by the superimposition of intervallic thirds.

tessitura: the parameters of highness and lowness of a majority of the notes in a musical work.

tetrachord: the first or last four notes of a scale.

texture: the density and manner in which sound is represented in a piece.

theme: an extended and complete melodic idea proposed as the basis for continued development in a work.

thirteenth chord: a superimposition of six thirds inclusive of the root, third, fifth, seventh, ninth, eleventh, and thirteenth scale degrees. A thirteenth chord requires at least a root, seventh, and thirteenth.

thorough bass: see figured bass and basso continuo.

through-composed music: music, especially of a vocal type, in which each successive stanza incorporates new material.

tie: a curved line or lines joining two or more notes.

tierce de Picardie: see Picardy third.

timbre: the quality of a tone as the result of the presence or absence of particular overtones (partials).

toccata: a keyboard piece, usually for organ or harpsichord, in the style of a fantasia (free structure) and containing rapid scalar passages and chordal sonorities executed as arpeggiations and full-chord sonorities.

tonality: the relatedness of all notes and harmony to a central pitch.

tone: the sound of a vibrating body representing pitch, intensity, duration, and timbre.

tone poem: synonymous with symphonic poem.

tonic: the first degree of a scale.

tonicization: the momentary emphasis of a key center.

tranquillo: tranquil, calm.

transposition: the shifting of a musical work to another key center.

triad: a three-note chord initially consisting of superimposed major and/or minor thirds.

trill: the rapid alternation of a principal note and its upper neighbor.

triple meter: the regular grouping of time units by three.

tritone: the interval of an augmented fourth or diminished fifth.

troppo: too much.

tune: in popular music, a song or instrumental piece.

tutta, tutti: all, the entire.

twelve-tone music: highly chromatic music based on

the use of all twelve pitches, not to be considered atonal or serial.

twelve-tone row: a predetermined sequence of the twelve pitches to be used in the composition of a work. Also called *series, set.*

unison: *see* prime.

un poco: a little.

upper-partial chord: a tertian constructed chord consisting of odd-numbered scale degrees above the octave.

vamp: in popular music, especially jazz, a prolonged accompaniment, used as an introduction, interlude, or ending.

variation: the harmonic, rhythmic, or melodic modification of a theme for the purpose of protraction.

variations: literally, the varied restatement of a musical idea (usually the theme), accomplished by one or more of the following techniques: inversion, retrograde, augmentation, diminution, ornamentation, rhythmic modification, or transposition, or by any other means of modifying the idea.

veloce: swiftly.

vigoroso: vigorously.

vivace: a spirited, bright, even style.

vivo: lively, spirited.

voce: the voice.

voice leading: the practice of correctly resolving harmonic and contrapuntal notes.

whole-tone scale: a six-tone scale comprised exclusively of whole steps.

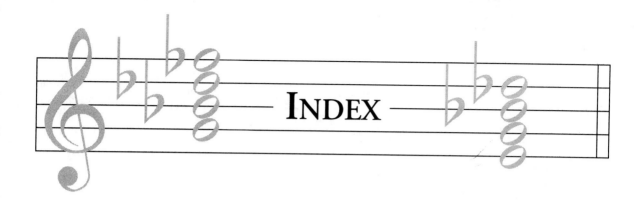

INDEX

Accents, 20–21
Acciaccatura, 203
Accidentals, 3–4, 459–60
Added-note chords, 478
   add 9 chord, 386, 391
   add 6 chord, 391
Aeolian mode, 44–45
Alla breve, 13
Alto, 132, 140, 142
Anacrusis, 21
Anchors, perfect fifth, 493
Anticipation, 207
Appoggiatura, 202–3, 402–3
Arabic numerals, 86, 110, 204, 488
Arpeggio, 259
Arsis, 21
Articulation, 24–25
Attack, 24
Augmentation, 238
Augmented chords
   elevenths, 389
   perfect-augmented quartals, 481–82
   perfect fourths, 483
   sixth chords, 363–75, 454

   voice leading, 153–61
Augmented intervals, 62, 78–79

Bach, Johann Sebastian, 132
Bar lines, 10–11. *See also* Staff
Baroque period, 86, 137, 462
Bass, 132, 140–42
Bass clef. *See* Clef
Bass note, 155
Beams, 5, 10–11
Beat(s), 5
   division of, 14–16, 23
   downbeat as, 19–20
   interpretation of, 24
   less than half-, 23
   pick-up, 21
   upbeat as, 19–20
   variable, 18
Bridge, 269

Cadences, 149, 228, 250–56
   augmented sixths as, 373

cadential six-four chords as, 149
   deceptive, 253–54
   evaded, 253
   half-, 251
   imperfect authentic, 251
   Landini, 254
   modifications of, 254–55
   in modulation, 273
   perfect authentic, 251
   Phrygian, 253
   Picardy third, 254
   plagal, 251–52
   in popular music, 91–93, 112,
      255–56
   semicadences, 251
Cadenza, 270
Caesura, 228
Cambiata, 209
Cells, 226, 241, 248
Changing tones, 210
Chorale style, 132, 137–38, 140, 190
Chordal tendencies, 176–79
Chord identification
   figured-bass system of, 85–88, 106

in popular music, 91–93
in unconventional root move-
    ments, 431
Chord movement, 179–80
    cyclic, 417–19
    mediant, 419, 423
    noncyclic, 417–19
    progressive, 179–80
    remote, 336
    retrogressive, 179–80, 191, 193
    stepwise, 314, 419–23
    tritone, 419, 424–26
    unconventional, 431
Chords, 80–81. *See also* Dominant
    chords; Interval(s); Intervallic
    configuration; Seventh chords;
    Triad(s); Upper-partial chords
    added-note, 478
    add 9, 386–91
    add 6, 391
    altered, 316, 386, 449
    augmented-augmented quartal,
        483
    augmented eleventh, 389
    augmented perfect fourth, 483
    augmented sixth, 363–75, 454
    borrowed, 330–33, 337
    change-of-quality, 333–36, 449
    compound quartal, 486
    embellishing, 187
    extensions of, 185–86
    in fifths, 490–493
    fourth, 488–89
    in fourths, 481–90
    hybrid, 113, 118, 386
    9, 11, 390
    nonfunctional augmented-aug-
        mented quartal, 483
    open fifth, 492
    in open position, 138
    passing six-four, 149–52
    pedal six-four, 150
    perfect-augmented quartal,
        481–82
    pivot, 273, 442, 445, 449, 450,
        452
    progression of, 177, 186–93, 488
    secondary, 332
    in seconds, 478–80
    structural, 187

sus 4, 391
    unconventional, 431
    voice-leading of, 153–61
Chord substitution, 183–86, 351,
    355–56, 426, 429
Chorus, 269
Chromaticism, 38, 183, 213, 270,
    273, 284–85, 292, 330, 335,
    417, 419, 431, 462–63
    in melodies, 232
    and modulation, 273–75, 440, 449
    and the Neapolitan chord, 346
    and pitch, 271–72
Circle of fifths, 41, 179
Circle progression, 179, 190, 192,
    292
Classical music, 240
Classical period, 18, 118, 137, 462
Clef, 2
Closed sections, 266
Closely related keys, 336
Close position, 84, 138
Clusters, 480
Common-practice works, 14, 24,
    111, 178, 249, 284
    influence of, on popular music,
        256
    suspensions in, 204
Common time, 13
Common tone, 146, 314, 442, 461
Composition, 177, 193, 240. *See also*
    Four-part writing; Notation;
    Part writing
Concerto, 270, 270n
Consonance, 64–65, 484, 493
Contemporary period, 119, 137, 351,
    462, 464
Counterpoint, 334. *See also* Composi-
    tion; Four-part writing
Counting, 19
    of beat divisions, 23
    and parallel minor key signature,
        40–41
CQ chords, 333–36, 449
Cut time, 13
Cycle of fifths, 41, 179

Decay, 24
Decrescendo, 269

Degrees. *See* Scale degrees
Diatonic intervals
    ninths, 383–84
    sevenths, 105–6, 112–13, 154
Diatonicism, 38, 183, 284
    and chord substitution, 183–86
    conventional functions of, 420
    and diminished chords, 307
    and melodies, 232, 284
    and modulation, 440
    and scale system, 38
Diminished chords, 307–21
    applications of, 309–14
    deceptive resolution of, 310–11
    embellishing function of, 308–9
    inversions of, 312–13
    pitch spellings of, 314
    voice leading of, 153–61
Diminished intervals, 62, 105
    diminished fifths, 78
    diminished sevenths, 105
    doubly diminished intervals, 63
    diminished triads, 78, 79, 307, 313
Diminution, 238
Dissonance, 64–65, 477, 481, 485,
    493. *See also* Nonharmonic
    tone(s)
    dissonant-appearing seventh inter-
        vals, 105
    dissonant intervals, 64–65
    in dominant seventh chords, 150
Distance
    alphabetical, 33, 41
    interval, 33, 57–59
    between pitches, 34
Dominant chords. *See also* Quintal
    harmony
    dominant eleventh chords, 387–88
    dominant ninth chords, 385–86
    dominant seventh chords, 118–19,
        150–53
    dominant triads, 77–79
Dominant (fifth) degree, 38, 44, 135,
    145, 491
Dorian mode, 44–45
Dots, 10–11
Double flats, 4
Double inflections, 489
Double periods, 262
Double sharps, 4

Doubly augmented intervals. *See* Intervals, augmented
Doubly diminished intervals. *See* Diminished intervals
Downbeats, 19–20
Duplets, 16
Duration, 15, 200, 225
Dyads, 56, 209, 492

Editing, 24
Eleventh chords, 199, 382, 387–90
  inversions of, 396–97
  natural-occurring, 387
  pitch tendencies in, 400–401
Embedded structures, 393–96, 463
Embellishing harmonies, 187, 286, 287, 292, 308–9
  with French, German, and Italian 6ths, 374
  of major triads, 332
Enharmonic alteration, 453
Enharmonic equivalents. *See* Enharmonic spellings
Enharmonic modulation, 275, 442, 453–59
Enharmonic names and pitches, 4
Enharmonic spellings, 3–4, 42, 315, 456
Escape tone, 203–4

Factors, 77, 184–85
Fake books, 112, 112n
F clefs. *See* Clef
Fifth (of triad), 78
Fifth degree. *See* Dominant
Figured-bass system, 85–88, 106
First degree. *See* Tonic
First inversion
  in seventh chords, 108
  in triads, 84, 147–48
Flags, 4, 10–11
Flats, 4. *See also* Accidentals, Circle of fifths
Form, 262, 266, 267
Four-part harmony, 140
Four-part writing, 133, 138–46
  nonharmonic tones in, 210–11
Fourth chords, 488–89

Fourth degree. *See* Subdominant
Free tones. *See* Nonharmonic tone(s)
French sixths, 368–70, 427
Fully diminished seventh chords, 157–59, 456–57
  alterations of, 316
  pitch spellings of, 314–15
Fundamental, 135–36. *See also* Root position

German sixths, 365–68, 374, 426, 454
Grace notes, 203. *See also* Appoggiatura
Grand staff, 2, 138
Gruppetto, 21

Half-beat values, 19–20, 20–22
Half-cadence, 251
Half-diminished seventh chords, 157–59, 316
Half steps, 3, 33, 35
Harmonic and nonharmonic tones, 200
Harmonic ideas, 138
Harmonic intervals, 56
Harmonic minor scale, 35–37, 40
Harmonic progressions, 176–93, 420–21. *See also* Resolution; Tension
Harmonic structures, 334, 393–96, 463–64. *See also* Embellishing Harmonies
Harmonizing, 188–93
Harmony, implied, 200. *See also* Four-part writing
Hidden fifths, 145
Hidden octaves, 145
Homophony, 210
Hook, 269

Impressionist period, 137, 351
Improvisation, 112, 270
Intensity, 24, 225
Interpolation, 238
Interpretation, 24–25
Interval(s), 56–69. *See also* Chords;

Diminished intervals; Intervallic configuration
  augmented, 62, 78–79
  characteristics of, 64–68
  compound, 63
  consonant, 65
  diminished, 62
  dissonant, 65
  distance, 33, 57–59
  doubly augmented, 62
  doubly diminished, 62
  dyads as, 56, 209
  equidistant, 481
  harmonic, 56
  identification of, 57
  inversion of, 63–64
  major, 59
  melodic, 56
  minor, 61
  perfect, 60
  quality of, 59–64
  resolution tendency of, 66–67
  simple, 63
Interval distances, 32, 56–57
Intervallic configuration, 249
  of French sixths and German sixths, 368
  of Italian sixths, 371
  of seventh chords, 115–17, 157
  symmetrical, 314, 419
  in triads, 77, 79, 90
Introduction, 269
Inversions
  of diminished chords, 312–13
  of intervals, 63–64
  melodic, 238
  of ninth, eleventh, and thirteenth chords, 396–98
  numerical labeling of, 110–12
  predominant, 313
  and progressive and retrogressive movements, 180
  of quartal chords, 486–87, 488
  retrograde, 238
  of secondary-dominant chords, 287
  of secondary-dominant seventh chords, 288
  in secundal system, 478
  of seventh chords, 109, 115, 156

six-four, 148–50
    of triads, 84–85, 88
    of upper-partial chords, 396–98
Ionian mode, 44–45
Italian sixth, 210, 371

Jazz, 119, 137, 319, 480. *See also*
    Popular music

Key(s), 38–40, 57–58, 189, 271
    closely related, 336
    D major, 38
    E major, 38
    remotely related, 336
Key change, 442, 461
Key regions, 319, 337–39, 440, 452
Keys (keyboard), 3, 38, 44
Key signature, 38–40

Landini, Francesco, 254
Leading tone (seventh degree), 37,
        38, 66, 137, 185, 315
    in four-part writing, 145
    and Locrian mode, 44
    pitch tendency of, 137
Leading-tone diminished triad, 420
Lead sheets, 319
Leaps, 314
Ledger lines, 2
Letter class, 77
Locrian mode, 44–45
Lower pedal tones, 209
Lutheran Church, 138
Lydian mode, 44–45

Major intervals, 59, 62
Major keys, 57–58
Major ninth chords, 385–86
Major scales
    construction of, 33–35
    diatonic intervals in, 105–6
    mode position relative to, 44
    relative, 35
    tetrachords of, 42–44
    triad derivation from, 81

whole- and half-step pattern in,
        33, 57
Major seventh chords. *See* Seventh
    chords
Measures, 10, 21. *See also* Staff
Mediant (third) degree, 38, 77–79,
        184
    and Phrygian mode, 44
    pitch tendency of, 134
Medieval chants, 481, 492
Melodic ideas. *See* Motives
Melodic intervals, 56
Melodic leaps in four-part writing,
        142–43
Melodic minor scale, 35, 37
Melodic movement, 334. *See also*
    Chord movement
Melody, 224–28, 230, 232, 464
    analysis of, 258–61
    chromatic, 232
    components of, 226–28
    development of, 238
    diatonic, 232
    harmonizing of, 188–89, 192
    melismatic style of, 210
    motion of, 232
    nonharmonic tones in, 213
    perception of, 224–26
    pointillistic, 232
    primarily ascending, 232
    primarily descending, 232
    rhythmically active, 232
    rhythmically calm, 232
    sawtooth, 232
    undulating, 232
Meter, 10, 12–14. *See also* Tempo
Metronome, 19
Mezzo forte, 24
Minor eleventh chords, 389
Minor intervals, 61. *See also*
    Interval(s)
Minor scale(s). *See also* Modes
    chord derivation from, 81
    construction of, 35
    diatonic sevenths in, 106
    harmonic, 35–37, 40
    melodic, 35, 37
    natural, 35, 36–37
    pure, 35–37

relative, 35–36, 177
Minor seventh chords. *See* Seventh
    chords
Minor triads, 78, 79
Mixolydian mode, 44–45
Modal mixture. *See* Chords, bor-
    rowed
Modal scales. *See* Modes
Modes, 44–49, 241. *See also* Minor
    scales
    relationship with tonic of, 46
    transposition of, 45–49
    triads in, 83–84
Modulation, 270–75, 337, 440–65
    cadences in, 273
    chromatic, 275, 449
    common-chord, 273, 442, 443–45
    common-tone, 442, 461
    diatonic, 273
    enharmonic, 275, 442, 453–59
    extensive, 462–63
    implied, 442, 459–61
    pivot-chord, 273, 442, 445, 449,
        450, 452
    remote, 464
    static, 442, 461
    types of, 273–75
Motifs. *See* Motives
Motion. *See also* Chord movement.
    contrary, 147
    by leap, 314
    of melody, 232
    oblique, 146–47
    passing-tone, 364–65
    primarily leaping, 232
    primarily stepwise, 232
    similar, 145
    skipping, 232
Motives, 226–27, 248, 259
Movement (section), 249
Movements. *See* Chord movement
Musical form, 262, 266, 267

Natural signs, 4
Neapolitan chords, 346–57, 364,
        420, 450, 452
    characteristics of, 347–52
    Neapolitan sixths as, 352–54, 364

part writing of, 352–54
in popular music, 351
spelling of, 346–47
as tritone substitution, 355
Neighboring six-four chord, 150
Neighboring tone, 150, 201–2, 313
Ninth chords, 199, 383–86, 391,
  396–97, 400
  inversions of, 396–97
  lowered, 385
  pitch tendencies in, 400, 401
Nonharmonic tone(s), 199–211
  anticipation as, 207
  appoggiatura as, 202–03
  cambiata as, 209
  changing tones as, 210
  chromatic pitch in, 271
  échappée as, 203–4
  embellished, 210
  escape tone as, 203–4
  in four-part writing, 210–11
  free tone as, 207–9
  as function of melody, 213
  neighboring tone as, 201–2
  organ point as, 209
  passing tone as, 201
  pedal tone as, 209
  retardation as, 206
  suspension as, 204
Notation, 81–83, 86, 110, 156–61,
  204, 248
Note heads, 4
Notes
  and beams, 5, 10–11
  and dots, 10–11
  duplication of, 89–91
  duration of, 4
  and flags, 4, 10–11
  groupings of, 16–17
  half-beat, 19–20
  and pitches, 1, 4
  single, 248
  and stems, 4, 10–11
  symbols for, 1, 4
  and ties, 10–11
  values of, 4–5, 18
Note spacing, 85
Numerals
  Arabic, 86, 110, 204, 488

figured-bass, 85–88, 106
  and labeling seventh chords, 110–11
  Roman, 81–83, 110, 113, 156–61,
    431
Octave(s), 33, 382
  hidden, 145
  perfect, 69
  tenor part and, 140
Open position, 138
Open sections, 266
Organa, 492
Organ point, 209
Overtones, 135–36

Parallelism, 423
Parallel keys, 331
Parallel major and minor scale
    forms, 40–41
Parallel movements, 141
Parallel octaves, 459
Parallel perfect fifths, 141
Parallel perfect octaves, 141
Parallel periods, 262
Partials, 135–36
Parts, 138
Part writing, 138
  of borrowed chords, 333
  of Neapolitan chords, 352–54
Passing tone, 201, 286, 364–65
Pedal point, 209
Pedal six-four chord, 150
Pedal tone, 209
Perfect intervals, 60, 62, 69
  perfect-augmented fourths,
    481–82
  perfect fifths, 41–42, 69, 491, 493
  perfect fourths, 65, 69
  perfect-perfect fourths, 481
  perfect unisons, 65
Performance styles, 85
Periods, 248–49, 262
  double periods, 262
Phrase(s), 227–28, 241, 248–49,
    256–62
  analysis of, 258–61
  antecedent, 228
  completeness and resolution of, 257
  consequent, 228

Phrase modulation, 442, 461
Pitch(es), 1, 2
  alteration of, 34
  as component of melody, 225
  fundamental, 135–36
  in the overtone series, 135
Pitch spellings, 314–16
Pitch tendency, 66, 133–35,
    400–402
Pivot chord, 273–75
  augmented sixths as, 454
  augmented triads as, 457–59
  modulation of, 442, 445, 449, 450
Planing, 423
Pop, 119, 284
Popular music, 137, 480. *See also*
    Jazz
  augmented sixths in, 372–73
  chords in, 91–93, 112, 251–52
  composition of, 240
  diatonic melody and harmony in,
    204
  formats of, 91
  harmonic progression in, 178
  Neapolitan in, 351
  seventh chords in, 112–13, 115
  song writing in, 240, 269, 401
  spellings of chord structures in,
    319
  structure of, 267–69
  suspensions in, 204, 388
  symbols in, 388, 392
Post-Romantic period, 119
Printed music, 24
Progressions, chordal, 176–78
Progressions, circle, 179, 190, 192,
    292,
Pulse, 9. *See also* Beat(s)

Quartal harmony, 481–90
Quintal harmony, 490–93
Quintuplets, 16

Raised chord factors
  eleventhchords, 387
  ninths, 385, 386, 390
Raised fourth degree, 374

Range
  melodic, 230
  voice, 145
Reiteration, (melodic), 238
Relative keys, 182, 331
Relative major scale, 35
Relative minor scale, 35–36, 177
Repetition (melodic), 238
Resolution, 66–67, 135, 150, 154,
  176. *See also* Harmonic progression
  of appoggiatura, 202
  deceptive, 151–52, 159–61,
    289–92, 310–11, 420
  of French sixths, 368–69
  of German sixths, 365–69
  of Italian sixths, 371
  of Neapolitan chords, 351
  of secondary-dominant chords,
    289–94
  of secondary-dominant seventh
    chords, 288–89
  of seventh chords, 150, 154–55,
    158–61, 313–14
  of suspended notes, 204
  unusual, 294
  of upper-partial chords, 403
  V7/IV, 292–94
Rests, 5, 19
Retardation, 204, 206–7
Retrograde, 238
Retrograde inversion, 238
Rhythm, 9–25
  of appoggiaturas, 203
  articulation of, 24
  modification of, 238
  notation of, 18, 21
Rhythmic stress, 189–90, 403, 460
Ringer, Alexander, 224–25
Rock, 137
Roman numerals, 81–83, 110, 113,
  156–61, 431
Romantic period, 18, 119, 137, 351,
  462
Root movements, 423–26, 431
Root position
  ambiguity of, 397–98
  of augmented sixth chords,
    363–64
  implied, 429–30

of Neapolitan chord, 351
  ninth additions to, 385
  seventh chords in, 104, 108
  of triads, 77–79, 85, 88, 146–47
Roots
  implied 429–30, 487–88
  unimplied, 465

SATB format, 132, 140–41
  in chorale style, 136, 138,
    145–46, 190–91
Scale, 32–38, 57, 241, 249. *See also*
    Modes
  Blues, 42
  chromatic, 38, 42
  C major, 39
  definition of, 32–33
  diminished, 42
  five-tone, 42, 481
  Oriental, 118
  pentatonic, 42, 481
  six-tone, 42
  twelve-tone, 38, 42
  whole-tone, 42
Scale degrees, 36, 38, 82, 392. *See*
    also Dominant (fifth) degree;
    Half step; Subdominant (fourth)
    degree; Tonic (first) degree, etc.
Scale formation, 57
SDR principle, 268–69
Secondary chords, 309, 332. *See also*
    Triads
Secondary-dominant chords, 286–88
Secondary-dominant seventh chords,
    288–98
  and circle progressions, 292
  inversions of, 288–89
  resolutions of, 288–94
Secondary fully and half-diminished
    sevenths, 310
Second degree. *See* Supertonic
Second inversion, 84, 109
Sections, 248–49
Secundal harmony, 478–80
Semicadences, 251
Septuplets, 16
Sequence, harmonic, 176–93, 420–21
Sequence (melodic design), 238
Seventh chords, 104–22, 157–61

diatonic, 105–6, 112–15
  dominant and nondominant,
    118–19, 150–53
  figured-bass numerals and, 113
  four-note, 394–95
  fully diminished, 157–59,
    314–15, 456–57
  half-diminished, 157–59, 310, 317
  hybrid types of, 112–15, 118
  intervallic configurations of,
    115–17
  inversions of, 106–9, 115
  major-minor, 454
  nondominant, 118–19
  numerical labeling of, 110–11
  in popular music, 112–13, 115
  preparation of, 313–14
  qualities of, 105–6
  resolutions of 150, 154–55,
    158–61, 313–14
  Roman numerals and, 113
  in root position, 104, 108
  third inversion in, 109, 156–57
  and upper-partial chords, 394–95
Seventh degree. *See* Leading tone
Seventh intervals. *See* Diatonic inter-
    vals
Sextuplets, 16
Sharps, 3–4. *See also* Accidentals,
    Circle of fifths
Sixth Degree. *See* Submediant
Song writing. *See* popular music
Soprano, 132, 140, 142
Sound mass, 479
Sound production, 24
Spread-position triads, 89–90
Stacked thirds. *See* Tertian harmony
Staff, 1–2, 140
  and grand staff, 2, 138
Statement-departure-return principle,
    268–69
Static modulation, 442, 461
Staves. *See* Staff
Stems, 4, 10–11
Structural harmonies. *See* chords
Structure, musical, 189, 248–75
  binary, 19, 262–67
  elements of, 248–55, 249
  expanded ternary, 268–69
  hybrid, 386

and improvisation, 270
polychordal, 491
of popular song, 267–69
ternary, 266
Subdominant (fourth) degree, 38, 44, 66, 134
Submediant (sixth) degree, 36, 37, 38, 66
and Aeolian mode, 44
pitch tendency of, 136
Substitution. *See* Chord substitution; Tritone substitution
Subtonic (minor seventh) degree, 38, 66
Superimposition
of fifths, 492
of thirds, 382
Supertonic (second) degree, 38, 66, 133–34
and Dorian mode, 44
and French sixths, 369–70
Sus 4, 388, 391
Suspension, 204, 388
Syncopation, 20, 21–23

Tempo, 9. *See also* Meter
Tenor, 132, 140, 142
Tenor clef. *See* Clef
Tension, 66, 176, 187
Ternary structure, 262, 266, 267
Tertian harmony, 81, 104, 122, 382, 477, 482–83
stacking of, 405
Tessitura, 230
Tetrachords, 42–44
Theme, 269. *See also* Melody
Third (of triad), 78
Third degree. *See* Mediant
Third inversion, 109, 156–57
Thirds (alphabetical), 32, 40–41
Thirteenth chords, 200, 382, 390–91
inversions of, 396–97
pitch tendencies in, 401
Tierce de Picardie. *See* Cadences, Picardy third
Ties, 10–11

Timbre, 24, 225, 225n, 248
Time. *See* Meter; Rhythm; Tempo
Time signatures, 10, 20–21
Tonic (first) degree, 38, 40, 46, 66, 133
and Ionian mode, 44
key areas related to, 336
Tonicization, 286, 292, 309, 364, 440–41
Tonic pitch. *See* Tonic (first) degree
Tonic triads, borrowed, 332
Transposition
of intervals, 58
of modes, 45–49
Treble clef. *See* Clef
Triad(s), 77–93, 122, 249
augmented, 78–79, 457–59
closely spaced root position of, 84
construction of, 79
diminished, 78–79, 307, 313
factors of, 77
fifth of, 78
figured-bass system and, 85–88
harmonic form of, 77
identification of, 80
inversions of, 84–85, 88
major, 78–79
melodic form of, 77
minor, 78-79
in modes, 83–84
note spacing in, 85
numerical designation of, 80–81
primary, 81
qualities of, 78–79
Roman numerals and, 81–83
root of, 78
in root position, 77–79, 85, 88, 146–47
in scales, 81–83
and seventh chords, 177
in spread position, 89–90
third of, 78
in upper-partial chords, 393–94
voice leading of, 146–48
Triplets, 14–15
Tritone intervals, 424
and augmented sixths, 426–30

in dominant seventh chords, 118
in four-part writing, 142
and fourth chords, 485
preparation and resolution of, 313–14
Tritone movement. *See* Chord movement
Tritone substitution, 256

Unisons, 69
Upbeats, 19–20
Upper-partial chords, 382–404, 464, 477
appoggiatura, 402–3
authentic, 402
and seventh chords, 394–95
triads in, 393–94
voice-leading of, 398–99
Upper pedal tones, 209

Verse, 269–70
Verse-bridge, 270
Voice, 132, 151
Voice-crossing, 144
Voice designation, 138. *See also* Voice leading
Voice leading, 132, 146–48, 153–61, 314, 431
of augmented chords, 153–61
of diminished chords, 153–61
of dominant-seventh chords, 150–53
of triads, 146–48
of upper-partial chords, 398–99
Voice-overlapping, 142
Voicing, 91, 398–400, 479
of notes in quartal chords, 484
in popular music, 91
Volume, 24
V/V resolution, 292

Whole step, 3, 33,35
Whole-step/ half-step pattern, 33, 35–37